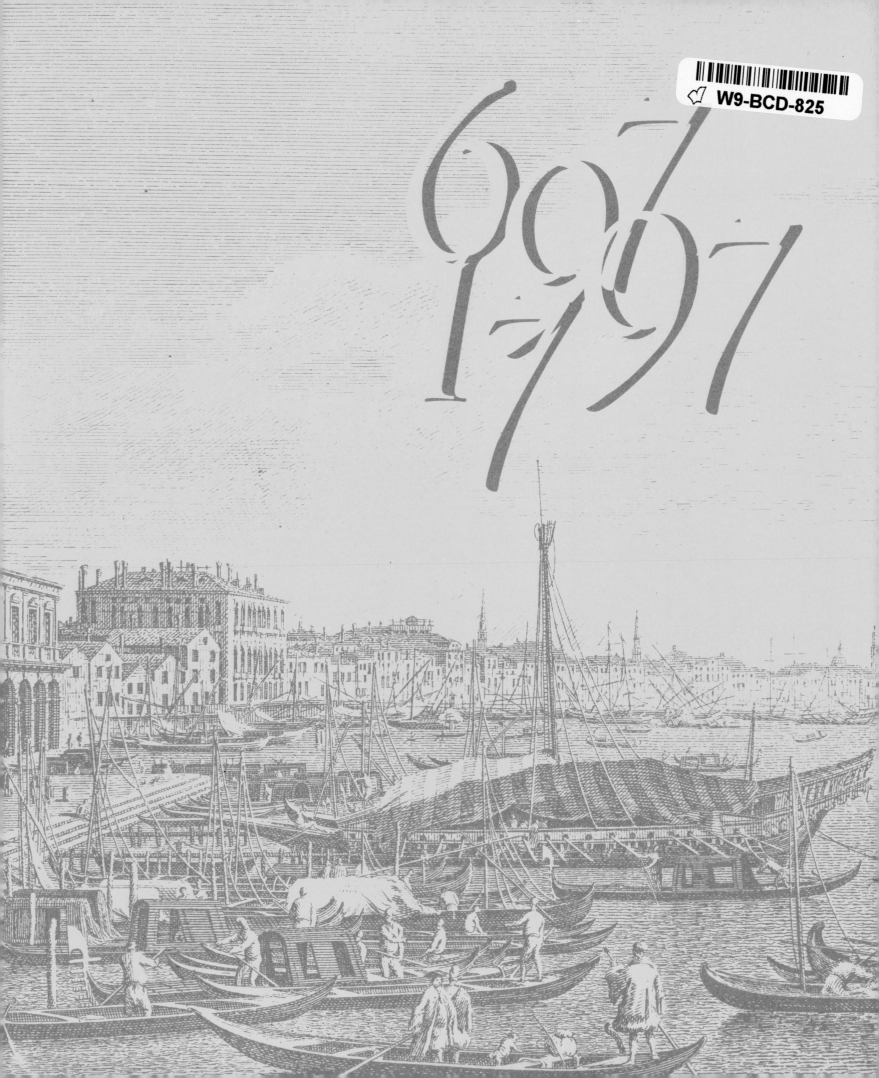

1997

A City, a Republic, an Empire

ALVISE ZORZI

VENICE 697–1797

THE OVERLOOK PRESS
PETER MAYER PUBLISHERS, INC.
Woodstock • New York

Opposite title page:
Panel from Paolo Veronese's *Pala Feriale* (1345),
depicting the miraculous discovery of the body of
St. Mark in one of the columns of the Basilica.
Museo Marciano, Venice.

English translation by Judyth Schaubhut Smith

First published in hardcover in the United States in 2001 by
The Overlook Press, Peter Mayer Publishers, Inc.
Woodstock & New York

Woodstock:
One Overlook Drive
Woodstock, NY 12498
www.overlookpress.com
[for individual orders, bulk and special sales contact our Woodstock office]

New York:
141 Wooster Street
New York, NY 10012

Library of Congress Cataloging-in-Publication Data

Zorzi, Alvise.
   [Città, una republica, un impero. English]
   Venice : a city, a republic, an empire / Alvise Zorzi.
      p. cm.
   Includes bibliographical references and index.
   ISBN 1-58567-132-0
   1. Venice (Italy)—History—697–1508. 2. Venice
   (Italy)—History—1508–1797. I. Title.
DG676 .Z59413 2001
945'.31—dc21
                                        2001021021

Printed and bound in September 2001
by Artes Gráficas Toledo, S.A.
Printed in Spain

D.L. TO: 2037 - 2001

First English edition: 1983
Revised English edition: 2001

CONTENTS

VENICE: MYTHS AND COUNTER MYTHS

The various myths and legends surrounding the birth of Venice are far more ancient than Venice herself. While the rest of the world was virtually unaware of the settlements on the Realtine Islands that were destined to become the city as we know her today, Cassiodorus, Roman minister to Theodoric, King of the Ostrogoths, would lend credence to these various accounts in a letter addressed to the "Maritime Tribunals." In his correspondence, he described an amphibious population who lived like marsh-birds, who tied up their boats to their dwellings instead of hitching up their horses, and who thought nothing of traveling "enormous distances" across the waters.

Cassiodorus was particularly impressed by the way in which the Venetians used their boats to go about their daily lives. Some fifteen hundred years later, Marcel Proust would be struck by the same phenomenon as he rode along the Grand Canal: "Just like the ladies in the Bois de Boulogne," the women of Venice "were leaning back against the cushions of their family's gondolas" as they meandered from one place to another, "even if they were only paying visits to family members or friends, or running everyday errands. . . ." For Proust, such an experience was tantamount to "going to a museum while on a boating excursion."

When Venice came into her own as a major European city, the legends surrounding her singular lifestyle would be reaffirmed time and again by her many admirers. The first to do so were the powerful rulers of the day, such as Henri III of France, whose state visit in 1574 was greeted with all the pomp and circumstance the Venetians could muster. As early as 1001, the Roman Emperor Otto III would pay his respects in relative obscurity, as would Emperor Joseph II in the year 1775. Other famous visitors arrived in absolute obscurity so as to enjoy a new sense of freedom as they wandered the streets and squares in search of a way of life "so different from their own."

Of no lesser importance were diplomats such as Philippe de Commynes, who described the Grand Canal as the most beautiful street in the world. For Prince Metternich, who would arrive in Venice some four centuries later, strolling around St. Mark's Square was the equivalent of taking a walk through one of the tales in A Thousand and One Nights.

As far back as the 13th century, St. Mark's Square would delight the likes of Ezzelino II da Romano, the noble head of such a warring clan that Dante compared him to a "spark" that could set half of Italy on fire. "On ne peut nulle part cacher si bien sa vie comme à Venise" ("There is no other place on earth where you can hide away more easily than in Venice,") wrote Count Giuseppe Gorani, the Milanese adventurer and Illuminist who had been treated so poorly by every important personage in Europe.

At a later date, the legend of "Venice, the city for lovers" was born, thanks to that most Venetian of institutions, the courtesan, whose role in Renaissance society was immortalized by poetess Veronica Franco, as well as the "dames gallantes" of Pierre de Bourdeille (better known as the Abbé de Brantôme), who so longed for "the happy, carefree life of the courtesan" that they would not even have exchanged places with "the empress of the entire universe!" Then, of course, there was Pietro Aretino, one of the city's most famous adopted sons, whose 16th-century writings firmly established Venice as the center of "licentiousness" and "lasciviousness," and Giacomo Casanova, whose celebrated memoirs two centuries later would only reinforce the image of a civilization dedicated to carnality and corruption. Among the 19th-century Romantics who would further perpetuate the myth of the "city for lovers," there were George Sand and Alfred de Musset, whose accounts of their idyllic sojourn in Venice confirmed what the world already knew. It was not until the early 20th century that Filippo Tommaso Marinetti and his Futurists would attempt to destroy this romantic stereotype when they exhorted the city to "murder the moonlight!" Despite their heroic efforts, the Venetian moon still shines on millions of honeymooners!

"Hier bin ich ein Mahler!" ("Here I can actually be an artist!") wrote Albrecht Dürer during his stay on the Grand Canal as a guest of the Fondaco dei Tedeschi (the complex of warehouses, offices and living quarters of the local German merchants). His remark reaffirmed yet another myth surrounding the city on the lagoon—Venice as the cultural capital of Europe. It was here that artists from throughout the continent enjoyed the respect and admiration of the entire populace. It was here that the ever-changing light captivated painters from Canaletto and Guardi to Turner, Whistler and Monet. It was here during the 17th century that outlawed noblemen would risk being captured rather than miss the final dress rehearsal of a new melodrama. It was here that Antonio Vivaldi served as impresario, conductor and violin soloist at one of the city's 14 theaters, while at another, Carlo Goldoni produced 16 new comedies in one season. Finally, it was here that the city's mayor (who was also a recognized poet) founded the Biennale, the first important exhibit of contemporary European art, at the end of the 19th century.

During the Renaissance, the legends surrounding the Republic's extraordinary system of local government would gain universal respect and admiration. Foremost among these were the balance of power embodied in her written con-

stitution, her state Senate, described as "la più gran testa politica che sia in Europa" ("the greatest political body in all of Europe," which ruled with a wisdom and authority unequaled elsewhere on the continent), the skill of her diplomats, the shrewdness of her secret agents, and above all, the love and loyalty she engendered in the most humble of her subjects. (This last phenomenon was acknowledged by none other than Niccolò Macchiavelli, whose general antipathy toward the Venetians was a well-established fact.) At the same time, the myth of Venice as the promoter of humanist ideals was born. Not only would she establish herself as a refuge for radical reformers, opening up the doors of her university in Padua to heretics and free thinkers alike; she would also dare to humiliate Maximilian, the Holy Roman Emperor, and even defy Julius II, the "papa terribile," who had first allowed Italy to be overrun by foreign invaders in order to thwart the Republic's expansionist policies, and who then seceded from the League of Cambrai with the proclamation, "Fuori i barbari!" ("Out with the barbarians!") Among those who personified the free spirits of 16th-century Venice were individuals as diverse as Bernardo Tasso, father of the poet Torquato, Bernardino Ochino, a Capuchin friar and eloquent orator whose sermons bordered on heresy, and Pietro Aretino, celebrated throughout Europe for his bold attacks on the rich and powerful.

Along with the myths there were, of course, the counter myths, the first being "Venice, the republic of predators," who had somehow managed to "fleece" every head of state in Europe. Rumors to the effect that the Venetians had their hearts set on founding a universal monarchy the likes of which had not been seen since the days of ancient Rome, spread by such influential figures as Niccolò Macchiavelli, which were already flying between court and chancery by the beginning of the 16th century, led to a series of anti-Venetian alliances that would culminate in the formation of the League of Cambrai.

During the Enlightenment, there were the terrifying legends surrounding the dreaded Venetian Inquisitors of State, along with the infamous "Piombi" (prisons situated under the "leads," or lead-covered roofs of the Doges' Palace) and "Pozzi" (the lower prisons, which Casanova's vivid imagination actually placed beneath the level of the Rio di Palazzo). At the fall of the Republic, there were also the negative images promulgated by the very forces that had brought about her demise, which would continue to fascinate writers, poets, artists and musicians throughout the Romantic Age, and which still persist to this day, thanks to popular culture.

Between the 19th and 20th centuries, any number of influential scholars took it upon themselves to systematically destroy the myths surrounding Venice's 500-year-old tradition of aristocratic governance (which had already come under severe attack by the leading figures of the Risorgimento, especially in light of Daniele Manin's revolutionary democratic Venetian Republic of 1848–49, and his resurrecting of the winged lion to the cry of "Viva San Marco!") In particular, the ruling class of the last years of the Serenissima, a favorite target of these moralistic historians, was variously described as "effete," "dissipated," "ineffectual," "incompetent," and above all, "corrupt." According to one author, who chose to totally disregard the libertine atmosphere of contemporary London, Paris and Versailles, they were by far the most corrupt nobility in Europe. This is yet another negative stereotype that has persisted to the current day.

In any case, none of these scholars was able to come up with a logical explanation for the 11 centuries of political independence enjoyed by Venice, or the 500 years during which she profited from the general consensus of her citizenry. It is only in the modern era that certain historians have emerged who are free of the prejudices of the past, and are willing to reopen the dialogue begun with such great insight and erudition by Samuele Romanin, who pursued his passionate defense of Venice in the most desperate of times. Among these, we are especially grateful to Frederic C. Lane, Fernand Braudel, Gaetano Cozzi and Alberto Tenenti, who have finally allowed us the opportunity of judging the events of those 11 centuries, in all their unique aspects, with clarity, honesty and a spirit of open-mindedness.

We would also hope that our own efforts, which have enjoyed 20 years of enthusiastic readership in Italy and abroad, will continue to contribute to a greater understanding of the historical realities surrounding the city, the republic, and the empire known as Venice, despite the fact that they are neither purely academic, nor are they meant to convey startling new discoveries or radically differing interpretations. Although this volume is now being published in revised form, complete with additional illustrations, charts and diagrams, it has remained faithful to its original purpose, which was that of offering the reader both a concise and accurate portrayal of Venetian history and culture and a thoroughly enjoyable literary experience. Ever mindful of Voltaire's famous maxim, "Tous les genres sont bons sauf le genre ennuyeux" ("All genres are fine except for the boring"), this writer fervently believes that there is no reason on earth why a historical work cannot be as readable as it is scientifically accurate. Thus far, his Italian, English, French and American readers have proved him right.

Venice-Rome, June 1999
Alvise Zorzi

"VENETIAE CAPUT MUNDI"

Opposite page: Detail of a painting by Gaspar von Wittel, illustrating what the Molo and the Doges' Palace must have looked like at the beginning of the 17th century, when Venice was famed for her enormous wealth and extraordinary beauty (Madrid, Prado Museum). As early as 1423, when the city had reached the height of her power, Doge Tommaso Mocenigo would proudly proclaim: "At this time of peace and prosperity, our city has 10 million ducats in capital funds, some of which are invested in ships, and some in galleys and other sailing vessels throughout the entire world. These bring in a profit of two million ducats in exports and another two million in imports. By now we have launched a total of 3,000 merchant vessels carrying anywhere from 10 to 200 amphoras and 17,000 crew members, 300 ships carrying a total of 8,000 crew members, and 45 galleys, both large and small, carrying upwards of 11,000 crew members. . . . The generations that came before us have made this possible. If you can maintain the current situation, you will be greater than all others. May God grant you the strength to govern wisely. . . ."

"The Venetians are bound and determined to establish a monarchy the likes of which has not been seen since the days of ancient Rome!" So said Enea Silvio de' Piccolomini, also known as Pope Pius II. "The Venetians have got their hearts set on founding a monarchy in the grand old Roman tradition!" Such were the words of Niccolò Macchiavelli, author of *The Prince*. "They are all so stubborn and pig-headed, always prowling around with their tongues hanging out, waiting to swallow up as much territory as they can, just to satisfy their lust for power, and rule the entire land of Italy!" Such was the opinion of Francesco Sforza, the Duke of Milan. But King Louis XII of France would take things one step further: "The Venetians will stop at nothing until they succeed in ruling the entire world!"

Even though these accusations were made at the height of the Renaissance, similar rumors had been flying between court and chancery from the time of the Middle Ages. Everyone had joined in the fray, from the chroniclers of Padua, Ferrara, Genoa and Greece to the great poets of Florence and the princesses of Byzantium.

The Venetians' opinion of themselves was quite a different story. Witness a stone marker in the atrium of St. Mark's Basilica dedicated to the memory of Doge Vitale Falier, which bears the following inscription: "He was the king of kings, the law of the land." In the Church of San Giorgio Maggiore, a similar memorial refers to Doge Domenico Michiel as "the terror of the Greeks," and "the bane of the Hungari-ans." Then, of course, there is the proclamation of the Lion of St. Mark, that proud heraldic beast who holds up the Gospel in one hand and brandishes his naked sword in the other:

> *I am the great lion himself,*
> *And my name is Mark the Evangelist!*
> *Whoever should attempt to defy me*
> *Shall be banished from my sight!*

Modern-day Venice. A winter's evening when the mist muffles the soft sounds of the lapping of the tide, and the rare passerby, chilled to the bone, wends his way through the silent streets. A bright summer's morning when the colorful, carefree caravan of tourists from every corner of the earth wends its way from canal to campiello. The everyday life of the common folk of Venice, captured so vividly by Goldoni's comedies, who still pursue their unhurried pace, from the traditional glass of white wine in the local bar to the cutting remarks of the women who sit gossiping as they thread their pearls. The cultured, sophisticated life of the Venetian nobility, who drift between concerts in town and conferences on the Island of San Giorgio, and the Carpaccios in the Scuola degli Schiavoni and the Accademia Gallery. The so-called high life lived by the local expatriots, immortalized forever in the novels of Ernest Hemingway. The decadent life of a city living on the brink of disaster, promulgated by Thomas Mann, Maurice Barrès and

Right: The earliest known map of Venice, contained in a manuscript dated 1346 and preserved in the Biblioteca Marciana. This precious document indicates that almost the entire city had already been laid out by that time. Excess water produced by the draining of nearby wetlands was either diverted into canals or flushed out into the lagoon. The schematic drawing at the bottom of the page gives us a clearer picture of the Grand Canal as it wound its way throughout the city:

1 The Lido
2 San Pietro
3 The Arsenal
4 The Island of San Giorgio
5 St. Mark's Square
6 The Rialto
7 The Island of Murano
8 Cannaregio
9 The Giudecca
10 San Nicolò

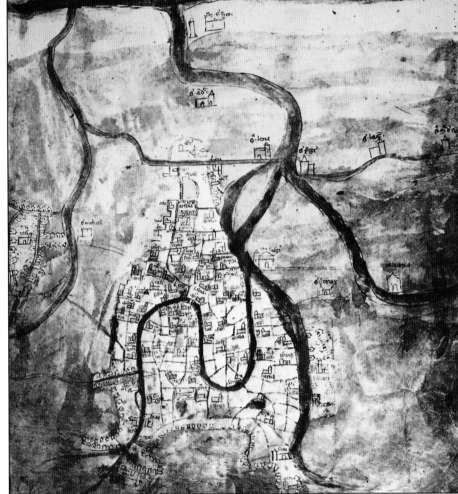

the Venetians themselves considered the ultimate compliment: *"Roma caput mundi, Venetiae secundi"*), the other European superpowers would finally set aside their own differences and form a united front against her.

For the average individual sipping an aperitif in one of the plush and slightly decadent salons of the Café Florian underneath the arcades of the Procuratie Nuove, it would be hard to believe that by the beginning of the 16th century, the problem of Venetian territorial expansion had become so pressing that her neighbors found it necessary to join forces against her. Could Venice possibly have represented as great a threat as Napoleon? Yet history tells us that it was not until the entire continent of Europe had been thrown into confusion by Bonaparte's conquests that another such coalition was actually formed!

In the year of our Lord 1508, the major European heads of state gathered together in France, where they entered into an alliance that would come to be known as the League of Cambrai, after the town in which the pact was signed. These included the pope, the kings of France, Spain and Hungary, the German emperor, and the Archduke of Austria. Shortly thereafter, lesser powers such as the dukedoms of Mantua, Ferrara, Urbino and Savoy would align themselves with the League as well. Even the King of England would stake a future claim on the partition of the Venetian territories! And Venice took up the challenge.

Luchino Visconti, and reinforced by a constant barrage of books and films.

Yes, the remains of a grand and glorious past are still to be seen. But they cannot even begin to convey a proper idea of that arrogant, overbearing Renaissance republic who aroused such hatred, fear and suspicion among her neighbors, all of whom were terrified at the thought of a universal monarchy. By repeatedly conjuring up the threat of a Venetian empire modeled after the grandeur of ancient Rome (which

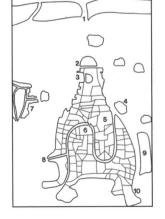

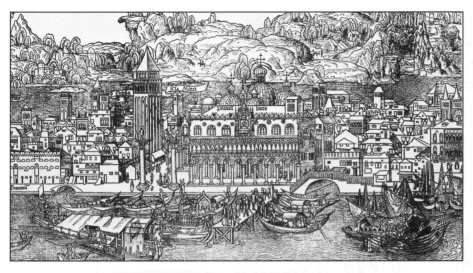

Above: An idealized sketch of Venice from a 15th-century illuminated manuscript that is now in the Bodleian Library at Oxford. Although it is obvious that the artist himself had never actually seen the city, he undoubtedly based his drawing on the accounts of merchants or statesmen who had visited the Serenissima.

Left: Fifteenth-century engraved illustration by Erhard Reuwich depicting the Bacino di San Marco, including the Molo, the Doges' Palace and the Piazzetta, from Breydenbach's Peregrinato. The number and variety of boats give us some idea of the amount of traffic on the Grand Canal during the city's golden age.

hand combat. Certainly, they deserve our respect and admiration, as they are truly the mightiest of men. . . ."

Despite all of the above, just about anyone alive today would find it almost impossible to comprehend the extent of power and influence that Venice wielded during the 400 years or so in which she reigned supreme (from 1100 to the end of the 1500s). It would be especially difficult to visualize the enormous amount of territory that she eventually controlled, whether directly or indirectly, not to mention the seemingly limitless mercantile and financial resources that she came to enjoy. Even the official textbooks published by the Italian government for the use of the nation's schoolchildren either ignore the subject of Venetian history entirely, or seriously misrepresent it. In so doing, they reflect the fact that other myths and legends (particularly those concerned with Italian unification) have taken precedence over everything else. The story of Venice has been erased from the slate, thanks to prejudices old and new, such as the vicious propaganda surrounding the sorry circumstances of the fall of the Republic, which was promulgated by the very forces that had brought it about! With the exception of those few individuals who are engaged in scholarly research, the rest of the world has been left with the image of a romantic getaway that has chosen to wallow in its own decadence.

And yet the amount of power wielded by the Republic of Venice for well over four centuries was so enormous that perhaps it can only be compared to that enjoyed by Victorian England at the height of her own empire. The type of criticism hurled at both superpowers is another parallel between them. In fact, certain anti-British propaganda sheets that were circulated toward the end of the British Empire recall almost to the letter the anti-Venetian pamphlets that were to become so popular at the height of the Renaissance!

During the years when the Venetian popes Eugenio IV Condulmer and Paolo II Barbo were presiding

Two of her territories on the mainland, the Veneto and Lombardy, were lost to the enemy shortly after the fighting began. From Santa Marta, San Nicolò and Cannaregio, the Venetians could see the glow of the campfires of the insurgents, who had pitched their tents no more than a stone's throw away. They could even hear the dull thud of artillery fire. But these same individuals had no intention whatsoever of surrendering. Instead, they reminded each other of those times in the past when they had found themselves in equally desperate straits. They remembered the year 1380, when the Genoese navy had joined forces at Chioggia with the armies of the Duke of Padua, the Patriarch of Aquileia and the King of Hungary, and how all would have been lost had Carlo Zeno's galleys not suddenly arrived from the East. And the time when the Hungarians invaded the lagoon itself in their small, skin-covered boats, only to meet death and defeat. And the year 801, when the Franks, under Charlemagne's son King Pippin, had penetrated so far into the labyrinth of canals that they were hacked to pieces by the townspeople at the site that is now known as the "Orphans' Canal."

I am the great lion himself, and my name is Mark the Evangelist! Whoever should attempt to defy me shall be banished from my sight!

Surrounded on all sides, and given up on by just about everyone, Venice would emerge from the war with the League of Cambrai more powerful and independent than ever before. In the words of a minister from France: "The people of Venice are a rugged race indeed. They dared to lie in wait in the open countryside for the four most powerful princes in Christendom, and with banners unfurled, they engaged in hand-to-

had managed to infuriate the entire population of Constantinople, and humiliate the Byzantine Emperor Manuel Comnenus himself, with the outrageous display of power and wealth put on by the naval ships that had escorted the Venetian ambassadors to Byzantium.

By the time Comnenus ordered the arrest of all citizens of Venice residing in his territory, her merchants were actively engaged in trade from the westernmost part of Europe to the Far East, and some 150 years had passed since the main cities and islands of Istria and Dalmatia had surrendered to Doge Pietro II Orseolo during the course of his triumphal crusade. And yet the borders of the city herself did not reach as far as the smokestacks and cranes of today's Porto Marghera. The same people who called their doge "the king of kings," "the terror of the Greeks" and "the bane of Hungary" were confined to a small, scattered archipelago protected by a thin strip of coastal islands in the part of the lagoon that extended from the source of the Isonzo to that of the Adige, or from Grado to Cavarzere. Such were the frontiers of what had once been a remote Byzantine province, then a city-state, and finally a republic unlike any other in the history of mankind, whose courage and fortitude had allowed her to withstand the onslaught of the great powers and superpowers of the day.

From the Early Settlements to the "Serenissima"

"Once upon a time, Venice was nothing but a deserted swamp . . . an uninhabited outback. . . ." These words, spoken by the Byzantine emperor Constantine Porphyrogenitus, exemplify to what extent the story of the birth of the city that would one day become a great metropolis at the crossroads of East and West has taken on mythical proportions. Despite the noise of the planes on their way to and from Marco Polo Airport, if we venture out to the remotest part of the lagoon as it is today, near Lio Piccolo and Lio Mazor, among the small islands covered by a thick carpet of blue-green grasses that turn a deep red in the fall, and along the fishing banks in the so-called *"valli da pesca,"* and the narrow canals that disappear into the swamps and shoals, we can easily see why the various accounts of the founding of Venice are reminiscent of the Biblical story of the creation of the universe!

Both tradition and legend attribute the establishment of the early settlements in this part of the lagoon

A late-15th-century iconographic map of Venice from Tolomeo's illustrated manuscript entitled Cosmographia *(Biblioteca Apostolica Vaticana, Rome).*

in Rome, they were constantly exposed to the savage attacks of the humanist Platina, who accused them and their fellow citizens of being not only arrogant, but ignorant as well. As early as the middle of the 12th century, the Venetians had been the objects of similar insults on the part of the citizens of Constantinople, whose outrage and indignation would eventually lead to the mass arrest and expulsion of all members of the Venetian expatriot community. Not only had these arrogant foreigners assumed almost total control over commerce and the sale of arms. They had also insisted on paying less customs duty than anyone else. Like the British in Shanghai, they had even taken over one of the more desirable neighborhoods in the city, which included a private square and adjacent church, as well as a foundry and well-equipped docks. Finally, they

catastrophe that took place somewhere between the fourth and 11th centuries.)

There was Grado, a small fortified town with its own harbor, which was only a short distance from Aquileia, a former capital of the Roman Empire. There was a Roman colony at Chioggia, and there must also have been a Roman settlement, however modest, on the Island of Torcello. There were probably a number of forts as well on the islands that make up the historic center of Venice (perhaps at Castello, or even San Marco). Then, of course, there was Altino, an important city that was located at the very edge of the lagoon.

As far as the fate of Attila, *"flagellum Dei"* is concerned, many locals still believe that a certain monumental stone located on Torcello was once his temporary throne. Legend also has it that his body is buried, along with boundless treasure, beneath the tiny island known as Monte dell'Oro. Even though we know for a fact that he nearly destroyed the city of Altino, he cannot take the blame, or the credit, for the mass migration to the lagoons.

Neither can Alaric, the King of the Visigoths, whose invasion of the mainland coincided with a famous medieval legend giving March 25, 421 A.D. as the actual date of Venice's birth. The migration of the inhabitants of the many prosperous communities situated in the Roman Veneto, such as Padua and Corcordia Sagittaria, and Altino and Coderzo, would hardly take place all at once, even if the onslaught of the Goths and Huns most probably prompted those individuals with enough means to seek immediate shelter among the islands of the lagoons. The major event that set in motion the mass exodus from the Veneto was actually the arrival of an especially primi-

Left: Early settlements in the Venetian lagoon, as depicted in a 10th-century manuscript written by Cristoforo Sabbadino (Biblioteca Marciana, Venice).

Above: The dockyard of the Arsenal. Detail of an engraved illustration by Erhard Reuwich from Breydenbach's Peregrinato.

to the successive incursions of barbarian tribes, and above all to the invasion of Attila the Hun, "the Scourge of God," who forced the inhabitants of the Roman cities on the mainland to seek refuge among these same small islands, and along these same fishing banks and narrow canals. As they fled from the fury of the invaders, they took with them their sacred relics, and those few belongings they had managed to salvage from the fury of their northern neighbors.

In reality, the lagoons that stretch from Isonzo to the Po had never been the deserted swampland described by Porphyrogenitus and so many others. (Today we have good reason to doubt that the lagoons actually existed at that time. Recent archeological finds would lead us to believe that the region was originally farmland that was irrigated by a series of canals, and that the lagoon itself was formed as a result of a natural

Right: Engraving by Berardi entitled View of the Lagoon, after a painting by Canaletto. Venice's natural setting, which has never failed to fascinate the world at large, was the very reason that she was able to survive. When the flourishing mainland cities of the Roman province of Venetia were pillaged and plundered by various barbarian tribes, their inhabitants sought refuge in a remote area of the lagoon, where they would come to consider the surrounding waters as the source of life itself. Protected by the marshes on the landward side from the threat of further invasions, and sheltered from the onslaught of the nearby sea by the lidi, this thousand-year-old maritime community would find the ideal environment. Opposite page: Detail of Jacopo de' Barbari's famous Pianta prospettica (1500), depicting the islands of Burano and Torcello.

Roman order as represented by Byzantium. In short, they had decided to uphold those age-old Romano-Veneto traditions that had their roots on the mainland.

Over the years, however, attitudes would begin to change, and the inhabitants of the "Maritime Province of Venice" found themselves aligned with one side or the other as they moved closer to absolute autonomy. In the midst of bloody reprisals, they would eventually reach the decision that the provincial ruler ("il Duca," who would later be called "il Doge") should be elected by popular vote. His official residence, which was also the capital city of what was by then a small confederate state, was moved from Cittanova to Malamocco. And it was here in the year 810 that the invasion of Pippin, the son of Charlemagne, would forever change the course of Venetian history.

Once again, it is Porphyrogenitus who tells us that Pippin, "who already ruled over the Pavians and others," swooped down on the Venetians "with his might and his army of men," intent upon reaching the Island of Malamocco "along with all of his horses." The Venetians stopped him dead in his tracks by barricading the harbor with rows of piles, and then "launching a counterattack from their ships with arrows and javelins." In response to Pippin's famous proclamation: "You are my subjects, because you belong to my lands and dominions," they promptly replied, "We wish to be the subjects of the Roman Emperor, and not yours!"

According to local chroniclers, Pippin's entire fleet was stranded in the shallow waters of the lagoon, and suffered severe losses as they were forced to retreat. According to Frankish chroniclers, Pippin had actually succeeded in imposing his rule over the Venetians. Whatever the case may be, Pippin and his father Charlemagne eventually had to resign themselves to the fact that "Maritime Venice" would remain under the authority of the Emperor of Byzantium.

By refusing to swear allegiance to the King of the Franks, Venice would save herself from a future of

tive, aggressive Germanic tribe known as the Lombards. Unlike the Goths and Huns, they had invaded Italy with the firm intention of staying for good!

During those years, if not centuries, of constant violence and guerilla warfare, at a time when the last vestiges of the crumbling the Holy Roman Empire of the German Nation (then under the sole authority of the Eastern Roman Emperor, who ruled from Byzantium) were besieged from all sides by the newly arrived "barbarians," individuals and institutions would eventually establish permanent settlements away from the mainland among the waters of the lagoons, which formed a natural barrier against further incursions on the part of the "landlocked" invaders.

New cities were born near Grado, which had already become the center of religious life, and on Torcello, which Porphyrogenitus himself would describe as a "great emporium." There were Cittanova, and Eraclea, which was established at the far end of a lagoon that has since disappeared. There were Metamauco, and Malamocco, which was situated at the edge of what is now the Lido. There was the cathedral at Torcello, founded in 639–40, where a stone marker imbedded in its walls proclaimed the ultimate authority of the Patriarch of Ravenna, the personal ambassador of the Roman Emperor on Italian soil (the same marker bore the name of Marcellus, who served as military commander and local governor), which shows us that the earliest settlers had already made a specific political choice. Instead of swearing allegiance to the new Longobard regime, they had opted to remain loyal to the ancient

In response to Pippin's famous proclamation:"You are my subjects, because you belong to my lands and dominions," they promptly replied, "We wish to be the subjects of the Roman Emperor, and not yours!"

feudalism and farming, and turn her face instead toward the sea, and the eastern lands that lay beyond it. After she had formalized her relationship with the Franks through an agreement signed in Constantinople (which would later be personally renewed by the doges and Charlemagne's successors), she would also become the official channel for dealings between the two great powers. In the end, this would lead to her dual role as the bridge of communications and trade between East and West.

As we can see from a number of contemporary documents, there was yet a third party that would soon enter into the picture. The nation of Islam, with its sprawling, overpopulated cities teeming with rich and poor alike, would also establish close commercial ties with the tiny maritime community. The Byzantine East, the Moslem East and the European West were to become the three sides of a triangle on which Venice would base her policy of economic expansionism, which would, in turn, become the very foundation of her future greatness.

King Pippin's abortive attempt to conquer the Roman province known as "Maritime Venice" would lead to yet another extraordinary series of events. In fact, it was at this point that the Venetians decided to abandon Malamocco once and for all, and move the center of government to the more important Realtine Islands (the historic center of today), where they would be protected from further invasions by the deeper waters and greater distance from the mainland. As they began docking their merchant vessels along the gently meandering Grand Canal, they also decided to call themselves the "City of Venice."

Just a few years later, in 829, the body of St. Mark the Evangelist, which had been removed by Venetian merchants from its final resting place in Alexandria of Egypt, was brought back in triumph to the city on the lagoon. According to ancient Romano-Veneto legend, Mark had been the founder of the Patriarchate of Aquileia, and the people of Venice greeted his arrival with wild enthusiasm. Once in possession of these precious remains, they felt that they had finally succeeded in forging a new identity for themselves. They had their own ruler, their own capital, and their own patron saint. From that moment on, they would dedicate their lives to political independence, as well as extensive territorial expansion. And on the site where they had buried the bones of St. Mark, they would erect one of the most beautiful churches in all of Christendom.

Even though Venice would continue to maneuver between the empires of Byzantium and the Franks (later known as the Germanic Holy Roman Empire) for many years to come, in no way did she ever depend on either of them. Over the years, her longstanding relationship with the Byzantines would gradually take on new dimensions through a series of decrees issued by the Eastern Emperors, who were to grant the Venetian merchants an ever-increasing number of special privileges. Those same citizens of Venice whom the courtly language of Constantinople insisted on calling "our dearest friends and subjects," had, in fact, become "our dearest friends and sovereigns!" The events of 1171, when the emperor Manuel Comnenus ordered the arrest and expulsion of all Venetian expatriots, would only confirm the current state of affairs. Those "dearest friends and subjects," who had established absolute control over the Byzantine economy, were also protected by a military machine the likes of which Byzantium had never seen before!

As far as Comnenus and his subjects are concerned, once the Venetian merchants had left their shores, they were obliged to look elsewhere for someone who could give a boost to their sagging economy. Unfortunately for them, the whole of the Mediterranean Basin was in the hands of the Italians. Aside from the Venetians themselves, the most powerful shippers and traders were the Genoese and Pisans. (The Amalfitani had been eliminated from competition many years earlier, while Ancona and Gaeta lacked the necessary means to compete on a grand enough scale.)

By severing his relationship with the Venetians, and abolishing those special privileges that had allowed them to monopolize the entire Byzantine economy, Comnenus would set in motion a series of events that were to culminate in the Fourth Crusade of 1204. With the conquest of Constantinople, and the parti-

tioning of what was left of the Eastern Roman Empire (the so-called "Partitio Romaniae"), Venice would begin to lay the foundations for what would one day become a vast colonial empire.

We shall return shortly to the subject of the "Partitio Romaniae," and how much of the Byzantine territory Venice had received as a result of the partition she was actually able to keep for herself. For now, suffice it to say that from the year 1205 on, Venice would gradually become as important a colonial presence as she was a mercantile power.

Why a mercantile power? The meager, barren soil on which the Venetians had chosen to settle themselves, much like the seagulls perched on top of poles throughout the lagoons, yielded only a modest crop of food. There were but a few wooded areas, and even fewer vineyards (such as the one located on the island that is still known as "Le Vignole"), and only where there were underground springs of fresh water. Except for scattered herds of cows and horses, nothing else was actually raised. But the same canals and fishing banks that fed the local population also contained endless amounts of salt. From time immemorial (certainly from the time of the Romans), salt works had existed throughout the lagoons, particularly in the area between the Realtine Islands and Chioggia. This precious mineral, which the Venetians would sell as far and wide as their barges could take them, was as important to the survival of the Middle Ages as oil is to modern man. As early as the time of the Gothic invasions, their ships would set sail over the "limitless horizons" of the Adriatic in search of corn and wine on the shores of Istria.

Aside from the Adriatic coast, their "customers" included towns and cities on the Italian mainland, where salt was transported through the waterways of the Po Valley by means of barges that often had to be drawn by hand along a towpath. One 10th-

which would then be sent to the Moslem East, together with large quantities of timber. (This last, the only other natural resource found in the lagoons, would actually float in on the tides of the Piave and Adige.) Both wood and iron were considered strategic materials, and popes and emperors from East and West did what they could to obstruct trade with the Saracens, whose ferocity and mobility kept the entire Mediterranean Basin in a constant state of crisis. But the Venetian merchants went on their way undaunted, even when faced with the threat of excommunication!

In exchange, they brought home all sorts of exotic spices, which the Western World considered almost as precious a commodity as salt. Pepper, which is mentioned in the earliest Venetian documents, was the universal drug of choice. (Coffee and tea had not yet appeared on the European scene, hard liquor was a rarity reserved for the rich, and tobacco was still *in mente Dei.)* Aside from urine, which the wealthy used to preserve game, there was no means available for keeping food from going bad, or even making it palatable when it was no longer fresh. Snow, which was hauled down from the mountains at an enormous cost, was used primarily to cool beverages such as wines mulled with cloves, cinnamon, ginger and coriander.

In a world in which money was also a rarity, and where ships' anchors were either rented or inherited, the city of Venice was to accumulate such enormous wealth that she would witness the birth of a new social class. The *nouveau riches,* who counted among their numbers not only business entrepreneurs and merchants, but master craftsmen as well, would gradually gain the acceptance of the old, aristocratic landowners (who were themselves more than willing to engage in commerce and the sale of arms). Eventually, the members of the aristocracy would be given new blood by intermarrying with their prosperous neighbors. Together, they became the driving force behind the power politics of the day.

As far as the "common folk" of Venice are concerned, it is somewhat difficult to comprehend exactly what role they and their "popular assembly" played in the political life of the city. Despite the fact that absolute power had long been restricted to a small circle of nobles (or wealthy merchants, since almost all of the merchants were nobles, and almost all of the nobles were merchants), the doge continued to be elected by popular acclaim, and the major decisions of the government were still ratified by the assembly.

century Pavian customs official would express his amazement at such a phenomenon in the following terms: "These people who don't even plough or sow can buy grain and wine wherever and whenever they want to!"

The Venetians would soon start trading more sophisticated goods from the Orient, such as fabrics, perfumes, exotic bird feathers, and even slaves. And while it seems that no one else was capable of making glass at that particular time, their own production of this precious material was so plentiful that the furnaces were eventually ordered to be moved to the Island of Murano to avoid further poisoning of the atmosphere with the noxious fumes from their chimneys.

Salt and glass were also transported by land, especially to Styria, where they were exchanged for iron,

Over the years, however, the common people would gradually be forced to take second place, until their participation in local politics was reduced to merely shouting their approval or disapproval of government policy in St. Mark's Square. This situation would come to a climax in 1297, when the members of the upper classes staged a sort of *coup d'état* (with the full approval of the government). Such was the famous (or infamous) *"serrata del Gran Consiglio"* ("Closing of the Great Council"), when the lower classes were literally "closed out" of the Great Council Chamber.

This particular episode, which so outraged liberal historians of an earlier age, and which still makes contemporary Marxist historians wrinkle up their noses, was the result of a series of events that should not be measured by today's yardstick, but rather in light of the social and political climate of the times. As the historian Frederic Chapin Lane has pointed out, there were originally no more than 40 individuals (wealthy, influential members of the business community, according to another historian, Yves Renouard) who were directly involved in political decision-making. By the time of the famous "Closing of the Great Council," however, all major decisions had been assigned to a political assembly known as the *Gran Consiglio*, which eventually numbered more than 2,000 members of the same social class. These "patricians," as they would eventually call themselves, were the sons of penniless nobles as well as wealthy merchants and craftsmen, the descendants of the old, aristocratic families as well as the heirs to recent fortunes.

For the next 500 years, the one and only requisite for active participation in political affairs would be membership in an elected political assembly. This extraordinary system of government (which was no more unusual than any other aspect of Venetian politics) seems to have been inspired by the Venetians' ultimate respect for "political expertise," which was passed down from one generation to the next, rather than the dominance of one particular social or economic class. (As we have already said, among those who were "closed inside" the Great Council, there were wealthy financiers, merchants, arms salesmen and entrepreneurs, but also aristocrats without a penny to their name.) As such, it was about as far removed from today's anti-populist politics as it could possibly be!

Were the members of the Great Council nothing but career politicians? Certainly not. But they were duty-bound to play an active role in the affairs of state. For those who belonged to the patrician class, there were absolutely no other alternatives. Yes, they could engage in commercial or shipping activities that might take them away from the city for long periods of time. But as soon as they returned to their native shores, they were obliged to participate in the political process. This responsibility was hardly limited to the legislative functions of the Great Council (which met as a rule on Sunday). It might well involve a stint as a foreign embassador, or provincial governor, or even military commander.

As time went by, these civic duties would become more and more onerous. During the 16th and 17th centuries, there were only two ways that a member of the patrician class who had reached the majority age of 25 could avoid being caught up in the web of the *cursus honorum*. He could either join the priesthood (all members of the clergy were automatically excluded from participating in politics), or, if he had the means, he could pay an enormous fine.

The effective result of the "Closing of the Great Council," however one may choose to judge it, was that while the rival city of Genoa would undergo constant political upheaval at the hands of warring political factions both at home and abroad, Venice would enjoy 500 years of total and absolute autonomy. Her ability to defend herself not only from possible foreign domination, but from internal threats to her security as well, is proof positive that the system of government she had chosen worked to her advantage. The final proof of this may well lie in the fact that she was able to maintain her integrity as an "Italian" city, whereas the rest of the Italians would be subjected to every sort of foreign influence from the time of the late Renaissance on.

almost all of the merchants were nobles, and almost all of the nobles were merchants

Venice: Incomparable, Unconquerable

Although the gradual process of stripping the popular assembly of all of its prerogatives had been relatively painless, the "Closing" itself would suffer a number of serious repercussions. On the morning of June 15, 1310, several of the city's "grandees," who could not

Opposite page: On the south side of the facade of St. Mark's Basilica stands the Treasury Tower, at the corner of which are two pairs of fourth-century porphyry figures representing Diocletian and his imperial colleagues. The walls are covered with alternating slabs of polychrome marble, decorative fragments of plutei and geometric bas reliefs dating from the ninth to the 11th centuries. On the front of the ledge that runs along the bottom are two late-13th-century putti being devoured by dragons. Over a span of three centuries, the lavish use of decorative elements for the facade of St. Mark's was a conscious attempt to reflect the growing importance of the Venetian Empire. At the very end of the 12th century, the spoils of war that began pouring into the city's harbors in the form of precious marbles, columns, sculptures and capitals were scattered throughout St. Mark's Square to proclaim the Republic's supremacy over all others.

resign themselves to the fact that they were no longer part of the power structure as a result of the new system of hereditary political rule, would attempt to overthrow the government in favor of an absolute dictatorship.

The organizers of this plot were the heads of the great families of Querini, Tiepolo and Badoer, who were led by Baiamonte Tiepolo, popularly known as the *"gran cavaliere"* ("grand gentleman"). Baiamonte was the heir to a family of nobles who had already given the city two doges, and who now had their hearts set on giving her a third. (His father, Jacopo, had also enjoyed such widespread popularity that he had been considered a serious candidate for the office of doge.) In the end, Baiamonte's attempt to impose himself as dictator would fail dismally because of the lack of popular support. In fact, among those who rallied around Doge Pietro Gradenigo and confronted the insurgents in St. Mark's Square, there were plenty of local craftsmen and common folk who made it absolutely clear that they preferred the political monopoly of the aristocracy to the personal dictatorship of a single individual.

So ended the famous Tiepolo-Querini Conspiracy, which would lead, among other things, to the establishment of the dreaded tribunal known as the Council of Ten, whose name still evokes memories that are almost as terrifying as those of the Spanish Inquisition, and whose nefarious activities have inspired a steady stream of novels, plays, operas and films.

Another conspiracy to overthrow the government came to a tragic end in 1335, when Marino Falier, the doge himself, took part in a plot that was actually promulgated by certain powerful representatives of the *"popolo grasso."* These last were members of the wealthy bourgeoisie whose hatred of the old aristocracy had prompted them to lend their financial support to alternative candidates throughout the length and breadth of Italy. The plot was discovered, and Falier lost his head for his failed attempt to rule "with an iron hand." This time as well, the common people refused to have anything to do with the conspirators. Once again, they joined their fellow citizens in St. Mark's Square in response to an urgent appeal on the part of the city fathers.

After this sorry episode in Venetian history (which has been exploited by everyone from Donizetti to Byron to Delacroix), the role of the central government would be established for the rest of time. The "Republic" of Venice, who had reached the height of her political and economic power by the first half of the 15th century, no longer had to concern herself with pressures from the outside world. Instead, she was free to engage in the painstaking process of debate and discussion that was so essential to her own survival. In fact, rather than diminishing the importance of a popular assembly, the "Closing of the Great Council" had

a formula for anything as complicated and complex as the City of Venice? From the earliest historical accounts to the "Patrician Republic" of Charles Diehl and the "Maritime Republic" of Frederic Chapin Lane, scholars have repeatedly failed in their attempts to find the proper formula. Both the Republic of Venice and the City of Venice are something so unique, so incomparable, and so complex that they literally defy definition.

Nothing could be more complicated than a map of Venice herself. Despite the infinite variety of artistic and architectural styles, and the jumble of streets and canals in the heart of the city, the overall effect is completely harmonious. By the same token, despite the jumble of rules and regulations that formed part of Venice's political structure at the height of her power, the overall effect is one of total harmony. These same rules and regulations illustrate to what degree the "powers that be" were able to give the citizens of Venice a balanced system of government that would stand the test of time. And what about the test of time? In Venetian history, "time" is measured in very large doses. Together with the Byzantine Empire, the Republic of Venice still holds the endurance record among all the states of Europe.

actually reinforced the idea of a parliamentary system of rule.

Is it possible to come up with a nice, neat definition of anything as complicated and complex as the class system and political structure of the Republic of Venice? For that matter, is it possible to come up with

THE KEYS TO POWER

Opposite page: Portrait of
Doge Leonardo Loredan, who
ruled Venice from 1501 to
1521, by Giovanni Bellini
(National Gallery, London).
Once considered the supreme
political and military authority,
the Venetian doge (whose name
derived from the Latin word
"dux," or "leader") would
gradually lose his rights and
privileges until he was little
more than an elected chief
magistrate. Leonardo Loredan,
who is depicted by Bellini in all
the majesty and dignity for
which he was renowned, was
head of the Republic at a time
when Venice "had the whole
world against her." In fact, her
increasing power and influence
would eventually force the other
great leaders of the day, Pope
Julius II, King Louis XII of
France, Emperor Maximilian
and Ferdinand of Aragon, to
enter into an alliance known
as the League of Cambrai
(1508). It was only through
the Venetians' extraordinary
political cunning that they able
to maintain control over their
territories on the mainland.

THE MOST SERENE REPUBLIC, "MAINLAND SENATE" AND "MARITIME SENATE," "THE COUNCIL OF FORTY" AND "THE COUNCIL OF TEN," "EL PARON DE LA REPUBLICA," "CACCIATI I PAPALISTI," A SYSTEM OF CHECKS AND BALANCES, VENETIAN CIVILIZATION

As the head of the Republic, or rather, the Most Serene Republic, as it came to be called in later centuries, surrounded by every possible outward manifestation of sovereignty, the doge was truly the living embodiment of the majesty of the state. He was clothed in the most sumptuous of garments, including mantles of brocade and ermine, gold and silver damask, and scarlet silk according to the season and the circumstances. On ordinary occasions, he would wear "*il corno d'uso*" (the "everyday" horn-shaped cap that was the Venetian equivalent of an imperial crown) over the "*camauro*," or "*rensa*," which was a type of bonnet made of fine linen woven in Rheims. Only on Easter Sunday, when he paid his annual visit to the Church of San Zaccaria, could he be seen wearing the "*zogia*" (*gioello*, or jewel), the far more opulent cap that he had been crowned with at the top of the Giants' Staircase in the Doges' Palace.

The so-called "ordinary" occasions were either religious processions that took place on important liturgical feast-days, such as Corpus Domini or Palm Sunday, or solemn state visits to this or that church, or this or that monastery. (There were enough of these to fill almost the entire yearly calendar. On January 6th, for example, the doge would visit the Cathedral of San Pietro di Castello for the feast of San Lorenzo Giustiani, the first Patriarch of Venice. On January 31st, he would celebrate the retaking of Padua from the League of Cambrai in 1512 at the Church of Santa Marina. On February 2nd, he would attend a service at Santa Maria Formosa in memory of the Venetian brides who been rescued from Narentine pirates in the

year 935.) On each of these forays, he would be escorted by all the trappings of Byzantine royalty, including the silver trumpets, the unsheathed sword, the *cero* (Paschal candle), the chair, cushion and damask umbrella, and the eight silk banners bearing the emblem of the Lion of St. Mark, two of which were white, two red, two violet and two blue, symbolizing respectively peace, war, truce and allegiance.

Along with his name, the doge's image was stamped on all coins of the realm as he knelt in adoration before St. Mark the Evangelist. It also figured on the signet ring that he wore on his finger, where there had once been written "*voluntas ducis*" ("the will of the doge"), and where there was now, instead, the phrase "*voluntas senatus*."

On Maunday Thursday, he would look as stately and majestic as any Caesar or pope while he stood between the two red columns of the colonnade in front of the Doges' Palace and presided over the celebrations taking place in the Piazzetta. (These annual festivities, which commemorated the defeat of the Patriarch Ulrico of Aquileia, traditionally culminated in the beheading of a bull and 12 pigs, an irreverent allusion to the prelate himself and his 12 canons!) On every Ascension Day, he would be rowed by shipyard workers from the Bacino di San Marco to San Nicolò del Lido to perform the Republic's annual marriage ceremony with the sea. During the journey on board his elaborately carved and gilded galley, which was known as the *Bucintoro* (Bucentaur), he was escorted by literally hundreds of gondolas and boats of every possible shape

The Procession of the Doge on Palm Sunday. *The original engraving, which measures four meters (13 feet) in length, was executed by Matteo Pagan between 1556 and 1559. It is now in the Correr Museum in Venice. The doge was the living embodiment of the grandeur and dignity of the state, as can been seen in this detailed rendering of a ducal procession, which was led by eight silk banners bearing the emblem of the Lion of St. Mark.*

and size, all of which were decked out in grand style. To the pealing of church bells throughout the city, and the thunder of the fleet's entire artillery, he would eventually arrive at the mouth of the port, and the open sea, where he would hurl a wedding ring into the waters of the Adriatic as he pronounced the famous words, "We wed you, o sea, as a symbol of our absolute and everlasting supremacy."

When the doge died, it was not his own body that lay in state on a bier in the *Sala del Piovego,* with his cap on his head, his sword by his side, and his spurs on his boots. His earthly remains had already been buried during the night, in the strictest of secrecy, in his family tomb. Instead, it was a dummy made out of straw, with the doge's features modeled in wax, that was escorted to

the requiem mass at the Church of SS. Giovanni e Paolo by a huge entourage, including important statesmen, ambassadors, patricians, and all the priests and monks in the city. (At the funeral of Doge Giovanni II Corner, there were said to be as many as 6,000 mourners.) It was the same dummy that was raised up in the air nine times by sailors in front of St. Mark's Basilica, each time to the cry of "Lord, have mercy!" In the end, it was merely *"un sacco de pagia e mascara de cera/el cadavere là del Serenissimo"* ("a sack of straw and mask of wax/that corpse of the Most Serene").

This extraordinary custom, which began with the death of Doge Giovanni Mocenigo in the first years of the 16th century, seems to have originated from the fear of contagion in times of plague rather than any

particular political motive. Whatever the case may be, it is profoundly illuminating: It was to the office, and not to the man himself, that all respect, devotion and honor were due. In fact, through a series of constitutional amendments, the doge's role as an absolute monarch in the first few centuries of the Republic had gradually evolved into that of a chief magistrate whose powers were extremely limited. The task of actually deciding how much influence the new doge would wield fell to a group of advisors known as the *"Correttori alla Promissione Ducale"* ("Revisors of the Coronation Oath"), who were promptly appointed on the eve of his election to the supreme office. It was their task to alter the *Promissione* by effecting new rules and regulations regarding the ducal rights and privileges. At

each succession, in fact, in an effort to discourage anything even remotely approaching a cult of personality, the power of the doge was limited even further, and his authority even more restricted.

Although the doge was one of the very few Venetian magistrates who did not have a fixed term of office, he was also one of the very few who was not permitted to carry out his mandate on his own. Upon the death of his predecessor (in the last 600 years of the Republic, only Francesco Foscari would abdicate in 1457), the new doge was elected by all patricians over the age of 30 who were members of the *Maggior Consiglio* by means of an extraordinarily complicated procedure involving a whole series of steps in which the participants were first chosen by lot, and then by ballot. The

Next in line were the silver trumpets, followed by the doge's chamberlains, the canons wearing their copes, the patriarch in his pontifical vestments, the members of the clergy, and the secretaries. Then came the equerries, who bore the ducal cap, and the gilded chair and cushion, and finally the doge himself, dressed in a mantle of ermine and gold. Behind him were the ambassadors, the symbolic sword, and the patricians dressed in robes of damask and velvet.

1

ASSERTING HER ABSOLUTE SUPREMACY: VENICE'S MARRIAGE CEREMONY WITH THE SEA

3

Desponsamus te, mare, in signum veri perpetuique domini. "We wed you, o sea, as a symbol of our absolute and everlasting supremacy." These were the words spoken by the doge on Ascension Day as he hurled a golden wedding ring into the sea from the upper deck of the *Bucintoro.* This proud acknowledg-ment of Venice's maritime power may well have had its origins in a *benedictio maris* (blessing of the sea) at the time that Doge Pietro II Orseolo led his famous expedition against Dalmatia (1000). After Venice had gained further freedom and glory as a result of having brought about a reconciliation between Pope Alexan-der III and Emperor Frederick I in 1177, this simple ceremony would be supplemented by the far more splen-did and ornate *desponsatio* as a means of confirming her absolute sovereignty over the Adriatic.

Following the traditional proces-sion in St. Mark's Square (5, from a painting dated 1515), the doge would set out in the *Bucintoro* along the route illustrated in Figure 3. After meeting the patriarch's barge in front of the Fort of Sant'Andrea, he proceeded to the port of the Lido (2), where he actually threw the ring into the sea. On his way out to the Lido, the doge passed through the Bacino di San Marco along the Riva degli Schiavoni (1, from a painting by Francesco Guardi). During the return trip, he would stop for mass in the Church of San Nicolò del Lido (6, from another painting by Guardi).

The marriage ceremony with the sea was connected to the legend of a poor fisherman who supposedly gave the doge a ring that he had received from the Evangelist on the tragic night during the reign of Doge Bartolomeo Gradenigo in which Satan had threat-ened the city with a terrifying storm (4, detail of a painting by Paris Bordon). Over time, the ceremony itself came to be viewed more as a colorful spec-tacle than a national event.

4

2

5

6

The Great Council Chamber in the Doges' Palace during an actual plenary session. Engraving by Paolo Furlani, 1566. The Great Council, which was the supreme governing body of the Republic, was comprised of every Venetian nobleman over the age of 25. In its great hall, laws were passed, and high government officials were elected. The important issues of the day were first examined by specially appointed committees, and then voted upon when the entire Council was in session. At such times, the doge himself would sit at the center of the "Tribunale," or "Bancale di San Marco," flanked by the "Serenissima Signoria," while the Council members occupied the seats along the walls and in the double rows of benches placed back to back.

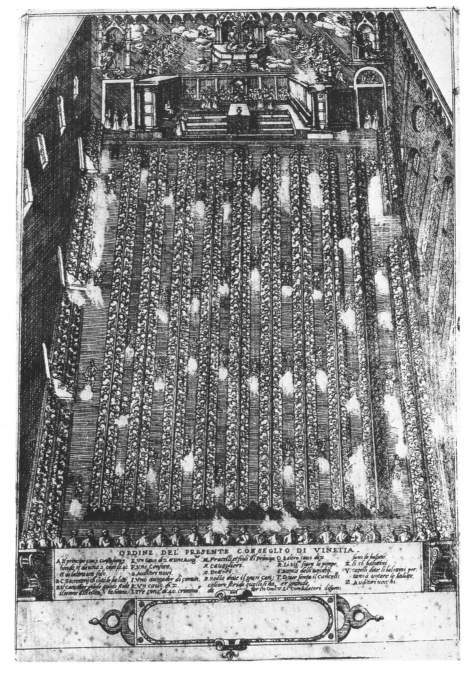

their balloting balls, since they could not be related to each other by birth or by marriage.

Twenty-one of the original 30 were then eliminated, again by lot, whereupon the remaining nine elected 40 new electors by ballot, 28 of whom were eliminated by lot. By a majority vote of at least nine, the remaining 12 then elected 25 new electors, 16 of whom were eliminated by lot. The remaining nine elected yet another 45 electors, whose numbers were reduced to 11 by lot. These last were the actual electors of the electors of the "Most Serene Prince of the Republic," a group of 41 individuals whose numbers could not include any of those who had been involved in the entire nominating process.

The election itself, which required a majority of at least 25 votes, took place during a conclave that might last an extremely short while (as was the case when Pietro Grimani was elected on the first ballot in 1744), or an inordinately long time (as was the case in 1655, when Carlo Contarini was elected after 68 separate ballots). There might be a number of candidates to choose from, or perhaps just one, as was the case when Marco Foscarini, the illustrious historian and man of letters, was elected in 1762.

Upon his election, the new doge assumed the exalted status that would be his and his alone. After being presented to the people in St. Mark's Basilica, he was paraded around the Piazza San Marco in his *"pozzetto,"* or circular sedan chair, on the shoulders of shipyard workers from the Arsenal while he and his relatives threw coins to the crowd. Then, of course, there was the coronation ceremony itself, which was followed by three consecutive days of feasting. Among the doge's first

process began with the entire body of nobles filing past an urn containing as many copper "ballot balls" (only 30 of which were gilded) as there were potential electors (usually more than 1,000, and sometimes as many as 2000). As each of them passed by, he would be handed a ball drawn from the urn by the so-called "ballot boy" (a child between the ages of eight and 10, theoretically chosen at random). At this point, only the 30 individuals who had received one of the *"balle d'oro"* ("gilded balls") were allowed to remain in chambers. Everyone else was obliged to leave the room, including the relatives of these 30 electors, whose names were "shouted out" by an usher as they were handed official duties, the most important by far was that of swearing his allegiance to the *"Promissione,"* or *"Coronation Oath,"* which contained the latest rules and regulations regarding his various rights and privileges, as well as the latest restrictions on his powers.

If we examine some of the richly illuminated copies of the *Promissione* that are still available in various Venetian libraries, we

can see just how many restrictions were actually placed on this highly decorative figure-head, whose coronation often marked the end of a long career of service to the Republic (on the sea, perhaps, or as an ambassador, or colonial governor, or member of the judiciary, or even as a member of parliament itself, whose duties were both endless and exhausting). First and foremost, he could not propose any measures to increase his own power. He could not abdicate unless he had been asked to do so. He could not receive anyone in an official capacity without his personal advisors being present, nor could he grant any private audiences. During public audiences, such as when he received foreign ambassadors (this was one of his prerogatives), how he would respond to a specific issue depended entirely on the reaction of his advisors. If anyone, under any circumstances, spoke to him privately about affairs of state, he was obliged to change the subject immediately. He could not display his own coat-of-arms in public, or have canopies placed over his throne. With the exception of close relatives, under no circumstances could he or his family members give or receive gifts. He could not let anyone kiss his hand, or kneel down before him. (Doge Agostino Barbarigo, who did allow such practices, became the object of such hatred that when he died, as a certain chronicler noted, "It was amazing to hear the curses hurled at him by one and all." Doge Lorenzo Celsi, who insisted on keeping lions and leopards in the ducal palace, and who had a page precede him wherever he went carrying some sort of a scepter, might well have ended up just like Marino Falier, if he had not died first of a broken heart, according to some, after one of his advisors had shattered the ill-fated scepter before his very eyes, and the Council of Ten had initiated legal proceedings against him.) He could not leave the palace except for official functions (even though more than one 18th-century doge is known to have slipped out in disguise for visits to the *Club dei*

If anyone, under any circumstances, spoke to him privately about affairs of state, the doge was obliged to change the subject immediately.

Filarmonici, located at the other end of St. Mark's Square, where a private room was set aside for their exclusive use), nor could he attend the theater, go to cafes, or participate in *conversazioni*. He could not even take a vacation without asking the government's permission, and proving that it was necessary for his health. Among the many prohibitions that affected the lives of his own sons and brothers, they could no longer vote in constitutional assemblies, nor could they accept any benefices or hold any ecclesiastical offices.

Give all of the above (and more), it is hardly surprising that certain of the important figures of the day dreaded the possibility of actually being elected. It was virtually impossible to bear up under the restrictions placed upon the doge and his family, and the incredibly demanding schedule that he himself was expected to keep (aside from the countless ceremonial occasions that he presided over, he participated in most of the sessions of the constitutional assemblies, as well as all meetings held by those government offices that had any degree of authority), without totally sacrificing his own life in the interest of the state.

It is no less surprising that the relatives of many a candidate for the *dogado* shuddered at the thought that their kinsman might emerge as the victor. Apart from everything else, they ran the serious risk of losing a substantial part of their personal wealth, in light of the fact that the doge's expenses usually far outweighed his considerable salary. (By the end of the Republic, three years' salary was barely enough to cover the costs of post-election festivities.) In addition, he had to pay for all the magnificent robes and mantles that comprised his extensive wardrobe, which alone were worth a fortune, and give expensive gifts to St. Mark's Basilica. Despite these obligations, he was prohibited from engaging in any commercial, industrial or financial activities that he might have been involved in before his election to the throne. Among his privileges, however, there was no exemption from paying his taxes!

Once the doge was dead, and the funeral service was over and the eulogies delivered, his personal finances were painstakingly audited by a group of individuals called the *"Inquisitori sul Doge Defunto"* ("Investigators of the Late Doge"), who nit-picked their way through the debits and credits recorded by

One of the ways in which ordinary citizens helped to maintain law and order was the anonymous letter, which could be dropped in any of the numerous "bocche di leone" ("lions' mouths"), or "bocche della verità" ("mouths of truth"), "mail-boxes" that were located along city streets and on the walls of magistrates' palaces. These accusations, denunciations, petitions and disputes between different parties were not taken seriously unless they mentioned at least two witnesses. Only when affairs of state were involved could the head of the Council of Ten and the doge's advisors, by a five-sixth majority, actually request an official investigation.

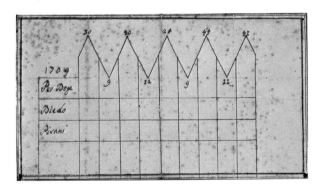

The election of the doge, which had originally been the prerogative of the popular assembly, was subsequently assigned to a limited number of individuals. The electoral process itself evolved gradually until it was codified in 1208. In order to avoid corruption, participants were first chosen by lot, and then by ballot, until the 41 members of the conclave were finally designated. The procedure began when all the members of the Great Council over the age of 30 filed past a young child known as the "ballot boy," who handed each of them a copper or gilded "ballot ball" that he had drawn from an urn. The 30 members who had received a gilded ball were then reduced to nine, again by lot. In turn, they elected another 40 electors by secret ballot, 28 of whom were eliminated by lot. The remaining 12 then elected 25 new electors, 16 of whom were eliminated by lot. The remaining nine elected yet another 45 individuals, whose numbers were reduced to 11 by lot. These last were the electors of the electors of the doge, whose responsibility it was to choose the 41 individuals that would participate in the conclave. After the 41 had proposed their candidates for the dogado, they voted for or against them by placing crimson ballots in as many urns as there were actual candidates. In the end, whoever had obtained at least 25 votes was elected doge. Above left: one of the ballots used in the election of Giovanni Corner in 1709. Above right: An engraving from the Venetian State Archives illustrating the complexity of the electoral process. Below: One of the election urns that was actually used.

the deceased under a provision in the law known as the *redde rationem*. If any irregularities at all were found, it was the doge's heirs who suffered the actual consequences. Even a great doge like Leonardo Loredan, who had been at the very center of the resistance movement against the League of Cambrai, was the subject of a post mortem inquest that lasted more than two years, and that eventually required his heirs to reimburse the state for 2,700 ducats thought to have been illegally appropriated as income. (As for the enormous sums that Loredan and his relatives had contributed to the war effort, these were considered voluntary donations, and in no way canceled out the alleged illegality!)

It is true, however, that whenever the *"Eccellentissimo Quarantuno"* ("Most Excellent Forty-one") elected an influential member of the community, or a particularly shrewd and skilled parliamentarian, limitations or not, the new *Serenissimo* could definitely assert his own authority. In fact, more than one doge was actually clever enough to resort to some form or another of subterfuge in order to hide his real ambitions. Such was the case of Agostino Barbarigo, and again of Andrea Gritti, a courageous general whose reputation as a despot obliged him to pretend to support the opposition in an effort to impose his own agenda. As for Francesco Foscari, the fact that he had sworn to obey the terms of the *Promissione* in no way prevented him from encouraging Venetian expansionism on the mainland as the head of a militant political party, nor did it keep Leonardo Donà dalle Rose from leading the desperate fight against Pope Paul V in defense of the sovereignty of the Venetian state.

Not all of the doges were of the same caliber as Silvestro Valier, "a great statesman and consummate politician," or Francesco Dandolo, or Nicolò Contarini, to name but a few of the most notable

ARBORE SIMBOLOGICO
Nel quale apertamente si scorge il Modo facile, e sicuro di elegger il Serenissimo Doge di Venetia

Il Serenissimo Maggior Consegio

A Con Balle d'Oro nu. 30. cauate à forte elegge 30. Nobili del medemo, che restano parimente à forte n. 9.
B Con 7. Balle, e non meno del predetto n.9. vengono eletti n 40. che à forte restano quelli n. 12.
C Con 9. Balle, e non meno del predetto n. 12. vengono eletti n 25. che à forte restano quelli n.9.
D Con 7. Balle, e non meno del predetto n.9. vengono eletti n 45. che à sorte restano n.11.
E Con 9. Balle, e non meno del predetto n. 11. vengono eletti n. 41. che con n.25. al meno aiutano al Trono Ducale, il Nobile fortunato, & eletto.

of those 120 individuals who held the office until the year 1797. In fact, during the 15th, 16th and 17th centuries, the doge's seat was often occupied for extensive periods of time by venerable old men whose decrepitude was usually coupled with immense personal wealth, and whose personalities were so weak that they were easily manipulated by others.

The Most Serene Republic

Who were the individuals who actually controlled the government at the height of Venice's power and influence under the terms set forth in her constitution? We have already noted that the doge himself was prohibited by law from making any decisions on his own. (He was not even permitted to open letters from ambassadors, or municipal or provincial governors, which were customarily addressed to him.) For that matter, in order for any of his actions to be considered legitimate, his personal advisors were required to be present. It was not the doge, but the doge and his advisors, who actually functioned as the heads of state.

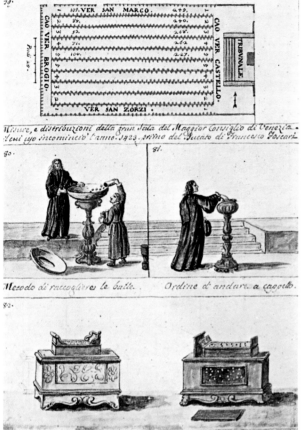

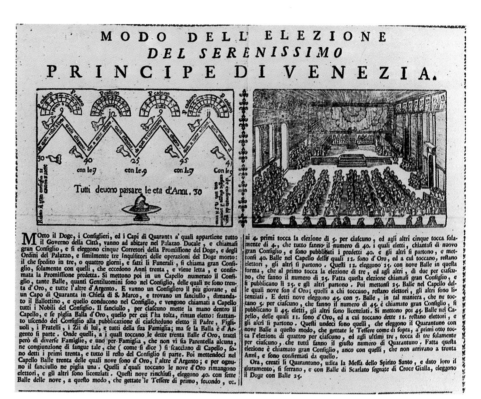

There were eventually six personal advisors to the doge, one for each of the city's six districts, or *sestieri,* which were Castello, Cannaregio, Dorsoduro, San Marco, San Polo and Santa Croce. All together, they made up what was originally known as the *Minor Consiglio,* or *Consilium Minus* (Lesser Council), as opposed to the Great Council, or *Maggior Consiglio.* Along with the doge and the three heads of the *Quarantia Criminal* (Criminal Court), the highest judicial authority, these individuals formed the *Serenissima Signoria* (Most Serene Signory), which was the supreme authority of the Venetian state.

Now let us take a closer look at the advisors themselves as they awaited the arrival of the doge in the *Sala degli Scarlatti* (Hall of the Scarlet Robes), which was their own private room in the Doges' Palace (named after their official robes, which were made of red damask). They could not be related to the doge, they served in office for eight months, and they were elected by the Great Council, three at a time, as needed. After their terms were up, they remained in the Senate for an additional two months, during which time they still had the right to vote.

The ever-changing role of these advisors (who were originally only two in number) was closely linked to the ongoing process of placing greater and greater restrictions on the doge's monarchical power. In 1033, when they appeared in public with Doge Domenico Flabianco, they were still merely puppets in his hands. By the year 1204, however, when Geoffroi de Villehardouin, the Marshal of Champagne, appeared before Doge Enrico Dandolo to request the loan of transport ships and vessels for what would be the Fourth Crusade, all six of them were seated next to the *Serenissmo* in their new role as "watchdogs" and special advocates, rather than personal advisors in the true sense of the word.

In fact, among their specific duties, they were not only expected to collaborate with the doge, but they were also charged with curbing and controlling his actions. At least once a year, during the first week of October, they would read him the entire *Promissione*

Above left: Floor plan of the Maggio Consiglio, and illustrations of voting procedures. Above right: Another page from the State Archives explaining the electoral process. Below: The "ballot boy," and the pair of wooden hands that he used to count the ballot balls at the final vote (Museo Correr, Venice).

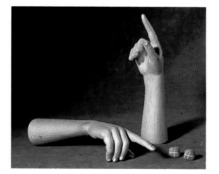

The Dogaressa Seated between Two Ladies-in-Waiting. *Engraving from Giacomo Franco's* Habiti d'huomeni et donne venetiane, *1610 (Biblioteca Marciana, Venice). The rights and privileges accorded the doge's consort, who was known as the* dogaressa, *were also laid down in the* Promissione, *as were the numerous prohibitions against such activities as accepting gifts, recommending individuals for public office, or entering into any kind of trade To compensate somewhat for these restrictions, her coronation ceremony was a lavish affair indeed, during which she was escorted from the Bucintoro to St. Mark's Basilica by the High Chancellor and four counselors of state, where she was personally received by the canons before swearing allegiance to the coronation oath and hearing the Te Deum. She then made her way solemnly to the Doges' Palace in the company of distinguished gentlemen and patricians, which had been decorated for the occasion by members of the various arts and crafts guilds, who exhibited their most precious wares in her honor, including carpets, tapestries, glass, and intricately carved weaponry. Opposite page, above: Engraving by Giulio Goltzio from G. G. Boissard's* Habitus (1581) *depicting the doge and dogaressa in splendid formal attire. Both the doge and dogaressa, as well as those of their relatives who resided in the Doge's Palace, were exempt from the city's sumptuary laws. In recognition of her exalted position, the dogaressa was also permitted to wear the ducal cap, or* corno, *although hers was smaller than the one worn by the doge.*

in order to remind him once again of its various stipulations. It was also their responsibility to admonish him whenever he seemed to be overstepping his bounds. Such was the fate of poor Doge Lorenzo Celsi, a most worthy, cultured and patriotic gentleman, and a personal friend of the poet Petrarch, whose insistence on having a scepter carried in front of him wherever he went was severely punished when one of his advisors shattered the hated object before his very eyes!

There were certainly plenty of other less dramatic, but equally significant, occasions when advisors felt it necessary to call the doge to account for actions that they thoroughly disapproved of. In 1464, for example, Doge Cristoforo Moro was supposed to have assumed command of the fleet for the crusade that Pope Pio II was attempting to organize against the Turks. However, besides being old and feeble, he was totally inexperienced in naval matters. After he had indicated that he had no interest at all in participating in such an endeavor, he was severely chastised by one of his advisors named Vettor Cappello, who told him in no uncertain terms, *"L'è necessario ch'el vada e che la terra (la città) non puol far de manco de adoperar la so persona per le occorenze de questi tempi"* ("It is absolutely necessary for you to go, for our city cannot do without your services in these times of need"). Two centuries later, Doge Domenico Contarini (who was as popular and well-loved as Doge Moro had been unpopular and disliked) made the mistake of sounding a little too authoritarian during his reply to a foreign ambassador, at which point his advisor, Piero Basadonna, interrupted him with these chilling words: *"Vostra Serenità parla da principe sovrano, ma la si ricordi che non ci mancheranno i mezzi per mortificarla quando trascorerà dal dovere"* (Your Serene Highness has the right to speak as a sovereign prince, but he should also remember that we are not lacking in the means to punish him when he neglects his official duties.")

In addition to monitoring the doge himself, the Most Serene Signory was ultimately responsible for the activities of his electors. If the members of the

conclave seemed to wasting too much time in political maneuvering, for example, it was up to the Signory to appear on their doorstep, whereupon they would peremptorily invite the *Eccellentissimo Quarantaun* to get on with it!

The members of the Signory played an important role in many other areas of government as well. For one thing, they were in charge of scheduling, and supervising, elections to various political offices and magistracies. The six advisors also took weekly turns at presiding over the *Maggior Consiglio*, during which time these *Consiglieri in Settimana* (Advisors of the Week) were expected to intervene in any violent disputes, to respond to members' requests for official explanations of government policies or actions, and to open and close the parliamentary debates themselves. Together with the doge, they sat in on all legislative and executive committee meetings, including those of the *Consiglio dei Dieci* (Council of Ten). Each of them, in turn, took part in the deliberations of the dreaded Tribunal of the Inquisitors of Sate. Finally, whenever the doge was away on vacation, the Signory itself was responsible for running the government, whereupon one of its members would assume the title and functions of vice-doge.

In turn, the members of the all-powerful Signory were themselves the subjects of any number of rules and regulations. While it was true that the doge was not allowed to leave Venice without two advisors dogging his heels, it was also true that none of them could leave the city for so much as a single day without the doge's permission. And just as the doge could not reply to any foreign ambassador without the collaboration of his advisors, they were not allowed to officially respond without the express authorization of the Senate. In fact, without the Senate's permission, the Signory could not make any decisions at all involving government spending or political appointments. Even their interpretations of the law of the land were subject to Senate revision. In the end, the *Scarlatti,* or *Rossi* (Reds), as the common folk called them, were as much

DVX VENETVS.   DVCISSA VENETA

a part of the system of checks and balances as the doge himself.

Which brings us to the Senate itself, in all of its power and glory. Francesco Maria della Rovere, the Duke of Urbino, who defined the upper house of the Venetian parliament as the wisest political head in the world, was not alone in his thinking. In 1582, Frederico Badoer, who was himself a skillful politician and man of letters, considered it a "perfect legislative body," in that its membership represent- ed all three stages of life: There were the young, who were daring by nature, and the old, whom experience had taught to be cau- tious and considerate, and the middle-aged, who were in full possession of their faculties, and both balanced and secure in themselves.

The *Consilium Rogatorum, or Consiglio dei Pregadi*, more commonly known as the *Pre- gadi* ("invited ones"), came into being around 1255, at which time its members were only 60 in num-

ber. In later years, this number was doubled by the institution of the so-called *Zonta (aggiunta)*, or "addi- tional 60 members," whereupon the election of all 120 was entrusted to the *Maggior Consiglio*. Over the course of the centuries, their numbers would continue to increase as more and more magistrates were per- mitted to participate, with or without the *"balla"* (the right to vote). By the time of the fall of the Republic, this supreme legislative assembly (the *Pregadi*, plus the *Zonta*, plus the magistrates, with or without the right to vote) numbered some 275 individuals, all of whom were elected, and all of whom had limited terms of office (one year for the *Pregadi* and *Zonta*, and variable terms for the magistrates). Among the Venetian patri- ciate, only the doge himself and the nine Procurators of St. Mark's were elected for life.

"Mainland Senate" and "Maritime Senate"

The miles upon miles of shelves in the cavernous Venetian State Archives containing the acts and debates of the Senate are divided into two major cate- gories, *Senato Terra* (Mainland Senate) and *Senato Mar* (Maritime Senate). Together, they give us a pretty good idea of the extent of the legislative and executive

Right: A page from the Promissione of Doge Andrea Dandolo, 1342 (Museo Correr, Venice). This was the doge's coronation oath, which defined both his rights and responsibilities. Above: The High Chancellor, who was head of the ducal chancery, depicted kneeling down before Doge Antonio Venier. Miniature from the Cronaca of Rafaino Caresini (Biblioteca Marciana, Venice).
Below: Portrait of a "consigliere," or ducal advisor, from the Capitolare dei consiglieri di Venezia (Museo Correr, Venice). Opposite page: The entrance to the Arsenal.

responsibilities assigned to the upper house of parliament. In fact, perhaps more than any other body defined in the Venetian constitution, it was closest to what we would nowadays call "the government." Just try to imagine a government of 275 individuals! But even in the worst of times, all 275 members of the Senate shared the responsibility for critical decisions involved in government policy-making. While it was certainly true that such an unwieldy number eventually led to many wrong decisions, and much waffling, if we consider that this particular form of assembly rule survived for a good 542 years, from the first *Consiglio dei Pregadi* to the fall of the Venetian Republic, it is obvious that it actually fared far better than many other governments that were in the hands of a single individual.

First and foremost among the responsibilities of the Senate was that of conducting foreign affairs. In early times, when Venice's very survival had depended on her relations with Byzantium on the one hand, and the Longobard Kingdom, the Carolingian Empire and the Romano-Germanic Empire on the other, skilled diplomacy had played a crucial role in maintaining her hard-won independence from such powerful and potentially dangerous neighbors. However, as the network of Venetian commerce continued to expand, so did the vast network of Venetian foreign affairs. New roads opened up for the caravans that struggled their way over the great land masses of the Alps, and down into the huge valleys of central Asia, through the snows of Pamir, the sands of the Trans Jordan, and the rocky terrain of the Gobi Desert. At the same time, fleets of mercantile ships mapped out new trade routes from West to East, from Southampton to Alexandria in Egypt, and Bruges to the Azov Sea. Thanks to

the extraordinary negotiating skills of her diplomats, treaties were signed, contracts drawn up, privileges secured, better tariffs granted, and any number of potential competitors defeated.

These same skills would be put to the test over and over as Venice's ever-increasing power and prosperity came up against the envy and hostility of her many rivals. There was also the constant threat of military action on the part of emerging national states such as France and Spain, not the mention the ever-present danger presented by a great multi-national power such as the Ottoman Empire. Time and again, the Venetian Republic would look to her diplomats to defend her on all sides. Whenever they returned from their vari-

ous diplomatic missions, the Venetian ambassadors were expected to report their findings directly to the entire Senate body. These documents, which have been preserved intact to this day, represent a vital source of information for modern scholars: Not only do they contain a wealth of detail on every possible facet of life in most of the great European states of the times (and many eastern countries as well); they also demonstrate the amazing insights displayed by the Republic's diplomatic corps as a whole.

In addition to their final reports, ambassadors were required to send daily dispatches to the Senate from the moment they actually left Venice until the moment of their return. These last were so incredibly detailed (no revelation regarding the lives of kings and queens, ministers and mistresses, or anyone else involved in the power structure of a particular country, no matter how intimate, was excluded) that we might well be tempted to attribute them merely to the Venetians' well-known predilection for gossip! In point of fact, they often provided the Senate with the necessary information to make reasoned decisions regarding foreign policy.

From earliest times, the permanent representatives of the Venetian Republic at the various royal courts of the day would play a vital role in the state's conduct of foreign affairs. Among the countless members of the ambassadorial corps who served so loyally throughout

"The Arsenal is at the very heart of the Venetian state." So stated the Senate in a document from the beginning of the 16th century, when the shipyards had already been in existence for four centuries. At that time, they covered almost as much space as they do now, and constituted the largest industrial complex and the greatest concentration of manpower in the world. If we take the vaporetto from the Bacino di San Marco, and turn into the Rio dell'Arsenale, we will find ourselves passing through the main entrance to the Arsenal, which is flanked by two towers. This canal, which leads us directly to the oldest section of the complex (A), is the same one that the Venetian galleys traveled through when re-

L'ARSENALE: THE HEART OF THE MARITIME REPUBLIC

turning to their fortified base. For security reasons, it was situated a good distance from the more exposed Bacino di San Marco, and protected from the rear by the muddy lagoon to the north of the city. Originally known as the *Arsenale Vecchio* (Old Arsenal), it was constructed in 1104, when it was made up of 24 building-slips (certainly not the only ones in the city), all of which were under the control of the state. At the beginning of the 14th century, it was substantially enlarged, first in 1303 (B), and then in 1325 (C), by using the shoreline of the Lake of Daniele (today , the *Darsena dell'Arsenale Nuovo*, or New Wet Docks) for the construction of additional building-slips. By the year 1423, when Doge Mocenico gave his farewell famous speech, there were some 16,000 *marangoni* (carpenters) employed at the site.

On the nearby Riva degli Schiavoni, there were two other important state enterprises, the *Magazzini dei Cereali* (Grain Warehouses), and the *Forni,* or Bakeries, which prepared the rations for all the Republic's ships as well as the overseas garrisons. Many of the other flourishing activities associated with the Arsenal were also located in the Castello district, as we can see from the street names that still exist today, such as the *Calle dei Bombardieri* (Bombardiers), *dei Corazzieri* (Armorers), *della Pegola* (Pitch), *del Piombo* (Lead), *delle Ancore* (Anchors), *degli Scudi* (Shields), and *delle Vele* (Sails).

In 1473, another large boat basin, known as the *Arsenale Novissimo*, was fitted out to the north of the *Arsenale Nuovo* (D). Further renovations were made inside the Arsenal's stout walls during the 16th century, first in 1539, with the addition of the *Vasca delle Galeazze* (Galleass Gate) (E), and then in 1564, with that of the *Canale delle Galeazze* (Galleass Canal) (F). Although large-scale efforts to modernize and retool continued up until the last years of the Venetian state, it was only under Austrian rule that the perimeter itself was further enlarged.

This huge state enterprise was administered by a council known as the *Eccellentissima Banca,* which was composed of three senators (the so-called *Provveditori del-*

San Francesco della Vigna

San Giovanni in Bragora

Canale delle Galeazze

Arsenale vecchio

Darsena Novissimetta

Darsena Arsenale Novissimo

Darsena Arsenale Nuovo

Darsena Arsenale Nuovo

Rio dell'Arsenale

Bacino di San Marco

Rio della Tana

Isola di San Pietro in volta

Canale di San Pietro

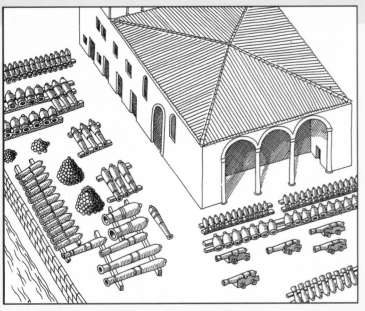

l'*Arsenale, or* Superintendents of the Arsenal), and three *patroni* from the *Maggior Consiglio.* Every two weeks, these individuals took turns at sleeping in the Arsenal itself, where they were responsible for keeping the keys to the warehouses and workshops, and checking on the guard during the night. On the technical end, the head of the Arsenal was the *Magnifico Ammiraglio* (Magnificent Admiral), who supervised the various *protomagistri,* or *proti* (site managers), from the ranks of whom the Admiral himself had come. These last were responsible for overseeing the different groups of skilled workers, such as the carpenters, caulkers, oar-makers, smiths, sawyers and gunpowder-makers.

The Venetian *Arsenale,* whose fame was such that it would lend its name to all arsenals that came after it, fulfilled the very same functions performed by any modern-day naval facility: It was a protected base fully equipped for construction, maintenance and repair, and a repository of supplies and weaponry. In 1590, when the Turks attacked Cyprus, 100 galleys (some of which were newly built, and others merely refitted with arms) were prepared for battle in the space of just two months!

The drawings contained on these pages give us some idea of the complexity and diversity of the yard's various activities. There were the all-important *corderi,* for example, who manufactured the hemp for ropes (before the introduction of iron in the 19th century, the main raw materials used in shipbuilding were hemp, pitch and wood). Their *Tana,*

or *Casa del Canevo* (Hemp Workshop), as it appears in an architectural drawing made by Antonio Da Ponte in 1579-83, measured 315 meters in length, and was divided into three naves with some 84 columns (1). Da Ponte was not the only great Venetian architect who worked on the Arsenal. Sammicheli constructed the building-slip for the *Bucintoro,* and Sansovino may well have designed the two covered wet-docks known as the *Gaggiandre* for the *Arsenale Novissimo* (1573) (2). At the fall of the Republic, the artillery storage area, which was called the "garden of iron" by those distinguished guests who were permitted access for propaganda purposes, contained all of 5,923 fire-arms (3). The building-slips occupied more or less the entire banks of the boat basins (6). The *Velerie,* which were the workshops where sails were cut out and stitched, were just as important as the shops where oars were manufactured (5). As part of the ongoing process of building and renovation to ensure that the Arsenal was functioning at top efficiency, a new wood-working shop was constructed in 1778 (4). It was here that the *squadratori* (wood-workers) made life-size drawings before cutting the timber for the latest type of battleship, which was called the *vascello.*

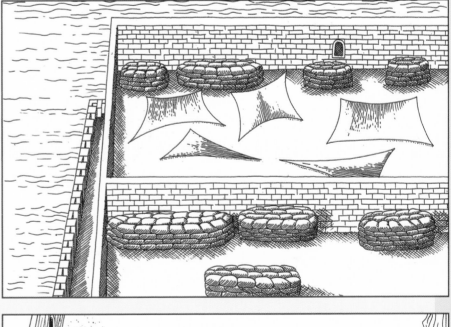

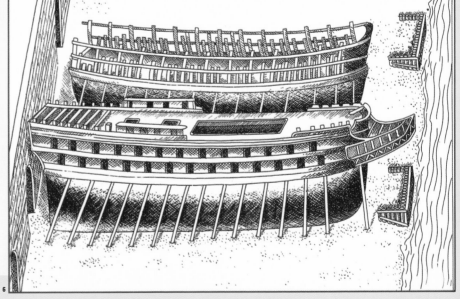

Above: Plan of the Arsenal dating from the 16th century (Museo Correr, Venice). Below: Engraving of a ship-yard worker by Grevembroch. These craftsmen enjoyed a privileged position in the Venetian social hierarchy: Not only did they work on the docks and in the port; they also served as fire wardens, and were the only manual laborers employed by the state mint.

the years, certain individuals have gone down in history not only for their diplomatic skills, but also for a devotion to duty that occasionally reached the level of true heroism. Perhaps the most extraordinary of these figures was Alvise Contarini, who was first named ambassador at the tender age of 25, and who then spent the rest of his life abroad, engaged in an unending serious of diplomatic missions, each more delicate than the last. In fact, in 1648, it was mainly through his own efforts that the long, drawn-out negotiations involved in drafting the Peace of Westphalia finally ended with the signing of a treaty that would restore the balance of power in Europe after the tragedy of the Thirty Years' War. In 1638, when he was acting as plenipotentiary in Constantinople, he himself was imprisoned by an enraged sultan after the *Provveditore* Marino Cappello had sunk 15 Algerian pirate ships in the Ottoman anchorage of Valona, Albania. However, even in those unpleasant, tenuous circumstances, he was able to maneuver in such a way as to avoid disastrous consequences for Venetian-Turkish relations. (The ambassadorship to Constantinople was always considered a risky business. The Turks were quick to arrest, and free with the scimitar, as Ambassador Marcantonio Barbaro, for one, would learn to his chagrin. After he was imprisoned in a lone tower, this cultured man of letters and patron of Paolo Veronese would go on negotiating until he was eventually set free. In 1648, the ill-fated Giovanni Soranzo was dragged in chains through the streets of Constantinople, where

he was subjected to public ridicule following the murder of his interpreter, or *dragomanno*. Ambassador-at-Large Giovanni Cappello actually died of torture and starvation while imprisoned in the Castle of Adrianople in 1652. His secretary, Giovanni Ballarin, would later die in the same prison after attempting to reopen diplomatic negotiations for eight long years!) In the course of their missions, other dedicated members of the Venetian diplomatic corps, such as Caterino Zeno and Giosafat Barbaro, would actually go to the extent of exploring remote, unknown regions in search of new economic ties that might prove useful to the Republic in the future.

In any case, we would be sadly mistaken if we thought of these indefatigable negotiators as merely smiling, silver-tongued diplomats, ready to compromise at any cost. Witness the reaction of Ambassador Giorgio Dolfin when Pope Julius II, a notorious hot-head, ranted and raved about reducing Venice to the fishing-village it really was, who replied, stony-faced, that the Republic would reduce the pope to the status of *"un curatello qualsiasi"* ("a humble country priest!")

Aside from foreign policy, the Senate also dealt with economic and financial affairs. Among its ranks, in fact, there were magistrates who were responsible for everything from collecting taxes and updating the taxpayer rolls (*Governatori delle Entrate, Dieci Savi sopra le Decime*, and *Provveditori sopra Camere*) to apportioning revenue (*Camerlenghi di Comun*) to collecting customs duty (*Provveditori sopra Dazi*) to keeping the government accounts (*Ufficiali alle Rason Vecchie, Ufficiali alle Rason Nove*, and *Provveditori sopra Conti*) to monitoring the banking system (*Provveditori sopra Banchi*). The upper house of parliament also elected a number of other important magistrates who were not among its members, but who nonetheless reported directly to it. First and foremost were the three *Deputati alla Provvision del Danaro* (Delegates for the Provision of Money), and the *Savio Cassier* (literally, the Wise Cashier), who together formed the Ministry of Finance. Then there were the *Scansadori alle Spese Superflue*, a group of "hatchet men" charged with reducing public spending, and the magistrates who supervised the many and varied activities of the state mint, including the coining of money, public and private deposits of precious metals, a savings bank, and an investment bank for state revenue. Finally, there was the *Depositario al Banco Ziro*, or Governor of the State Bank, which was founded in 1619.

In addition to the above, the members of the Senate elected any number of individuals who supervised the city's food supply, storage facilities, and price controls. (Judging from the rare instances of food shortages in Venice in comparison with the rest of Europe, they must have carried out their duties in exemplary fashion indeed!) They also nominated the five *Savi alla Mercanzia* (Commercial Experts), who were charged with investigating new ways and means to favor the expansion of Venetian trade, and as of 1707, the *Inquisitor delle Arti* (Superintendent of the Arts), who fulfilled the same function with regard to industry and arts and crafts. In the last years of the Republic, when the Venetian economy found itself in ever more dire straits, both these institutions were obliged to come up with a steady stream of new proposals to curb public spending. Unfortunately, many of these were not taken seriously enough, or were not implemented at all. (By then, neither the Senate nor the institutions themselves had any direct control over remedial action.) Such was the dilemma of Andrea Tron, one of the most prominent political figures of the day, whose reports to the Senate while he was serving as "Superintendent of the Arts" are a model of clarity and accuracy. Despite his attempts to save the situation, the economy was already so depressed that there was really nothing more to be done. Along with Venice herself, the Republic's finances would soon come to a sorry end.

Another series of institutions that fell under the aegis of the Senate, and that somehow managed to function efficiently in the last days of the Republic despite the general state of decline, were those concerned with flood control and soil conservation. Both issues were of critical importance to this amphibious community, which depended for its survival not only on the surrounding lagoon, but also on its territories on the mainland. On terra firma, in particular, there was the constant threat of flash floods due to the many rivers, large (the Po and the Adige) and small (the Piave, the Sile and the Tagliamento, among others), that cut through the Venetian possessions. A number of these same waterways, like the Piave, Sile, Brenta, Bacchiglione and Musone, also opened up directly into the lagoon.

Flood control was the direct responsibility of the three *Esecutori alle Acque* (Water Commissioners), who, along with three *Savi* (Experts), one additional *Inquisitor* (Supevisor), and three *Provveditori all'Adige* (the so-called "Superintendents of the Adige," who were the individuals who were actually charged with looking after the most troublesome of the rivers in the Veneto), formed part of the *Collegio delle Acque* (Maritime College). Ultimate responsibility for the lagoon itself

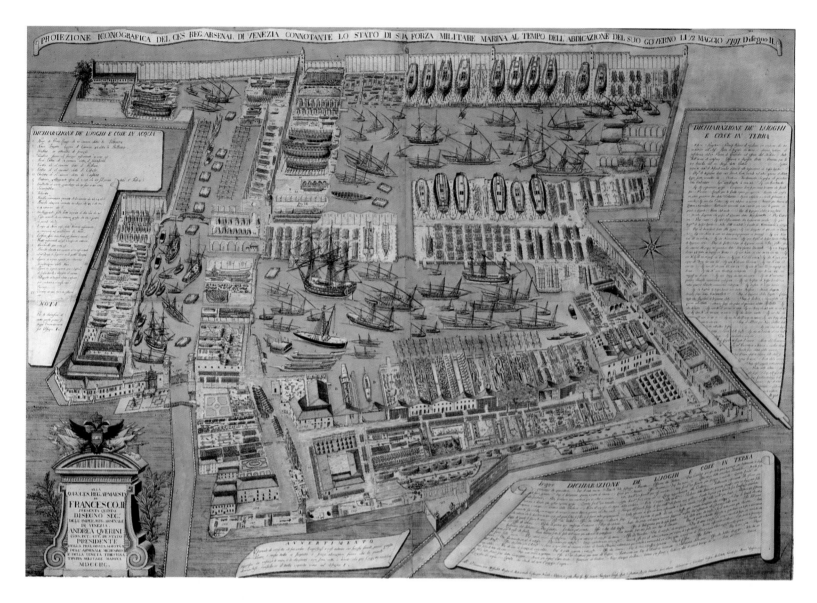

Above: Plan of the Arsenal by Abbé Giammaria Maffioletti, 18th-century naval author and instructor at the Scuola dell'Arsenale. Opposite page, above left: Engraving of the facade of the Arsenal by Michele Marieschi (first half of the 18th century). This enormous complex, which served both as a naval base and construction site, was founded by Doge Ordelaf Falier in the year 1104, and enlarged several times thereafter. At the height of the Republic, it employed as many as 16,000 workers.

fell to the three *Provveditori ai Beni Inculti* (Superintendents of Uncultivated Territory), who were concerned with basic ecological issues such as wetlands preservation and land reclamation.

Unlike many of their modern counterparts (at least in Italy, which has often suffered the tragic consequences), these various state agencies employed the services of the most qualified consultants and experts they could find. The wisdom and farsightedness of the acting magistrates and members of the Senate who reviewed their recommendations, and ultimately decided on the best course of action to follow, is more than obvious when we contemplate the enormity of the preventive measures that were actually adopted. Only a few short years before the fall of the Republic, the architect Bernardino Zendrini undertook the monumental task of reinforcing the *lidi* on the Adriatic side with the famous *murazzi*, or massive Istrian-stone sea walls, that line the coasts of Malamocco and Pellestrina.

Given the lack of cranes or other types of heavy machinery for transporting the great boulders of Istrian stone from the opposite shores of the Adriatic, it was truly an impressive feat of engineering. As early as the Middle Ages, rivers were diverted to prevent the lagoon from silting up, and two of the five natural channels through the *lidi* were blocked to minimize flooding, in a continuing effort to maintain the integrity of the vast, sheltered, impenetrable port that represented Venice's only real means of protection, and the instrument of her good fortune.

The considerable amount of time and effort spent by members of the Senate in dealing with the eternal problem of the lagoon is in stark contrast to the lack of professionalism and political maneuvering that surround the same issues today. This is not to say that special interest groups, and sometimes overwhelming political pressures, did not exist in earlier times. Obviously, in such a parliamentary system, every party had

the right to be heard. But from what history tells us, the opinions of the experts were taken into far more serious consideration, and their recommendations far more readily implemented, than they are nowadays.

Upon the recommendations of the *Provveditori ai Beni Inculti* (Superintendents of Uncultivated Territory) and *Provveditori ai Beni Comunali (Superintendents of State-owned Territory)*, the Senate was also responsible for government policy-making in the area of agricultural reform. The various problems associated with farming on the Venetian mainland had always been acute, and the members of the Senate were just as fearful of the possibility of a famine as they were of the recurring plagues. (The physical well-being of the citizenry was entrusted to the *Provveditori alla Sanità*, or "Commissioners of Health," whose methods of combating disease proved to be so efficient and illuminating that even an avowed enemy of Venice such as Napoleon Bonaparte was impressed!) Eventually, state-subsidized land reclamation and farming would solve the chronic problem of a shortage of grain (wheat, corn and rice), which had nearly always been imported in the past. In the process, however, much of the land that had traditionally been set aside for grazing sheep was severely compromised. The consequent shortage of wool would seriously affect the clothing industry, which had long been an extremely important part of the Venetian economy, and would prompt the Senate to appoint a special commission to investigate remedial action. Although many of their recommendations were not able to be implemented because of

the fall of the Republic, others resulted in such enlightened measures as the publication of a government handbook for farmers, which was ultimately circulated in the thousands.

The educational system, yet another of the Senate's responsibilities, was overseen by three *Riformatori allo Studio di Padova* (Superintendents of the University of Padua), whose jurisdiction included not only the state university (one of the oldest and most illustrious in Italy), but also the public elementary and secondary schools, and the all-important printing industry. Their absolute dedication to providing the university with the best possible instructors led to Padua's acknowledged superiority in many academic disciplines, particularly those involved in the hard sciences. In fact, students were able to take courses from the acknowledged scientific experts of the day, including Mercurialis, Vesalius, Fallopius, Fabricius of Acquapendente, Morgagni, Vallisnieri and Galileo. The results are obvious, if we remember that among the student body there was none other than Nicolaus Copernicus!

Despite the admonitions of the State Inquisitors, the *Riformatori* continued to extend a warm welcome to heretics and the persecuted alike so as not to lose the interest of the young scholars who flocked to Padua from the Germanic

Above: The Doge and the "Most Serene Signory" (engraving by L. Ziletti, 1575). The members of the Signory represented the supreme authority of the Venetian state. Charged with monitoring the doge's every action, they were required to sit in on all legislative and executive committee meetings that he himself attended. As of the 13th century, their numbers included the doge's six personal advisors (each of whom represented a different district in the city, and who served in office for a period of eight months), and the three heads of the Quaranta al Criminal (Criminal Court). Below: Scribes of the doge and Signory, from Giacomo Franco's Habiti.

and Slavic worlds. This attitude was very much in keeping with the Venetian's traditional spirit of independence when it came to dealings with the Roman Curia. Both before and after the Council of Trent, the Republic had chosen to go her own ideological way, particularly in light of the ever-increasing importance of the printing industry. (As far as the Inquisition itself was concerned, the Republic viewed it more or less as a necessary evil. In fact, the three *Savi all'Eresia* appointed by the Senate to protect its own citizen-

ry from the excesses of the Inquisitors were a real thorn in the flesh of the Roman popes, as their primary function was to prevent the papal representatives assigned to Venice from taking too much power upon themselves.)

Senato Mar. The maritime industry was yet another critical area of concern to the Senate, particularly with regard to the all-important merchant fleet and the state Arsenal (the same one that had so fascinated Dante as to make him draw the famous comparison with hell!), which manufactured not only warships, but many other types of sailing vessels as well.

In the early days, there was a great deal of confusion between the public and private maritime sectors. Among the galleys that took part in the great expeditions of the Fourth Crusade and the conquest of Constantinople, for example, many belonged to private citizens. In the mid-13th century, responsibility for policing the jealousy guarded Gulf of Venice (the Adriatic), was actually entrusted to a single individual who happened to possess an armed galley. On the other hand, state-owned galleys were put up for auction every season, and contracted out to the highest bidder from one voyage to another.

By the end of the 12th century, the traditional barges and small sailing-boats that had served as coasting-vessels (which were probably something like today's

bragozzi, burchi and *trabaccoli)* were replaced by other kinds of ships that were far sturdier and more capacious. This was the heyday of the galley, whose swiftness and easy maneuverability was essential for both war and trade. Although equipped with sails, it was powered mainly by oars. (At that time, the oarsmen themselves were hardly *galleotti*, or condemned criminals, in the modern sense of the word, nor were they poor souls recruited overseas from places like Dalmatia and Greece. Rather, they were natives of Venice herself, who actually volunteered their services in the hopes of making a little extra money on the side from the enormous amount of trading that went on between East and West.) The galley was eventually replaced by the galleass, which gave way to the cog, *cocca* and carrack because of conditions on the Atlantic routes. These cargo ships then spawned the galleons and warships that were used during the centuries of Venice's decline.

This picturesque world of adventure was also under the direct jurisdiction of the Senate through the offices of specially appointed magistrates. As far as the Arsenal was concerned, the cast of characters charged with overseeing its many and varied activities ranged from *Provveditori* to *Inquisitori* to *Patroni*. The crafts guilds, which represented the different categories of skilled workers, such as the *calafati* (caulkers), *marangoni* (carpenters) and *cordai* (rope-makers) (who enjoyed any number of special privileges, some nominal and some real), were supervised by a whole series of foremen, technical experts and nautical engineers. These last reported directly to the *Magnifico Ammiraglio* (Magnificent Admiral), who had come up through the ranks like the rest of them. Although hardly a member of the aristocracy, the Admiral himself carried the ducal standard during the newly elected doge's triumphal procession around St. Mark's

IL PALAZZO DUCALE: THE CENTER OF POWER

La Porta della Carta (1), the monumental ceremonial gateway to the palace, may have taken its name from the decrees that were posted there, or perhaps the proximity of the *depositi cartarum* (State Archives), or even the benches used by the public scribes *(magnacarta)*. The portico (2) measures 75 meters (246 feet) in length, and has 18 arches.

The Doges' Palace, which is the largest municipal building in Venice, was the work of several centuries. At the very heart of the Venetian state, it contained the doge's private apartments, as well as government offices and the assembly rooms of the collegial magistracies, the most important of which was the *Maggior Consiglio*. Conference rooms, armories, courtrooms, and even prisons were housed under its roof.

It was here that some 100 doges also took the oath of office. Just as many died here, including Marino Falier, who was beheaded for treason.

Within its solid walls, which were restored and rebuilt more than once, a thousand years of history would unfold. It was from here, in fact, that Venetian patricians masterminded the conquest of an empire, fought back against a European coalition, confronted the pope, made war on the Turks, and administered justice, always managing to endure through their wisdom and shrewdness until they were forced to abdicate in May of 1797.

The *Loggia Foscara* (3) was specially decorated by members of the various arts and crafts guilds, who organized an exhibition of their wares for the dogaressa after her coronation ceremony in the Basilica. Death sentences were traditionally read to the public from the ninth arcade on the left.

The votes cast by members of the *Maggior Consiglio* were verified in the *Sala del Scrutinio* (Counting-room) (4), where the committees appointed to elect the doge and

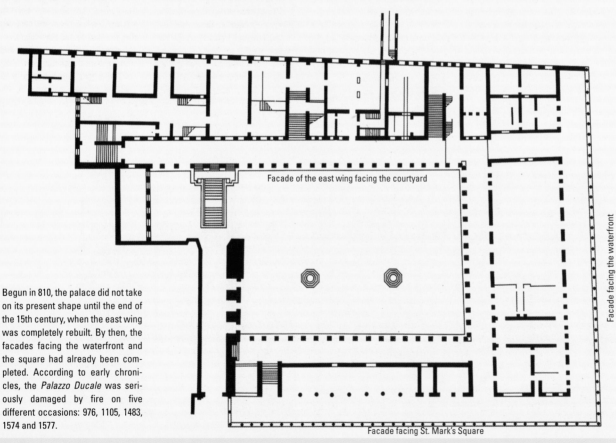

Facade of the east wing facing the courtyard

Facade facing the waterfront

Begun in 810, the palace did not take on its present shape until the end of the 15th century, when the east wing was completely rebuilt. By then, the facades facing the waterfront and the square had already been completed. According to early chronicles, the *Palazzo Ducale* was seriously damaged by fire on five different occasions: 976, 1105, 1483, 1574 and 1577.

Facade facing St. Mark's Square

Floor Plan of the Doges' Palace

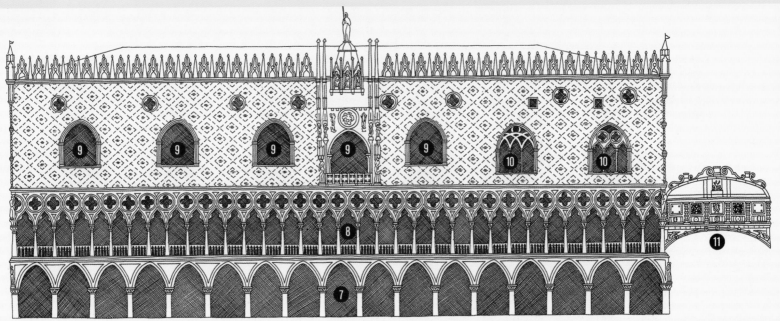

various other magistrates also met.

The *Sala della Quarantia Civil Nuova* (5) served as the court of appeals for civil suits involving possessions on the mainland and overseas.

The two windows closest to the lagoon (6) corresponded to one of the shorter sides of the *Sala del Maggior Consiglio* (Great Council Chamber).

The waterfront facade is the oldest in the palace. Its portico, which is 71.5 meters (234 feet) long, has 17 arcades (7). It was here the galley captains hired their crews, and paid them an advance.

Behind the central arches of the loggia (8) (from the 14th on the left to the 26th on the right) is the *Sala del Piovego*, or State Property Office. It

was also here that the body of the dead doge was brought to lie in state for a period of three days.

The largest room in the palace is the Great Council Chamber, which measures 54 meters (177 feet) in length by 25 meters (81 feet) in width by 13.4 meters (44 feet) in height (9). This was the seat of the lower house of the Venetian parliament, whose membership was comprised of all nobles over the age of 25. When in session, they took their places on benches that ran the length of the chamber, while the doge and the Most Serene Signory presided over the proceedings from the front of the room.

Off the corridor leading to the Great Council Chamber (10) was the Armory, which housed the ceremo-

nial arms of the Council of Ten, as well as captured tropies and gifts to the Republic, and the *Sala della Quarantia Civil Vecchia*, which adjudicated civil suits involving more than 1,500 ducats in value.

Il Ponte dei Sospiri (Bridge of Sighs) (11) connected the palace with the state prisons. Legend has it that the "sighs" were those of the condemned criminals.

From the top of the grandiose *Scala dei Giganti* (Giants' Staircase) (12), the newly elected doge would swear allegiance to the laws of the land, and receive the *corno,* or ducal cap.

In the east wing, at the level of the loggia, there were the offices of the Chancery (13), the *Milizia da Mar* (14), who recruited members for the navy,

the *Avogaria* (15), whose members prepared certain cases to be brought before the *Quarantia*, and who also kept the *Libro d'Oro* (the Italian equivalent of *Burke's Peerage,* in which the names of noble families were registered), and the Censors (16), who were responsible for monitoring the morals of the patriciate, and preventing corrupt voting practices.

The doge's personal living quarters were located on the *primo piano nobile* (second floor), which overlooked the *Rio del Palazzo. The Sala Grimani* (17) was the doge's private audience chamber. In the *Sala degli Scarlatti* his advisors and other high dignitaries of state would gather to await his arrival (18). In yet another room (19), the *Quarantia Criminal*

(Criminal Court) adjudicated the most serious crimes of all.

Il secondo piano nobile (top floor) housed some of the most powerful branches of government, including the members of the Signory, who convened in the *Sala del Collegio* (20), and the Senate, whose assembly room was located directly behind it. The dreaded *Consiglio dei Dieci* (Council of Ten) (21), charged with judging cases of high treason, was also situated on this floor, along with its three chief magistrates (22). Finally, there were the offices of the State Inquisitors (23), which had an inner staircase that led directly to the torture chamber, and the so-called *Piombi* (the prisons located under the lead-covered roof).

Opposite page: A view of the magnificent waterfront facade of the Palazzo Ducale. Constructed in 1340 to accommodate an enlarged Great Council Chamber, it represents the oldest section of the palace. Following the devastating fire of December 20, 1577, it was partially rebuilt, along with the Sala del Maggior Consiglio. Above left: Fragment from the Paradiso, which the Paduan artist Guariento frescoed on the wall above the Tribune in 1365. The Republic commissioned Guariento to provide the decorations for the Great Council Chamber after he had established his reputation as an important artist while working for the Carraresi family in Padua. Above right: Detail depicting armed angels from the private Carraresi chapel, now preserved in the Museo Civico di Padova.

Square. He was also in command of the *Bucintoro* on the solemn annual occasion of Venice's marriage ceremony with the sea.

Since the *Pregadi* were also responsible for matters involving national defense, the top military and naval officers were answerable to the them as well, from the *Provveditore Generale da Mar,* who lived in Corfu, and who commanded the fleet in times of peace, to the *Provveditore Generale* at Palma (Friuli), who was charged with protecting the Republic's borders from both the Turks and the Hapsburgs, and who operated out of his great, star-shaped fortress, which was built at the end of the 16th century, to the *Presidenti alla Milizia da Mar* (Maritime Police Commissioners), to the *Governatori alle Galere de' Condannati* (Superintendents of Prisoners' Galleys), who dealt with problems involving crew members (the galleys were indeed rowed, alas! by condemned criminals and Turkish and Barbary prisoners of war as of the middle of the 16th century), to the *Provveditori alle Artiglierie* (Artillery Commanders), to the *Provveditori alle Fortezze* (Fortress Commanders).

Incredibly, in times of war, the upper house of parliament also assumed the role of supreme military commander. Even more extraordinary is the fact that an army of men who reported to the entire collegial body of the Senate suffered no greater number of serious defeats or military setbacks than their counterparts throughout the Mediterranean Basin. This does not mean, however, that there was any lack of com-

plaints on the part of the field commanders themselves, who often blamed the Senate (so far away, and yet so omnipresent) for unnecessary delays!

"The Council of Forty" and "The Council of Ten"

We have just seen to what extent the *Pregadi* exercised control over almost every aspect of Venetian life, whether political, economic, military or diplomatic. They were even involved to some degree in the judicial system, although they wielded no actual power. However, the three *Avogadori di Comun,* who functioned first and foremost as the heads of the State Prosecutor's Office (which also included the members of the *Quarantia Criminal,* or Criminal Court, and the Council of Ten), were members of the Senate as well. Among their other responsibilities, they were charged with keeping the official records of the *Libro d'Oro,* or "Golden Book," of the Venetian nobility, and verifying their personal qualifications for admission to the Great Council.

The *Quarantia,* or Council of Forty, was first instituted between 1207 and 1222, when it served as a purely political assembly. (One of its most important acts took place in 1284, under Doge Giovanni Dandolo, when the first Venetian *zecchino,* or gold ducat, was minted. This particular coin, which soon became the medieval equivalent of today's dollar, remained the most stable form of currency in the Mediterranean Basin right up until modern times, thanks to its weight, and the purity of its gold.) Over time, however, the *Quarantia* assumed more and more judicial functions, and was eventually split up into three separate and distinct tribunals: the *Quarantia Civil Vecchia,* which adjudicated all civil suits involving sums in excess of 1,500 ducats, and acted as the court of appeals for civil sentences passed by the lesser tribunals in the city; the *Quarantia Civil Nova,* which judged appeals from courts on the Venetian mainland; and the *Quarantia Criminal,* which served as the court of assizes for the most serious crimes committed in the Republic and the *dogado* (the actual territory covered by the original Byzantine province, whose borders stretched from Grado to Cavarzere), as well as the court of appeals for criminal sentences handed down by the lower courts.

The members of the *Quaranta* (whose three chief magistrates were also part of the *Serenissima Signoria*), served for eight months on the *Civil Nova,* whereupon they were automatically transferred to the *Civil Vecchia*

Opposite page, center: Two pages from the famous Libro d'Oro. At the beginning of the 16th century, the distinction between the members of the noble class, who were entrusted with all high government offices, and the commoners, who were excluded from participating in any form of public policy-making, received its official sanction in the Golden Book. This was the record of the Venetian peerage, which consisted of the Book of Patrician Births, begun in 1506, and the Book of Marriages, begun in 1526. The requirements for inclusion in the book, which was kept by the Avogaria until the fall of the Republic, were not always that strict. Above: Venetian patricians of the 14th century, from Livy's Prima Deca, which was illuminated by the Venetian artist Giannino Cattaneo.

for an additional eight months, after which they moved on to the *Criminal*. (This type of rotational system harked back to much earlier times, and the so-called College of Fifteen, who were charged with adjudicating civil suits involving sums between 200 and 800 ducats, and the College of Twenty-five, who passed judgment on cases where higher sums of money were concerned.)

At the bottom of the judicial pile, there was the intricate maze of Venetian courts, both civil and criminal, whose jurisdictions were so complex that is it really not worth our while to go into them in any extensive detail. Among these were the *Signori di Notte*, whose job it was to watch over the safety of the citizenry by night, the *Giudici del Piovego*, who fulfilled the all-important function of policing the waters of the lagoon, particularly in the Middle Ages, the various magistrates concerned with protecting the private rights of citizens (the *Giudici del Petizion, del Procurator, del Forestier, dell'Esaminador* and *del Mobile*), and finally, the *Auditori Vecchi, Novi* and *Novissimi*.

At the top of the pile, in all its power and majesty, stood the *Eccelso Consiglio dei Dieci* (Most High Council of Ten), as it was officially known until the last days of the Republic.

Among the elected by the Senate, there were also the Censors, whose jurisdiction included not only corrupt voting practices, but also, curiously enough, "salaries and special payments to servants," and "boatsmen who make money on the side by using their masters' boats," and "who start brawls when their masters are on board." Then there were the four *Esecutori alla Bestemmia*, who held office for one year, and whose job it was to adjudicate cases involving "Blasphemers, and those who use profanity in Temples and Sacred Places," as well as swindlers and seducers of young maidens (who were obliged either to "marry the deflowered damsel, or bestow on her a suitable dowry"), and those responsible for obscene prints or publications.

Even in the bland, easy-going atmosphere of 18th-century Venice, offenders were often punished severely for such crimes. Remember the ill-fated character called Pandolfo in Carlo Goldoni's *Bottega del Caffè*, who was slandered by Don Marzio, and then publicly whipped! (In earlier times, punishments in general were far more severe. During the last decade of the 15th century, the nobleman Giovanni Zorzi was found guilty of cursing in public, and lost his tongue and his right hand for it—although we should add, in all fairness, that he had also been found guilty of "exporting" a nun from a certain convent in Treviso! In the 16th century, foul-mouthed priests were exposed

Notisi che l'epoca premessa di questi nomi non è quella in cui ottien il candidato cavata la palla d'oro cioè nel dì di S. Barbara di quell'anno, ma si quella in cui si presenti per goder di questi privilegi. Dagli altri patrizii, specialmente di Marco Barbaro, risulta effettivamente quando ottien cavata la palla d'oro —

to the elements in an iron cage that was hung outside the Campanile. One of these poor souls was *pre* Agustino, a gambler, womanizer, and protagonist of a very unusual rhyme, who was confined to the cage at the beginning of the century. However, there were also those who somehow managed to escape!)

Let us return for a moment to the Most High Council of Ten. A popular Venetian rhyme relates how "in the year one thousand three hundred and ten, in the middle of the month of cherries, Baiamonte crossed over the bridge (Rialto), and so was formed the Council of Ten." These magistrates, who were originally appointed as temporary criminal judges in the case brought against the co-conspirators of Baiamonte Tiepolo, would later become a permanent institution with jurisdiction over crimes of high treason. (As far as their name was concerned, they were *The* Council of Ten, not just another of the various ten-member commissions in Venice, or even in Florence, with its famous *Dieci di Balìa*.) Over time, their authority was extended to cover all matters judged to be top secret, as well as the crimes of sodomy, counterfeiting, illegal possession of a firearm, felonies committed on shipboard or by persons in disguise, and corrupt practices on the part of municipal and provincial governors. While certain of their powers were conferred by the *Maggior Consiglio* or the Senate, others they simply took upon themselves: During their 487 years of existence, the members of the *Eccelso* meddled so often in the affairs of state that the central government was eventually forced to intervene on a regular basis in an attempt to curb their powers, and exert more and more control over their various activities.

The real authority exercised by the Council of Ten derived from their jurisdiction over all felonies, misdemeanors and minor infractions of the law committed by members of the aristocracy. This was a far cry from their original mandate, which was that of supporting their fellow patricians in their quest for ultimate political power at a crucial point in the Republic's history. In fact, no sooner had the nobles asserted their absolute control over the administration of government than the Council of Ten (who were themselves chosen from the noblest and most respected families in Venice) became their harshest critics and avowed enemies! This turn of events, which has no precedent in the entire history of Europe, illustrates to what extent the state was concerned with defending the integrity of the *Maggior Consiglio* from the influence of a supreme oligarchy, and establishing a system of checks and balances to discourage any further seditious attempts on the order of the Tiepolo-Querini Conspiracy.

The fact that the members of the Council of Ten would ultimately take advantage of their extraordinary powers through repeated attempts to establish an oligarchy of their own was certainly not what its founders had foreseen. However, in each instance, the Venetian political system proved itself more than capable of reacting swiftly and surely to prevent such a disaster.

More foolish things have been said about the dreaded Council of Ten than perhaps any other government agency in the history of mankind. Even now, there is talk of grim, shadowy rites and rituals, inhumane prisons, and extreme cruelty. Another legend surrounding the Ten that persists to this day involves the "lions' mouths," those sinister mailboxes designed to receive secret denunciations,

Above: Portrait of a Capitan Grande, *who functioned more or less as the chief of police, from Vecellio's Habiti.*
Below: *Also from Vecellio's* Habiti, *portrait of one of the heads of the Council of Ten. The three members who presided over the Council were elected on a monthly basis. It was their responsibility to open all correspondence, and to schedule Council meetings.*

Elsewhere in Europe, there were the barons, counts, marquises, and so on. In Venice, high-born families were part of a hereditary nobility that made no distinctions whatsoever in rank. The Venetian aristocrat was either called by the title N.H. (for *Nobilomo,* or Nobleman), or was referred to as a patrician, and that was that.

Even before the year 1000, the more important members of Venetian society were claiming descent from the old noble Roman families that had sought refuge in the lagoon from the barbarian invasions. Later on, they often touted the fact that they were direct descendants of the tribunes who had governed the city before the first doges.

The "old" aristocratic families were 24 in number. At the time of the "Closing of the Great Council" (1297), they were joined by the "new" families that had been officially recognized as members of the nobility. A third group, known as the "very new," was added during the war against Genoa in 1381, and still others were admitted "on payment" in the mid-17th century to cover the expenses of the War of Candia.

During the 14th century, when the city had a population of 120,000, the membership of the Great Council included some 1,200 adult male patricians from hardly more than 150 families. By the middle of the 16th century, the

Council's numbers had reached their peak, with a total of 2,050 members out of a population of 150,000. Over time, however, the aristocracy began to decrease in numbers, despite the admission of new members. By the year 1797, the *Libro d'Oro* mentioned only 1,030 nobles from 111 families, who represented a mere 3.2 per cent of the total population.

By right of birth, political power was concentrated in the hands of the noble class through their participation in the lower house of parliament, known as the Great Council, which was the only stepping-stone to the upper house, or Senate.

All male patricians over the age of 25 born of legitimate marriages (which were duly recorded in the

Golden Book) were eligible for membership in this, the larger of the two legislative assemblies. (The only exception to this rule were the 27 patricians under the age of 25 who had drawn a gold balloting ball on St. Barbara's annual feast day.)

When the Council was in session, its more than 1,000 members crowded into the Great Hall of the Doges' Palace (2).

Those aristocrats who chose to become career politicians had to take a number of different factors into consideration, not the least of which was their own economic situation. Although all nobles were *de jure* equal, many political offices represented a heavy financial burden. In light of this, patricians from less affluent families were granted

government scholarships to allow them to study at the Academy of Nobles or the University of Padua. Young aristocrats often gained their first real work experience in the area of trade on board either their families' ships, or those belonging to the Senate (9). Although they might eventually choose to serve the state in some official capacity, this did not necessarily mean that

they would abandon their own commercial or financial interests.

If his family possessed the financial wherewithal, a patrician (1) usually began his career in government service as a *Savio agli Ordini,* at which time he could sit in on meetings of both the Senate and Great Council, and perhaps gain some practical experience while working in a Senate office. The main advantage of wealth, however, was that it allowed a young man the possibility of joining one of the more prestigious (and costly) *Reggimenti,* or even serving as an ambassador (4). In between, he could gain further experience as a *Savio di Terraferma,* or member of the Senate (10) or the Council of Ten (5). Eventually, he

could aspire to even higher offices, such as those of doge's advisor, or *Savio del Consiglio,* and finally, Procurator of St. Mark's (3), which also made him a lifetime member of the Senate.

A young aristocrat from a somewhat less affluent family could work his way up the government ladder by serving as a judicial magistrate, which would lead to membership in the Council of Forty. Later on, he could become head of the *Quaranta al Criminal Superior,* which automatically made him a member of the Signory.

Those with even less means had the possibility of working in one of the humbler magistracies, such as the Grain Office or Customs House, or

THE PATRICIANS: BORN TO RULE

joining one of the minor regiments. Alternatively, they could pursue a legal career, which might eventually lead to membership in the *Avogaria di Comun* (8), or the Council of Forty (5).

Many of those who chose to pursue a military career first started out as *Nobili di Nave,* or *Nobili di Galera,* after which they could work their way up to the highest rank of all, the *Provveditore Generale da Mar* (Commander of the Fleet) (6). Others, who joined the military after having served in politics, might well become *Provveditori Generali* (Provincial Governors) in such places as Dalmatia or Albania.

Since these various government positions were more or less interchangeable, it was not uncommon for individuals to transfer from one to another with a versatility that was unique to the Venetian patriciate.

(Soldiers might become brilliant diplomats, for example, or merchants great sea captains.)

Members of the nobility who chose a career in the church were automatically excluded from participating in the *Maggior Consiglio*. They also had to obtain the Senate's permission before they could become bishops or cardinals (7).

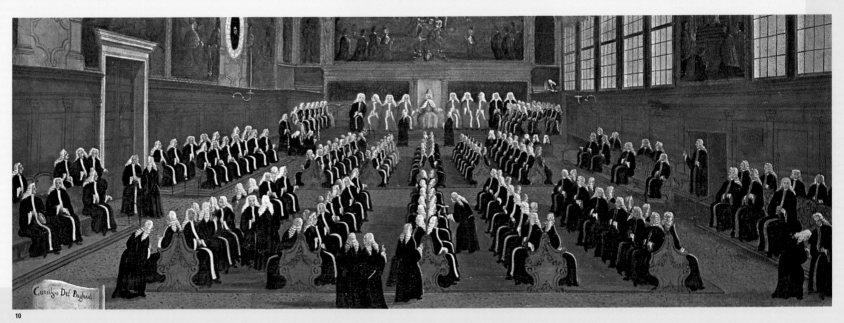

Above left: The Pisani Family, by Alessandro Longhi. Above right: Detail from Titian's Pala Pesaro *depicting Jacopo Pesaro, who commissioned the altarpiece, along with members of his family. The Venetian nobility viewed its position in society as less of a privilege than a civic duty. No member of the aristocracy was exempt from government service, and the cursus honorum very often represented a heavy burden indeed. From earliest times, it was also common practice for the patrician class to engage in various commercial activities, which were often the source of great personal wealth. Even the doges indulged in trade (which was considered a "most noble occupation") until they were forbidden to so by the* Promissione *at the end of the 10th century.*

which often made the difference between life and death for so many innocent folk who were sacrificed to the pride of the patrician class. All of these accusations are either literary inventions or pure propaganda without a single grain of truth.

There is no question that the Council of Ten (whose membership also included the doge and his six advisors), endowed as it was with such extraordinary power, was far more severe than any other Venetian judicial authority, and that its deliberations, which were cloaked in utmost secrecy, brooked absolutely no outside interference. It is also a well-established fact that they did not hesitate to suppress those individuals who were judged to be a real menace to society. (Such was the fate of the "grand gentleman" Baiamonte Tiepolo, who continued to conspire against the Republic after he had been exiled to Dalmatia following his abortive plot to overthrow the government.)

In their various roles, however, the Ten displayed an integrity that is sorely lacking among the magistrates of many of the so-called civilized societies of today, Italy included. A good example of this is the way in which they handled the secret denunciations that were placed in the notorious "lions' mouths." If they were anonymous, they were automatically examined by the three heads of the Council (who were elected on a monthly basis, and were responsible for initiating proceedings and conducting trials), together with the six personal advisors of the doge, who needed a unani-

mous vote in order to pass them on to the Council itself. The full membership then required a five-sixth majority before it could recommend yet another examination, after which a four-fifths majority was necessary before any definitive action could be taken.

But let us not delve any further into the complicated "rites of the Most High." Suffice it to say that under this particular legal system, the accused were accorded far greater protection than their counterparts in many countries today.

As far as the defense was concerned (which could only be presented in written form), there was the magistracy known as the *Avvocati dei Prigioni* (Public Defenders Office), which was established in 1443 to represent those who could not afford to hire their own counsel. During any and all legal proceedings involved in a criminal trial, at least one of the three *Avogadori di Comun* was required to be present to monitor the decisions of the Ten. These individuals also had the right to "intervene" whenever they deemed it necessary by suspending or appealing a particular sentence. (The sentences themselves were decided by majority vote, as were the penalties imposed. Furthermore, throughout the entire trial, any member of the Council was allowed to reopen the case as well.)

With regard to the prison system, and the infamous *Piombi* (the so-called "Leads," which no longer exist), they were simply the garrets in the Doges' Palace, which took their name from the lead-covered roof.

(Balzac made the witty remark that in Paris, there were plenty of people who paid a fortune in rent to live in similar quarters!) The even more notorious *Pozzi* were hardly below the water level of the *Rio,* as that rogue Giacomo Casanova would falsely claim. In fact, they were, and still are, on the same level as the offices occupied by the President of the Biennale until some 30 years ago! Still and all, the *Piombi* and *Pozzi* were an integral part of a criminal justice system that would eventually fall under the jurisdiction of the dreaded Supreme Tribunal, or State Inquisition, which came into being as a result of the constant restructuring of the Council of Ten.

Countless myths and legends have grown up around the activities of these individuals as well. In reality, they were first elected in 1539 to stem the growing tide of gossip involving state secrets (which was one of the very worst habits of the Venetian politicians), at which time their membership was composed of two representatives from the Council of Ten, and one of the doge's personal advisors, each of whom served for a period of one month. However, at the point where the Venetians found themselves surrounded on all sides by the Hapsburg dominions, they would be forced to grant the Supreme Tribunal further authority as part of their desperate attempt to maintain their independence from foreign enemies who were considerably more powerful than the Republic. As a consequence, the Inquisitors were allowed to operate in even greater secrecy, and proceed far more swiftly and efficiently than their predecessors. In the end, their influence was such that they would play an increasingly important role in Venetian politics, whether through intervening any number of government matters, or

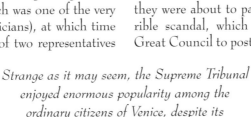

Strange as it may seem, the Supreme Tribunal enjoyed enormous popularity among the ordinary citizens of Venice, despite its constant meddling in the affairs of state, and its obvious abuse of power.

corresponding directly with ambassadors and provincial governors (which the Council of Ten had also done). At the fall of the Republic, they themselves were more or less in charge of monitoring the nobility, as opposed to the members of the Council of Ten.

Strange as it may seem, the Supreme Tribunal enjoyed enormous popularity among the ordinary citizens of Venice, despite its constant meddling in the affairs of state, and its obvious abuse of power. Witness the reaction of the general populace at the time of the major dispute between the *Querinisti* and *Tribunalisti,* which was one of the last of the *Maggior Consiglio's* great debates. As the story goes, the *Avogador di Comun,* Angelo Maria Querini, had been arrested and imprisoned on the order of the Inquisitors as a result of his having challenged a sentence that they were about to pass down. This gave rise to a terrible scandal, which prompted the members of the Great Council to postpone their renewal of the authority of the Council of Ten until all government rules and regulations regarding the various commissions and colleges had been thoroughly reviewed. This task was assigned to a committee of five *Correttori,* or Revisors, who were required to report their findings directly to the *Consiglio.*

As usual, two opposing factions were formed. First there were the *Querinisti,* who in the name of the poor *Avogadore* that had been unjustly arrested, took the position that it was high time for the authority of the State Inquisitors to be subjected to certain limitations. Then there were the *Tribunalisti,* who maintained that the extraordinary powers accorded the Inquisitors were absolutely necessary in terms of discouraging the members of the nobility from overstepping their bounds. According to them, the dreaded reputation of the Tribunal was ultimately a guaranty of liberty and justice for one and all.

During the actual debate, every great orator's voice would eventually be heard, including those of Marco Foscarini, the leader of the *Tribunalisti,* and Paolo Renier, his counterpart among the *Querinisti,* both of whom would one day be elected as doge. To add to the general state of confusion, public opinion ended up taking the opposite side to that which everyone had

Left: La Camera degli Imprestidi (The Chamber of Loans). *Illumination from the parish register of San Maffeo di Murano, 1391 (Seminario Patriarcale, Venice). The state looked to its private citizens to meet its financial needs through voluntary or obligatory loans. Below: Two busts by Tullio Lombardo (Ca' d'Oro, Venice).*

Above: Eighteenth-century engraving showing the heavy boat traffic at the Rialto. Below, left and right: Gondolas from the 15th and 18th centuries, by Carpaccio and Guardi. The gondola was designed specifically to navigate the narrow, shallow canals. Originally, it was painted in a variety of colors, only becoming black by order of the Senate in 1562. Opposite page: Detail from Gentile Bellini's Miracle of the Cross. *The portrait of the young African reflects the mixed nature of 15th-century Venetian society.*

expected! According to the crowd that thronged St. Mark's Square each day to hear the results of the latest vote, those in favor of placing restrictions on the powers of the Inquisitors were actually trying to assert their own power as patricians! Little did the common folk care about the doctrines of Montesquieu and the Enlightenment, or even the false arrest of the Avogadore Querini! By the same token, those who were in favor of endorsing the full powers of the Tribunal were looked upon as popular heroes, and applauded for their efforts at protecting the general populace against the power-hungry patricians!

After a memorable speech by Paolo Renier, which lasted for five hours, and Marco Foscarini's formal rebuttal, the members of the *Maggior Consiglio* finally approved the appointment of three *Correttori Tribunali* by a majority of just two votes. This decision caused a near-riot in the square, where an angry mob of over 6,000 townspeople cheered on the supporters of the *Tribunal Supremo*, and threatened to besiege the homes of the "liberal" members of the opposition.

Aside from the usual crowd hysteria, this particular episode clearly illustrates the relationship between the people and the patricians, and the people and the political system. More than anything else, the ordinary citizens who gathered in St. Mark's Square to applaud the State Inquisitors were showing their unanimous support for the five-century-old tradition of confining the privileges and prerogatives enjoyed by the nobility to those directly connected with the legitimate exercise of judicial power.

On the other hand, no one would ever hope to claim that Venetian society was egalitarian. Even Gasparo Contarini, a future cardinal and leader of a profound reform in the Catholic Church that was a good 400 years ahead of its time, based all of his arguments on the existing class structure. Let us not forget about those *beaux esprits* of the 18th century, whose open admiration for the Turkish social system (where there were no privileged classes whatsoever between the monarchy and the commoners) was undoubtedly a reflection of their dissatisfaction with their own situa-

PROTECTING THE LAGOON:
A MILLENNIUM OF PREVENTIVE MEASURE

Maintaining the ecological balance of a living organism as delicate as the Venetian lagoon is no easy task. Given the constant threat of encroachments on the part of the sea, which tend to erode the fragile line of sand bars that protect it from the Adriatic, and the alluvial deposits carried by rivers, which constantly silt it up, the lagoon would long since have disappeared had it not been for the intervention of mankind. Throughout the centuries, in order to safeguard the lagoon's precarious existence, the Republic undertook any number of preventive measures. First and foremost, the tides were given free play, which kept the city canals clear, and allowed the rivers to drain properly. (In this regard, every possible effort was made not to reduce the size of the lagoon itself, which meant prohibiting land-fills, closing down the salt-pans, and excavating the so-called "Tagli Gar-zoni".) The lower reaches of those rivers that emptied directly into the lagoon were then diverted, and other preventive measures taken, such as the construction of dams. But the most ambitious engineering project of all, which would be carried out over the course of many centuries, was that of diverting the flow of the major rivers away from the lagoon and into a series of canals.

The various phases involved in this mammoth undertaking are indicated on the map displayed on these two pages. In 1540, the Bacchiglione River, which originally emptied into the Chioggia Lagoon through the

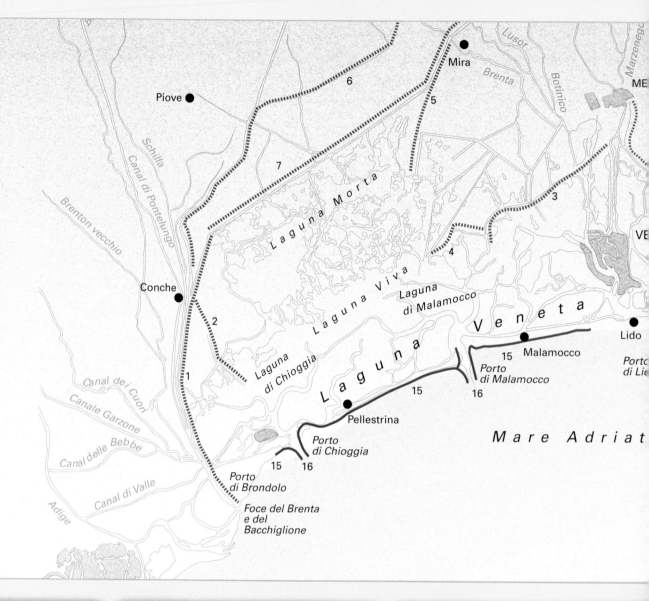

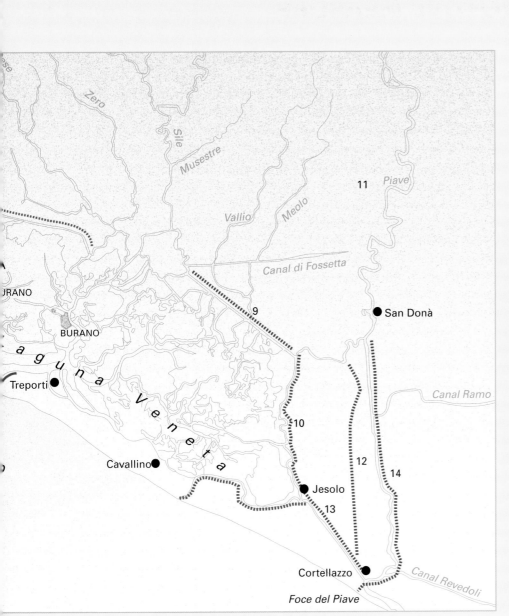

Montalbano Canal (2), was diverted into the Canal del Toro (1), from where it flowed into the open sea. In 1324, the estuaries of the Brenta River, which were situated opposite the city herself, were moved farther south through the Corbola Canal (3). This same canal was extended as far as the Malamocco Lagoon in the year 1452 (4). In 1531, the waters of the mighty Brenta were diverted into the Mira Canal (5), which, together with the Corbola Canal, could redirect its flow to one part of the lagoon or another as needed. In 1507, the Brenta had already been diverted into a canal that extended from Dolo, through Conche, as far as the Chioggia Lagoon via the Canal di Montalbano (6). Finally, in 1613, the Mira Canal (7) and the Taglio Nuovissimo were completed. These last diverted the waters of the Brenta, Botinico, Lusor, Brentella and Musone rivers away from Venice and into the Chioggia Lagoon. (At a later date, they were diverted into the Canale del Toro, which empties into Brondolo Harbor, along with the waters of the Bacchiglione River.)

The Canale dell'Oselin (8), completed in 1507, diverted the waters of the Marzenego, Zero and Dese rivers to the east of Venice. In 1683, the Sile River, which emptied into the lagoon in the vicinity of Burano, was diverted to the original bed of the Piave River (9) via the Taglio del Sile (10).

The Argine di San Marco (11) was constructed in 1534 to protect the lagoon from the flood waters of the Piave, which was first diverted in 1579 via the Canale del Re (12) to the Nuova Cava Zuccherina (13), where it emptied directly into the open sea. After it had broken its banks at Landrona, a new canal was excavated in 1683 (14), which ran as far as Cortellazzo.

The massive Istrian-stone sea walls known as the *murazzi* (15) were constructed during the 18th century to protect the lagoon from serious flooding.

Today, the Venetian lagoon communicates directly with the sea via three mouths, or ports, which are protected by a series of dikes that were built between the 19th and 20th centuries (16). It is through these openings that the tides flow into the lagoon, which contains some 800 kilometers (500 miles) of canals.

Below: How mankind has modified the lagoon: Enclosures made of earth and wood, which were used by the lagoon's first settlers as fish traps and salt pans (a). Dikes built before the year 1000 from stones and withies (b). Early dock made from wood and pebbles (c). Cross-section of a 17th-century embankment made from green oak piles called *topli*, cross-bars, and Istrian and Lispidan stone (d). Another embankment, which was used between the end of the 17th and the beginning of the 18th centuries, stood some 4.50 meters (14 _ feet) high, and had a wider base than the earlier type (e). Cross-section of the famous *murazzi* constructed between 1740 and 1782. These solid vertical walls, which were 14 meters (46 feet) wide at the base and stood 4.50 meters (14 _ feet) above mean high tide, were made of large blocks of Istrian stone and broken rock held together by pozzolana mixed with lime (f).

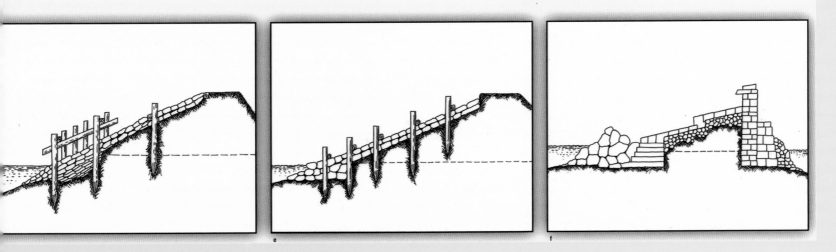

tion, where there were perhaps too many privileged classes. In the end, however, the severity of the measures adopted by tribunals and magistracies alike in their dealings with the aristocracy were specifically intended to protect the Venetians' most prized possession: their legal system. As the French historian René Guerdan so aptly noted, the motto of the *Serenissima* might well have been the same as that of the French Republic, with one all–important exception: Instead of *Liberté, Egalité, Fraternité*, the Venetians would have used the words *Liberté, Légalité, Fraternité!*

The entire political structure of Venice was based on an intricate system of checks and balances that was designed not only to prevent any single branch of government from prevailing over any other, but also to prevent any member of the politically privileged noble class from controlling any other member of society. We have already mentioned several times the Tiepolo-Querini Conspiracy, which had demonstrated just exactly what could happen when the nobles overstepped their bounds. The same was true of Marco Falier's abortive plot to bring about a bourgeois revolution, if we accept the fact that one of the co-conspirators, a certain

Isarello Bertucci, had joined the ranks of Falier's supporters because he had been slapped in the face by a member of the noble Dandolo family.

So it was that the Venetian political system, although governed by the patricians themselves, made it a point of honor to force them to set an example for the entire community. In fact, crimes and misdemeanors committed by the nobility were punished far more severely than those committed by the general populace, to the point where the doge and the Council of Ten sometimes treated their peers with unwarranted cruelty.

In this regard, there was the notorious case of Doge Antonio Venier, whose son, Alvise, had been found guilty of playing a rather nasty joke on a certain individual named Dalle Boccole. (What he had actually done was to tack onto the fellow's front door what some said was a bunch of horns, which implied that he had been cuckolded, and others the head of a goat, which implied stupidity). While awaiting trial in prison, Alvise had fallen seriously ill, which prompted the magistrates to suggest letting him out on bail. However, the doge himself (who had worked extremely hard during his administration to curb the outrageous behavior of many

of the young nobles) ultimately opposed such a move, and let his son die behind bars. This tragic episode led to the doge's own death shortly thereafter, when he succumbed to a severe form of depression.

No less notorious was the case of Gasparo Valier, a young nobleman who had been condemned to death by the Council of Ten in 1511 for having murdered a poor tax collector in Treviso. At the time he was convicted, Valier had everything going for him, including good looks, plenty of money, and an impeccable pedigree. However, when the Patriarch of Venice himself intervened to beg the Ten for clemency, he was promptly turned away, and told that the Council fully intended to carry out the sentence that they had already imposed. Even when the three *Avogadori di Comun*, who had originally brought the charge against the accused, actually knelt down in front of the three heads of the Council of Ten to plead for a suspended sentence, they were met with the icy reply: "You are no longer worthy of this magistracy. However, you may rise." Immediately thereafter, they were removed from office, and were never allowed to serve in the same capacity again.

"El paron de la Republica"

As we continue our search for the supreme governmental authority, let us return for a moment to our discussion of the Venetian political structure in and of itself. The *Pien Collegio*, which functioned as a sort of appendix to the Senate, was actually somewhere between a parliamentary commission and a ministry of state. Its members, who included the doge, the *Serenissima Signoria*, and 16 *Savi*, or Sages, met in the *Sala del Collegio*, which led directly to the larger *Sala del Senato*.

The title *Savio*, which was used for any number of other magistrates as well, was always attached to extremely important government officials. Among those who actually participated in the *Pien Collegio* were the five *Savi agli Ordini*, who had originally been concerned with naval affairs. Although they lost some of their authority during the last years of the Republic, they were always considered a stepping-stone for anyone who wished to pursue a high-level political career. Then there were the five *Savi di Terraferma:* the *Savio*

was over, they could not be re-elected for another six months.

Each and every morning, the *Signoria* and the *Collegio* would meet in the doge's apartments to discuss the business at hand, and prepare whatever proposals were to be presented to the Senate, which usually convened on Thursdays and Saturdays. This not only gives us some idea of the importance of the *Collegio;* it also gives us a clue as to why it would eventually degenerate to the point where it excluded the Senate from participating in the decision-making process. In fact, in the very last months of the Republic, all important government policy was made during the *"consulte negre"* ("black conferences"), named for the black robes worn by the *"Savi Usciti,"* or "Retired Members," who were actually allowed to be part of the deliberations despite the fact that their terms were up. This truly was the end of the Republic, because the political system that had been so carefully constructed over the course of five centuries had been completely dismantled on the pretext of secrecy and urgency.

However, we are getting ahead of ourselves. We have yet to consider the workings of the supreme governmental authority that we have been searching for: *"El paron de la republica,"* otherwise known as the *Maggior Consiglio.*

We have already mentioned the early days, when the entire citizenry was involved in matters regarding the general well-being of the state through its participation in a popular assembly, whose responsibilities included, first and foremost, the election of the doge. This particular form of government came into being at least as far back as the eighth century, after a whole series of doges had been removed from office as a result of warring political factions (about which history tells us very little), at which point every free man in the *ducato*, from Grado to Carvazere, was invited to participate in the election of Doge Maurizio (or Galbaio, as he was commonly called). (Before we go on, however, we should add that for those poor souls who had been dethroned, there were often terrible punishments in store as well, such as the barbarous Byzantine custom of putting out their eyes! Later on, they were simply tonsured, and then shut up in a convent! This milder form of punishment probably originated in France!)

The various "dynasties" that had formed around the early doges (the last of which involved the Orseolo family, who lost all their power just after the year 1000) were eventually replaced by popular vote. In fact, from the time of Doge Pietro Flabianico on, doges were

Above: Fashionable wedding clothes of the 15th century (Fieschi manuscript). Below: Engraving of a merchant's wife (after Giacomo Franco). Opposite page: Portrait of a Lady by Carpaccio (Rijksmuseum, Amsterdam). Venetian women of means adorned themselves with all manner of elegant clothing, jewels and cosmetics. However, there was also the popular saying: "Che la piasa, che la tasa, che la staga a casa" ("Just look pretty, keep your mouth shut, and stay at home where you belong!")

Cassier, who was responsible for various financial matters, the *Savio alla Scrittura,* or Minister of War, the *Savio alle Ordinanze,* who was in charge of organizing and maintaining the efficiency of all mobile land troops (the famous *Cernide,* whom Ippolito Nievo poked such fun at in his *Confessions of an Italian),* the *Savio ai Cerimoniali,* who arranged the state visits of foreign rulers, ministers and ambassadors, and the *Savio ai "Da Mo',"* who was responsible for seeing that all emergency legislation enacted by the government was carried out (so called because his official reports always began with the words *"E da mo',"* which was a shortened version of *"La parte che andò mo' . . . ,"* meaning "the law that has just been voted in"). Last but certainly not least, there were the six *Savi del Consiglio,* or *Savi Grandi,* who were a cross between a parliamentary commission, the presidency of the Council of Ministers, the Ministry of Foreign Affairs, and many other things besides. These six were usually consummate politicians, worldly-wise, and thoroughly experienced in handling the most difficult, and most prestigious, of government assignments. Like all the others, they were elected on different dates, three at a time, so that their membership would always overlap to some degree. After their term of office

Later on, the *Consilium Sapientium* (or *Maggior Consiglio*, as it was then called) would number some 100 individuals, who were eventually joined by the members of the *Quarantia* and the *Consiglio dei Pregadi*. At this point, the *Gran Consiglio* was made up almost exclusively of the heirs to the great noble families who could trace their roots all the way back to the tribunes of the earliest maritime settlements, as well as the nouveau riches, who came from the ranks of prosperous seamen, artisans, merchants and manufacturers.

The "Closing of the Great Council," which was carried out by Doge Pierazzo Gradenigo at the suggestion of the *Quarantia* in February of 1297, would both extend and restrict the composition of what was by then the real decision-making body of the Venetian state. Numerically speaking, the Council as a whole was enlarged, but participation was now restricted to those who were currently elected members, or had once been elected members, and to the descendants of those who had been elected members within the last 125 years, with the exception of certain *"uomini nuovi"* ("new members"), who were to be chosen by a specially appointed electoral college.

From a total membership of 586 in 1297, the Maggior Consiglio would gradually increase to more than 1,000 participants by 1311, and to 2,000 or more by the 16th century. Despite their swelled ranks, these individuals continued to represent an absolute oligarchy. Having deprived the *arengo* of any role whatsoever in the affairs of state, the patrician class would remain in complete control of the parliamentary system until the end of the Republic.

Over the years, however, membership in the Great Council would become even more restricted. Among the nobles recorded in the *Libro d'Oro* (which was kept up to date by the *Avogadori),* only those born of marriages contracted between two individuals of equal social standing were eventually considered eligible. (Marriages between members of the aristocracy and women of the servant or plebeian class were totally disregarded. "Equal social standing" meant that marriages could only be made with women from the patriciate, or daughters of secretaries to the Senate, lawyers and notaries, doctors and apothecaries, nobles from the mainland, and master glass-blowers from Murano.)

Once they had reached the age of 25, all males born of legitimate marriages that had been approved by the *Avogaria* had the right to participate in the *Maggior Consiglio*. This was their right, but it was also their duty. Unless, of course, they chose to enter the priesthood, whereupon they were automatically excluded from participating in any and all aspects of political

elected by the *arengo,* or popular assembly, which soon stripped the nobility of many of its traditional prerogatives as well. At that point, the *arengo* might well have been defined as government by popular acclaim, as was manifested by the crowd that thronged St. Mark's Basilica (which was not much different from the way it is now) to applaud Doge Enrico Dandolo for his decision to participate in the Fourth Crusade.

However, by the year 1143, a new legislative body had assumed the ultimate responsibility for governing the affairs of state. This was known as the *Consilium Sapientium,* or *Consiglio dei Savi*. At the beginning of the 13th century, its membership, which numbered some 35 individuals, was no longer determined by the popular assembly, but rather by a *Collegio* of three electors, who in turn had been elected by three of the so-called *"Trentacie."*

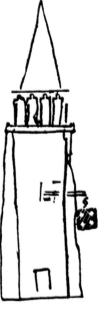

life (despite the fact that the Great Council and the Senate interfered directly in the affairs of the church by electing the bishops!) They would also be part of the Council until their death, thanks to the endless array of public offices from which to choose. Even the Council's octogenarians were expected to serve in the role of *Decano d'Età* (Elder Deacon)!

If we were looking for the very essence of the complex Venetian political system, we most certainly have found it. The *Maggior Consiglio* was indeed a Valley of Jehoshaphat in that it comprised every single eligible member of the aristocracy (all of whom were theoretically equal, at least as far as the right to vote was concerned), from the doge to the senators, from the Ten to the Forty, from the very rich to the very poor, from the influential to the unknown, from the oldest to the newest families. It was the *Maggior Consiglio* that elected the electors of the doge, the 60 members of the *Pregadi*, the 60 members of the *Zonta*, and the Ten and the Forty. It was within the ranks of the *Maggior Consiglio* that the vote of any one member was worth that of any other, from those who had little or no influence to the *Savio Grande* himself.

We should also mention, however, that such a practice would eventually lead to a number of serious problems, the most obvious of which was the buying and selling of votes. As was noted by the chronicler Marin Sanudo at the beginning of the 16th century, *"Chi vol honor bisogna dar danaro ad alcuni poveri zentilhomini"* ("Those who wish to be honored are obliged to give money to certain impoverished gentlemen"). During the 18th century, even as cultured and universally respected a figure as Doge Marco Foscarini would resort to bribing less affluent members of the nobility in order to obtain their votes. (These last were nicknamed the *"Barnabotti"* after the free housing given to them by the state in the neighborhood of San Barnaba.) In fact, the *Broglio* (so called *ab antiquo* because it had once been part of a vegetable garden kept by the nuns of San Zaccaria), which referred to the area directly in front of the Doges' Palace where members of the Council would meet during breaks in parliamentary sessions to discuss the candidates for various governmental offices, eventually became synonymous with bribery and corruption.

However, there were any number of positive aspects of the system as well. There was not one member of the *Consiglio*, no matter how powerful his title or important his role in the parliamentary process, who could not be done in by a single vote. Anyone who attempted to overstep his bounds ran the serious risk of being voted down, or even removed from office.

On such occasions, the *Maggior Consiglio* would not hesitate to use the full extent of its authority. We have already mentioned the time when the Consiglio postponed voting on whether or not to renew the Council of Ten because they had authorized the arrest and imprisonment of poor Angelo Mario Querini. During the years in which they reigned supreme, the Ten had doubled their numbers by means of the *Zonta* (or addition), which was composed of the most influential members of society. Toward the end of the 16th century, the *Consiglio* would once again castigate the Ten by suppressing the *Zonta*, first by refusing to elect anyone who presented himself as a candidate for membership, and then by an actual vote!

On other occasions, the *Consiglio* might choose to put a politician in his place by electing him to an office that was obviously beneath his dignity. Whenever this occurred, rather than undergoing the humilia-

Above: Members of the Confraternity of Merchants, depicted by Domenico Tintoretto in their ceremonial garb (Galleria dell'Accademia, Venice). The two individuals in the foreground are the Savi alla Mercanzia. *Opposite page, left to right: Various aspects of the arts and crafts industry, including weavers, wax refiners, the doge's personal tailor, firemen, a mirror-maker and a fishmonger (from Giovanni Grevembroch's* Varie venete curiosità sacre e profane, *1755-65 (Museo Correr, Venice).*

tion of serving as *Podestà* of Camposampiero, or perhaps *Castellano* of Quero, the individual so elected could avoid fulfilling his duties by paying a heavy fine, and "atoning by default," which meant that he could not be elected to any other office for the entire duration of the one that he had just turned down.

Under normal circumstances, the *Maggior Consiglio* was responsible for all major policy decisions regarding the Venetian state. As we have seen, it was also responsible for electing those who held the most important positions in the government, including ambassadors and *Capitani Generali da Mar* (the supreme commanders of the maritime fleet). Then there was the seemingly endless task of electing magistrates from among its own membership, who would go on to serve in various political, administrative, judicial, naval and commercial capacities, or perhaps in one of the so-called "regiments," as maritime or mainland governors. Finally, there were the military officers, including the *Sopracomiti*, the galley commanders and the *Governatori di Nave*, who were in charge of the sailing-ships.

The *Sala del Maggior Consiglio* (Great Council Chamber) was also the setting for great political debates. This enormous hall, which was destroyed by fire in the year 1578, had originally been decorated by none other than Titian, Carpaccio, the Bellinis and the Paduan artist Guariento, whose monumental fresco of the *Coronation of the Virgin* once covered the wall behind the *tribunale* of the doge and the Signory, where there is now Jacopo Tintoretto's colossal painting of *Paradise*. On less solemn occasions, such as the state visit of King Henry III of France and Poland in 1576, it was also used as a ballroom and banquet hall. In far more dramatic circum-

Who was it who said that the Venetians placed all of their faith in St. Mark, just enough of their faith in God, and little or none of their faith in the pope?

stances, it would be the scene of the riotous debates that took place during the tumultuous days of May 1797, which marked the end of one thousand years of independence enjoyed by the *Serenissima*.

"Cacciati i papalisti"

"Prima veneziani e poi cristiani!" How many times has it been said that during their golden age, the Venetians considered themselves first and foremost Venetians, and only then Christians! And who was it who said that the Venetians placed all of their faith in St. Mark, just enough of their faith in God, and little or none of their faith in the pope?

At the height of the Republic, the pontiff was not only a formidable temporal power, but also one of the Italian princes whose territories shared a common border with those of the Venetian state. This set of circumstances was more than enough to justify a certain diffidence on the part of the Venetians with regard to the Vicar of Christ, who was actively engaged in encouraging the sailors, merchants and shipowners in the ports under his control to compete directly with their neighbors.

First, there had been a serious conflict between the pope and the Republic regarding the ultimate fate of Comacchio, a small town in the Romagna that had dared to interfere with Venice's commercial activities along the rivers of the Po Valley, particularly in the area of salt exports. After the Venetians had attacked it a second time in the year 932, under Doge Pietro II Candiano, and had actually deported its citizens to get them out of the way, the Vatican reacted accordingly. Then there had been Ancona, which had eventually been forced to give up all hopes of competing with Venice for trade with the East. Finally, in the late 16th century, when the Venetians had managed to sabotage the major renovations undertaken by Pope Clemente VIII at the port of Goro in the Polesine, Pope Aldobrandini threatened to stop acting like a "lamb" and start acting like a "lion," and personally shut down the Po River Canal, which had been built by the Venetians to remove the accumulation of soil and gravel deposited in the river-bed.

Even though the Republic had openly sided with Pope Alexander III at the time of his historic clash with the German emperor Frederick Barbarossa, and had been instrumental in bringing about the reconciliation between the two great rivals, the relationship between Venice and the Roman pontificate, which lasted for over a millennium, would be marked by endless disputes and quarrels. The last and most serious conflict came about in 1606 when the Venetians refused to hand over to the Roman tribunal two priests who had been arrested for having committed common crimes, and chose instead to judge them before the Council of Ten. Infuriated, Pope Paul V used the interdict itself, the most powerful weapon in his spiritual armory, to teach the Republic a lesson once and for all. After Venice had promptly declared the interdict null and void based on the fact that it was canonically illegal, the rest of Europe looked on in complete amazement as the two sides squared off for a battle that would last the better part of a year. In the end, the Venetians could claim at least a partial victory.

The main protagonist in this stormy episode was a monk of the Servite order named Paolo Sarpi, whom the Senate had appointed as special counsel to the Republic to advise them on both theological and judicial matters. Despite inordinate pressures and constant threats on the part of the papal authorities (whose Spanish faction epitomized the bigotry and religious fanaticism that the Venetians had been struggling against for the last 80 years), it was well known that Sarpi himself was at the root of the opposition that was being waged by the leading politicians of the day, including Doge Leonardo Donà and Nicolò Contarini, both of whom would appeal directly to the Venetians' strong sense of patriotism, whatever their actual convictions might be.

Despite his religious and inquisitorial zeal, the Borghese pope had only succeeded in reinforcing the Republic's overwhelming sense of civic pride. Perhaps the famous motto, "right or wrong, my country," applies as much to the citizens of the Republic as to those of Victorian England, whose patriotism gave rise to any number of similar anecdotes.

Few people on earth practiced a more spectacular or solemn form of Catholicism than the Venetians themselves. Fewer still were in a position to defend their rights and privileges as private citizens against the weight of Rome. In regard to the official relationship between Church and State, these rights and privileges were jealously guarded indeed. The doge himself attended more religious functions than the bish-

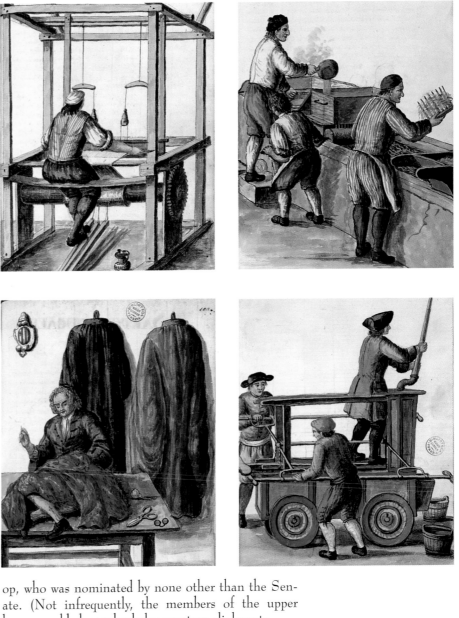

op, who was nominated by none other than the Senate. (Not infrequently, the members of the upper house would choose bachelor senators, diplomats or other parliamentarians for this particular office. Amazingly enough, they usually made exemplary bishops!) All sentences handed down by the ecclesiastic courts had to be ratified by members of the lay judiciary, the clergy as a whole had no say whatsoever in the affairs of state, and whenever the *Collegio* met to discuss matters pertaining to religion, or relations with Rome, the first order of business was to remove from chambers the so-called *"papalisti"* (those who had relatives high up in the Church, or who were in

CONFRATERNITIES AND GUILDS

The very first *scuole*, or confraternities, were more religious organizations and mutual aid societies than professional associations per se. In fact, their membership, which gathered in meeting-houses that adjoined a particular church or monastery, often represented a number of different trades. These early societies eventually became the model for the various guilds that were formed to look after the interests of the arts and crafts industry as a whole. Most importantly, they represented the lower and middle classes who were automatically excluded from the political process, and who used the confraternities to promote their professional activities and assert their prerogatives as valued members of the community. At the beginning of the 11th century, there were already societies of craftsmen who freelanced in workshops throughout the city. By the 14th century, there were some 100 religious, trade and craft associations, large and small. The universal admiration and respect enjoyed by these diligent and highly skilled craftsmen is more than obvious in the Romanesque bas reliefs of the central arch of St. Mark's Basilica depicting their various trades (reliefs 5 -8: blacksmiths, carpenters , bakers, and vintners), as if in homage to the flourishing guilds that had contributed so much to the city's greatness. The confraternities themselves, which were allowed a certain amount of autonomy, were regulated by a series of statutes known as *mariegole* (1, a page from the *mariegola* of the furriers' guild), which dealt with everything from the governance of the organization itself to abuses such as unfair competition, poor workmanship, overly long hours (especially with regard to night shifts) and defective materials. When certain of the *scuole* had become so powerful that they could actually price their own merchandise, the three *Giustizieri* (whose office had been created in 1173 to supervise the city's merchants), intervened on more than one occasion to prohibit such practices, and establish a more equitable system (9, butchers' price list). The *mariegole*, which were formulated by a specially appointed committee of the *scuola*, were then approved by the entire membership, and ratified by the *Giustizieri*. Officers, who were elected on an annual basis, generally included the president *(gastaldo),* vice-president and certain board members (who formed the executive committee), as well as the treasurer, secretary, cashier, two auditors, and one or more assessors, who were responsible for apportioning membership dues. Journeymen and apprentices were excluded from the election process, which was entirely in the hands of master craftsmen. The confraternities all had their own banner, which was kept in their meeting-hall, and which traditionally displayed the image of their patron saint, the tools of their trade (4, painted wooden panel depicting members of the furriers' guild), their official seal (2 and 3, seals of the masons and oil vendors), and their chest. Assembly meetings, and the annual banquet in honor of newly elected officers, were held in the main hall and refectory respectively (4, the main hall of the Scuola Grande di San Rocco). All major decisions of the general assembly had to be ratified by the three *Giustizieri* as well. New members were selected on the basis of good character and a strong sense of commitment. In fact, once they had reached the age of 12, the so-called *garzoni* were expected to serve an apprenticeship of five to seven years, and spend another two to three years working as skilled craftsmen, before they were given the ultimate title of *maestro*, or master craftsman, at which point they could also open

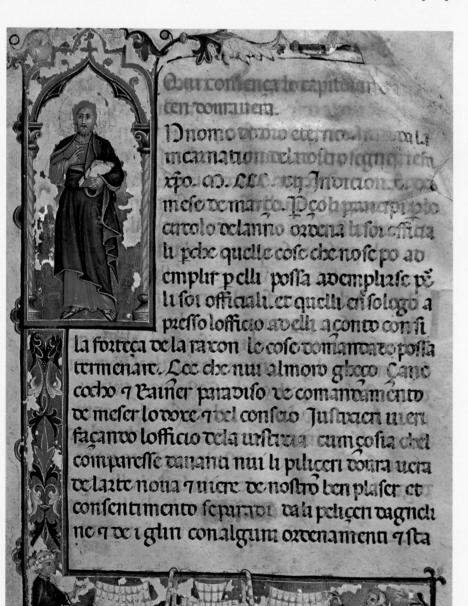

4

their own shop. In addition to their annual dues, guild members paid a personal income tax. They were also responsible for settling any disputes that arose within their ranks, and ensuring that the organization as a whole remained loyal to the state. Finally, they and their fellow members played an extremely important role in Venetian society, giving financial aid to the poor and infirm, providing pensions for widows, looking after the welfare of orphaned children, and founding almshouses. As of the year 1539, all skilled and unskilled workers were required to become guild members. Among their rights and responsibilities, they provided conscripts for the galleys, and played an active part in religious festivals and public ceremonies, when they proudly displayed their emblems and banners to the public at large.

9

7

8

Right: Romanesque bas relief depicting shipbuilders from the central arcade of St. Mark's Basilica. The respect and admiration enjoyed by the Venetian scuole is evident not only in the grandeur of their great halls and their participation in many of the formal ceremonies of the day, but also in paintings and sculptures representing the various trades themselves. Opposite page: Engraving from Franco's Habiti. As part of the doge's official coronation ceremony, he was carried around St. Mark's Square in his pozzetto (which was a type of circular sedan chair) on the shoulders of 50 strong young workers from the Arsenal while he and his relatives threw fistfuls of coins to the enthusiastic crowd. This was one of the ways in which the Republic sought to maintain good relations among the various social classes. According to statistics published by Gaetano Cozzi in 1586, the city had a total population of 150,000. Of these, the nobility accounted for 6,039, the "citizenry" 7,600, and the common people 19,000. There were also 2,507 monks, 1,205 friars, 447 beggars, 1,111 poor people in almshouses, 536 priests and 1,694 Jews. Man servants accounted for 3,680, and maids for 6,000.

any way beneficiaries of the papacy). In such cases, the official minutes would always begin with the phrase, *"Cazzadi (cacciati) i papalisti . . ."* ("The followers of the pope having been removed. . . .").

It has also been said time and again that the Venetians were good orthodox Catholics (more orthodox than Rome, according to some). In fact, religion was everywhere. The city was literally crammed with churches and pious societies, and devotional activities were a large part of everyone's social life. But in the end, it was the strong sense of patriotism, at every level of society, that reigned supreme in the citizens' hearts and minds. In this regard, there is a famous anecdote about Brother Mauro Camoldolese, a cosmographer who proudly presented one of the members of the Senate with his magnificent planisphere (now in the *Biblioteca Nazionale Marciana*). "And where is Venice?" the senator asked immediately. When Brother Mauro showed him, he was stunned, and demanded to know why he had made her so small, whereupon the poor friar launched into a long scientific explanation that boiled down to the fact that Venice was just a tiny spot on the entire globe. "Then shrink the globe," exclaimed the senator indignantly, "and make Venice bigger!" The tale itself might not be true, but it makes a wonderful story!

Even though John and Sebastian Cabot were sailing under the British flag, the first thing that they did when they discovered Newfoundland was to raise the banner of St. Mark. "Because," noted one chronicler offhandedly, "they were Venetians."

During the Republic's golden age, her citizens actually saw themselves as God's chosen people. After all, they were the descendants of the Romans who had sought refuge among the waters of the lagoons rather submit to the will of barbarian tyrants. Not a day would go by that they were not reminded in some way of their glorious past As for the patricians and the

political power that they wielded after the "closing" of the Great Council, they saw themselves as the elite among God's chosen people.

The members of the Venetian aristocracy were fiercely proud of their heritage, which for certain families (such as the houses of Marcello, Valier, Venier, Gradenigo, Falier and so many others) was undoubtedly Romano-Venetian. In fact, within their own circle, there were definite social distinctions made according to how far back they could trace their roots. First there were the *"case vecchie"* ("old houses"), which had originated before the ninth century, including the 12 so-called "apostolic houses," whose ancestors had supposedly participated in the legendary election of the first doge in the year 697 (Badoer, Barozzi, Contarini, Dandolo, Falier, Gradenigo, Michiel, Morosini, Memmo, Polani, Sanudo and Tiepolo). Then there were the *"case nuove"* ("new houses"), which had entered the ranks of the nobility after the ninth century but before the "Closing of the Great Council," and the *"case novissime"* ("newest houses"), which had been admitted to the patriciate in 1381 for distinguished service to the Republic during the last stages of the dreaded war with Genoa. Finally, there were the great families on the mainland, who had been admitted on the basis of merit throughout the course of the Middle Ages.

In his role as a member of the *Gran Consiglio*, each male patrician was theoretically eligible for the doge's throne, and was treated in as princely a manner as any of his foreign peers: *"Tot nobiles veneti, tot reges."* However, all this vanity and pretentiousness meant nothing when compared to civic pride and fulfilling one's patriotic duty. In the 17th century, when the sultan of the Turks decided to take Crete for himself, and a brutal military conflict drained the Republic's finances and decimated the ranks of the aristocracy, it was the nobles themselves who made the momentous decision to put themselves up for sale. In fact, on Feburary 16, 1646,

VILLAS OF THE VENETO: A TOUR OF TERRA FIRMA

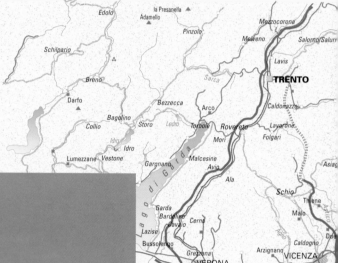

After two decades of internal strife (the terrible "Italian Wars," which lasted from 1509 to 1529), the country as a whole was once again at peace. Members of the Venetian aristocracy and the upper middle class soon took advantage of the situation to close down their businesses in the city, and invest their funds in the more stable real estate market on terra firma. For the remainder of the 16th century, the entire Veneto region would experience a "building boom" in country homes the likes of which had never been seen before. Although many of these villas no longer exist, and others are sorely in need of restoration (the Italian government is now providing

Golfo di Venezia

Polesine (C), and then proceeds to Villa Pisani at Montagnana (D), Villa Pojana at Pojana Maggiore (E), Villa Pisani at Bagnoli di Sopra (F), and finally, the overwhelmingly beautiful Villa Rotonda (Villa Almerico-Capra-Balmarana), which is near Vicenza (G). The Veneto is literally covered with Palladian villas, but the most spectacular ones of all are in the neighborhood of Asolano: Villa Emo at

Fanzolo di Vedelago (whose walls were entirely frescoed by Giambattista Zelotti) (H), and Villa Barbaro (now known as Villa Volpi) at Maser (I), with its magnificent frescoes by Paolo Veronese. Andrea Palladio was not the only great architect who worked in the region. There were other master builders, such as Vincenzo Scamozzi, who designed the Pisani Castle at Lonigo (J). Among the

countless villas constructed in the 17th century, there is the majestic Villa Manin (3) at Passariano di Codroipo in Friuli (K), where Napoleon Bonaparte signed the Treaty of Campoformido, which gave Venice and the Veneto over to Austria. There are also splendid frescoes by Tiepolo in Villa Valmarana, Villa Cordellina and Villa Loschi-Zileri, all three of which are close to Vicenza (5).

funding through the auspices of the *Ente Ville Venete* for the conservation of so rich an artistic and historical heritage), there are several itineraries available for those who wish to enjoy the magnificent architecture and splendid scenery of the Veneto. The most popular route follows the banks of the Brenta River, from Malcontenta (A), with its Palladian masterpiece known as Villa Foscari (2), and ends up at Stra (B), with its grandiose 17th-century Palazzo Pisani, whose walls were frescoed by Giovanni Battista Tiepolo. For those who are primarily interested in the Palladian villas, there is a second itinerary that starts with Villa Badoer (la Badoèra) (1) at Fratta

Above: Detail showing a barber shaving the doge's beard from one of a series of painted panels depicting the various arts and crafts guilds, which originally adorned the walls of the Doges' Palace. (Museo Correr, Venice).

matter whether they were professionals, or merchants, or even members of the lower class. They were now permitted to mingle socially with the most illustrious descendants of the early tribunes, and participate on an equal footing in all parliamentary affairs, including the election of government officers and magistrates. Eventually, they would marry into the ranks of the original patrician families as well.

Notwithstanding the fact that the members of the old Venetian aristocracy suddenly found themselves in a painfully inferior position with regard to their European counterparts, whom they had always looked upon with a certain amount of disdain, they were still bound and determined to put the interests of the state ahead of their own. Nevertheless, their sense of patriotism and civic pride did not discourage them from making definite social distinctions among their own ranks, which often led to open warfare. A classic example of this was the ongoing conspiracy among certain members of the "new" and "newest" aristocracy, who continued to vote against the heirs of 16 of the oldest families during elections for the dogeship. This "blockade," which went on for two whole centuries (from the death of Michele Morosini to the election of Marcantonio Memmo), automatically precluded any member of the Barbarigo, Donà, Foscari, Grimani, Gritti, Lando, Loredan, Malipiero, Marcello, Mocenigo, Moro, Priuli, Trevisan, Tron, Venier and Vendramin from seeking the ultimate office.

On more than one occasion, the disputes between the so-called "long" and "short" houses (the old houses and the new) actually reached the breaking-point. In the 17th century, there were violent disputes between the "older conservatives," who were ardent supporters of the papacy and the Counter Reformation, and the "younger liberals," led by Doges Leonardo Donà and Nicolò Contarini, who were calling for major reforms in governmental policy-making and religious practices.

In the following century, the most serious conflicts among the various members of the aristocracy involved the widening gap between the "haves" and the "have-nots" within the nobility itself. Given the economic straits of many of the grand old families, and the every-increasing wealth of the privileged few, the heavy financial burdens connected with public service had gradually given precedence to those who could still afford to hold government office. This sorry state of affairs would eventually lead to the last great parliamentary debate of the *Maggior Consiglio,* when Carlo Contarini and Giorgio Pisani, two brilliant lawyers who were themselves members of the aristocracy, urged the Council to enact new legislation to break the monopoly of the rich and powerful once and for all,

they submitted a legislative proposal to the *Maggior Consiglio* that would have accorded patrician status to anyone from the city or the mainland who agreed to support 1,000 soldiers for a period of one year, or who donated 60,000 ducats in cash to the war effort.

In the end, the proposal itself, which was defended by none other than the dogal *Consigliere* Giacomo Marcello (using arguments that might well be relevant to this day and age), was not approved. Despite this earlier decision, the Council was eventually obliged to open its doors to each and every family that had donated 100,000 ducats to help the government defer the costs of war. Given the circumstances, no one was about to quibble over the particulars. Along with the Zaguris, who were nobles from Zara, and the Labias, who were enormously wealthy merchants from Florence, there were the Correggios, who were fur-traders from San Giovanni Crisostomo, the Tascas, who owned a clothing-store called "The Golden Tree," and the Lombrias, who were direct descendants (so it was said) of the Rolla family's cook.

Time and again, the members of the Great Council would be forced to resort to the same measures in the interest of the state. Thanks to the financial support of the nouveau riches, Francesco Morosini was able to mount a successful military campaign against the Turks, and actually conquer the Peloponnese. In return, those who had actually bankrolled the campaign were freely admitted to the ranks of the nobles, no matter how humble their ancestry. Little did it and allow full participation in government policy-making on the part of its entire membership.

The tragic consequences of this debate marked the beginning of the end of the Republic herself. When the State Inquisitors had the two leaders of the opposition arrested, the same *Maggior Consiglio* that had reacted so violently to the arbitrary arrest of the *Avogadore* Querini just a few years before, and had fought so hard for his release, the same *Maggior Consiglio* that had condemned Doge Giovanni Corner and his family in the previous century for their obvious abuse of power, now chose to remain silent. Worse yet, it actually approved a motion to give a round of applause to the Inquisitors themselves!

Despite a final impassioned plea on the part of Doge Paolo Renier, who cunningly resorted to the threat of foreign domination in an effort to revive a sense of patriotism among his fellow aristocrats, claiming that the Republic's neighbors were now so concerned about the decadent state of her internal affairs that they were considering some form of direct intervention, the system had broken down to the point where the nothing could save it.

During the 18th century, one of the obvious signs of a decaying society was the growing disinterest on the part of the nobility in fulfilling their civic duties, which were still obligatory for all members of the aristocracy from the age of 25 until their death. Increasing numbers of wealthy patricians chose to pay enormous fines rather than engage in active government service, while those with less means often joined the priesthood

Above: Panel depicting the Guild of the Peateri, whose barges transported goods from one part of the city to another. Below: Panel depicting the Marengoni, or Arsenal Woodworkers' Guild, restored in 1753 (Museo Correr, Venice). The term marengoni *covered all types of workworkers, including master carpenters and joiners. Given the constant demand for lumber for the construction of ships and buildings, this particular guild was one of the busiest, and most famous, in the entire city.*

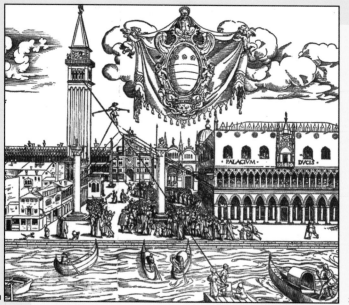

FEASTS AND FESTIVALS

Beginning in the Renaissance, the ruling aristocracy used public celebrations and games as a means of keeping the general population under control. In fact, these events brought the entire community together in joyous celebration of their Venetian heritage, and helped to foster solidarity among the various social classes. Curiously enough, several of the popular games harked back to earlier times, when rival political factions often ended up settling their differences in hand-to-hand combat. (Such practices died out of their own accord after the nobility took over the government, and the population as a whole was no longer directly involved in politics.) These were the so-called "mock wars" between rival neighborhoods that took place on the city's bridges, which were either fought with fisticuffs (8) or sticks (6) (engravings by Franco). They were eventually prohibited in the interest of maintaining law and order.

On the most festive occasions, the city herself became a stage, and the people the actors and audience. Among the local celebrations that have survived to this day, the most important is the "Historic Regatta," which commemorates the great maritime power that Venice once was (7, the Riva degli Schiavoni, from a 17th-century drawing; 3, the Grand Canal, from an engraving by Zucchi dated 1740, showing the "machina," which was the finish line, and the place where prizes were awarded). Official ceremonies such as the doge's annual visits to different locations and institutions throughout the city, and the wedding ceremony with the sea, were also extremely significant, as

were the religious feasts (2, the "Festival of the Redeemer," from an engraving after a painting by Canaletto, which shows the traditional bridge of boats to the Giudec-ca). Then, of course there pure fun and games, such as "Killing the Cat with the Shaved Head," "Catching the Duck," "Catching the Goose" (9, from an illustration by Franco), and

"Chasing the Bulls," which allowed women to participate as well (4). Acrobatic feats included human pyramids known as the "Pillars of Hercules" (5, from an 18th-century engraving), and the so-called "Flight of the Turk," when certain daring individuals walked a tightrope between the Campanile and the Bacino di San Marco (1).

Right: The Votive Bridge Built for the Festivities in Honor of the Madonna della Salute *by Luca Carlevaris (The Wadsworth Atheneum, Hartford, Connecticut). This national holiday, which is celebrated each year on the 21st of November, commemorates the Senate's decision in 1630 to erect a great church in honor of the Virgin Mary for having delivered the entire population of Venice from a terrible plague. As part of this special occasion, the citizens themselves build a pontoon bridge between the two banks of the Grand Canal so that celebrants can visit the sanctuary itself, after which everyone enjoys the traditional meal of "castradina," or smoked, salted mutton.* Below: *A typical puppet stall, which must have been a common sight in the public squares of Venice (from Grevembroch).* Opposite page: *A gilded wooden sculpture from the last of the Bucentaurs, which was built in 1729 (Museo Correr, Venice). Aboard his magnificent personal galley, the doge would pay an annual visit to the waters of the Adriatic, where he performed the famous marriage ceremony with the sea. This was one of the most cherished of all Venetian traditions.*

instead. (We should add, however, that these practices were not as widespread as certain critics have suggested.)

All members of the patrician class were permitted to use the title "N.H.," or *"Nobil Uomo"* ("Nobleman"). When they were called by their Christian names, they were referred to as *"Ser"* (Sire), except for the Procurators of St. Mark's, who were known as *"Missier."* They were dressed in floor-length robes fastened by a belt at the waist, which were edged with fur during the winter, and which were colored according to their official rank: red for the doge's advisors, blue or violet for other magistrates, and black for those who were currently out of office. Over their shoulders, they wore the *stola,* or *bàtolo,* which was edged in gold for those who also bore the title of *"Cavaliere."* The magnificent purple robes with large, capacious sleeves (known as *"alla ducale,"* "in the doge's style") were reserved exclusively for the nine Procurators of St. Mark's. These included the three *de supra,* who were charged with superintending both the physical plant of the Basilica and the countless treasures that it contained, the three *de citra,* and the three *de ultra,* whose duties included acting as legal guardians for widows and orphans, and estate executors for any Venetian citizen who chose to appoint them in that capacity.

Throughout the 18th century, which was in some respects the most frivolous time in all of Venice's long history, there was a constant tug-of-war between the patricians, who had decided not to wear their official garb in public, and the State Inquisitors, who were against their wearing an ordinary *tabarro,* or cloak, which they felt was not in keeping with the "patrician character." What the patricians really wanted was to be able

to blend in with the rest of the crowd. Why? Because while ordinary citizens and foreign visitors could do just about anything they liked so long as they kept their noses out of politics, the behavior of the nobles themselves was under constant scrutiny on the part of the government. Even in the last days of the Republic, members of the aristocracy were expected to keep up appearances in accordance with their exalted status. They were also potential victims of the government's extreme paranoia with regard to spying and the possible revelation of state secrets, which had forever plagued the rulers of a Republic that was surrounded by hostile foreign powers.

The most glaring example of the tragic consequences of such a policy was the so-called "Foscarini Affair," which occurred several years after the arrest and execution of Angelo Badoer, an influential member of the Senate and *Savio di Terraferma* who had been exposed as a spy, and the expulsion of the Marquis of Bedmar, the Spanish ambassador to Venice, who had been accused of openly conspiring against the Republic. In the year 1622, Antonio Foscarini, the heir to an old noble family who had served his government well as ambassador to England and France before being elected as senator upon his return to Venice, was arrested, tried, strangled to death in his prison cell, and then hung by one leg between the columns of San Marco and San Todaro in St. Mark's Square "for having met pri-vately and in secret with the ministers of foreign powers . . . and having revealed to them verbally or in writing the most intimate secrets of the Republic."

Shortly thereafter, the Council of Ten discovered that Foscarini had in

Castelfranco. Among the specialties of the kitchen gardens in the lagoon, which extend all the way from the islands of Sant'Erasmo, Burano and Torcello to Cavallino and Treporti, there are delicious artichokes, including the famous *castraùre*, which have a slightly more bitter taste, and fresh spring peas, which are the main ingredient of a creamy rice dish called *risi e bisi*. The traditional rice and vegetable soups that are often served as a first course are usually made with celery and tomatoes, Savoy cabbage, potatoes or beans. Another typical first course is *bigoli in salsa*, a pasta dish made with thin slices of onion sauteed in olive oil, and chopped anchovies or sardines. For the past three centuries, *polenta* has also been an important staple of Venetian cooking. It is served steamed, baked, or fried, and is often used as a bed for a wide variety of fried or baked fish, including the tiny squid known as *sepolline*, and steamed or baked eel. Among the traditional *antipasti* are the famous *sardelle in saòr*, fried sardines marinated for a day or more in frying oil flavored with vinegar and onions (with or without pine-nuts and raisins). Other extremely popular seafood dishes are soft-shelled crabs, called *molèche* in Venetian dialect, which are often fried in an egg yolk batter, hard-shelled crabs, known locally as *mazanéte*, which are generally served in the month of December, and boiled shrimp called

caparozzoli (clams).

The most famous meat dish on the Venetian menu is the classic *fegato alla veneziana*. Among the lesser known traditional dishes is the *castradina,* which is actually smoked, salted mutton from Dalmatia or Albania, which is then boiled and served with mountains of Savoy cabbage as part of the festivities that take place on the national holiday in honor of the Madonna della Salute.

Wild ducks from the so-called *valli*, or wetlands (2), such as coots, teals and mallards, are also a popular item on the Venetian menu, including the delicious *màzori* (mallards) *alla vallesana*, a specialty of the house on the Island of Burano. (The lagoon's extensive wetlands, which are mainly used as fish farms, represent an essential part of the city's food supply. We should also mention that as a result of the growing concern for preservation of wild life, more and more nesting sites for water fowl species such as herons and ospreys are now being prohibited by law to hunters.)

Any number of traditional dishes that are no longer served at home can still be found in restaurants and *trattorie* throughout the city, including

THE ART OF VENETIAN COOKING

Venetian cuisine is based on both quality and variety. (For the most part, this has helped the city to withstand the onslaught of cheap pizzerias and fast-food restaurants that cater to foreign tourists throughout the rest of the world.) If we take a leisurely walk through the lively, colorful outdoor market at the Rialto Bridge (1), we can get a pretty good idea of just how tempting, and plentiful, these ingredients really are. First there are the fresh fish stalls (3),

which offer a wide choice of seafood, often at very reasonable prices, from the Adriatic and the waters of the lagoon. Then there are the vegetable stalls overflowing with rich produce from the lagoon and the mainland. Seasonal specialties of the terra firma include white asparagus from Bassano, *radicchio rosso*, a crisp, long-leafed, red-tinged variety of chicory from Treviso, and *radicchio verde*, a pale-green variety from

canoce. The Venetian version of *baccalà* is the stockfish, which can be prepared in any number of ways, including *baccalà mantecato*, where it is ground up with garlic and olive oil until it reaches a creamy consistency, and then served as an antipasto on slices of fried *polenta*. Other seafood staples include *peòci* (mussels) and

"Harry's Bar," which was immortalized by Ernest Hemingway, and is now owned by Arrigo Cipriani. Among the many classic items on its menu is the ever-popular *carpaccio*. Another local Venetian tradition is the so-called

1

ombra, a small glass of white wine that is generally consumed in one of the city's many *osterie* (taverns and wine bars, the most modest of which are called *bàcari),* together with tempting cold snacks known as *cicheti.*

2

3

both the *Avogadori di Comun* and the Signory. In fact, the structure of the entire government was based on an intricate system of checks and balances that functioned primarily to prevent the abuse of power.

We have already seen several examples of what could happen when one branch of government attempted to assume total control over another. Among the doges who would eventually overstep their bounds, there was Marino Falier, who paid with his life, Lorenzo Celsi (who may well have been innocent of the charges brought against him), who was subjected to public humiliation, and Agostino Barbarigo, whose reputation was literally destroyed after his death by the "Revisors of the Coronation Oath," who immediately introduced any number of cautionary measures to prevent his successor from "attempting to make himself all-power like Missier Augustin Barbarigo." As for the Ten, the *Maggior Consiglio* threatened time and again not to elect any more members to the dreaded Council, and let it die out instead.

In the last decades of the Republic, the system of checks and balances would break down to the point where the State Inquisitors were allowed to arrest the heads of opposing political parties with absolute impunity, and the *Pien Collegio* no longer bothered to forward important dispatches to the Senate. Such practices soon led to the formation of ad hoc committees and illegal assemblies whose members took it upon themselves to discuss important government policy without the participation of their peers. Even during the last session of the *Maggior Consiglio,* which was held on May 21, 1797, the act of abdication that signified the end of Venetian independence was enacted by less than a full quorum. *Libertà, Legalità, Fraternità* were no more.

Given a parliamentary system based wholly on the checks and balances built into the Republic's constitution, the government had been able to absorb the attacks and counter-attacks on its authority so long as all of its members had played by the rules. In fact, within the ranks of the ruling class, who had excluded the rest of the population from participating in the voting process, the concept of universal suffrage determined every major decision. The members of the oligarchy, who were justly proud of such an egalitarian system, never missed an occasion to remind the public, and themselves, of how it really worked. A classic example of this was the ritual known as *"sbassando stola,"* which was performed by all candidates for public office, who would go out to the *Broglio* in the company of their relatives and *piezi* (supporters), where

fact been the innocent victim of unjust accusations on the part of a secret agent who bore him a personal grudge. To atone for the fatal blunder that they had committed, the Ten made an open confession of their crime to all the courts of Europe, and then attempted to rehabilitate poor Foscarini, for whom they decreed a public funeral. Despite all this, even in the easy-going atmosphere of the 18th century, patricians who were seen in the company of foreign ambassadors ran the serious risk of paying for it with their own lives.

Oh, what a blessed city this is! What divine laws, which require a man with so much personal power and authority to carry out his civic duty after he has returned to his homeland!

A System of Checks and Balances

At this point, we have made a complete tour of the various branches of government that comprised the Venetian Republic. We have also established the fact that the *Maggior Consiglio* was indeed the supreme legislative body of the state inasmuch as it was responsible for all laws of any consequence, and all important elective offices. But we have also learned that the members of the nobility who participated in the deliberations of the Great Council were answerable to the Council of Ten and the State Inquisitors, whom they themselves elected. With regard to the members of the Senate and *Pien Collegio,* which functioned as the supreme executive body of the state, they in turn were answerable to the *Maggior Consiglio,* as were the doge and the members of the Signory, all of whom were elected by the *Consiglio* as well. Finally, the Council of Ten was answerable to the

It must have been quite an experience indeed to witness the victor of Lepanto humbly submitting to the rules of the parliamentary game, even though he had been the supreme commander of such an important naval operation! Episodes of this nature help us to understand just how seriously the members of the ruling class took their responsibilities, and how much respect they had for the constitution.

Let us now take a look at several other social strata within the populace as a whole. The so-called "citta-

they introduced themselves to the electors by bowing their heads until their stoles would slip from their shoulders and fall into their hands.

During one of his famous speeches, Marco Foscarini recounted the following episode, which was meant to be a morality tale for one and all:

"I shall never forget something that I read in my youth, which was written by a chronicler in the last century. There was once a certain Spanish nobleman who decided to visit Venice. . . . He had been here many years earlier during the Battle of the Curzolari . . . and had come to know well the great warrior and statesman named Sebastiano Venier . . . who used to go about in public with a cortege of one hundred or more nobles, all of whom were under his command. When asked . . . what had impressed him most about our city, the Spaniard replied, 'For me, the greatest wonder was to observe Sebastiano Venier bowing his head in supplication under the arches of the Procuratie Nuove. I remember a poor, humble Greek who served in the fleet during the war, and who would pass by him without even removing his hat. . . .' He ended his account by exclaiming, 'Oh, what a blessed city this is! What divine laws, which require a man with so much personal power and authority to carry out his civic duty after he has returned to his homeland!'"

dini originari," or "original citizens," represented the most privileged members of the bourgeoisie. From their ranks came the High Chancellor, who was the only elected official besides the doge and the Procurators of St. Mark's to hold office for life. Although he was not a patrician, he wore the same magnificent purple robe with wide sleeves as did the Procurators, and the gold-lined stole of the *"Cavalieri della Stola d'Oro."* As the head of the state bureaucracy, he was in charge of all the *"segretari"* who served the various government offices. Just as the magistrates were recruited exclusively from the aristocracy, the "secretaries of state" were selected from the ranks of the privileged upper middle class.

Many historians of the past who attempted to define this particular group of individuals referred to them as the "people's nobility," particularly in light of the nouveau riches who bought their way into the ranks of the European aristocracy during the 16th century. These "original citizens," as they were called, took their name from the medieval tradition of dividing the populace into four distinct categories: *de jure, de gratia, de intus* and *de extra*. The last three of these, which were designed to support the

A CITY UNLIKE ANY OTHER

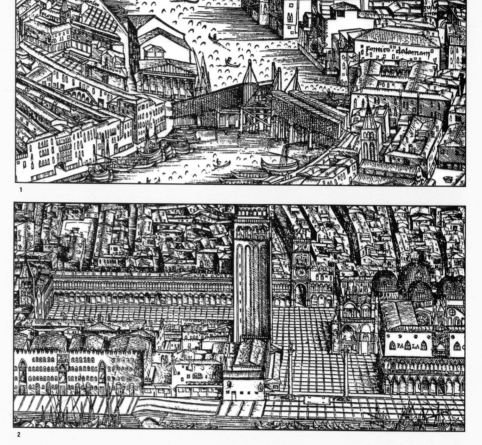

Venice owes her existence to an accident of nature known as the Realtine Islands, which lie at the center of the waters and wetlands of the lagoon, and which are actually more sandbanks than solid ground. She is also the product of man's ingenuity and farsightedness in harnessing the forces of nature to meet the needs of an urban environment. On the map at the bottom of the page, we can see how the city gradually developed over the centuries from the very first settlements to modern day. The areas shaded in yellow indicate more or less what the islands must have looked like in the seventh century, based on the original foundations of the earliest churches. These, together with the areas in pink, give us a fairly accurate idea of ninth-century Venice, at the time when the center of government was transferred from Malamocco to San Marco. If we then add the areas marked in light green, we can imagine the city limits as they appeared in the 11th century. By the middle of the 12th century, the city's topography was not all that different from what it is today, as we can see when we include the light brown areas. Finally, if we add the areas shaded in violet, we can visualize what the city actually looked like at the end of the 15th century.

We have also reproduced several details from Jacopo de' Barbari's famous *Pianta prospettica* (1500) to illustrate how certain sections of the city gradually took on a distinct character of their own. The "Rialto" (1), which was once the only bridge that spanned the Grand Canal, was originally made of wood, and could easily be raised to allow vessels to pass underneath. From the time of the 11th century, it would serve as the center of commerce and industry. The area of the city that would eventually become the "banking district" was located under the arcades of San Giacomo, where the money-changers kept their stalls and account books. The canal side of St. Mark's Square that overlooks the Bacino di San Marco, which is still known as the "Molo," was the historic center of the Venetian harbor. The port itself included the Riva degli Schiavoni, the Grand Canal (before it became a residential neighborhood for the wealthy), and the Zattere, which are located on the Giudecca Canal. On the promontory that divides the Grand Canal from the Giudecca Canal, there were the warehouses of the Customs Office (3). The salt warehouses were located nearby.

The *"Palatium dei Parteciaci"* (the modest dwelling on the Campiello della Casona that became the first Doges' Palace in Venice) would ultimately deter-

Seventh-century boundaries

Ninth-century boundaries

Eleventh-century boundaries

Mid-12th-century boundaries

Sixteenth-century boundaries

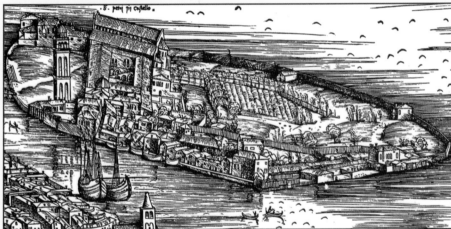

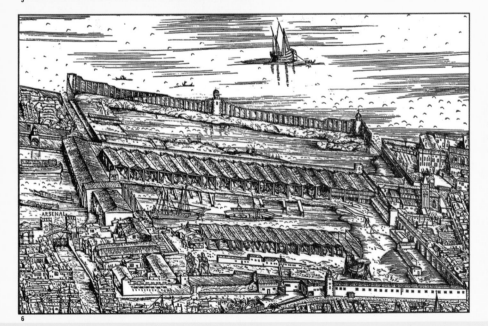

mine the center of the city's political and spiritual life. As seen from de' Barbari's perspective map (2), the Doges' Palace, the Basilica of St. Mark's, the Procuratie Vecchie, the Piazzetta and the Piazza looked very much the way they do today. The area known as the Piazzetta was originally an arm of the Bacino di San Marco, and the Piazza itself was crossed by a rio. The city's political and commercial centers were linked by the Mercerie, which led directly from St. Mark's Square to the Rialto. The various arts and crafts industries were scattered throughout the city, including the neighborhood of Cannaregio, where there were once foundries on the site of what would later be the Jewish Ghetto. With the construction of the Arsenal shipyard, however, the eastern part of the city would become the main "industrial zone." In Figure 6, we can see that the Lago di San Daniele was already the site of the Arsenale Nuovo. Although the boat basin of the Arsenale Novissimo was protected by a wall, its banks had not yet been fitted out.

Venice's "dual" transportation system allowed the populace to travel by boat along the countless canals and rios, or on foot, through the maze of calli, campi and fondamente. Until the 19th century, the Rialto Bridge was the only "land route" over the Grand Canal, and therefore the center of pedestrian traffic. As was typical of all medieval cities, rich and poor lived side by side. The patrician palaces often adjoined the dwellings of craftsmen and commoners, so that the city formed more or less of an organic whole. There were exceptions to the rule, however, particularly in the neighborhood of Castello (4), whose state-subsidized "public housing" included a number of sailors' residences.

The Island of Olivolo, now known as San Pietro di Castello (5), which is located off the eastern shore of the city, was the center of religious life. Perhaps as early as the year 775, when Obilerius of Malamocco was appointed as the first bishop, it served as the official seat of the Venetian diocese. In 1451, when the metropolitan see was transferred from Grado to Venice, it became the home of the Patriarch of Venice. It was not until 1807, after the fall of the Republic, that his title was transferred from Castello to San Marco. De' Barbari's map also shows a number of empty fields, pergolas and walled gardens.

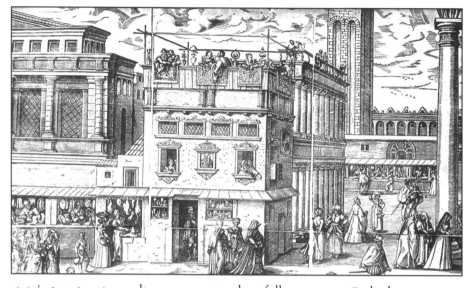

state's immigration policy, were assigned as follows: After a 10-year residency in Venice, foreigners were eligible to become citizens *de intus,* which gave them the right to hold certain public offices, and engage in some of the most important arts and crafts industries. After six more years, they became citizens *de extra,* which allowed them to "sail under the protection of the banner of St. Mark" (that is, to practice the "noble art" of commerce while protected by the combined forces of the Venetian military, diplomatic service, etc.) Subject to approval by the *Maggior Consiglio,* citizens became *de gratia* if they had resided in Venice for at least 25 years, during which time they had neither engaged in manual labor nor lived solely on a private income.

Toward the middle of the 14th century, after a series of epidemics had decimated the city's population, *de intus* citizenship was granted to all those who had moved to Venice along with their families, and who were officially registered with the *Provveditori di Comun.* At an earlier time, silk-weavers from Lucca who had fled their native city in the wake of civil disorders had already been welcomed with open arms, and granted *de gratia* citizenship. These craftsmen were the first to bring the silk industry to Venice, which soon became an important part of the city's economy. Certain of them would eventually acquire such enormous wealth that they became members of the nobility.

The only members of the population who enjoyed the status of *de jure* citizenship were those who had been born in Venice of a legitimate marriage between two individuals who were themselves Venetian citizens, and who had never engaged in any form of manual labor. Within their ranks, there were not only merchants, businessmen, lawyers, notaries, doctors, apothecaries and landowners, but also former members of the aristocracy who had married outside their social class, and had thereby forfeited all rights and privileges,

including participation in the proceedings of the *Maggior Consiglio.* Among them were descendants of the Barbarigo, Contarini, Gradenigo, Foscarini, Bragadin, Venier, Celsi, Foscolo, Tron, Zen, Zorzi, Querini and Dolfin families.

At the time of the fall of the Republic, there were some 176 noble houses residing in Venice. There were also 286 families who descended from the so-called "original citizens," who bore names such as Alberti, Zon, Dardano, Imberti, Busenello, Giacomazzi, Sanfermo and Tornielli, and who could themselves lay claim to a long and illustrious past. In fact, many of them had already bought noble titles and coats-of-arms elsewhere (which were generally looked upon with utter disdain by the Venetian patricians themselves). Among the wealthiest of these families, there were those who competed fiercely with the old aristocracy in terms of art collections and palatial homes, including the Coccinas (or Cuccinas), who built the magnificent Palazzo Tiepolo-Papadopoli on the Grand Canal, not far from the Rialto, and who commissioned none other than Paolo Veronese to paint their portraits (both canvases are now in the National Gallery of Dresden). The Amadi (or Amai) family would eventually acquire such an impressive collection of classical antiquities and musical instruments that they attracted the attention of the Cardinal of Lorena himself, who paid a personal visit to their palazzo at Santa Croce in 1576.

In terms of social prestige, the "cittadini ordinari" were responsible for the entire bureaucratic infrastructure that comprised the Doge's Chancery. This particular branch of the government, which was under the authority of the High Chancellor, was divided into four separate categories: the four secretaries to the Council of Ten and the 24 secretaries to the Senate, who were called the *"Circospetti"* ("Prudent Ones"), and the 44 "ordinary" and "extraordinary" ducal notaries, who were known as the *"Fedelissimi"* ("Most Faithful").

Whether they were assigned to the *Maggior Consiglio, Pregadi, Collegio, Dieci , Inquisitori di Stato,* commanders of the fleet, major "regiments" and important embassies abroad, or diplomatic missions to minor foreign powers such as the Duchy of Mantua, the Grand Duchy of Tuscany and the Kingdoms of Sardinia and Naples, these bureaucrats were expected to exercise the utmost discretion in the execution of their official duties. Such was

the case of Marc'Antonio Busenello (a future High Chancellor), who actually swallowed a coded message rather than let it fall into enemy hands when he was arrested by the Imperialists while residing in Mantua. Giovanni Ballarin, secretary to Ambassador-at-Large Giovanni Cappello, died in Constantinople as a prisoner of the sultan in 1666 while attempting to reopen diplomatic negotiations after Cappello himself had succumbed to starvation and torture. No less dramatic was the fate of the *Circospetti* Sanfermo and Giacomazzi, who continued to forward classified information from their respective posts in Basel and Turin up until the very last days of the Republic.

Whereas the Venetian magistrates were constantly rotated thanks to the intricate electoral system (terms of office rarely exceeded two or three years), the members of the bureaucracy were often allowed to serve in the same capacity for extended periods of time. In fact, this silent, omnipresent class of civil servants eventually became so powerful that certain courageous politicians such as Ranieri Zeno and Nicolò Contarini felt obliged to warn the Council of Ten, the Senate and the Great Council of the dangers inherent in allowing a single group of individuals to become so involved in the machinery of state that they often wielded far more influence than the elected politicians whom they supposedly served. In the tragic case of Antonio Foscarini, there were those who suspected that the real culprits were to be found among certain bureaucrats who were known to have clashed with the ill-fated ambassador on more than one occasion, and who eventually took their revenge by falsely accusing him of espionage.

The ultimate manifestation of the wealth and influence enjoyed by the "*cittadini ordinari*" lay in the grandeur of their "*scuole*," or guild halls. Foremost among these were the six "*Scuole Grandi*," or Great Guilds, which were the among most powerful of the many Venetian confraternities. These grandiose structures, which are the still subject of admiration on the part of modern-day visitors, are located throughout the city, starting with the Scuola Grande di San Marco, whose monumental Renaissance facade overlooks Campo SS. Giovanni e Paolo, and proceeding to the Scuola Grande di San Rocco, the Scuola Grande di San Giovanni Evangelista and the Scuola Grande di San Teodoro. (On the former site of the Scuola Grande di Santa Maria della Carità there is now the Galleria dell'Accademia, while the Scuola di Santa Maria della Misericordia has been converted to a municipal sports arena.)

As we can see from Tintoretto's elaborate decorations in the Scuola Grande di San Rocco, no expense was spared on the part of guild members when it came to hiring the services of the most celebrated painters, sculptors and architects of the day. Apart from the luxuriousness of their private residences, the magnificence of their meeting-houses was a clear message to the members of the nobility who had excluded them from the exercise of political power that they, too, were a force to be reckoned with.

Of the countless fraternal organizations that existed during the height of the Republic, more than 300 were still active at the time of her demise. While certain of these were strictly religious or charitable organizations, such as the Scuola dei Zotti, which provided assistance to disabled war veterans, the vast majority functioned as trade associations and mutual aid societies. Besides the local guilds, there were the so-called "*scuole nazionali*," which functioned as social clubs for foreign nationals and citizens of foreign extraction. Among these, the most notable were the Scuola degli Albanesi (Albanians) and the Scuola degli Schiavoni (Dalmatians), with their magnificent painting cycles by Carpaccio, the Scuola del Volto Santo dei Lucchesi (natives of Lucca), the Scuola dei Milanesi (natives of Milan), which was dedicated to Saints Ambrogio and Carlo, and the Scuola dei Greci (Greeks).

Although the statutes of a number of medieval guilds have indeed been published, the story of the Venetian *scuole* and the all-important role that they played in the lives of the common citizenry has yet to be written. This tale would constitute an extraordinary chapter in the history of the Republic in terms of the courage and strength exhibited by these marvelous people, whose hard work and generosity contributed so much to the health and well-being of Venetian society.

The proliferation of arts and crafts guilds also reflected the enormous variety of trades practiced by the city's skilled workers, whose products were sold far and wide. Despite fierce competition, changing fashions, and political and social upheaval, these craftsmen continued to flourish from the early Middle Ages until the fall of the Republic, as manifested in the endless array of exquisite items displayed in their pavilions at the annual fair that took place on Ascension Day in St. Mark's Square.

The industry as a whole had its ups and downs, of course, particularly with regard to the textile manufacturers, who reached peak production in the 15th century, and then lost their foothold in the international market to the point where they were barely able to sur-

The enormous prosperity enjoyed by the Republic of Venice for a period of more than 500 years was reflected in the extraordinary proliferation of magnificent public and private buildings.

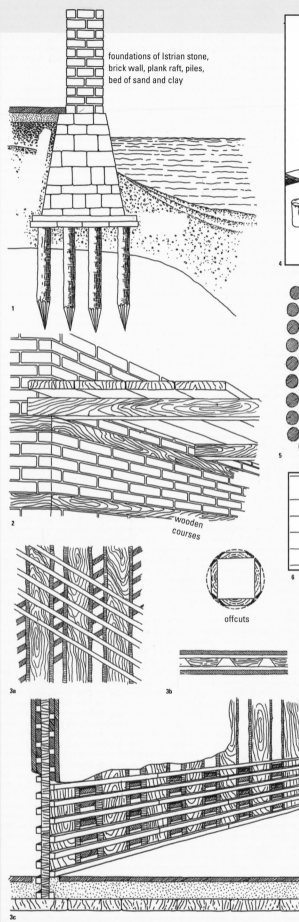

foundations of Istrian stone, brick wall, plank raft, piles, bed of sand and clay

wooden courses

offcuts

3a 3b

3c

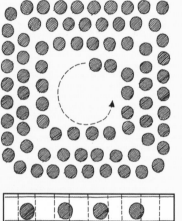

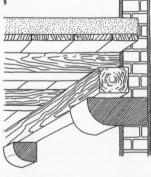

THE CONSTRUCTION TRADE AND THE VENETIAN LAGOON

Venice's unique natural environment required a great deal of ingenuity and expertise on the part of the members of the construction trade. First and foremost, buildings had to be light-weight and flexible in order to survive on the unstable floor of the lagoon. Foundations were made from piles that were driven into the ground (1) until they reached the bed of sand and clay known as "caranto" (4, pile-drivers at work, after an 18th-century engraving by Grevembroch). These were either arranged in several rows around the perimeter of the building (6), or they covered the entire surface area if the structure was designed to be very heavy (5). On top of the piles was placed a raft of planks that supported the foundations of Istrian stone and the walls above ground.

Wood was used in great quantity, even for the tie-beams, which may have been a technique that originated in the shipbuilding industry. The reme (2), which were horizontal courses placed at regular intervals inside the walls to distribute the weight of the floor-beams evenly, were also made of wood, as were the dividing walls themselves, which consisted of a row of offcuts reinforced by horizontal (3b and 3c) or diagonal (3a) joists called cantinelle. The entire surface was then covered over with plaster. Wood was employed as well for the projecting buttresses that adorned the facades Venetian houses, sometimes along an entire calle (7). By using a row of wooden corbels, it was also possible to allow the building's facade to project beyond the ground floor.

With the exception of certain monumental structures, where the main beams were crossed by joists that supported the floor-planks (8),

the flooring was placed on top of beams that ran across the shorter side of the room. These were either fitted straight into the wall above a rema (2), or were placed on top of a beam that ran parallel to the wall, which was supported by stone cor-

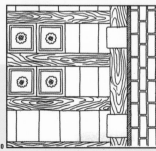

1

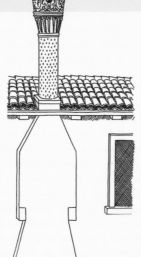

14

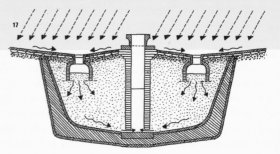

17

part of a rather complicated system designed to provide potable water to the city's inhabitants. The well itself stood in the center of a sand-filled cistern (17) equipped with impermeable walls that collected rainwater from two or four gutters. The water was then filtered through the sand on its way into the well.

To complete our brief tour of Venetian architecture, we have included the floor plan of a 15th-century residence located in the neighborhood of Castello, which

bels (9). This technique prevented the floor-beams from weakening the infrastructure of the walls, and allowed them to absorb less moisture. The wooden ceiling was either covered by a layer of woven reeds and then plastered over, or the beams were left entirely exposed (10).

Functional elements were harmoniously

ing-room (11). Other interesting aesthetic devises were external staircases (20, from a drawing by Jacopo Bellini), roof gardens, loggias (12, also from a drawing by Jacopo Bellini),

15

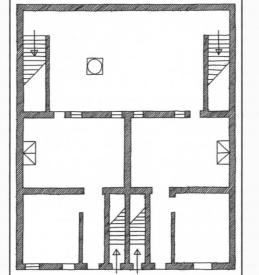

18

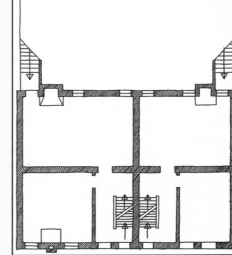

19

16

2

blended with decorative elements throughout the history of Venetian architecture. The Gothic windows that grace the facades of so many magnificent palaces resulted from the dual necessity of reducing the weight of the facade itself and providing enough light for the main liv-

and the picturesque chimney-pots that dot the city's rooftops.

Even the windows of less imposing facades were often designed with graceful double arches and shutters (15). The wooden architraves used for storefronts were supported by a row of stone pilasters (16).

Highly decorative wellheads, which were a common feature of Venetian architecture, were found in courtyards, campi and campielli (13, a wellhead built with recycled construction materials from the ninth and 10th centuries). These were

was eventually converted to a six-unit apartment house (18 and 19). The two living units on the first floor have private entryways at the front of the building, while access to the four apartments on the upper floors is via two separate staircases. Each unit is comprised of two rooms, and at least one fireplace. Behind the building is a courtyard with a wellhead, and two external staircases (20).

20

Above right: The Ca' da Mosto on the Grand Canal is a typical Veneto-Byzantine palazzo from the 12th and 13th centuries. The private dwellings of prosperous Venetian merchants served as living quarters, warehouses and places of business at one and the same time. Although they were originally inspired by the magnificent palaces of Byzantium, the city's architectural masterpieces were as functional as they were beautiful. Below right: Campo di San Boldo.

vive some three centuries later. To a certain extent, the same was true of the age-old shipbuilding industry, which had remained in the hands of private contractors located throughout the city (during the Middle Ages, there were even shipyards on the Grand Canal) until the construction of the huge state-subsidized Arsenal.

Even if a shipwright's pay might have seemed extremely modest compared to the enormous profits made in the real estate industry throughout the Republic's history, the skilled craftsmen employed by the Arsenal were most definitely among the privileged members of the working class. The most privileged of all, however, were the glassblowers from Murano. In fact, every possible effort was made on the part of the state to keep these workers in Venice for fear of their taking their skills and the secrets of their trade elsewhere, including a special government dispensation that allowed those individuals who had been born of a marriage between a member of the nobility and a glassblower's daughter to participate in the proceedings of the *Maggior Consiglio.*

Despite the obvious social and economic distinctions that characterized Venetian society as a whole (which were well documented from the 16th century on), the plight of the average manual laborer was far from desperate. The peasants on the mainland were considerably worse off, as

were the gardeners and vintners who toiled on the islands in the lagoon, and who often ended up huddled together under the city's bridges in freezing weather after a particularly bad harvest. Worse still were the living conditions of the fishermen. As for the common sailors and poor souls who comprised the *"galleotti,"* or galley crews, they were often defrauded by the state itself, which would dock their wages for the slightest infraction, and find every possible way to delay paying them for their services.

Given these circumstances, it is not surprising that there were frequent riots and demonstrations throughout the city, particularly on the part of sailors and galley crews who had been driven to the breaking point by the deceitful practices and delaying tactics of the government. At times, the level of discontent would erupt into serious episodes of violence, as was the case in 1437, when an angry mob looted the city's shops and stalls, and killed or injured a number of municipal guards. Had it not been for the intervention of a much beloved sea captain by the name of Pietro Loredan, things might have progressed even further.

In general, seamen were badly paid, badly treated and often badly recruited. In fact, many of those who ended up as sailors or members of a galley crew were unable to find employment elsewhere. In those rare cases where they were fortunate enough to sail under a captain who was a little more humane and understanding, or perhaps more influential, they often became passionate defenders of his cause. During the conclave that elected Carlo Contarini as doge in 1655, for example, the sailors of the fleet provoked a major riot because they themselves had supported the election of "their Foscolo," the extremely popular *Provveditore Generale* Leonardo Foscolo. Four centuries earlier, the election of Lorenzo Tieplo had aroused such enthusiasm on the part of the maritime workers that they had insisted on bringing their galleys right up to the quay of St. Mark's Square so that the new doge could hear them cheering in his honor.

Such public displays of emotion were hardly restricted to the seamen. Giovanni Sagredo, an accomplished diplomat, politician and historian who was about to be elected doge in August of 1676, found himself facing an angry mob in the sqaure, all of whom were shouting, "Don't choose Sagredo! We don't want him!" In this case, however, the riot had been organized by Sagredo's political rivals. As a result, the frightened members of the Signory immediately cancelled the list of 41 electors who had declared themselves in favor of Sagredo, and Alvise Contarini became the new doge.

As we proceed with our general survey of Venetian society, we have yet to mention various sectors of the

population who played a less conspicuous role in the life of the community, but whose contributions were nevertheless extremely important.

First and foremost, there were the members of the clergy. Although the provincial Metropolitan, who was known as the Patriarch of Grado (the title of Patriarch of Venice was eventually merged with that of Bishop of Castello, when the metropolitan see was transferred from Grado to Venice in the 15th century), as well as the bishops of the local dioceses and the abbots of the more important monasteries, were originally members of the city's legislative assemblies, they were eventually excluded from any activity that was even remotely connected with politics. The same was true of the *Primicerio,* or Prelate, whose responsibilities included the supervision of St. Mark's Basilica, and the management of the church's local institutions and real estate holdings. (In this regard, we might mention that the Basilica did not become the official cathedral of Venice until the year 1806, when the government was in the hands of Napoleon Bonaparte. In fact, until the fall of the Republic, St. Mark's was under the direct patronage of the doge. As such, it served not only as his private chapel, but also as the church of state.)

If the numbers of lay clergy (many of whom originally acted as notaries) were impressive, those of the regular clergy were literally staggering. In fact, the local convents and monasteries were filled to overflowing, partially as a result of the widespread practice of cloistering young girls in order to avoid paying for their dowries. This sad state of affairs was one of the principal causes for the rampant corruption in Venetian convents, which neither the

Above: Two 15th-century Gothic palaces on the Grand Canal. On the left, Palazzo Giustinian. On the right, Ca' Foscari, one of the most splendid examples of the many ogival buildings that can still be seen in Venice. By merging traditional Byzantine motifs with the classic Gothic style, local architects devised the famous central arch that characterized the windows of Venetian palaces, whose main function was to lighten the overall effect of the facade.

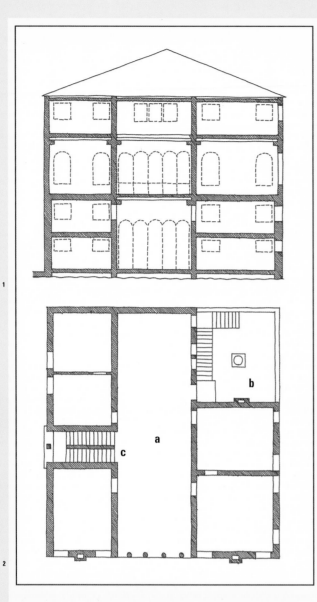

1

2

a

b

c

5

The magnificent palaces that lined the banks of the Grand Canal would not only make it the "most beautiful street in the world," but would also serve as the warehouses and places of business for the Venetian merchant class. Although these same premises eventually represented no more than the stately homes of the rich and powerful, particularly from the time of the Renaissance on, they still retained their original design, which included two separate entrances, one from the Grand Canal, where the docks were used to receive personal visitors as well as commercial deliveries (7), and the other from the intricate maze of streets and alleyways that eventually led to an inner courtyard with its wellhead and external staircase. (In this regard, we should mention the extraordinary spiral staircase of Palazzo Contarini, the so-called "Scala a Bovolo," 4, which is a classic example of the fantasy and creativity that characterized Venetian architecture as a whole.)

Among the other architectural features that originated in the Middle Ages was the triple row of windows on the facade, and the tripartite layout of the palace itself, which consisted of a long, rectangular space that was flanked on both sides by a series of smaller rooms. The main reception hall corresponded to the row of graceful windows on the *piano nobile,* or second floor (5). Until the time of the Renaissance, it was also common practice to place the windows of the side rooms at the corners of the facade (2). The windows themselves were designed to give an overall effect of lightness and elegance, which was heightened by the use of Istrian stone for the cornices and the surfaces of the outer walls.

THE VENETIAN PALACE: MIXING BUSINESS WITH PLEASURE

4

3

If we examine the floor plan (1) and elevation (2) of a late-15th-century palace that was originally designed to serve as both living quarters and business premises, we can easily see how the system actually worked. The first-floor atrium (a), which could be reached from either the dock or the courtyard (b), was the area where merchandise was loaded and unloaded in the days before it became the *androne,* or grand entrance hall. The inner staircase (c) led directly to the main reception room on the second floor. The smaller rooms on both sides of the atrium, which were used as storage areas, often contained a mezzanine reserved for office space.

On the second floor, the *portego,* or main reception room, was used primarily for entertaining and displaying merchandise to clients, while the series of smaller rooms on either side served as the actual living quarters. The third floor was set aside for servants and business employees.

On the facade itself (6, 15th-century Gothic), the windows were also designed in terms of the dual function of the palace, with those in the center being arranged in rows, and those on the side being single. The first row, which corresponded to the main reception hall, was always considerably larger and more ornate than that of the floor above.

The main characteristics of these palaces were derived from the so-called *"casa a torresele,"* which was a late Romanesque construction with portico and loggia that was set between two small towers. This particular style can still be seen in the Fondaco dei Turchi (7), built between the 12th and 13th centuries, which first belonged to the dukes of Ferrara, and then to the Priuli and Pesaro families, before becoming the Turkish emporium in 1621.

After the Romanesque period, as exemplified by the Fondaco dei Turchi and Ca' da Mosto (page 92), and the Gothic period, as typified by Ca' Foscari (page 93), the basic design of the Venetian palace would not change in any significant way until the middle of the 15th century, despite the fact that it became increasingly elegant and luxurious. At the time of the Renaissance, however, Venetian architects began to incorporate many of the classical motifs that can still be seen in Palazzo Vendramin-Calergi (8), which was begun by Mauro Codussi, the celebrated architect from Bergamo, and completed by Tullio Lombardo in the first decade of the 16th century, and Palazzo Manin (9), which was designed for the Dolfin family by

Jacopo Sansovino in the mid-16th century. Palazzo Pesaro (10), which was begun in 1652 by Baldassare Longhena, is a magnificent example of the Baroque period.

A large number of the palaces along the Grand Canal date from the last four centuries of the Republic, when the class of prosperous merchants who had contributed so much to the city's prosperity was gradually becoming a dying breed. Although these later structures were no longer designed to meet the dual necessity of living quarters and business premises, they continued to reflect the basic aesthetic principles that had inspired Venetian architects from time immemorial. Their enduring grace and beauty are a living testimonial to this grand tradition.

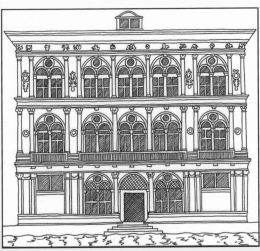

Above: Detail from Carpaccio's Return of the Ambassadors. *Although the building in the background is purely imaginary, it serves to illustrate how reluctant Venetian artists were to fully embrace the aesthetic principles of the Renaissance. The population as a whole had developed such a taste for lavish decorations and contrasting colors and lines that they objected to the simple proportions and plain surfaces that characterized much of Renaissance art (Galleria dell'Accademia, Venice). Opposite page: Detail from Gentile Bellini's* Procession of the Cross in St. Mark's Square, *depicting the Doges' Palace, the Campanile and the Ospizio Orseolo, which was demolished in 1582 to allow space for Scamozzi's Procuratie Nuove (Galleria dell'Accademia, Venice).*

Council of Ten, nor the patriarchs, nor the apostolic nuncios themselves were ever able to root out.

The members of the Jewish community were first relegated to the Island of the Giudecca, then to Mestre, and finally to the neighborhood of Cannaregio, where they founded the first so-called "ghetto" in Europe on the site of a former foundry. (The word "ghetto," which would later be associated with one of the most tragic episodes in Western history, derived from the Venetian dialect for "foundry.") While these individuals, who were obliged to wear a distinguishing badge in accordance with the laws of the Catholic Church, were constantly in and out of public favor according the circumstances of the moment, they were forever subjected to blackmail on the part of the city's exchequers. This was due to the enormous sums of ready cash that they had at their disposal in light of the fact that they were not permitted to invest in any form of real estate. They were, however, given the right to pursue their own religion and cultural traditions within the confines of the ghetto itself, where they eventually built any number of magnificent synagogues.

The Fondaco dei Tedeschi was the complex of warehouses, offices and living quarters of the local merchants from Germany, Austria and neighboring states. Located at the foot of the Rialto Bridge, it was also the site of elaborate decorations, including the early-16th-century frescoes by the fashionable painters Giorgione and Titian that adorned the outer walls. The Germans were by far the most numerous of the hordes of foreigners who crowded the narrow streets of the Rialto's business district, where the most important banking, insurance and commercial operations of the day were carried out against the backdrop of the noisy, bustling meat, fish and vegetable markets.

With its endless array of boarding-houses, inns and taverns, the Rialto was also the center of prostitution, which thrived on the constant comings and goings of businessmen, sailors and tourists. As prostitutes gradually began to spread throughout the city, the municipal authorities did everything in their power to restrict them to a small section of the Rialto called the Castelletto, but to no avail whatsoever. In fact, during the height of the Renaissance, most of the city's prostitutes abandoned the Rialto entirely, and camped out instead in the former dwellings of the noble Rampani family (known as the "Carampane"), which were situated in the neighborhood of Sant'Aponal, while their more ambitious counterparts sought the favor of the city's privileged classes. These last, who would become known as "courtesans," were often elegant, refined women who sold companionship as well as love. As such, they were

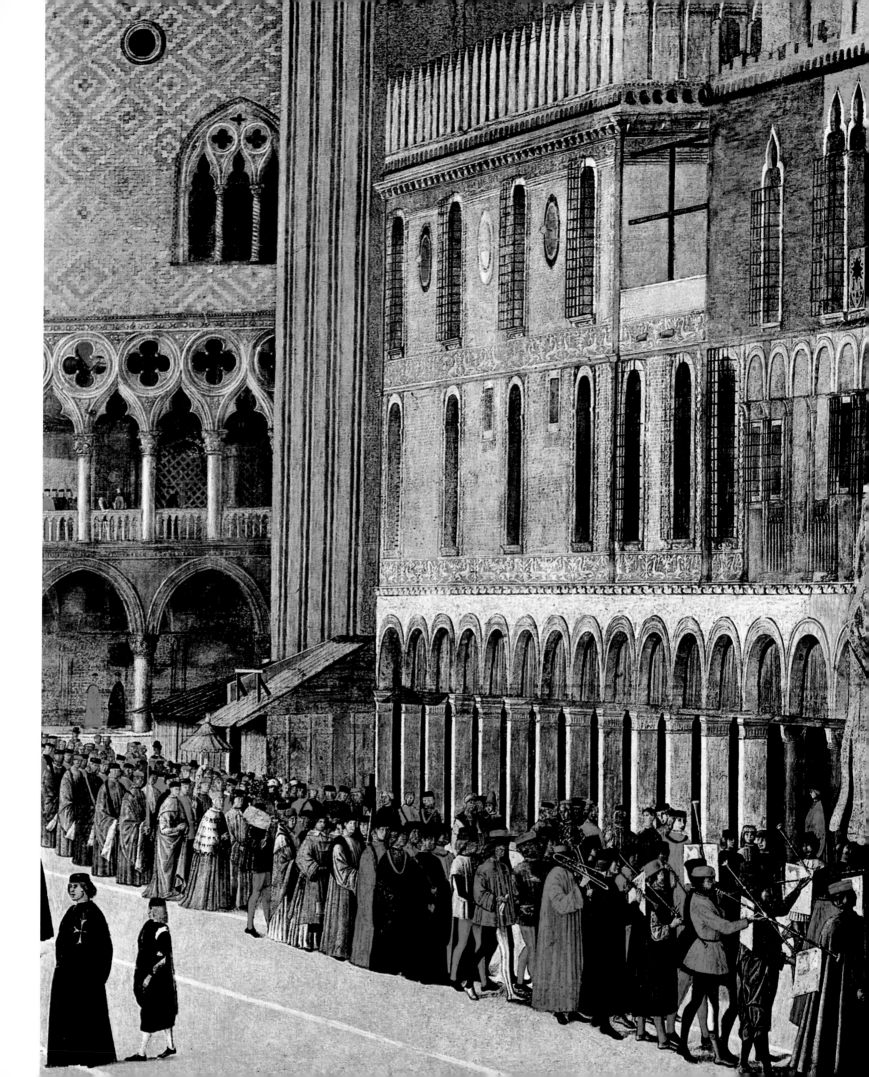

"THE GRAND TOUR"

For those of you who are about to set out on a tour of Venice, there is, of course, the Grand Canal (A), which is a "must" for all visitors. Perhaps the best way to get a feel for the city as a whole, however, is simply to wander her streets and canals with no partic- ular destination in mind, and let your- self be surprised by the many marvels you meet along the way. However, if you wish to make the "grand tour" with the aid of a map, we would sug- gest the following itinerary: As you cross the Ponte di Canonica from St.

3

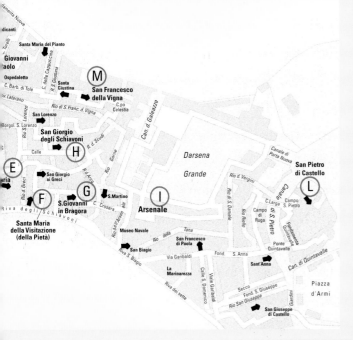

Mark's Square (B), be sure to take a look at the beautiful Romanesque cloisters of Santa Apollonia (C). Then walk through Campo SS. Filippo e Giacomo (D) until you reach the Church of San Zaccaria (E), with its facade by Mauro Codussi, its great altarpiece by Giovanni Bellini, its frescoes by Andrea del Castagno, and its polyptychs by Giovanni d'Alemagna and Antonio Vivarini. Along the Riva degli Schiavoni is the Church of S. Maria della Pietà (F), with its splendid frescoes by Tiepolo (2) (where Antonio Vivaldi served as choirmaster for many years). Then walk over to the Church of San Giovanni in Bragora (G) to see Cima da Conegliano's famous *Baptism of Christ*. Nearby is the Scuola di San Giorgio degli Schiavoni (H), the site of the great series of paintings by Vettor Carpaccio. Also nearby is the Arsenale (I), with its stately Porta del Lepanto, and the pride of lions that were brought back from Greece by Doge Francesco Morosini. Next follow the map along the winding streets until you arrive at the Church of San Pietro di Castello (J), the grandiose former cathedral of Venice. On your way back to the center of the city, stop at the Church of San Francesco della Vigna (K), designed by Sansovino, with its magnificent Palladian facade. As you enter Campo SS. Giovanni e Paolo, you will see Verrocchio's imposing equestrian statue of Colleoni. While you are there, be sure to pay a visit to SS. Giovanni e Paolo (L), the Pantheon of the doges, with its splendid paintings and sculptures. The next stop along the way is the Church of Santa Maria dei Miracoli (M), a masterpiece of Renaissance architecture that has recently been restored (5).

Another possible itinerary would begin at the Church of San Salvador (N), with its astounding *Annunciation* by Titian, (3). Then walk through Campo San Bortolomìo to the Church of San Giovanni Crisostomo (O), with its altarpieces by Giambellino and Sebastiano del Piombo. Along the bustling Strada Nuova is the Misericordia (P), and then the Gothic Church of the Madonna dell'Orto (Q), where Tintoretto lies buried below his two monumental canvases. On your way to the Scuola Grande di San Rocco to see the extraordinary series of paintings by Tintoretto (R) is the lively Rialto market. Then head in the direction of the Church of San Polo, with its *Via Crucis* by Giandomenico Tiepolo, until to you come to the Gothic Church of Santa Maria Gloriosa dei Frari (S), with

4

its magnificent *Assumption* (4) and *Pesaro Altarpiece* by Titian. Nearby is the Church of San Pantalon (T), with its

splendid *Coronation of the Virgin* by Giovanni d'Alemagna and Antonio Vivarini.

5

sought after by painters, princes, politicians and poets alike. Although the authorities once again made a vain attempt to curb their activities, they were so popular that even King Henri of France demanded to spend a night with the famous courtesan and poetess Veronica Franco on the occasion of a state visit to Venice.

As early as the 10th century, Venetian merchants had engaged in the buying and selling of slaves, many of whom, particularly the Africans and Tartars, could be seen rowing gondolas and waiting at table in the city herself. While the legendary beauty of the female Circassian slaves made them the favorites of the rich and powerful, most of the households of wealthy patricians and merchants kept elderly slave women to look after the wardrobe and pantry. This practice died out during the 16th century, and eventually the word slave was applied to prisoners brought back from the Turkish wars, who were condemned to row Venetian galleys in the same manner that Venetian prisoners were condemned to row Turkish galleys!

The general well-being of the Venetian state was absolutely essential to her survival. No matter how wealthy or powerful the individual citizen might be, he was expected to put the public good ahead of his own private interests.

Among those who lived on the margins of society, there were the vagabonds and gypsies ("gajuffi"), who were particularly troublesome in the 16th and 17th centuries. Then, of course, there were the infamous "bravi" of the 17th century, who were professional bullies employed by the worst of the noble class to intimidate their personal enemies. In all fairness, we should mention that their numbers were rather modest when compared to the hordes of thugs who terrorized Spanish-controlled Lombardy. Even so, their deeds all too often went unpunished. During the course of the century, however, many of them joined the ranks of the young toughs who fought in the Turkish wars.

Another group of outcasts were the actors and actresses of the European stage, whose profession was thought to be beneath the dignity of the solid middle class. Despite the prejudices of their neighbors, the Venetians themselves, who loved every form of public spectacle, soon embraced these thespians as a vital part of their daily lives. In fact, the theaters were always filled to overflowing, as were the opera houses and concert halls, as part of a society in which music and drama reigned supreme.

Venetian Civilization

As we near the end of our survey, let us take one last look at the city that routed the forces of the ill-fated Pippin in the year 810 to become the capital of a province, a duchy, a municipality, a republic, and an empire. Her earliest years were centered around the fortified palace of the doge and the bishop's cathedral, while she gradually developed into an urban society, attracting many of the inhabitants of the outlying islands along the way. After centuries of dredging and land reclamation, she gained complete control of the small islands of the archipelago around the Grand Canal, whose rapid development sent real estates prices skyrocketing.

Right next to the Doges' Palace, she built the great basilica that would become the national shrine of St. Mark the Evangelist, and began to fill her *campi* and *campielli* with churches of every size and shape. As she grew ever more prosperous, the members of her noble class constructed elegant palaces of their own, many of which originally served as both living quarters and places of business. Unlike the other city-states throughout the Italian peninsula, whose wealthy residents built private towers to protect themselves and their families from angry mobs and political enemies, the two small towers that characterized the early Venetian palaces were for decorative purposes only!

During the more than five centuries that her citizenry enjoyed enormous wealth and power, her stately homes were rebuilt and embellished by every available means according to the fashions of the times. Even in her declining years, she remained faithful to the cult of beauty that was such an integral part of her character. In fact, the last decades of the Republic witnessed a virtual frenzy of artistic activity.

After Napoleon Bonaparte's lightning-strike campaign against Italy, his unexpected victories, and his even more unexpected treaties with the Austrian Empire, Venice would finally forfeit the independence that she had so jealousy guarded over a period of 11 centuries. However, when Bonaparte and his troops finally arrived at her doorstep, they were met with the most extraordinary array of art and architecture they had ever seen. Despite her heavy losses at the hands of looters, vandals, city administrators, urban planners, antiquarians and amateur art collectors, she is still the proud possessor of untold artistic riches.

No matter how splendid the works of art commissioned by her private citizens, religious orders and guilds, her great artists and architects were first and foremost at the service of the state in order to ensure that nothing and no one could possibly rival the Republic herself in terms of her beauty, elegance and majesty. In fact, at the height of her power and influence, each and every public building was a work of art

in and of itself. Although a large proportion of this extraordinary patrimony no longer exists, the Doges' Palace and St. Mark's Basilica are living proof of the magnificence of the Republic that once was.

No single individual can be credited with having designed the basic structure of either of these two elaborate buildings. Rather, they are the result of a collective effort on the part of any number of architects who refurbished and renovated their premises throughout the course of the centuries. The same is true of the artists and artisans responsible for the decorative motifs that adorn their walls. More importantly, however, they are the result of a collective effort on the part of the citizens themselves. In the case of St. Mark's Basilica, when Doge Domenico Contarini turned to the people of Venice to assist him in raising the funds to reconstruct this national monument, which had already been destroyed once before, their overwhelming support allowed him to build an even more impressive structure that was directly inspired by the magnificence of the great cathedrals of Constantinople. In the following century, the Procurators of St. Mark's

took it upon themselves to further embellish the basilica by commissioning the premier artists, sculptors and artisans of the day, including Paolo Uccello and Andrea del Castagno.

As far as the Doges' Palace is concerned, its architectural design was hardly the work of Filippo Calendario, who was involved in Marino Falier's plot to overthrow the government, and was later hanged from one of the loggias together with his fellow conspirators. In fact, it was largely the result of a collective effort on the part of the patrician class, who considered the palace not only their own personal venue, but also the most obvious manifestation of their political power. Consequently, the various renovations and restorations that took place over the years were always subject to prior legislation.

In the end, perhaps the most important thing that we have learned from our survey is that the general well-being of the Venetian state was absolutely essential to her survival. No matter how wealthy or powerful the individual citizen might be, he was expected to put the public good ahead of his own private interests.

Above: The Lagoon Frozen Over, *by Francesco Guardi (Ca' Rezzonico, Venice). This was a rare event indeed, and the natural exuberance of the population seems to have risen to the occasion.*

THE VENETIAN EMPIRE

VENICE AND BYZANTIUM, THE BENEFITS OF A GOOD BARGAIN, DIVIDING THE SPOILS, MARITIME AND MAINLAND TERRITORIES

On Ascension Day of the year 1000, an armed Venetian fleet took to the high seas. Doge Pietro II Orseolo himself was in command, and his ultimate destination was the Dalmatian coast. For centuries, Venetian ships had traded with the cities on the opposite side of the Adriatic, but this time, they were part of a military expedition in the grand old style. At Ossero, both the Latin and Slavic locals immediately swore a solemn oath of allegiance to the doge. This scene was repeated at Zara, where representatives from the islands of Arbe and Veglia joined their neighbors in declaring themselves his loyal subjects.

These were peaceful, festive ceremonies, but things went very differently with regard to the rest of the Dalmatian Slavs. Once Orseolo had forced the inhabitants of the islands of Pasman and Vergada into submission, he captured a convoy of Narentine Slavs, who had been bitter enemies of Venice for hundreds of years. After a long, hard fight, he also conquered the Island of Curzola, and then Lagosta, which had been a traditional haven for pirates. From there, he made his way back in triumph along the entire length of the Dalmatian coastline.

Venice had been hankering for an open confrontation with the Slavs, especially the Narentine pirates, who supposedly abducted a group of Venetian brides during a collective marriage ceremony in Santa Maria Formosa in 946 or 948. While this particular episode has never been historically proven, what we do know for sure is that they captured none other than Pietro Badoer, the son of the reigning doge and himself a future doge, on his way back from a diplomatic mission to the Orient in 912. We also know that Doge Pietro Candiano lost his life in a skirmish with the Narentines in the year 887. (The Saracens had once posed a similar threat to the northern Adriatic, but had been routed in no uncertain terms.)

Orseolo's expedition, which was the most spectacular in a series of repeated attempts on the part of the Venetian fleet to establish right of way in the Adriatic, marked the legendary beginning of the city's dominion over Dalmatia and Istria. In fact, from that moment on, the doge would assume the official title of "Duke of the Venetians and Dalmatians."

Eight years earlier, Orseolo had scored an even greater victory when he obtained the "Chrysobol," or "Golden Bull," from the Emperor of Byzantium, which recognized the Venetians' absolute supremacy in terms of maritime traffic between Italy and Constantinople, and whose concessions gave them ultimate control over the trade route. Although the "expatriot colony" in the Bosphorus was still in its first stages, Venice had already invested heavily in Byzantium, and these privileges granted her a far more favorable position than that of her chief rivals, including Amalfi and Bari.

that Venice had always enjoyed with Byzantium. First and foremost, her military support enabled the Byzantines to stem the tide of Arab aggression. When the Normans invaded the south of Italy, scoring one victory after another until the entire territory lay in their hands, and then proceeded to the Dalmatian coast and the conquest of Byzantium, the Venetians fought side by side with their Byzantine allies during the ensuing military encounter. Guglielmo di Puglia, a renowned poet and chronicler who was then in the employ of the Norman Robert Guiscard, recorded the awe inspired by the warriors of "that populous city, overflowing with men and means," and "her people, so courageous and expert in the art of naval warfare . . . who travel by boat from one house to another when they are back in their native city. . . ."

Despite the conflicting accounts of a number of chroniclers, Byzantium ultimately emerged as the final victor. In recognition of the support of his most powerful ally, the Eastern Emperor issued yet another "Golden Bull" in 1082, which gave the Venetians privileges that far exceeded those granted in 992, particularly in terms of duty-free trade with any number of ports and inland cities. These territories extended from the lower Adriatic to the Mediterranean and Aegean, including Durazzo, Vaona and Corfu, Modon and Corone in the southernmost part of the Peloponnese, Nauplia in the northernmost part of the peninsula, the Isthmus of Corinth, Athens and Thebes, Negropont and Demetrias in the Bay of Volos, Thessalonica, Chrisopolis and Peritherion in Thrace, and Abydus, Andrianople, Rodosto and Selymbria on the Sea of Marmara, not to mention the imperial capital itself. Along the coast of Asia Minor, similar concessions were granted with regard to the cities of Phocaea, Ephesus, Chios, Strobilos, Antalya, Tarsus, Adana, Mamistra, Antioch and Laodicea.

Little did it matter whether or not these thriving centers of trade were still under the direct control of the Byzantine Empire. Their fate was forever sealed, as was that of Amalfi, which was then in the hands of the hated Normans, and which had aligned itself too closely with the Moslem world to be able to seek similar concessions from Byzantium.

Even more important, however, was the fact that the Emperor's "Chrysobol" of 1082 had officially sanctioned the existence of the Venetian expatriot community, whose commercial headquarters were located in the very heart of Constantinople. This local enclave included two churches, San Nicola "de Embulo," and Sant'Acindino, which was situated in the area

The next 90 years would lay the foundations for the enormous wealth and influence that the Venetians continued to enjoy for many centuries to come. In fact, the events that took place in the Mediterranean Basin during this period could not have been more propitious with regard to the privileged relationship

As far as the Italian peninsula was concerned, the powerful republics of Genoa and Pisa would eventually agree to participate in the crusade in the hopes of enormous personal gain. Venice herself, however, was more than hesitant to become involved, knowing full well that her great ally, the Emperor of Byzantium, was concerned that the crusaders would make little distinction between what belonged to the Arabs and what belonged to the Byzantines.

Genoa, which had been granted an entire district of Antioch, including a church, a square, and 30 houses, for having participated in the battle for its conquest, was the first of the Italian city-states to come forward for the pope. Although Antioch was

Opposite page, above: Treaty signed by Henry V, dated June, 1111. Opposite page, below: Treaty signed by Frederick Barbarossa, dated September, 1177 (Archivio di Stato, Venice). Above left: Ninth-century patera of a Byzantine emperor in Campiello Angaran. The events of the ninth and 10th centuries would firmly establish the city of Venice as a great naval and commercial power, which allowed her to finally assert her independence from Byzantium. With this came official recognition from various foreign powers, including Emperor Henry IV, who personally attended the consecration of St. Mark's Basilica in 1094. In 1177, Venice was also the site of the famous reconciliation between Pope Alexander III and the German emperor Frederick Barbarossa.

where weights and measures were kept for the buying and selling of oil and wine. (In the year 1107, when Doge Ordelaf Falier granted Sant'Acindino to the Patriarch of Grado, the latter would describe the church *"cum toto suo thesauro,"* or "with all its elaborate decorations and precious manuscripts," including the *"ergasteria,"* or "commercial storage space!") There were also two shops, a mill and a foundry. Finally, the Venetians had their own well-equipped docks, and duty-free warehouses where they could store and sell their goods without having to worry about any interference on the part of the Byzantine customs officials.

Several years later, the Venetian enclave in Constantinople, complete with all the necessary accouterments, a fresh water supply, and perhaps even public baths, would be extended to another strategic area of the Mediterranean Basin as a result of the First Crusade. When Pope Urban II launched the expedition with the intention of recapturing the holy lands of Syria and Palestine from the Moslems, most of the fiefdoms of Western Europe responded to his appeal with great enthusiasm, including the valiant knights of France and Lorraine, as well as the Normans themselves, who could not wait to resume their conquest of the East.

ΧΑDRIA·PERGIT NAVGIO ALEX ADRIA·RADIT GALIAM TUR RAVIT MANS & SYA

Mosaics from St. Mark's Basilica portraying Venetian sailors and soldiers in search of fame and fortune in foreign lands. Above left: St. Mark's Journey to Alexandria, *from the Zen Chapel, depicting a 13th-century sailing vessel.* Above right: Fourteenth-century mosaic of the doge in the company of armed soldiers, *from the Chapel of San Isodoro.*

considered a part of Byzantium, and Venice had already been granted duty-free rights by the emperor, she still could not make up her mind with regard to the expedition to the Holy Land. However, after a violent clash with the Pisan fleet in defense of Byzantine interests in Laodicea, the Venetians eventually came forward as well. In exchange for their pledge of military support in recapturing the coastline from Acri to Tripoli, Godefroi de Bouillon, the newly crowned King of Jerusalem, promised them not only a church, foundry, well, warehouse and marketplace in each of the conquered territories, but also the entire city of Tripoli, with exemption from all existing tariffs.

Even though the Venetian navy ultimately failed to fulfill the terms of this agreement, which gave the Genoese the lion's share of the spoils, Venice herself would finally lay claim to a third of the cities of Tyre and Ascalon after she had lent her support to a successful military campaign in 1124. It was at this moment that she became one of the acknowledged "colonial powers" in the region, along with Genoa and Pisa, all of which now enjoyed not only trade concessions, but jurisdictional privileges as well. In the end, however, it would not be the *Serenissima's* presence in Syria and Palestine that was destined to be the foundation of her great empire.

Venice and Byzantium

During the same period, Constantinople continued to play a critical role in terms of Venetian commercial interests abroad. Despite the presence of other Italian cities in the prestigious Byzantine capital and throughout its many territories, which was often the cause of serious disputes, Venice succeeded in maintaining her ultimate supremacy until the year 1124, when Emperor John Comnenus decided not to renew the privileges that had been granted to her in 1082. This action prompted Doge Domenico Michiel to set sail for the Archipelago, where he laid waste to Rhodes, Samos, Lebos and Modon in defense of his citizens' rights. In Cephalonia, he established a military base from which he continued to besiege the Byzantine territories until Comnenus agreed to renew the "Golden Bull."

Although Venice and Byzantium would eventually join forces against the Normans, who along with their king, Roger II of Sicily, were threatening the coasts of Greece and Dalmatia, the reconciliation was of short duration. In fact, the Byzantine chroniclers Cinnamus and Nicetas would tell the world in no uncertain terms how much the Greeks had grown to resent their

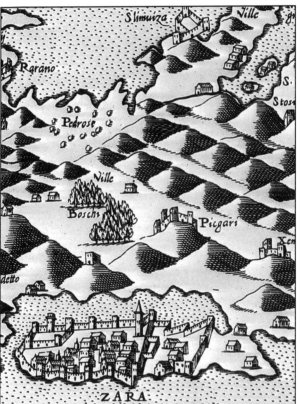

former ally. While they could hardly deny the fact that Venetian naval power had come to their defense time and time again, they were also keenly aware of the price they were expected to pay. Even the last military expedition against the Normans had gained enormous advantages for Venice, including the freedom to trade throughout the territories of the empire, and total exemption from the excise taxes that still applied to the Byzantines themselves. At least they could have shown a little gratitude! Their arrogance was entirely out of proportion to the concessions they had been granted! The more they received, the more they demanded! Worse yet, while any number of them had intermarried with the Greeks, they continued to affect a total disdain for a population that could in no way match their own wealth and influence!

The fact is that the Venetians were everywhere. Aside from the thousands upon thousands of merchants and citizens scattered throughout the empire, there were those who resided in the Byzantine capital itself, and who had "invaded" one neighborhood after another. (As was the case in other foreign cities where private citizens and religious institutions held property, such as the Patriarchate of Grado, the Basilica of St. Mark's, and the Abbey of San Giorgio Maggiore,

the Venetians in Constantinople did not actually live in their own commercial district.)

Among the expatriots who have gone down in history as extraordinary entrepreneurs, there was Romano Mairano, whose farsightedness made him one of the great merchant shipbuilders of the Middle Ages. Then there were Domenico Mastrocoli and Dobramiro Stagnario (the latter of whom evidently had Slavic blood in his veins), highly successful olive oil merchants from Corinth who traded not only with the West, but with every major port and market square in Byzantium as well. Among the more notable members of the Venetian aristocracy who engaged in commerce along the Venice-Jerusalem-Constantinople trade route were Colomanno Bembo and Marino Michiel, whose products included silk exported from Constantinople, wool cloth, wrought iron, carpentry and weapons from Venice, and spices and cotton from Palestine.

Toward the end of the 12th century, when tensions at home and abroad had reached the breaking-point as a result of Venice's refusal to support Manuel Comnenus' attempt to regain control of the Adriatic Gulf, the Emperor organized a secret plot whereby all Venetian citizens residing in his dominions would be seized, their goods confiscated, and their property handed

Above left: Fourteenth-century warrior. Above right: Map showing part of the Dalmatian coast and the fortified town of Zara (Zadar). Venice's hegemony in the Adriatic was established during the 11th century, beginning in the year 1000, when Doge Pietro II Orseolo conquered Dalmatia and signed peace treaties with the Narentines and Croats, and ending in 1085, when she defeated the Normans a second time. Once she had become "Queen of the Adriatic," she was assured of free passage to the East.

Above: A view of Pirano (Piran) from the sea. Below: The town hall in Capodistria. Opposite page: The facade of the "Lassa Pur Dir" Palace in Pirano, in Venetian Gothic style. The expatriot communities that established themselves in seaport towns along the various trade routes were an important part of the Republic's commercial success, which can be summed up by the popular saying, "Coltivar el mar e lassar star la terra" ("Cultivate the sea and leave the land alone"). As is obvious from the exquisite photographs contained on these pages, the Serenissima would leave an indelible mark on the territories that she occupied.

over to the Greeks. On March 12, 1171, when the massive police "round-up" began (with the complicity of the Genoese), the Venetians were completely taken by surprise. After it was all over, only a handful of expatriots had managed to escape on board a ship belonging to Romano Mairano, and the emperor's prisons were filled to overflowing. Worse yet, the powerful fleet that immediately set sail under the command of Doge Vitale Michiel would ultimately suffer a

disastrous defeat at the hands of the Byzantines, due in part to the plague, which broke out in all its horrors during the military expedition, decimating the Venetian contingent.

For a number of years thereafter, Venice would have to look elsewhere to trade. But he who laughs last laughs best. In the year 1182, when Emperor Andronicus Comnenus ordered the massacre of all Latins residing in Constantinople, the Venetians could only thank their lucky stars that they were not there to share the fate of the Pisans and Genoese.

This was the set of circumstances that would eventually lead to the Fourth Crusade some two decades years later, which would also witness the birth of the Venetian colonial empire in the East. In the meantime, a treaty signed between Venice and Byzantium in 1198 temporarily put an end to their constant wrangling by offering some degree of compensation to the Venetians for the damages caused by Manuel in 1171, and opening up other markets to their merchants. These included Yannina in Epirus and Castoria in western Macedonia, Skopje in the Macedonian interior, Zagoria in Bulgaria, Philippopolis in Thrace, the Cyclades, Crete, Zante, Levkas, the islands of Samos, Mytelene, Rhodes and Cos, as well as Philadelphia and all of Lydia in Asia Minor. Despite these numerous concessions, trade was nowhere near as profitable as it had once been, and both sides continued to view the other with apprehension and suspicion.

The Benefits of a Good Bargain

In return for the role that they had so astutely played in bringing about the reconciliation between Pope Alexander III and the German emperor Frederick Barbarossa in 1177, the Venetians would assume a position of far greater importance among their European contemporaries. In fact, as the Western World prepared to embark on the Fourth Crusade, the French, Flemish and Germans lost no time in dispatching an embassy to Venice to request the loan of transport ships for their troops, horses, armaments and attack weapons. This latest expedition to the Holy Land was spearheaded by Lothario dei Conti di Segni, otherwise known as Pope Innocent III, who had his

heart set on recapturing the Kingdom of Jerusalem, which had been lost after the Moslems' victory at Hattin.

Despite the huge crowd of 10,000 local citizens that assembled in St. Mark's Basilica in April of 1201, whom the chronicler Geoffroi de Villehardouin described as having been totally swept away by religious fervor and the lust for revenge, the Venetians themselves had in no way committed themselves to participating directly in the crusade. The only document that Doge Enrico Dandolo had actually signed was a contract stipulating that Venice would supply the necessary transport ships for 4,500 calvary officers, 4,500 horses, 9,000 grooms and 20,000 foot soldiers (including provisions for one whole year), and 50 armed Venetian galleys, which represented his personal contribution to the cause. In exchange, the crusaders were expected to pay the enormous sum of 85,000 silver marks, plus half of the profits made on the entire expedition. Although the final destination of the ships, which were to be ready by June 29, 1202, was not specified in the contract, according to Villehardouin, it was most probably Egypt, which was considered the heart of the Moslem empire.

By the 29th of June, the Venetian transport ships and *"uscieri"* (vessels specifically designed for the caval-

ry troops) had been fully equipped, and the necessary provisions gathered. In other words, Venice had kept up her end of the bargain. As far as the crusaders themselves were concerned, instead of arriving in Venice at the appointed time, most of the European princes and barons had already set sail for Palestine by other routes, or chosen instead to proceed on foot, taking with them the promised sum of 34,000 marks of silver. After consulting at length with the Marquis de Montferrat and the Counts of Flanders and Blois, who had arrived in Venice with only a fraction of their original troops, Enrico Dandolo proposed the following: In exchange for the missing funds, they would help Venice to recapture the city of Zara, which had placed itself under the protection of the King of Hungary.

In the end, despite the Pope's outrage and eventual excommunication of the Venetians, the fact that the citizens of Zara and the King of Hungary were Christians, and not infidels, was not a good enough reason for the papal legate, Cardinal Pietro Capuano, or the crusaders themselves, to refuse the doge's final offer. In fact, the siege of Zara was considered a necessary evil that would finally allow the crusade to get under way.

While encamped in Zara awaiting the approach of spring to continue on their pilgrimage to the Holy

Land, the crusaders were visited by envoys from the Byzantine prince Alexius, who had fled from Constantinople to his brother-in-law, Phillip of Swabia, after his father, Emperor Isaac Angelus, had been dethroned and imprisoned by his uncle Alexius III. The young Alexius had already appealed directly to the French barons for their help in regaining the throne for himself and his father when they had met him at the court of Philip of Swabia en route to Venice. Having been told nothing about this original encounter, the Venetians themselves were still engaged in a desperate attempt to improve relations with the new emperor, Alexius III, in order the further their own commercial interests.

This time, however, the ambassadors sent by Prince Alexius and the powerful Phillip of Swabia came armed with a concrete proposal. In exchange for the pilgrims' help in restoring Isaac Angelus to the imperial throne, they were prepared to pay the sum of 200,000 silver marks, place a contingent of 10,000 Greeks at the crusaders' disposal for the wars in Palestine, and bring about the union of the Greek Orthodox and Roman Churches. These negotiations took place in early January of 1203.

Historians have generally credited the political foresight of Doge Dandolo for the seemingly absurd decision to lay siege to Constantinople instead of Egypt, and wage war against the Christian Byzantines instead of the Moslems. The truth is that the last of the surviving barons, headed by Conrad of Montferrat and Baldwin of Flanders, were more than tempted by the possibility of enormous financial gains. They also argued that once the city was theirs, they would be able to take up the military challenge in the Holy Land

with a far greater chance of success. Even the pope was convinced that they would be furthering the sacred cause of religion in effecting the union of the Eastern and Western Churches. None of them had the slightest idea that this decision would ultimately lead to the conquest of the Byzantine Empire..

Once they had seen that the crusading barons were generally in favor of such an enterprise, the doge and his entourage began to realize that restoring the old man Isaac Angelus and placing his son Alexius on the throne might not be such a bad thing after all. At the very least, in exchange for what they owed to the Venetians, the two would be sure to grant them any number of important concessions. Apart from everything else, they were confident of the ultimate victory over the Greeks.

After the usurper, Alexius III, had been easily overcome, and it seemed that there was nothing left for the French and Venetians to do but extract from father and son the rewards that they had been promised, they found themselves face to face with the outrage and indignation of the Byzantine people themselves. While Alexius III had not been a particularly popular monarch, the new sovereign, Alexius IV, had been imposed on the Greeks by force, and was considered nothing less than a puppet in the hands of the crusaders, and therefore a traitor and a lackey.

Alexius himself, who was well aware of the hatred and resentment he engendered in his subjects, went so far as to

Above: Crusaders and Saracens in the Holy Land, *a miniature from Marin Sanudo the Elder's* Liber secretorum fidelium Crucis, *dated 1321.* *Below: A page from Mathew Paris's 13th-century* Historia Anglorum, *depicting St. John of Acri, now known as Akko, which is situated on the coast of Israel. After the city was sacked by the crusaders in 1189-90, it became the most important stronghold in the Holy Land.*

Right: The earliest known map of Constantinople, dating from the beginning of the 15th century, which illustrates the extraordinary number of natural and manmade fortifications that the crusaders were forced to overcome. Below: Mosaic tile dated 1213 from the floor of the Church of San Giovanni Evangelista in Ravenna, depicting an episode from the Fourth Crusade.

ask the crusaders to stay on in Constantinople until the spring of 1204. Given the enormous investment that they had made in transport vessels and military equipment, which had already remained unproductive far too long, the Venetians were not at all pleased with this possibility. More importantly, they understood the Byzantine people well enough to expect serious trouble if they maintained an armed presence in the midst of such a hostile environment.

In fact, hostilities between the two camps did break out shortly thereafter. Hoping to regain the respect and support of his own people, Alexius IV eventually turned against his foreign protectors, but to no avail whatsoever. In the wake of a massive popular uprising, he was deprived of the throne, and replaced by Alexius V, Ducas Mourtzuphlos, a member of the Greek national resistance movement, who demanded the immediate expulsion of the Venetians and their allies. At this point, the Latins had already suffered one guerilla attack after another on the part of the local populace. They had also barely escaped losing their entire fleet after the Greeks had set fire to it during the

night. Finally, they had been obliged to seek refuge in the outlying area of Pera after the city itself was set on fire, and the most important neighborhoods were completely destroyed. All they could do now was fight to save the fate of the fleet and their own skins.

By and large, historians have credited the Venetians with instigating the second attack on Constantinople. The truth is that Enrico Dandolo took it upon himself to open up last-minute negotiations with Mourtzuphlos, and only when the latter refused to make the slightest concession did the allies resort to combat. Before they actually embarked on the assault, however, the doge and the supreme commander of the crusading armies, Conrad of Montferrat, signed a treaty that would redefine the entire purpose of the crusade, and forever change the face of the Byzantine Empire.

First and foremost, the treaty determined that Byzantium would now have a Latin emperor, chosen by an equal number of Venetian and French electors. The empire itself, which had been structured in accordance with eastern tradition, would be subject to the criteria of western feudalism, which meant that its territories would be divided among the future emperor, the crusaders and the Venetians. The new Patriarch of Constantinople, who would obviously represent the Roman Church, would be chosen from the ranks of the French or Venetians, depending on which of the two contingents the emperor himself represented. Rules and regulations were also drawn up regarding the division of secular fiefdoms and ecclesiastical properties. Finally, the agreement bound the signatories to remain in Constantinople until the end of March of 1205. All those who defaulted would run the risk of being excommunicated.

After a long, hard fight, the mighty city itself, which had been devastated by yet another fire, at last surrendered to the allies. For the next two days, April 12th and 13th, the victors engaged in a systematic sacking and plundering of its countless treasures, during which time priceless works of art were either destroyed or stolen, and precious relics and reliquaries made their way back to Venice, along with the four bronze horses from the hippodrome that still adorn the facade of St. Mark's Basilica. The local chroniclers, horrified at the desecration taking place before their very eyes, have left us vivid accounts of the senseless acts of violence that ultimately destroyed what had been the most magnificent city in Europe.

Perhaps the strangest aspect of this entire episode is the fact that a series of completely unforeseen events had led to circumstances that no one would ever have

the new Latin emperor had been granted, which comprised a fourth of the total Byzantine territory.

Although Enrico Dandolo ultimately rejected the idea of his being elected emperor for fear of offending the French barons (even if he did manage to see to it that Baldwin of Flanders was chosen instead of Conrad of Monferrat, whom he considered to be a little bit too cozy with the Genoese), he was absolved from paying homage for his fiefs, and was allowed, in proper Greek fashion, to wear the purple buskins that attested to his own sovereignty. Nothing was more important, however, than the towns and cities that fell to the Venetian Republic.

Detail of a mosaic tile from the floor of the imperial palace in Constantinople, depicting a serpent and eagle.

dreamed possible, least of all the citizens of Venice. But the fewer than 50,000 inhabitants who were confined to a small, scattered archipelago protected by a thin strip of coastal islands in the part of the lagoon that extended from Grado to Carvarzere were ready to take up the challenge of a vast eastern empire, and reap from it the greatest possible advantage to themselves and their city.

Dividing the Spoils

Under the terms of the *Partitio Romaniae*, which was the official document that partitioned the former territories of Byzantium (now known as "Romania") among the new emperor and his Latin allies, Venice suddenly found herself in possession of a huge slice of the sovereign empire to which she herself had once been subject. In fact, it was such a huge slice that the doge assumed the title of "Lord of One-fourth and One-eighth of Romania," which his successors bore until the year 1356. In the end, it was even larger than

First of all, they would now hold three-eighths of the capital city itself, including the most important harbors in the "Golden Horn." Then they were granted the province of Adrianople, the port of Rodosto, and the entire coast of Greece as far as the Dardanelles, as well as the ports of Oreoi and Karistos in Euboea, the islands of Aegina and Salamis in the Gulf of Athens, the western coast of the Peloponnese, including the fortified towns of Modon and Corone, Patras on the Ionian Sea, Kalavrita in the Bay of Corinth, and Sparta and all of its territories on the mainland. They were also allotted the Ionian islands of Corfu, Levkas, Zante and Cephalonia, and the territory west of the Pindus Mountains, which included Epirus, Aetolia and Aroania. Finally, the doge himself acquired the Island of Crete from Conrad of Montferrat, which he considered extremely advantageous in terms of foreign trade.

In addition to these spoils, the Venetians were accorded the great honor of the Patriarchate of Constantinople, which meant that the clergy of St. Sophia was also in their hands, giving them the right to consider themselves the spiritual leaders of the new empire. Last but not least, they were finally in a posi-

The Conquest of Constantinople by the Crusaders, *executed by Palma il Giovane in 1202 (Doges' Palace, Venice). The surprising outcome of the Fourth Crusade gave Venice any number of new territories that extended from the lagoon to the Black Sea, which became a vital part of her trade with the East. The extraordinary circumstances surrounding the conquest of Constantinople would finally place the Republic in the ranks of the most important nations in Europe, thanks to her control over the Cyclades and much of the Aegean Archipelago, whose islands were given in fief to the more powerful among her patricians. Although the ancient Doge Dandolo ultimately rejected the idea of his being elected emperor for fear of offending the French barons, he did assume the title of "Lord of One-fourth and One-eighth of the Roman Empire," which his successors bore until the year 1356.*

tion to prevent their rivals from trading with the whole of the eastern Latin world.

Although this last clause in the contract was the source of much satisfaction at home and abroad, the most influential members of the local business community and political establishment were far from convinced that certain of the concessions that had been won would actually serve the interests of the Republic. Despite the prestige of Doge Dandolo, they were painfully aware of the fact that much of the territory that had been allotted to Venice was in the hands of the Greeks themselves, who had no intention whatsoever of submitting to a foreign power. Furthermore, they were well informed as to the actual numbers of crusaders who had been entrusted with maintaining law

and order in the new empire, who were far outweighed by the local population. Even the Republic herself, whose maritime supremacy was undisputed, was totally ill-equipped to deal with the rough terrain and mountainous regions of inland Greece and Thrace.

When the Bulgarians promptly responded to the current state of affairs by conquering Adrianople and imprisoning Emperor Baldwin, and conflicts began to develop between the Republic's contingent in Byzantium and the government at home, the Venetians knew that their instincts had been right all along. As usual, their wisdom and pragmatism would ultimately save the day. Doge Pietro Ziani, who was elected in 1205 after the death of the great Enrico Dandolo, shrewdly negotiated a settlement between Venice and

her eastern representatives that allowed the latter to elect a local governor, or *"Podestà,"* who was given the doge's own title of "Lord of One-fourth and One-eighth of Romania." This individual, who was authorized to sign agreements with the emperor and confirm the fiefs of his fellow citizens, also had the ultimate power to concede Adrianople to the Greeks, and the Island of Corfu to the Venetians.

The real story behind this novel solution was undoubtedly the Venetians' realization that it was in their best interest to stay out of administrative affairs in the East as much as possible, thereby avoiding potential embarrassment to the doge and the local government. Among the many sensitive issues that could possibly create strife both at home and abroad were the refusal of certain concessions allowed by the *Partitio Romaniae,* the allotment of feudal holdings, and even the day-to-day dealings with the empire, which was already beginning to show signs of weakness. In fact, for the next two decades, the doge always made sure to ratify *a posteriori* whatever decisions had been made by the *Podestà.*

Among the most powerful of the patrician overlords was Marco Sanudo, the nephew of Enrico Dandolo. Sanudo was no ordinary private citizen. Besides negotiating the acquisition of Crete in the name of the doge himself, he had served as a judge in the expatriot

colony in Constantinople. He had also participated in the conquest of Corfu, Modon and Corone. After a long, hard journey back to Venice to ask for Doge Ziani's personal blessing, Sanudo took command of a small armada composed of fellow nobles, and set sail for the Aegean Islands, where he presented himself to the local population as their friend and protector

The old walls of Constantinople, which date back to the time of Theodosius.

After the conquest of the legendary capital of the Eastern Empire, Venice was literally flooded with priceless works of art and precious objects in gold and marble that had been brought back by her own citizens. Above: The sacred icon known as the "Madonna Nicopeia" ("Bringer of Victory"), located in the left transept of St. Mark's Basilica, was one of the images traditionally carried by the emperors of Byzantium as they led their troops into battle. Opposite page, above left: Among the 800-year-old spoils of war that are part of the Treasury of St. Mark's Basilica is a 10th-century Byzantine icon of St. Michael. Opposite page, above right: This incense burner in Arab-Byzantine style, which dates from the 12th century, may have been crafted in southern Italy. Opposite page, below: The four superbly gilded bronze horses that dominate the facade of St. Mark's, which once stood before the hippodrome in Constantinople, may well be Greek-Alexandrian works from the third or fourth century B.C.

against the raids of the Genoese and Turkish pirates that continued to infest their waters.

With the support (or at least the tacit approval) of the local citizens, Sanudo and his friends took over a number of islands of greater or lesser importance, and promptly declared themselves the feudal lords of these territories. So it was that a second colonial system came into being that was made up of the fiefdoms of patrician families, who were pledged to concede their holdings only to their compatriots.

For himself and his descendants, Marco Sanudo established the Duchy of Naxos, or the Archipelago, which encompassed the better part of the Cyclades, including Naxos, Syra, Sifnos, Amorgos, Milos and Ios. Marino Dandolo installed himself on Andros, Andrea and Geremia Ghisi took over Tinos, Mikonos and the Boreal Sporades (Skiros, Skopelos, Skiathos and Alonissos), Giacomo Barozzi laid claim to Santorini, and Giovanni Querini settled on Stampalia. All of these aristocrats were actually vassals of Sanudo, the Duke of the Archipelago, except for Philacalos Navigajoso, who declared himself lord of the large island of Lemnos, and received the title of grand duke directly from the emperor. Members of the Venier and Viaro families, on the other hand, were considered vassals of the Republic as the overlords of Cerigo and Cerigotto.

In terms of her own feudal holdings, Venice would be somewhat less fortunate. While the towns of Modon and Corone in the southernmost part of the Peloponnese (known as the "eyes of the Republic") remained firmly in her hands, the Island of Corfu, which she had liberated from the Genoese pirate Leone Vetrano, was seized in 1214 by Michael Angelus, the Greek ruler of Epirus. (Angelus, who had already taken over the whole of Pindus except for Durazzo, would eventually become an ally of Venice.) The Venetians also failed to secure the other Ionian islands for themselves. Sparta and the western coast of

For himself and his descendants, Marco Sanudo, the nephew of Doge Dandolo, established the Duchy of Naxos, or the Archipelago, which encompassed the better part of the Cyclades.

the Peloponnese, which represented a precious source of oil and silk, was eventually seized by Geoffroi de Villehardouin, the nephew of the famous chronicler of the Fourth Crusade. (In the end, the Republic succeeded in maintaining sovereignty over this territory by declaring it a feudal protectorate, and granting Venetian citizenship to Villehardouin.)

As for Oreoi and Karistos, the fortified towns in the north and south of Euboea, the Venetians had apparently lost faith in their own ability to control these two important strongholds, since they eventually decided that the island should be divided into three separate fiefs, which were granted to the Veronese nobles Pegoraro dei Pegorari, Gilberto da Verona and Ravano dalle Caceri. Once again, however, the Republic would maintain sovereignty over the territory until such time as she herself could take formal possession.

Last but not least, there was the all-important island of Crete. This extensive mountainous region, which was so rich in grain and wine, was then in the hands of Enrico Pescatore, the Count of Malta, who was among the worst of the Genoese pirates. After he and Alamanno da Costa, another of the Genoese buccaneers, had successfully defended themselves against an assault led by Ranieri Dandolo, the son of Doge Enrico, in 1207, the two dangerous intruders were left undisturbed for a number of months. However, by the time that Pescatore had actually starting thinking about assuming the title of King of Crete, he was faced with the threat of another assault. When his native city, which was then engaged in disputes with both Pisa and Marseilles, failed to come to his aid, he eventually agreed to leave the island in 1212 in exchange for a large sum of money. Five years thereafter, as the result of a treaty that was signed between Venice and Genoa, his fellow pirate Alamanno da Costa, who had long terrorized the local inhabitants, was finally gotten rid of as well.

The Treaty of Nymphaeum, which was drawn up between Genoa and the Greek ruler of Nicaea in 1261, would mark the beginning of the end of the Eastern Latin Empire. After less than 60 years of struggling desperately to survive, the feudal *signorie* established by many of the original crusaders gradually died out, leaving the Venetians as the sole survivors of the *Partitio Romaniae*. In fact, two and a half centuries later, their own eastern dominions would be stronger and more vital than ever.

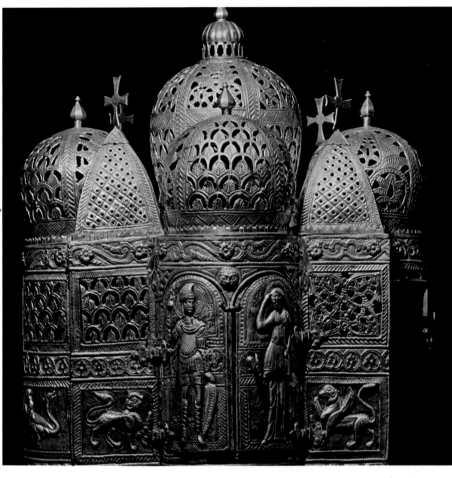

Maritime and Mainland Territories

Perhaps this would be a good time to take an overall look at the various territories held by the *Serenissima,* starting with the maritime communities. However, before we actually set out on this journey, let us not forget that during the centuries that witnessed the greatest expansion, the Venetian state in Italy was still confined to the city and the *dogado,* with the exception of a few modest settlements on the mainland. In fact, the Republic would have to wait until the acquisition of Treviso in 1338 in order to gain a real foothold in the Veneto. By then, nearly six and a half centuries had passed since the supposed election of the first doge, a little more than five centuries since the capital had been transferred from Malamocco to Venice herself, and 134 years since the signing of the *Partitio Romaniae.*

First and foremost, there were the communities established by Venetian merchants in the major cen-

Three panels from the "Pala d'Oro," depicting The Discovery of the Body of St. Mark *and* Christ Appearing to St. Mark *(above), and* St. Mark the Evangelist *(below). This extraordinary altarpiece, with its magnificent 14th-century frame by Gian Paolo Boninsegna, is covered with precious stones and cloisonné from the 10th to the 12th centuries, some of which came from the sack of Constantinople, and others from the first "Pala D'Oro," commissioned by Doge Pietro I Orseolo in the 10th century, and enriched by Doge Ordelaf in the 12th century, by Doge Pietro Ziani at the beginning of the 13th century, and by Doge Andrea Dandolo in the 14th century. Measuring 3.48 meters (11 feet 5 inches) in width and 1.01 meters (40 inches) in height, it contains more than 80 precious enamels.*

ters of commerce in the eastern Mediterranean, which were organized along the same lines as the expatriot settlement in Constantinople (whose inhabitants would somehow manage to survive any number of adversities, including the Turkish conquest.) In fact, their local judicial system, which was what actually defined them as an "overseas colony," would survive until the fall of the Republic in 1797.

As the successor to the *Podestà*, who had been elected by the Venetians of Romania after the conquest of Constantinople, the *"Bailo"* not only represented the Republic at the imperial court, but fulfilled a number of important administrative functions as well. From his palace among the vineyards of Pera (the area that the Turks still refer to as *"Beyoglu,"* or *"The Prince's Son,"* in memory of Alvise Gritti, the illegitimate son of Doge Andrea and himself a great Ottoman lord), he served as the "Governor General" of all the Venetian colonies in the eastern Mediterranean.

The Black Sea was also the commercial headquarters of any number of Venetian merchants. At Tana (modern-day Azov), which was the base camp for caravans from Asia, as well as the main supply depot for essential trading commodities, a Venetian consul fulfilled more or less the same functions as the *Bailo*, with the assistance of 12 advisors elected by the local business community. Uzbek, the district that had been set aside for the Venetians by the Khan of the Tartars, was sacked by Tamerlaine during the invasion of 1395, but somehow managed to survive until 1475. Other important commercial centers were located at Cetatea Alba on the coast of present-day Rumania, and at Trebizond, where another *Bailo* was installed.

The Venetian headquarters on the Sea of Marmara and in the Dardanelles (where the Dandolo and Viaro families had taken possession of Gallipoli, and two of the Querini brothers had laid claim to Lampsacus) would not outlive the fall of the Latin Empire. Like the signories of Tarsus and Samothrace, they were occupied by the Venetian Republic for a brief period in the second half of the 15th century before being swallowed up by the Turks. The same was true of Lemnos, the great fiefdom of the Navigajoso family, which eventually passed into the hands of the Gattilusi family from Genoa. However, the Venetians were able to hold on to the island fortress of Tenedos from 1204 to 1261, and again from 1364 to 1400, despite fierce competition from the Genoese, and yet again from 1656 to 1657 during the War of Candia.

The Republic's dominion over Thessalonica, which had always hosted a large contingent of Venetian merchants, would last all of 14 years, during which time she spent enormous sums of money on fortifications that still did not prevent the city from being conquered by the Turks in 1436. This strategic Macedon-

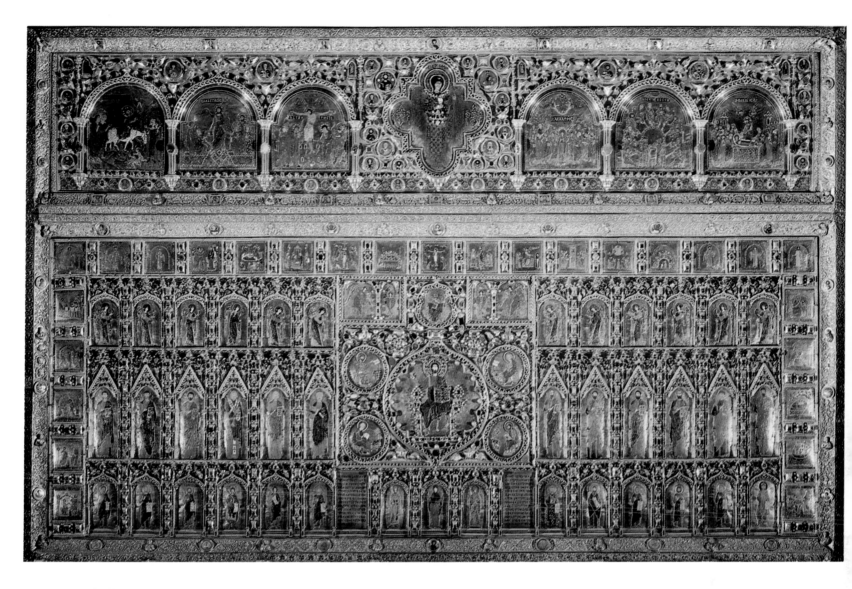

ian port marked the beginning of an important trade route that followed the Greek coast as far as the Thermopylae Pass and the massive fortress of Vonitsa, and then skirted the Island of Euboea and the fertile Negropont, which Venice considered the "pearl" of her eastern territories. (In the words of one voyager, this region produced "an extraordinary abundance of all things, including grain, vegetables, wine, oil, silk, cotton, wax, sheep and cattle.") When her precious jewel was lost in 1470, the leaders of the Republic were utterly stunned. According to a local chronicler, their sense of hopelessness and despair at the news that their eastern capital had actually been conquered by the Turks was almost palpable.

The fact that barely two years after their crushing defeat at Negropont, the Venetians were able to acquire the Kingdom of Cyprus, over which they gained complete control by 1489, is yet another example of the resiliency and shrewd diplomacy of the Venetian politicians. The details of this extraordinary event will be discussed at a later time. For now, suffice it to say that from the moment that they took possession of the island to its conquest by the Turks, they would enjoy 82 years of absolute supremacy.

The Island of Crete, or Candia, another of the strategic areas in the Mediterranean, would remain in Venetian hands for no less than 450 years. When they were eventually forced to defend this territory against the onslaught of the Turks, they did so with great courage and dignity. After more than 25 years of constant strife that drained the resources of the Republic and decimated the ranks of the nobility, they literally found themselves on the verge of bankruptcy. Despite the bitter end, when they were obliged to hand over the

All glitter and gold, the sumptuous "Pala d'Oro," which stands behind the main altar of St. Mark's Basilica, is one of the most extraordinary examples of exquisite craftsmanship in existence today.

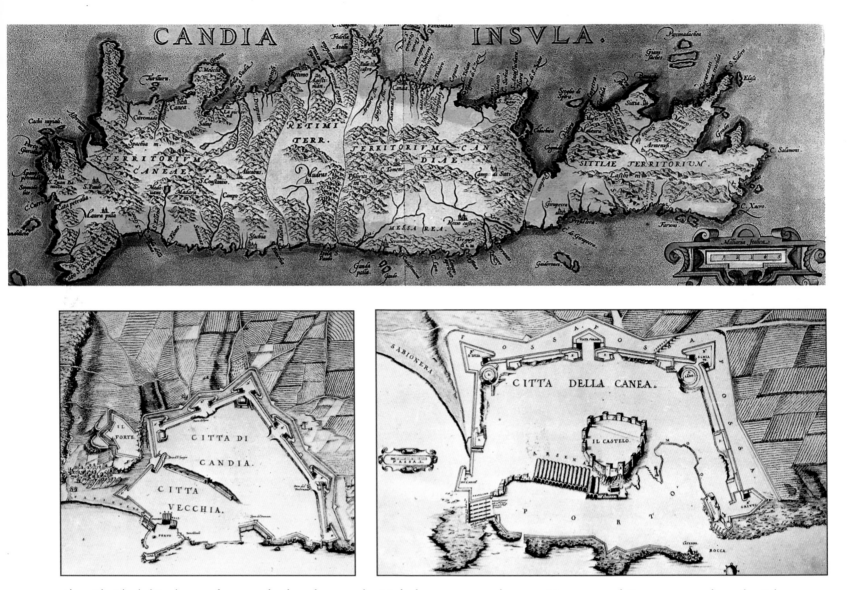

CANDIA INSVLA.

CITTA DI CANDIA.

CITTA VECCHIA.

CITTA DELLA CANEA.

IL CASTELO.

Above: The Island of Candia (Crete), as depicted in Abramo Ortelio's Theatrum Orbis Terrarum *(1570). Below: The cities of Candia (Iraklion) and Canea (Khania), as depicted in Angelo Oddi's* Città, fortezze . . . del regno di Candia *(1607). Despite fierce competition from the Genoesi, Venice took possession of Crete shortly after the end of the Fourth Crusade. Until 1671, when it was turned over to the Turks following the disastrous War of Candia, the island would serve as a strategic base of operations for the Republic's affairs in the East.*

keys to the kingdom to the Turkish insurgents, the heroism and endurance of their military leaders would be considered one of the most glorious moments in the Republic's history.

Besides Candia, there were the Aegean Islands, where Marco Sanudo and his fellow patricians had established a number of important fiefdoms that extended from the Cyclades to the northern Sporades. With a few notable exceptions, these territories were all lost to the Turks in 1540. Fortunately, the overseas route from the eastern Mediterranean to Venice herself always avoided the stormy Cyclades, which were constantly buffeted by high winds. Before reaching the fortified cities of Modon and Corone in Messenia, the Republic's ships would pass by the islands of Cerigo and Cerigotto, both of which remained in her hands from 1205 to 1797.

Navarino and Patras, situated on the Peloponnese coast, were only temporary possessions. There would come a time, however, when the whole of the Peloponnese belonged to the Venetians, thanks to the military victories scored by Francesco Morosini, which allowed the Venetians to maintain control of the entire region until the Treaty of Passarowitz in 1718. Little more than a century before the fall of the Republic, this brilliant general would show the world that the lion's claws were just as sharp as ever. In fact, only two months after his departure from Venice on June 8, 1684, he conquered the Island of St. Maur (Levkas). By September 29th, he was already in command of the fortress at Prevesa. The following summer, when he recaptured Corone, he stripped the Turkish general (the *"seraschier)* of his own standard with its three horses' tails, which was placed with much ceremony in

the Chiesa dei Tolentini. In the spring and summer of 1868, he took Modon and Navarino, and Nauplia and Argos, which had been lost some two centuries earlier. A year later, Patras, Lepanto, Rumelia, the Bay of Corinth, Athens and Aegina were all under his command, and Venice was able to replace Candia and Cyprus with the kingdom of Morea.

Given the lack of sufficient means to govern and colonize such a vast territory, which had been so depopulated and impoverished by Ottoman rule, this great victory would last no more than 20 years. However, during the brief period during which she reigned supreme, the Republic introduced a number of important measures in the areas of agricultural reform and repopulation. At Argos, Acrocortinth and Naples in Romania, she also constructed massive new fortresses. What she managed to achieve in so short a space of time, and with such limited resources, is yet another example of the intelligence and ingenuity of her leaders.

Among Morosini's conquests in Epirus, only the strongholds of Arta, Preveza and Vonitsa, and the offshore island of Levkas, would remain in Venetian hands until the fall of the Republic. The Ionian islands of Zante, Cephalonia, Ithaca, Paxos and Corfu, which had long been under the Republic's rule,

pean continent, which was slightly north of Zara, the capital city of Dalmatia, and to the west of Nona.

Among the chain of offshore islands, there were Cazza, Lagosta, Meleda and Curzola, which lay opposite Ragusa, and Lissa, Lesina, Brazza and Solta, which were located near the coast of Spalato. Pago, which was situated across from Nona, extended into the Gulf of Quarnaro along with Arbe, Veglia, Cherso, Ossero and Lussino. Farther north, there were Istria, Pola, Rovigno, Pirano and Capodistria, as well as the Montona Forest, which was under the direct jurisdiction of the Council of Ten. Beyond these territories lay the Gulf of Trieste, the lagoons, the *dogado*, and the Venetian capital itself. (As fierce competitors for domestic and foreign markets, the citizens of Trieste themselves had been placed under Venetian rule for a brief period of time, during which their neighbors made life as hard for them as they possibly could. Venice would pay for this in full during the 18th and 19th centuries, when Trieste once again became her commercial rival with the blessings of the Hapsburg regime.)

On the Italian coast of the Adriatic, beyond the Po, the Republic's conquest of Cervia, Ravenna, Bertinoro, Faenza, Rimini, Forlimpopoli, Sant'Arcangelo, Fano and Montefiore, all of which were papal cities, would seriously damage her relationship with the Holy See. In Ravenna, which was the last of her dominions to be lost, the magnificent fortress whose walls display the winged lion can still be seen, as can Dante's funeral monument, which was erected by the local *Podestà*.

At one time or another, Venice also controlled the Apulian cities of Bari, Brindisi, Monopoli and Lecce, among others. These strategic seaports, which had first been conquered by the Byzantines and then by the Normans, were absolutely vital to the defense of the Gulf. However, thanks to the vagaries of politics and war, the Republic was eventually obliged to give them back to the Kingdom of Naples, which was then under Spanish rule.

The great cities of Romagna, which were part of the Republic's extensive territories on the mainland, were treated as possessions rather than colonies. The same was true of the Veneto, Friuli and Lombardy, whose ancient civilizations and rich cultural heritage had played such an important role in Venice's own history. Although she considered them her loyal subjects, her regime was far milder and more benevolent than that of Austria, Spain, or even the papacy itself. Over the course of the next several centuries, the confines of this vast region, which were established by the Treaty

would also remain hers up until the very end. As the key to the Adriatic, Corfu itself would become the permanent headquarters of a naval squadron under orders from the "Captain of the Venetian Gulf," whose duty it was to block any and all potential intruders.

In many respects, this picturesque Greek isle still reflects the influence of hundreds of years of Venetian rule, including the citizens themselves, many of whom married into the patriciate, as did their neighbors in Cephalonia and Zante. On the nearby island of Paxos, which has just recently become the site of international tourism, instead of building the usual fortress, the Venetians would plant magnificent olive groves.

Even though Scutari was eventually lost to the Turks after a lengthy battle with Mehmed II, Venice's Adriatic territories extended all the way from Albania to the Velebit Mountains. There was Budua, the sleepy little town with a distinctly oriental atmosphere. There were the Straits of Cattaro, nestled in the winding ravines at the foot of the craggy mountains of Montenegro along with Perasto and Castelnuovo, which were second only to the Bay of Navarino as an ideal area for mooring ships. Aside from the tiny republic of Ragusa, which had somehow managed to remain independent, there were Marcarsca and Almissa, Spalato and Traù, and Sebenico and Scardona. There were also the rocky cliffs of Clissa and Imoschi, recaptured from the Turks, who thought nothing of attacking territories that had an age-old bond with Venice. Finally, there was the border with the Euro-

By and large, Venetian ships were able to sail the open seas without having to worry about interference on the part of foreign powers as a result of the intricate system of security measures that had been put in place by the central government. These included a naval squadron that was permanently based on the Island of Corfu, where a series of fortifications guarded the entrance to the Adriatic, as we can see from the above illustration, which dates from the 17th-century (Museo Storico Navale, Venice). Opposite page: Along with Corone, the fortified outpost of Modon, located on the southwest coast of the Peloponnese, was destined to become the "eyes and ears of the Republic" because of its strategic importance.

hands until the Treaty of Passarowitz in 1817), the amount of territory that they still controlled was more or less the same.

Any attempt to evaluate the extent of the Republic's empire in terms of population figures would be a complicated undertaking indeed. Instead, we can take a look at her annual income at certain moments in her history, keeping in mind, of course, that the currency values differed widely from one time frame to another. According to the historian Marino Sanudo, the city's income for the year 1464 was 698,500 ducats, while that of her mainland territories came to 317,400 ducats (the highest figures were 75,000 ducats for the province of Brescia and 65,500 for the province of Padua), and that of her maritime provinces totaled 180,000 ducats.

Forty years earlier, in April of 1423, Doge Tommaso Mocenigo had quoted far higher figures during his farewell speech to the *Signoria:* 774,000 ducats for the city herself, 464,000 for her mainland territories, and 376,000 for her maritime provinces.

Apart from the differences in currency values (in this case, the ducats were gold), the wide discrepancy between the two sets of statistics was undoubtedly due to the fact that the Venetian economy had deteriorated significantly during the 40 years after the death of Mocenigo. We can lay most of the blame for this sad state of affairs at the feet of his successor, Francesco Foscari, the leader of the expansionist party, who was the very person that Mocenigo himself had cautioned

the government not to elect as doge. In the end, Foscari's policies would result in the conquest of additional territory on the mainland, but at the expense of countless lives and enormous sums of money.

Statistics from the 18th century estimate the total income of the Venetian state at 7,160,000 ducats (this time in silver), of which 3,000,000 were attributed to the city and the *dogado,* 2,460,000 to the mainland, and only 800,000 to the maritime provinces. From these figures, we can see that the percentages had changed somewhat in favor of the mainland territories, while those for the maritime territories had remained more or less constant. In fact, the profits received from her overseas colonies would never represent a vital part of Venice's great wealth. Until the very end, in fact, the state and its private citizens continued to derive the major portion of their income from trade.

In all fairness, however, we should make certain distinctions among the colonies themselves in terms of their individual contributions to the well-being of the Republic. While certain of these functioned simply as trading-posts, and others served as naval bases and lookout points that were essential to national defense, there were also those possessions that brought in considerable amounts of money. Such was the case of Cyprus, which supplied Venetian merchants with sugar, cotton and potash, and the Peloponnese, which produced grain and silkworms. On Crete, after the turbulent years of local insurrections during which the

Certain of the allegorical sculptures on the facade of the Doges' Palace were specifically intended to be part of a "morality tale" for the good of the general public. Below left: On the corner facing the Piazzetta, the depiction of Adam, Eve and the serpent, which symbolizes the original sin, is located directly below the image of the Archangel Michael (above left), who is portrayed with his famous sword, which is drawn to defend mankind from the temptation of the devil. Below right: On the corner facing the Ponte del Paglio are the figures representing the drunkenness of Noah, with two of his sons, Shem and Japheth, who are attempting to cover his nakedness, while a third son, Ham, stands to one side. These are situated below the image of the Archangel Raphael (above right), who is depicted in the act of leading the young Tobias on the adventurous journey during which he would protect him from the forces of evil. As the "guardian angel" of all mankind, Raphael's location on the palace's facade allows him to extend his protection to the ships departing from the harbor, and to greet those who have returned home safe and sound.

Senate had actually blocked agricultural production in the fertile Mesarea region, the island would once again become the source of fine wines and wheat.

Although her troops were eventually forced to destroy the olive groves on Paros and several other islands during the wars against the Turks in order to cut off enemy supplies, the Republic continued to promote a series of agricultural reforms throughout her realm that yielded extraordinary results. Legislation passed in 1565, for example, made it obligatory for the inhabitants of Brazza to cultivate the wild olive groves that had long existed on the island. On Cephalonia, new crops such as cotton, indigo and coffee were introduced. On Zante, major land reclamation projects were undertaken, and extensive vineyards were planted, which turned out to be a veritable "gold mine." Even the famous voyager Saint-Sauveur, an avowed critic of the Venetian Republic, had to admit that Zante had become an essential part of the enormous trade in Corinthian grapes, including the raisins that the English market could not do without.

Contrary to the assertions of any number of historians, rather than draining the lifeblood of their colonial territories, and forcing the local population to engage in industries that were detrimental to the local economy, the Venetians invested precious time and money in revamping their industries and revitalizing their economies, knowing full well that their own prosperity depended first and foremost on trade. Thanks to a whole series of innovative measures, the balance-sheets of these colonies were most often heavily in the black. Such was the case on the Island of Cyprus in the year 1491, when the income derived from agricultural production and customs duties yielded a net income of 5,734 gold ducats. With the exception of Cyprus itself, which would always be exploited in the interest of the state, they were also meticulous about sharing the profits with their subjects. Killing the goose that lays the golden egg was definitely not a part of their merchant mentality!

Below left: On the corner of the palace that faces St. Mark's Square, the Judgment of Solomon, which is meant to symbolize the importance of human justice, is situated below the image of the Archangel Gabriel (above left), who represents divine justice and the promise of salvation. These sculptures were executed between the end of the 14th and the beginning of the 15th century. Although they are the work of different artists, they are remarkably similar in terms of their composition.

THE LOVE OF HER SUBJECTS

THE COLONIES, A CENTRALIZED SYSTEM, "EQUAL JUSTICE FOR ONE AND ALL"

"Our subjects must all be treated as friends." So said Doge Paolo Renier in a famous speech before the Maggior Consiglio in the year 1780. However, this noble, high-sounding phrase was put in the proper context when he went on to warn the Council members in no uncertain terms: "Those princes who possess no real power have to base their security on the love of their subjects." This admonition, which was the complete reverse of the classic Roman motto: "Let them hate me as long as they fear me," made it clear that the Republic was obliged to make herself loved, since she no longer had the means to make herself feared.

As we begin to examine in more depth the administrative structures that governed her colonial empire, we should think carefully about such statements, keeping in mind that at the time they were made by Doge Renier, they were intended to frighten the *Maggior Consiglio* with the specter of the extreme weakness of the state, and the consequent need for absolute unity, so as to stifle any real opposition to his own policies.

The truth is that Venice did not treat all her subjects in the same manner. With regard to the cities on the mainland, most of which had voluntarily surrendered themselves and their surrounding territories to their Venetian neighbors, she presented herself as their vindicator and protector against the injustices and oppressive tactics of other would-be rulers. In those instances where her dependents were particularly vulnerable to foreign invasion, she portrayed the image of the all-powerful defender of their sovereignty. As such,

she granted them a great deal of autonomy, which included leaving their own laws intact, and respecting their local customs. At the very most, if she felt that the less privileged of her subjects were suffering at the hands of the ruling class, she intervened on their behalf. (At the time that the Republic annexed the Treviso region, for example, the local peasants were placed under the protection of the *Podestà,* to whom they could appeal for assistance in defending themselves from violence or injustice on the part of the nobles and wealthy landowners.)

Things were more or less the same in the cities of Istria and Dalmatia, all of which had sworn a solemn oath of allegiance to Doge Pietro II Orseolo during the course of his triumphant military campaign against the Slavs in the year 1000. However, as opposed to the mainland, where there had never been any serious uprisings (on rare occasions, there were anti-Venetian conspiracies, such as in Padua, which had been conquered after a long, hard battle, and minor defections during times of crisis, which were always instigated by the local nobility), the constant rebellions that took place in Istria and Dalmatia forced the Venetians to resort to repressive military tactics, particularly with regard to Capodistria in the early days, and later on with regard to Zara (Zadar).

Thanks to all of seven bloody uprisings on the part of the local populace, Zara became a real thorn in the Republic's side. Time and again, the Venetians found themselves obliged to take up arms against these

Throughout the entire range of the Republic's overseas colonies, she would leave an indelible mark on the local people and their surroundings, from the sophisticated atmosphere of certain urban centers, especially in Istria and Dalmatia, to the "campielli" on Corfu, to the countless fortifications whose grandiose structures are a living testimony to the ingenuity and farsightedness of the *Serenissima* herself. In Istria, the last vestiges of the Venetian world can still be seen in any number of places, including Capodistria (5), Pirano, Buje, Montona (where the portable altar used by the great warriors Bartolomeo Colleoni and Barolomeo d'Alviano is preserved), Parenzo, Sanvincenti (with its Grimani Castle), Valle d'Istria (with its Bembo Castle), San Lorenzo del Pasenàtico, Dignano, Rovigno (4), Pola, and the islands of Arbe, Veglia and Cherso. Despite the ravages of the recent war, Dalamatia also bears the imprint of her Venetian neighbors, above all in the charming cities of Zara,

A BRIEF TOUR OF THE EASTERN TERRITORIES

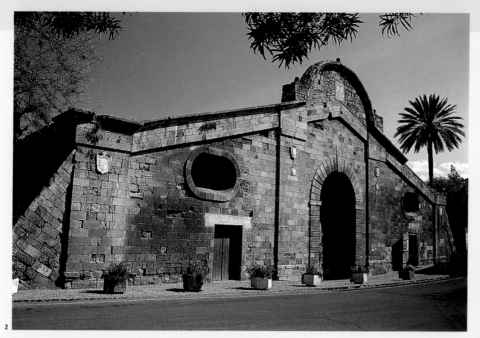

2

Sebenico and Traù (with its superb Tower of St. Mark, its splendid Orsini Chapel, and its loggias and palaces), and on the islands of Lesina and Curzola. A tour of the Venetian fortresses in the Ionian Islands begins in Corfu, with its great citadels, and goes on to Prevesa and Arta along the coast of Epirus, and Leucade and the Island of Kithyra (Cerigo). In the southern-

4

most region of the Peloponnese, there are the magnificent remains of Methoni (Modon) and Koroni (Corone), and the fortified city of Monemvàssia (Malvasia). Farther north are the imposing fortresses of Nàfplion (1) (Nauplia, or Napoli di Romania), including the Citadel of Acronauplia, which was built in 1706, and the Fortress of Palamedi, which was constructed by the *Provveditore Generale* Agostino Sagredo between 1711 and 1714. Aside

3

from the great walls of Iraklion and other fortifications, the Island of Crete is filled with impressive monuments and landmarks commemorating the 400 years of Venetian rule, including the Bembo, Sagredo and Morosini Fountains (3), the loggia and church of St. Mark in Iraklion, and the ancient quarter of Hanià (Canea). Venice left her mark as well on Eubea, the Aegean Islands and Cyprus, where the fortifications at Famagosta, which are situated in what is now the Turkish sector (2), held out against the onslaught of the Turks in 1576.

5

Map labels:
LIA
MAZIA
Knin
Spalato
Imoschi
Macarsca
Narenta
Ragusa
Cattaro
Budua
Scutari
Dulcigno
fredonia
Trani
Bari
Durazzo
Cruia
Monopoli
Brindisi
Valona
Salonicco
Kavala
Adrianopoli
Costantinopoli
Taranto
Lecce
Otranto
TASSOS
LEMNO
Larisa
CORFÚ
MITILENE
Prevesa
Arta
Mare Jonio
LEUCADE
Vonizza
Lepanto
Eubea
SKYROS
CHIO
Smirne
CEFALONIA
Atene
ANDRO
SAMO
ICARIA
Mare Jonio
ZANTE
Corinto
Nauplia
PARO
NAXOS
MOREA
COS
Modone
Corone
MILO
SANTORINO
CERIGO
CERIGOTTO
SCARPANTO
RODI
CRETA
Candia
Crotone

Above left: During the centuries that they were under Venetian rule, the territories on the eastern coast of the Adriatic would be fortified with any number of citadels and naval bases. Sebenico (Sebenik), which is still partially encircled by the massive walls constructed by the citizens of the Republic, is also the site of the Fortress of San Nicolò, which was built by Michele Sammicheli in 1546. Above right: The Orsini Palace is one of the many local residences erected by the Venetian patricians. Below right: Detail of a frieze from the Cathedral of St. James, whose restoration was begun in the year 1431. Opposite page: The side entrance to the cathedral, with its magnificent main portal.

to the land of Syria, we have already mentioned that they were all more or less organized along the same lines. At one time, the size and importance of the colonies on the Syrian coast also justified the presence of a *Bailo*, one of whom, Marsilio Zorzo, left behind a diary containing a wealth of fascinating details. Later on, when they became part of the Ottoman Empire, they were once again placed under the authority of the *Bailo* of Constantinople.

The first *Bailo* of Negropont, ser Pietro Barbo, seems to have been firmly entrenched in his post by the year 1216. As part of his official duties, he solemnly accepted an annual tribute of 700 gold pieces and any number of luxurious fabrics from the *"terzieri,"* or feudal overlords, in the name of the doge and the *Serenissima Signoria*. The last *Bailo*, Paolo Erizzo, who was in office during the Turkish invasion of 1470, met with a truly terrible end. After holding out as long as he could despite the lack of adequate naval support, he was finally forced to capitulate, at which point he was promised by Sultan Mehmed II that his own head would be spared. In fact, only his body was sawn apart as he lay fully conscious between two wooden planks.

The entire kingdom of Negropont, which was destined to become the "eyes and ears of the Republic," was taken over by the Venetians in the year 1390, when the *Comune* assumed direct control of the city of Chalcis, which was the seat of the local government. The rest of the territory was initially left in the hands of the powerful feudal overlords. Over the course of time, however, many of the more desirable fiefdoms eventually became the property of the state, who apportioned them among the most loyal of her patri-

cian subjects at home. So it was, for example, that a large percentage of the land that had belonged to the Dalle Carceri dynasty was given over to the Zorzi in 1470. This was the same family that had secured the great fief of Bodonice (modern-day Mendenitza) at Thermopylae by marrying ser Nicolò Zorzi to Guglielma Pallavicino, the widow and heiress of the Marquis Zaccaria de Castro. (As we shall see, Venice never hesitated to use the institution of marriage as a means of consolidating her position in the world.) In light of the strategic and economic importance of Euboea, especially after the defeat of the Catalan hordes who had devastated all of Attica, the Republic would make sure that the local *Bailo* controlled both the governance and the finances of the entire region.

Given the fact that her territories were scattered far and wide, and sometimes located at a great distance

Above, from left to right: Seventeenth-century sextant in brass and bronze; Clemente da Venezia's columnar sun-dial in ivory (1638); Lienhart Miller's ivory sun-dial with magnetic needle (1612); 17th-century compass and sun-dial in an ivory case; Descrolieris's astrolabe in brass and bronze, dated 1571 (Museo Correr, Venice); 16th-century armillary sphere (Antiquities Collection, Museo Correr, Venice). Opposite page: La burrasca by Francesco Guardi (Castello Sforzesco, Milan). Here we can see that the painter himself, who was a Venetian through and through, fully understood the perils involved in spending one's life on the open seas.

at agricultural reform. Whenever the occasion arose, they also lent their support to the Greek sovereigns of Nicaea, and then Constantinople, who were determined to regain the island. To make matters even worse, a number of the Venetian overlords eventually sided with the local inhabitants. The revolt that took place in 1363, which was provoked by a tax that was considered by many to be an unnecessary financial burden (even though it was destined for the development of port facilities in Candia), was staged by none other than two Gradenigos and two Veniers from the great patrician families of Venice.

After the revolt had been crushed with extreme severity, the Republic finally realized that a policy of reconciliation was absolutely necessary in order to improve her relationship with the islanders. Although these measures did extend certain privileges to the Byzantine archons, they did not provide for any greater involvement on the part of the local populace in the actual governance of the region.

In Negropont and the Peloponnese, the Venetians took an entirely different position, which was much closer to the principles preached by Doge Renier in 1780. In 1347, for example, when the Greek peasants of Modon and Corone complained about the excessive burden of local taxes, the two *Rettori*, or "*Castellani*," who had just gone out of office, would successfully plead the islanders' cause in front of the Venetian Senate as soon as they arrived back home. The same situation occurred in 1362, which prompted the Senate to provide the *Castellani* of Messenia with the necessary means to prevent further exploitation of the local peasantry.

In addition to the *Regimen* itself, which consisted of the *Castellano* and his personal advisor (the first of whom was paid 400 ducats and the second 200 in the year 1402), Modon was governed by an administrative body known as the *Consiglio dei Dodici,* or Council of Twelve, who were also elected from among the members of the Venetian patriciate. Since their primary function was to assist the *Regimen* in running the local bureaucracy, when they themselves overstepped their bounds during negotiations with the Greek despot of Mistra, they were promptly admonished by the Senate in Venice. In Negropont, instead, there was actually a *Maggior Consiglio,* as there was in Crete, and later on, in Corfu. Time and again, the colonies would adopt the same system of government that they had known at home.

Over the course of the years, as had already occurred on the mainland, the members of the colonial aristocracy would gradually assume most of the public offices

for themselves, particularly from the 16th century on. This was not a major cause for concern, however, as the responsibility for important policy-making decisions was still firmly in the hands of the *Regimen*, which continued to take orders directly from Venice. On Tinos and Zante, there are still families who proudly claim descent from the nobles who once participated in the governance of their own islands, as opposed to the local aristocracy of Crete, who were completely excluded from holding public office. With regard to Corfu, the influential members of the nobility were to play a significant role in the liberation and unification of Greece at the beginning of the 19th century, after which they would figure prominently in the ranks of the new ruling class. Such was the case of Count Capodistrias, the first Prime Minister of the independent Hellenic Republic, whose noble title had originally been conferred on his ancestors by the Venetian Senate, as had those of the Teotochi, Bulgari, Petretin and Lunzi families, to name but a few.

In Dalmatia, where there were any number of local aristocrats, many of whom, at least as of the beginning of the 16th century, were virtually penniless, the wealthy members of the bourgeoisie would come to resent bitterly the fact that their noble counterparts were allowed to participate in the affairs of government, while they themselves were not. On the Island of Lesina, this state of affairs eventually led to open rebellion between the years 1511 and 1514. Unfortunately, the Republic herself, who was going through a period of serious political and military upheaval, chose not to listen to the voices of reason that were raised in the Senate, and opted instead to resort to extremely harsh measures to quell the local riots. (Let us keep in mind, however, that the Venetians were far more concerned with the general security of the area, which was essential to the defense of the Gulf, at a time when they simply could not afford to contemplate alternative solutions.)

"Equal Justice for One and All"

There were various ways in which the colonial population could make itself heard in the capital city of Venice. We have just seen, for example, how the *Rettori* of Modon and Corone took on the role of spokesmen for the peasantry of Messenia. In fact, with the exception of Crete, where only the resident Venetians were allowed the opportunity of dealing directly with the Republic, the local inhabitants of all of the territories that comprised her empire, both on land and overseas, had the right to send their own "nuncios" and delegates to the city herself. In light of the fact that the Venetian state continued to expand in both size and complexity, the task of handling these specific complaints and requests was eventually entrusted to the *Avogadori di Comun*. (As we have noted elsewhere, these three individuals, who functioned first and foremost as the all-important heads of the State Prosecutor's Office, had the power to "intervene" in criminal trials by suspending or appealing the sentences passed down by a number of other magistracies, including the *Reggimenti*.)

At the beginning of the 15th century, however, a special magistracy, known as the *Auditori Novi,* was created to hear the appeals brought by the inhabitants of the mainland and Istria. By the same token, the overseas colonies dealt directly with the *Collegio dei XX.* All non-judicial matters of any significant nature were brought before the *Signoria, Pien Collegio* and Council of Ten by the colonial nuncios, who functioned as ambassadors to the mother country. Over the course of time, these individuals would come to be known officially as "delegates," and would establish permanent "missions" in the capital city. In addition to the above, there was the typically Venetian magistracy known as the *Sindici Inquisitori,* which represented the ultimate court of appeals for colonials seeking redress from the injustices of the local *Rettori.*

Throughout the colonies and mainland territories, the *Regimen* was responsible not only for local governance, but also for the administration of justice. On the mainland itself, the title given to the head of the local Regiment was usually that of *Podestà* (or *Praetor,* as he was known in all official Latin documents). Those who served in the same capacity in the overseas colonies were sometimes called *Bailo,* as we have already explained at length, or *Duca,* as was the case in Candia. Still others carried the title of *Provveditore,* as in Zante, Cephalonia, Cerigo, Parenzo, Admissa,

Capodistria, Cittanova and elsewhere, in which case they also fulfilled the function of military commander. In Istria and Dalmatia, the *Rettori* of Arbe, Brazza, Cherso, Curzola, Lesina, Nona, Pago, Pola, Sebenico, Spalato, Traú and Zara were given the ancient Hungarian title of *Conte.*

While the *Rettori* of the lesser territories personally administered the law with the aid of their own chancery, those who governed the more important regions worked within a judicial system that replicated that of the mother country on a smaller scale. (Depending on the individual circumstances, local customs were often taken into account as well.) In the Venetian colonies of Romania, for example, there were local magistrates who corresponded almost exactly to those in Venice, such as the *Advocatus,* who was the equivalent of the *Avogador di Comun,* and the *Signori di Notte,* whose function as a police court was the same as that of their Venetian namesakes. During the Middle Ages, there were three *Advocati* on Crete, just as there were in Venice, and four *Signori di Notte,* whose role as public safety officers often included acting as the local coroners. (Among their official duties was the unenviable task of removing the bodies of murder victims, and assisting those who had been seriously injured in public brawls). Crete was also one of the larger territories in which only the most important trials were conducted by the *Duca* himself. These primarily involved charges

of murder, lese-majesty, and treason (including embezzlement and theft of public funds).

Minor criminal offenses, such as brawling and burglary, were adjudicated by the *Giustizieri* and *Capitani* of the local cities, and the Castellans of the *castellanie*. There were also four *Capitani* who were responsible for cases of robbery, but not in the capacity of judges. Rather, they were expected to review the charges, and then proceed to arrest the culprits, if they could actu-

ally catch them! The civil courts, which also mirrored the judicial system of the homeland, had their own *Giudici del Proprio* and *Giudici del Petizion*. On the Island of Crete, it seems that there were also magistrates known as *Presoppi,* or *Prosopi,* whose task it was to litigate civil suits involving Greeks and Jews.

As part of their "commissions," the colonial *Rettori* were cautioned by the Senate to adhere to a system of "equal justice for one and all," particularly with regard to the native population, the Jews, and the members of the foreign community. What this really meant was that the state was extremely concerned that all local residents be treated in the same manner as the Venetians themselves. In fact, despite its reputation for severity, the Venetian judicial system was known to be far more equitable than that of its counterparts in the various Greek, Italian, Hungarian and Croatian dominions. In comparison to the Moslem system of justice, and the proverbially corrupt practices of the foreign sovereigns who held territories in Italy, it was so far superior that no one could possibly dispute its sense of fairness and decency.

As we have already seen, this policy of equal justice for one and all, which was an integral part of Venetian life from its very beginnings, was reflected in the intricate system of checks and balances that characterized the entire government. Even on the Island of Crete, which was in a constant state of turmoil, the conscientiousness with which criminal trials were conducted was unheard of in the rest of the civilized world. The legislation passed by the *Maggior Consiglio* in the year 1290 forbidding judges to inflict corporal punishment (which was then a common occurrence) on those who were under the age of 14, or who had been certified as mentally ill, was yet another example of the ultimate concern for human rights.

Once again on the Island of Crete, the Senate itself ordered that physical torture, which was then a standard part of the interrogation techniques of every country in the world, could not be used on a suspect without the prior consent of its own membership and that of the Council of Twelve. This was yet another example of the workings of a judicial system that was far more humane in certain respects than those of a number of contemporary western cultures, Italy included. With regard to those who were found innocent during the course of a criminal trial, there was also compensation provided for damages sustained as a result of their having been unjustly imprisoned.

Now let us look for a moment at the role of the *Sindici Inquisitori.* Despite the many positive aspects of the colonial system of justice, we should not automatically assume that all *Rettori* were models of virtue, or that the Venetian Empire was any kind of heaven on earth. (There were, of course, some truly great *Rettori*, such as Sebastiano Venier, who served as *Duca* of Candia and *Podestà* of Brescia before winning the Battle of Lepanto as *Capitano Generale da Mar*, and whose guiding principle is as relevant today as it was then: "Indulging the wicked is tantamount to tyrannizing the good.") As we all know, there is no such thing as perfection in this world, especially in situations where one human being is given the power to control the lives of other human beings. The leaders of the Republic, who were well aware of the instances of corruption, injustice, and incompetence among the ranks of the *Rettori*, were principally concerned about such issues as bribery on the part of the privileged classes in order to weigh the balance of justice in their favor, and personal ambitions on the part of the *Rettori* themselves that might prove to be detrimental to the general well-being of the *Serenissima.*

For these reasons, as soon as the *Rettori* went out of office, they were required to return promptly to Venice, where their entire administration was meticulously reviewed by the Council of Ten, the *Avogadori di Comun,* and various treasury officials. While still in office, they also were supervised by teams of inspectors from home on both a regular and emergency basis. Originally, these inspections were carried out exclusively by the *Avogadori di Comun.* (Interestingly enough, one expert in judicial affairs would suggest that this particular responsibility should be assigned only to "those who combined talent with great physical stamina, because even the strongest constitutions would be challenged by the complexities of the task at hand.") In fact, as late as 1410, an *Avogador* was sent to Candia to investigate the activities of an advisor to the *Reggimento* and his brother.

Above left: Facade of the Sponza Palace in Ragusa (Dubrovnik), in classic Venetian style. Above right: Statue of Admiral Leonardo Foscolo, situated in the couryard of the Papalic Palace in Spalato (Split), whose valiant defense of Dalmatia, Albania and Candia against the Turks included the conquest of the Fortress of Clissa.

On January 10, 1363, shortly before the revolt of the feudal lords on Crete, in response to a barrage of negative reports about the discontent of the local populace, the Senate approved a proposal from heads of the *Quaranta* to the effect that three special *Provveditori* be dispatched in person to the island territories. These individual were to be elected from among the patricians who had not served as *Rettori* in any of the colonies of the Eastern Latin Empire in the last 10 years, and who had no relatives that were currently *Rettori* or magistrates in the same region. They were to visit Crete, Corone, Modon and Negropont, where they were expected to listen to the complaints of the entire community. They were also cautioned to remain together at all times, and not to conduct any business or accept any gifts. If they could not agree on certain courses of action by majority vote, upon their return to Venice, they were to appear before the Senate, which would then make the final decisions based on the information received. Although this particular inspection did not prevent the outbreak of the bloody rebellion in Crete, or its equally brutal

repression, it undoubtedly played a significant role in the Republic's later decision to adopt a policy of conciliation with regard to her tumultuous island realm.

As of the end of the 14th century, these so-called *Sindici di Levante,* armed with specific instructions from the Senate, set sail every five years for Crete, Durazzo, Corfu and Negropont, where they listened, and read, and carefully considered the matters brought before them. In 1432, pursuant to a report submitted by the *Sindici,* the Senate sentenced the nobleman Secondo Pesaro, a former advisor to Candia, to two years in prison, a fine of 796 ducats, and permanent suspension from public office for having committed the serious crime of "accepting bribes in return for government positions and fiefdoms in our Cretan kingdom." Shortly thereafter, the Senate also granted the *Avogadori* permission to initiate proceedings against Pesaro's colleague and accomplice, *ser* Domenico Bembo, who was eventually given the same sentence. At the beginning of the following year, *ser* Pietro Mudazzo, the former *Rettore* of Rethimnon, found himself in a sim-

thorough investigation of the facts, during which the local inhabitants were given every opportunity to express their concerns, and the accused were provided with the best possible defense. According to F. Thiriet, an eminent authority on the Venetian Levant, these practices were specifically intended to protect the rights of the local citizenry above all others. The constant supervision of the activities of her colonial governors and functionaries was the most efficient way in which the Republic could assure her subjects that she herself was ultimately responsible for their welfare.

When Doge Paolo Renier reminded his colleagues in parliament that the colonials "must all be treated as friends," he was merely reaffirming a policy of equity and justice that had long been in effect. Such was the opinion of another doge, Marco Foscarini, when he proclaimed that the establishment of the office of *Sindici Inquisitori* had been inspired "by the love of our subjects." Although she was often harsh with

ilar predicament. At a later date, Daniele Loredan, the extremely powerful *Bailo* of Negropont, was found guilty of a number of shady dealings that led to his being sentenced to one year in prison, a fine of 400 ducats, and five years' suspension from public office.

Such severe measures were only adopted after a her rebellious territories, and always insistent on the unconditional loyalty of her dominions, at the height of her power the Republic of Venice was able to afford her colonies an equal system of justice for one and all. In the end, this was the main reason why so many foreign communities chose to place themselves under her tutelage.

THE TERRITORIES OF ST. MARK

CRETE AND CYPRUS, THE IONIAN ISLANDS, DALMATIA, FROM THE QUIETO TO THE ADDA, ST. MARK ON THE MAINLAND

By the time of the 13th century, which represented the height of her colonial empire, Venice had gained possession of the Ionian Islands, a large part of Albania, Epirus, Attica and the Peloponese, the Sporades, Cyclades and many other islands in the Aegean, Crete and Euboea, the European coast of the Dardanelles and the Sea of Marmara, and three-eighths of the city of Constantinople, including the arsenal itself. More than anything else, this vast amount of territory represented new opportunities for commerce and trade, which would remain the driving force behind her expansionist policies. Opposite page: The triple walls of Acrocorinth, on the slopes of which there was once the great acropolis of the city of Corinth. Given its strategic location in the northeast corner of the Peloponnese at the head of both the Gulf of Corinth and the Saronic Gulf, this ancient city was hotly contested by the various foreign powers during their attempts to gain control of Greece. From the years 1687 to 1715, when the Venetian Republic managed to control Corinth despite fierce competition from the Turks, she herself built one of the fortifications on top of the original walls.

Readers who are familiar with the amazing exploits of the two main characters in Emilio Salgari's celebrated oriental saga, Sandokan, the Tiger of Malaysia, and Janesz the Portuguese, his loyal friend and fellow adventurer, will also remember the proud, disdainful figure of Sir James Brooke, the white rajah of Sarawak, whose attempts to thwart the hero were always doomed to failure in the end. Brooke himself was hardly a figment of the vivid imagination of the Veronese author. Rather, he was the prototype of the versatility and courage displayed by Britain's colonial governors at the height of her empire, when they were known throughout the Victorian world for their ingenuity and pragmatism.

Sir James was born in India in the year 1803 to a family of English civil servants. During the time that he was a military officer in the ranks of the East India Company, he entered the employ of the Sultan of Brunei in Borneo, where he succeeded in putting down the rebel Dayak tribes of Sarawak on the northwest coast of the island. In exchange for his services, he was given the entire territory of Sarawak as his personal realm, whereupon he immediately placed himself and his kingdom under the protection of the British Crown, which bestowed on him the title of Consul General for Her Majesty in Borneo and Governor of Labuan.

Over the course of the years, Brooke (who was made a baronet in 1847) would become an important pawn in the British power games in Indonesia. Given his semi-independent status, he was able to dispose of the pirates that had infested the Sound in any way that he deemed necessary, without having to directly involve the Crown, which could always wash its hands of him in the name of political expediency. At the same time, he founded a local dynasty that reigned for over a century, until his great-grandson, Sir Charles Vyner Brooke, was forced to abdicate in 1946.

There is no possible way of knowing whether or not Sir James was aware of the circumstances surrounding the establishment of the Venetian Empire. However, in light of the fact that the British have always shown a great interest in the history of the Republic, such a possibility cannot be entirely excluded. What we do know for sure is that there are extraordinary similarities between the enemy of Sandokan and Enrico Dandolo's nephew, Marco Sanudo, who managed to found a feudal dynasty in the Cyclades while his fellow nobles ended up with only minor fiefdoms on the Aegean Islands.

After having served as a judge in the expatriot colony in Constantinople, and then as a *Sopracomito di Galera*, Marco set sail for the Cyclades and northern Sporades with a handful of other Venetian nobles stationed in the Byzantine capital, armed with the personal blessing of Doge Pietro Ziani, who had assured them of the protection of the *Comune*. The pretext for their occupation of these islands was the same one that Sir James had used to gain control of his own territory: protection against pirates. Like Brooke himself (although Sanudo had received his official title of Duke of Naxos from the Eastern Latin Emperor), he and his companions, who had declared themselves the

After the partitioning of the Byzantine Empire, Venice found herself faced with the problem of establishing her authority over the Greek possessions that she had been granted. The pragmatic Venetians came up with a solution: By granting her native citizens title to many of the islands and other regions that were now under her rule, she was able to absorb them into her own sphere of influence without the slightest risk of outside interference. So it was that Marco Sanudo, the nephew of Enrico Dandolo, became the founder of a great duchy in the Cyclades for himself and his heirs, which would forever maintain close ties with the Serenissima. Above: A Venetian fortress at Chalcis on the Island of Naxos, which was built to defend the inhabitants against the incursions of the Barbary pirates.

feudal overlords of other islands in the region (some as his vassals, and others not), were still members of the Venetian nobility. Once again like Sir James, Duke Marco was destined to become the head of a feudal dynasty that would endure for many decades to come.

When Marco first took possession of the Aegean Archipelago, which has now become a major tourist attraction, with its rocky islands set against the sparkling blue waters of the most beautiful sea in Europe, the area itself must have seemed both very remote and very familiar to him. The coastline itself, which was situated just off the main routes of the Venetian merchant ships, was dotted with countless bays and inlets, where Sanudo made sure that these vessels could always find shelter from storms and pirates' attacks. (It was also known, however, for its treacherous shoals, and its many dangerous cliffs that were constantly battered by the rough sea and high winds.)

Marco himself was an extraordinary individual whose lifestyle reflected both the myths and realities of the medieval Mediterranean world. From noble Venetian merchant, he had gone on to become a great feudal lord, but this was still not enough to satisfy his thirst for adventure. Once again, he took to the high

seas, this time headed for Asia Minor, where he claimed the city of Smyrna as his personal fief, only to find himself shortly thereafter the prisoner of Theodorus Lascaris, the Greek emperor of Nicaea, who had promptly attacked the Venetian fleet, and recaptured his former territories. However, Lascaris in turn was so captivated by this charming European nobleman that he not only set him free, but actually gave him the hand of his own daughter in marriage!

At Duke Marco's death in 1227, he was succeeded by his son Angelo. In 1371, after almost a century and a half of dynastic rule, his direct line became extinct when Fiorenza Sanudo was first married to Givanni dalle Carceri, the heir to one of the great feudal families of Negropont, and then to her own cousin, Nicolò Sanudo.

As the largest and most fertile of the Cycladic islands, whose rocky mountains sheltered lush valleys that were famous for their abundant crops and cattle farming (even today, it is probably the only place in the area where you can still find a good steak), Naxos was the perfect setting for Sanudo's feudal court, as was Kyparissia for the Villehardouin, and Athens for Otto de la Roche. On a more modest scale, there were the

Aegean courts of the Ghisi on Skiros, and the Querini on Stampalia, among others. Although Marco's own kingdom (whose local peasantry, or "pareci," seem to have benefitted from far better treatment than they had received at the hands of their Byzantine rulers) would eventually become home to any number of Venetian squires and sergeants, as well as craftsmen, merchants, pedlars and minstrels, it was still relatively isolated from the world at large. The treacherous seas themselves made it more difficult to enjoy the traditional pleasures of tournaments and hunts, as well as visits from famous troubadours and wandering poets such as Rambaldo di Vaqueiras (who did manage, however, to appear at the court of Conrad of Montferrat in Thessalonica).

Added to this, there was the need for constant vigilance due not only to the strained relations with the Byzantine world, both before and after the recapturing of Constantinople on the part of the Greek Emperor of Nicaea, but also the imperialist ambitions of certain members of the Latin community itself. Foremost among these was the greedy Villehardouin, who were then the princes of Morea (and whose adherents had actually succeeded at one point in taking over the territories of certain of the overlords in the Archipelago), and the ever-belligerent Genoese. There were other traitors in their midst as well, such as Licario of Vicenza, a nobleman from Negropont who actually sold himself to the Greeks in order to help them regain possession of a number of islands, which were eventually recaptured at great expense to the Latin world.

Once again, the various hurdles involved in the desperate attempt to survive in such a hostile environment closely resembled the experiences of Sir James Brooke, who also found himself far from home, and therefore extremely vulnerable to outside interference, while continuing to maintain close ties with the mother country. In the end, after making sure that his grandson would succeed him, Brooke would retire to an estate in Devonshire, where he lived out the rest of his days. Marco Sanudo actually died in his castle overlooking the port of Naxos, whose crumbling remains still exist today. At the time of the "closing" of the Maggior Consiglio, his direct descendants would finally make the journey back to Venice, along with the Ghisi and Dandolo and Barozzi and Zeno, to claim their birthright as members of the Venetian patriciate.

After the house of Sanudo had become extinct, and the Venetian fleet had helped to rout both the princes of Morea and the Greek insurgents led by Licario, the Crispo family, who may have come from Verona, and

even today, tourists who visit Naxos can see the vestiges of more than three centuries of Venetian rule

who claimed to be distant relations of Fiorenza Sanudo, would ultimately inherit the Duchy of Naxos. Despite family feuds, Turkish invasions, and a series of interregna, the great island fiefdom remained in their hands until the Turkish-Venetian peace treaty of 1540, which was only signed after the infamous Algerian pirate Khair-ad-din Barbarossa had succeeded in devastating their lands, driving out their own heirs, and taking any number of their subjects as slaves in the year 1537. The actual loss of their sovereignty did not signal the end of their presence on the island, however. Like the Gozzadini in Folegandros, Sikinos and Sifnos, and the Sommaripa in Andros, the Crispo were allowed to stay on in Naxos as long as they were willing to pay a tribute to the sultan.

Thanks to the political machinations of one of the most colorful figures in the entire Mediterranean cast of characters, Giacomo IV Crispo was finally forced to abandon Naxos once and for all in 1566. This individual was Josef Nassì, also known as João Miquez, a Jewish banker who had fled from Lisbon to avoid religious persecution, and had eventually ended up in Constantinople, where he became the personal advisor and favorite of Sultan Selim II. Nassì himself, who has been credited not only with the blame for having caused a war in Cyprus, but also for his attempt to create a homeland for the Jews in Palestine a good 350 years before Theodor Herzl, was eventually granted the fiefdom of Marco Sanudo.

The task of administering Sanudo's former duchy was assigned by Nassì to a Jewish refugee called Francesco Coronel, a "Marrano" who had fled from Spain some 13 years earlier. From what little is actually known of his rule, we can assume that he fulfilled his duties admirably. In fact, the former kingdom of Enri-

Although captured by Doge Vitale Michiel in 1172, the Island of Chios would not remain under Venetian rule for any significant length of time. After having been fought over by the restored Byzantine Empire and the Turkish pirates who had invaded this part of the Mediterranean, it eventually fell into the hands of the Genoesi. Above: A view of the Island of Chios in the 15th century, which bears the following inscription: "Along with many other islands of the archipelago, the city and island of Chios remained in the possession of the Giustiano family of Genoa for more than 200 years. Its loss to the Turks in 1566 was a glorious victory for 18 young Giustiniani, who entered the Kingdom of Heaven after having been martyred for their faith in Jesus Christ" (Biblioteca Marciana, Venice).

Modon, or Methoni, as it is now called, which is situated in the southwestern part of Morea, was not only an important outpost, but also the crossroads of the navigational routes from Venice to the Levant. Along with nearby Corone, it was considered one of the "eyes and ears of the Republic." As the "maritime information center," it was the stopping-off point for all ships returning from the East, whose captains would exchange the latest news about the movements of pirates and other vessels in the immediate area. As can be seen in the two photographs above, it is the site of any number of Venetian ruins. Left: The eastern gate of the Loredan Fortress. Right: The inner walls of the city, with a column that was once adorned by the Lion of St. Mark. Below: A sketch of warriors laying siege to a tower, from Livy's First Decad. Opposite page: On the eastern coast of Morea, Venetian ships often stopped at Nauplia (Naphlion), where there are still the picturesque remains of the Bourtzi Fortress.

co Dandolo's nephew would enjoy a certain amount of autonomy at least until the year 1601, when a representative of the Holy See reported to Rome on the existence of a Greek duke by the name of John Comnenus, who had taken over the territories of Naxos, Paros, Syra, Andros, Milos and Santorini. He also indicated that this "good Christian and true Catholic" had obtained the fief from the Grand Turk for the sum of 50,000 *zecchini*, plus an annual tribute of 15,000.

After suffering hundreds of years of oppression at the hands of the Ottoman Emperor, Naxos was again liberated, at which time it became a part of the modern country of Greece. Even today, however, tourists who visit the area can see the vestiges of more than three centuries of Venetian rule, starting with the ruins of the old fortress, with its original wooden doors still intact, and the more modest castles and towers scattered throughout the countryside, with their Guelph and Ghibelline crenellations. Then there are the doorways that line the narrow medieval streets, some of which still bear Venetian coats-of-arms, and certain of the modern name-plates and local shop signs, which are also reminiscent of ancient times. According to one individual, who visited the island about three centuries ago, there were still members of the Crispo, Sommaripa and Barozzi families living in the palaces clustered around Sanudo's city walls.

In 1814, a French tourist happened to run into a group of local residents who claimed to be the heirs of the original "castellan families." In fact, they had just celebrated a marriage between a Crispo, who descended from the last Duke of the Archipelago, and a Coronello, whose ancestor had once governed the island on behalf of the only Jewish feudal lord in the history of the Aegean. We ourselves met an individual named Sommaripa, who was probably a direct descendant of the feudal overlords of Andros, and another person named Dellarocca, who may have descended from the de la Roche family, who originally held the fiefdom of Athens.

Crete and Cyprus

Thanks to his compatriot Nikos Kazanzakis, whose portrayal of Zorba the Greek would earn him lasting fame, the Cretan author Pandelís Prevelakis has been

ARSENAL

unjustly relegated to second place in the realm of great literature. His charming tales, which are set against the gentle, sleepy background of *fin de siècle* Rethimnon, tell the story of a number of Candian gentlemen with high-sounding Venetian names, such as Mocenigo, Dandolo and Contarini. One of the island's most celebrated poets is named Marinos Falier, no less, just like the hapless doge who was beheaded in 1355. Can we assume that such individuals are the direct descendants of feudal overlords whose heirs became part of the Cretan community at large? Absolutely.

Over the course of time, certain of the wealthier Venetian overlords would return in triumph to their native city of Venice. However, there were also those families that had suffered serious financial losses, who would eventually find themselves so powerless that they were forced to join the ranks of the local peasantry, which had always been their nemesis. Even today, there are typical Cretan farmers from Messarea, or perhaps the Lassithi Plains, complete with breeches and moustache, who turn out to be descendants of one the "old houses" of the Venetian nobility, such as the Muazzo, Zancaruol, Semitecolo and Baseggio, which reigned supreme before the *serrata* of the *Maggior Consiglio*.

After the first two centuries of local unrest had finally come to an end, the mutual hostility that isolated the Venetians from their Cretan subjects would gradually give way to far friendlier relations, which sometimes resulted in mixed marriages. (This was true of the rest of the Greek colonies as well. The mother of Doge Antonio Grimani, for instance, was a member of an influential family from Modon.) Any number of young Cretans also went on to study in Venice, or at the state university of Padua. Certainly the most famous example of this phenomenon of assimilation was the Cretan artist Domenico Theotokopoulos, known to the world as "El Greco," who began his career by painting Madonnas (or *"madoner,"* as they were then called) for the domestic market, and was then given the opportunity to study directly with some of the great masters who were working in Venice at the time.

Although many of the Cretans of Venetian extraction chose to return to their city of origin when the island was finally lost to the Ottoman Empire, many others, who felt that they could not abandon their roots, opted instead to stay behind. But they themselves were not the only vestiges of Venice's rule that would survive the test of time. Despite the ravages of the Turks, the local city planners (who actually razed to the ground the magnificent walls of Rethimnon), and the bombings of the last war, Crete is still the site of any number of bastions, fortresses, castles, strongholds

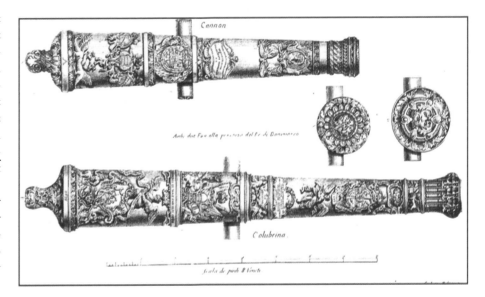

and public and private buildings. The magnificent fountains of Candia, the loggia where Venetian merchants once gathered, and the Church of St. Mark, to name but a few, are reminders of a daily existence that must have been rather peaceful and quiet, although a good deal less stimulating than that of Venice herself.

Throughout the Greek world, there would always be a certain amount of friction between the official Catholic Church and the members of the local clergy, the latter of whom had been forced to take second place to the Roman bishops, who were invariably Venetian citizens themselves. Although such a policy was extremely unpopular with her subjects, the Republic had adopted this position as a security measure in light of the rabid nationalism of the Greek Orthodox Church. Wherever possible, however, she made sure to safeguard the principle of freedom of worship, even in the most rebellious of her colonies. Furthermore, the

Opposite page: Ships at anchor off the Arsenal, from Jacopo de' Barbari's panoramic view of Venice. Above: Designs for the manufacturing of cannon and culverins, from Gasperoni's Venetian Artillery, 1708. *Below: Sixteenth-century culverin from the Doges' Palace. Maintaining control of the eastern Mediterranean depended not only on the supremacy of the fleet, but also the latest available weaponry. In fact, the Venetians were prohibited by law from selling their ships to foreigners as long as they were considered to be in good working condition.*

Right: The Castle of Morea at Rhion, situated at the mouth of the Gulf of Corinth. During the 13th and 14th centuries, the Venetians had control of a narrow strip of land along the eastern Mediterranean coast, which allowed them to establish a whole series of strategically placed naval bases.

fact that she herself elected the heads of the ecclesiastic community (which was standard practice with regard to the Catholic Church) against the wishes of the Roman Curia could hardly have displeased the Orthodox clergy.

It is also worth nothing that the local religious orders and institutions that now fell under her jurisdiction would benefit greatly from her tutelage. A prime example of this was the Convent of St. Catherine of Sinai in Candia, whose financial well-being was a direct result of its having been exempted from paying taxes immediately after the island was conquered by Doge Pietro Ziani. The famous Monastery of St. John on the Island of Patmos would also prosper for many centuries to come due to the protection afforded by the Republic.

At the time of the Council of Florence (1439), when it was decided to bring about the union of the two churches, the Cretan clergy made it absolutely clear that they had no intention whatsoever of renouncing their own beliefs. The Venetian Senate, which was initially unsure of what course of action to follow, finally agreed to support unification after the Turkish advance and the conquest of Constantinople had flooded the island with refugees whose religious leaders were considered highly untrustworthy. Although this experiment, which is still being discussed some five centuries later, would fail dismally in the end, it at least had the effect of normalizing relations between the Venetian authorities and the Cretan ecclesiastics.

During the long reign of the Lusignan family, who were extremely strict Catholics, the Island of Cyprus would become home to a powerful ecclesiastical hierarchy as well as several religious orders. Although the churches built by this local dynasty and many others throughout the Greek colonies were converted to mosques some 400 years ago, the magnificent Gothic cathedrals of Famagosta and Nicosia, designed by architects from Champagne, are a far more dramatic reminder of the adventures of the crusades than any written account could ever hope to be. Set in a typically Mediterranean landscape of olive groves and cypress trees against the background of a violet-blue sea, the Cistercian Abbey of Bellapais, in classic Romano-

Gothic style, could almost be the symbol of the Latin kingdom of the Levant.

The Venetians' acquisition of Cyprus, which came about as the result of the marriage of King James II de Lusignan to the beautiful Venetian patrician Caterina Corner in 1472, is yet another example of the Signory's ability to act first and foremost in its own interests. In fact, this union, which was the culmination of years of friendship and close business associations between the rulers of Cyprus and the extraordinarily wealthy and powerful Corner clan from Venice, was promoted and protected by the Republic herself.

Federico Corner, the founder of this financial dynasty, would go down in history as the individual who declared the highest personal income in the entire Republic in the year 1379, when the Treasury appealed directly to the local citizenry for additional support during the war against Genoa. As of 1366, Corner had begun lending enormous sums of money to King Peter I of Cyprus, in return for which he and his brothers were given the fiefdom of Piscopi. As one of the few regions on the island that was traversed by an open waterway, this territory was ideal for the cultivation of sugar cane. In fact, it was here that the Corner family established a plantation and refinery that would eventually realize enormous profits. (Sugar was then a commodity that was widely used by the medical profession, and therefore both expensive and in great demand.) They also increased the productivity of the local sugar-cane industry by importing large numbers of freemen and slaves. With regard to the precious water supply, it was used not only to irrigate the land, but also to power the mills that processed the cane, and to refine the sugar itself, for which purpose the brothers had brought in two huge copper cauldrons from Venice.

the Dodecanese in the year 1306. Given the close commercial ties between the Lusignan and Corner dynasties, and the blood relationships of the Corner clan with the Latin overlords and the Greek imperial family, the Republic settled on Caterina as the ideal bride for King James.

The storm that broke out in the Mediterranean after the wedding actually took place is dramatic proof of the tremendous coup that the Venetians had staged when they found the perfect excuse for intervening in the family feud that followed the death of King John II of Cyprus. As the story goes, his illegitimate son, James II, attempted to take the throne for himself, his sister Charlotte,

Preveza, which is part of the region of Epirus, was under Venetian rule from 1499 until 1530, when it was captured by the Turks. In 1684, it was reconquered by Francesco Morosini. Above: Bas relief from the main gate of the local fortress. Left: View of the entranceway to the Aighialos Castle in Zante (Zakynthos).

When we consider that Caterina's mother was Fiorenza Crispo, a descendant of Marco Sanudo and daughter of Valenza Comnena, whose father was the Greek emperor of Trebizond, we can further understand the political and financial implications of such a marriage. We should also mention that another branch of the Corner family from Crete had enlarged the territory controlled by Venetian feudal lords in the Aegean when it took over the Island of Scarpanto in the wife of Louis of Savoy and King John's only legitimate heir, used the support of the Genoese (who were then subjects of the powerful Visconti family from Milan) to have her brother deported from the island. This was all the Venetians needed to play their own political card, but without making their intentions too obvious. The fact that it was the Sultan of Egypt, the main supplier of spices to the *Serenessima*, who supported James in driving out Charlotte and taking pos-

After a good deal of soul-searching, she finally realized that she had no choice but to surrender her crown. In exchange, the members of the Corner family were given 14 additional island fiefdoms, which they used to increase production of sugar and cotton, as well as salt and potash.

Once the Venetians actually had control of the island (which also involved paying an annual tribute to the Sultan of Egypt, whose demands were nothing when compared with the profits that they hoped to reap from their new kingdom), they appointed any number of administrators to protect their own interests. In the city of Nicosia, besides the *Luogotenente,* there were two advisors "who represented the high court, and judged the actions of all feudal lords and gentlemen," and two chamberlains, "whose task it was to collect and distribute all income with receipts countersigned by the aforementioned *Luogotenenti* and *Consiglieri.*" In Famagosta, there was a *"Capitano del Regno"* who was the only official authorized to judge capital crimes, as well as two castellans. There was also a captain in Paphos, a castellan in Cerina, and another captain in Salines. With regard to military defense, each region had its own *Provveditore Generale,* whose duties were sometimes combined with those of *Luogotenente,* as was the case of the famous Sebastiano Venier.

The *Rettori* themselves were responsible for nominating the Viscount of Nicosia, who was chosen from among the ranks of the local nobility (whom Venetian sources described as poor but proud). This individual fulfilled a number of functions, both judicial and administrative, with the aid of a *Mathessep* elected by the island's inhabitants, who was charged not only with checking weights, measures and prices, but also performing certain police duties, and who carried a silver cane as a symbol of his office. The resident Syrians, Maronites and Copts had recourse to a judge known as the *Rais,* who was usually of western descent despite his Arab title.

Above: Despite the fact that her territories ranged far and wide, and her own citizens were scattered throughout the empire, the Venetian Republic never ceased to be the ultimate center of power, where major decisions were always made in the interest of the state itself. A prime example of this policy was the Senate's official adoption of Caterina Corner, whose marriage to James II de Lusignan assured them of a major stake in the Island of Cyprus. After providing the young bride with a huge dowry, the Venetians promptly dispatched her to Cyprus, where her wedding was celebrated in the year 1472.

session of Cyprus speaks louder than any documents that the Venetians must have placed carefully under lock and key.

The wedding itself infuriated not only Genoa and the Visconti, but also the Duke of Savoy. Ferdinand of Aragon, the King of Naples, who had set his sights on James, hoping to adopt him and acquire the Island of Cyprus for himself, would now join in the fray as well. In fact, when King James died the following year, Ferdinand began conspiring to marry the young widow off to one of his own relatives. However, when Caterina's uncle, Andrea Corner, who had been one of James's most trusted advisors, was murdered right before her eyes, the Venetians immediately set sail for Cyprus with the intent of taking the entire situation in hand.

Following the birth of Caterina's only son, who was given the title of James III, the Signory provided the young queen with the advice and counsel of three Venetian nobles, who were charged with supervising her every move during the long regency that lay ahead. However, when the child died in infancy, and Caterina found herself the sole heir to the Kingdom of Cyprus, the Republic first declared the territory a protectorate of the Venetian empire, and then dispatched Caterina's brother Giorgio to the island to help them persuade her to abdicate in favor of her compatriots.

Under the rules of the new government, the Venetian overlords also found themselves regimented into the *Maggior Consiglio*, whose membership automatically included all of their patrician compatriots. (Originally, the local administration had considered granting some 100 additional fiefs to aristocrats from home as had been done in Crete, but later abandoned the idea.) At the time of the dramatic events that led to the loss of the kingdom, the Council numbered 145 individuals, some of whom represented families from the Veneto mainland. In 1573, those among them who had managed to survive the terrible massacre that took place between July and August of 1571 in celebration of the Turkish victory were given a public subsidy in recognition of their loyalty.

The Ionian Islands

At the fall of the Republic, the Ionian Islands, along with Cerigo, Cerigotto and the Epirote strongholds of Preveza and Vonitsa, were under the direct command of the *Provveditore Generale da Mar*, whose official headquarters were situated on Corfu. This last island had initially come under the Republic's rule as a result of the *Partitio Romaniae*, at which time the Venetian fleet had rid the territory of the Genoese pirate Leone Vetrano, who was then hanged from the top of the mast of a galley belonging to Doge Enrico Dandolo's son Ranieri. In the following years, the *Serenissima* would lose control of the island, only to regain it, and lose it yet again. It was not until the death of the current ruler, Charles III of Anjou, the King of Hungary, when the local Citizens' Council would vote unanimously to cede the territory to Venice, that she was able to establish permanent sovereignty. According to the resolution itself, which was dated June 9, 1386, "as the island is virtually without protection . . . and coveted by rivals and neighboring populations, and constantly besieged by Arabs and Turks, and as her safety, security and well-being are all equally desired," the Council members "with one accord, and no dissenters, have chosen, designated and ordained as their defender, ruler and lord the venerable *Comune* of Venice. . . ."

Shortly thereafter, a delegation comprised of six Council members, one of whom was Jewish, appeared before Doge Antonio Venier to plead their cause, at which time they expressed their certainty that under Venetian rule, "we shall live by our own laws and under our own roofs, and enjoy our own wealth . . . and Corcira (Corfu) shall have nothing to fear with the Lion to guard her. . . ." Although the reference to wealth leaves little doubt as to the social status of the Citizens' Council and the delegation itself, there is reason to believe that they had also been influenced by the local populace, who had even waved banners bearing the image of the Lion of St. Mark during the public demonstrations that took place in the days immediately preceding the Council's deliberations.

The final agreement that was drawn up between the Republic and the Citizens' Council included a clause to the effect that Venice would provide for the defense and well-being of all her subjects on Cyprus. In accordance with the laws of the Republic, the administration of justice would be entrusted to the duly elected *Rettori*, who were expected to seek the advice and council of local judges whose own authority allowed them to argue appeals directly before the Venetian courts. With regard to the protection of personal property, the local citizenry was assured of the same rights as the overlords themselves. The prerogatives of the local church were also taken into consideration. Finally, there were two clauses that reflected the Republic's ultimate concern for fairness and equity, the first of which stipulated that any individual who had been arrested by a feudal lord could be tried only by the Venetian *Rettori*. The second provision allowed for the use of the Greek language in the drafting of certain legislation, which was tantamount to an official recognition of this bilingual community.

The cordial relations that existed between the two societies from the very beginning of Venetian rule would inspire the politician Gaspare Contarini to define Corfu as a "confederation with Venice" rather than a "colony." Even religious differences were eventually overcome. In fact, until the end of the Republic, an ecumenical service was held annually in the Church of St. Arsenius, which was celebrated by both Latin

Above: Portrait of Caterina Corner, attributed to Titian. The marriage between Caterina and James II of Cyprus, which ended when the king died one year later, was also marked by the premature death of their son, James III. In response to the various plots to overthrow the government after her husband's tragic death, the Venetians hastened to Caterina's side, and eventually convinced her to abdicate in favor of the Republic. Although she was received in Venice with all the honors befitting her station, and given a handsome lifetime allowance, Caterina would spend the rest of her life as an exile in the city of Asolo. Opposite page: The court of Caterina Corner at Asolo, attributed to the school of Giorgione (Attingham Park, Shropshire).

One of the major reasons that relations between the Venetians and their subjects on the Ionian Islands were so harmonious was the latters' need for protection against the constant assaults of the Turks. Corfu, which was taken over from the Anjou dynasty of Naples in 1386 at the behest of the local grandees, would eventually become the headquarters of the commander of the naval fleet for the Gulf (right: the remains of the Arsenal). Although the island was attacked by the Turks in 1537, and again in 1716, the sultan's troops were unable to get past the heavily fortified walls. Below: During the second siege, which lasted for 42 days, the inhabitants were saved by Count Schulenburg, a Prussian general whose statue by Antonio Corradini overlooks the same fortress in which he fought.

and Greek clergy "in such perfect harmony that one side sang the psalm while the other intoned the verses." Sixteen years after assuming leadership of the island, the Venetians also stabilized relations with Charles III's heir, Ladislas of Naples, who was only too pleased to hand over Corfu on August 24, 1402, in exchange for 30,000 gold ducats in cash.

The acquisition of St. Maur (Levkas), Cephalonia, Ithaca and Zante was a far more complicated affair. These islands, which were given to Venice in 1205, were to become the personal fiefdom of the Tocco (or del Tocco) family. While Leonardo del Tocco, the Palatine Count of Cephalonia, was still a minor, the Republic had used every possible means, from diplomacy to bribery to physical force, to regain control of the region, but to no avail whatsoever. The ever-present Turks, encamped at the entrance to the Adriatic, were also a part of the equation.

In the end, the Senate's spasmodic attempts to secure these maritime bases, combined with the Turks' stubborn resistance, would seal the fate of the unfortunate populace. When Venice was forced to give Cephalonia back to the sultan

in 1484 as part of a diplomatic agreement, the Senate ordered the *Provveditore* of Corfu to raze the territory to the ground, making sure to destroy "all that is good and useful on the island," and even deporting the local inhabitants, in the hopes that the Turks would decide to abandon what little was left. By the year 1499, when the Venetians finally called a halt to such tactics, they had succeeded in occupying first Zante, and then Cephalonia, where the Senate now busied itself with repopulating the countryside by importing veterans and refugees from the Peloponnese, and supplying them with building materials, plants, and seeds.

The colonies of Zante and Cephalonia were both governed along the same lines as many of the Republic's other territories. In each case, the local nobility participated in a Great Council (or General Council), whose membership elected the 150 representatives of a Lesser Council, which was also known as the "Council of One Hundred Fifty." In 1683, when a *serrata* limited the number of rightful members of the Great Council to 93, the *Provveditore* of Zante, Daniele Dolfin, noted with a certain amount of cynicism that the friction between the Venetian aristocracy and the local grandees was a necessary element in maintaining control over the island: "This antagonism should be tempered so as to avoid any possibility of grievous incidents, but should not be eliminated, since harmony between the members would be . . . suspicious and dangerous."

In Cephalonia, participation in the Great Council, which was established in 1505, was originally limited to wealthy landowners. However, "either with the tacit approval of the Venetian representatives . . . or on one

pretext or another" (in the words of the *Provveditore* Giustinian), by the year 1608, its membership had reached a staggering total of 900 individuals. In fact, the situation had gotten so out of hand that it was almost impossible to gather the troops for a legislative session, during which the doors to the chamber itself had to be guarded "with weapons in hand to stop the many, many people who wanted to enter by force." Worse still, according to the *Provveditore Generale da Mar,* Filippo Pasqualigo, "Once a . . . peasant has been in the Council, he claims the right, with all his line, to be exempt from any further voluntary service, including galley duty." In other words, the *Gran Consiglio* of Cephalonia had become the province of the local farmers, who were using their membership as a means to avoid being drafted for galley duty as members of the peasantry.

Several years later, the total number of voting members in the Council had risen to 1,000. In 1750, the *Provveditore Generale,* Vitturi, discovered that there were actually more than 6,000 individuals who claimed the right to participate in legislative sessions!

Despite these incredible figures, it is worth noting that no one ever raised the subject of a possible *serrata.* On the contrary, until the fall of the Republic, this particular assembly, which was so heavily criticized by the Venetian representatives, who were aristocrats to the core, survived as a democratic institution. Although it never really approved of the Council, the Senate, in its proverbial wisdom, chose not to press the issue for fear of antagonizing the islanders, who had become loyal subjects of St. Mark.

At some point during the 14th century, the Latin Duke of Athens, Gautier de Brienne, signed St. Maur (Levkas) over to *ser* Graziano Zorzi of San Moisè in payment of a debt that he had been unable to meet. After the island was lost, regained, and lost yet again, it was finally reconquered by Francesco Morosini in 1684, and remained under Venetian rule until 1797. It was here that the Republic established a truly autonomous government, with a single council under the jurisdiction of a *Provveditore,* which was responsible for electing judges, public officials and various other administrators. In the end, however, it seems

The old fortress of Corfu, dating from 1550, which was built by the Venetians on a promontory with twin peaks after the first Turkish attack.

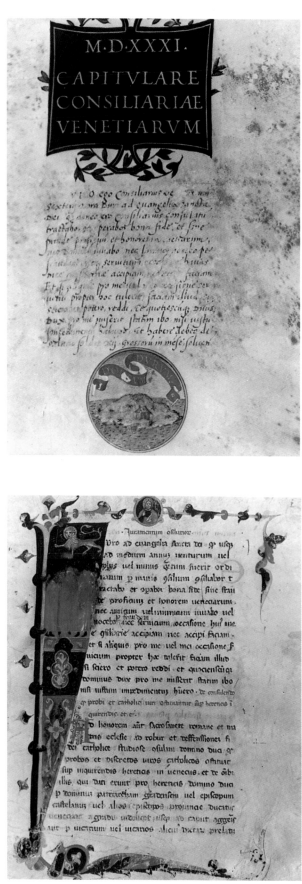

Two advisors' capitulars dated 1531 (above) and before 1396 (below), which were the oaths of office that were read during the swearing-in ceremonies of the six personal advisors to the doge (Archivio di Stato, Venice). These all-powerful politicians, who comprised the Consiglio Minore, were also members of the Signoria, along with the three heads of the Quaranta al Criminal Superior. Although they were responsible for monitoring the doge's every move, they themselves were the subjects of a number of rules and regulations. They could not hold any other official position, not could they leave the city for so much as a single day without the doge's permission. They were also forbidden to receive foreign ambassadors or delegates without the express authorization of the Senate, and to make any decisions whatsoever regarding political appointments. Opposite page: View of the western coast of the Island of Cephalonia.

mans had further reinforced the Republic's supremacy in the Gulf.

Maintaining control of this strategic position, however, was a constant struggle. On the one hand, there was the perpetual problem of piracy and foreign aggression, which forced the Venetians to take responsibility for policing the entire area (a burdensome, dangerous task that their neighbors were more than willing to leave in the hands of the Republic). On the other, there were the never-ending challenges to Venice's monopoly over trade in the southern Adriatic, particularly with regard to the Orient. Over the course of the centuries, she found herself dealing not only with the Normans, but also the Angevins and Aragons, all of whom would eventually rule the Kingdom of Naples.

When the Spaniards emerged as the first of the great modern nations to compete for ultimate control of the Gulf, the Venetians held out against them with a staunchness that verged on the foolhardy, given that there was a Hapsburg on the throne in Madrid as well as in Vienna. (The Austrian Hapsburgs were just as determined to rid themselves of the Venetian presence in Trieste and the Gulf of Quarnaro at the opposite end of the Adriatic, where they encouraged the dreaded Uzkoks, the Slavic pirates who had taken the place of the Narentines, to keep the Republic in a constant state of alarm.) Then, of course, there were the Turks, who could always be counted on to resurface at one point or another with all the might of their Eurasian territories behind them. There were also minor annoyances, such as the free merchants from Ragusa, who would conspire with anyone available in their constant battle for survival. In one way or another, all of these opposing forces were focused on the Dalmatian coast.

Despite the storms in the Gulf of Quarnaro, the coast itself was by far the safest and most convenient overseas route. With its long chain of islands, which formed a kind of natural jetty, and its deep bays and sheltered harbors, it actually extended almost as far as the Island of Corfu. For this reason, the *Provveditore Generale* for Dalmatia and Albania, who was second in command over the entire Venetian fleet, was stationed directly in Zara.

Firmly entrenched in the fortresses of Clissa and Imoschi, the Republic would be forced to live with this constant state of guerilla warfare and open aggression until the very end of her existence, including the period between the last decade of the 16th century and the first three decades of the 17th, when she faced a major crisis in the Morlacca Channel. This strategic sea lane, which wound its way south from the Gulf of

Several views of the Fortress of St. Maur on the Island of Levkas. Above right: The last vestiges of the walls themselves. Below right: The remains of a number of buildings located within the walls of the fortress. Below left: The emblem of the Lion of St. Mark. Opposite page: View of the eastern ramparts. Levkas was signed over to ser Graziano Zorzi by the Latin Duke of Athens, Gautier de Brienne, in payment of a debt that he had not been able to meet. After having been lost, regained, and lost yet again, it was finally reconquered by Francesco Morosini in 1684.

ner) would not be able to fulfill their duties while sitting comfortably at home. Accordingly, on September 6, 1747, Marco Foscarini proposed to the *Pien Collegio* that they nominate three *Sindici Inquistori*, just as they had done in the good old days, so that a proper on-site investigation could be carried out. The *Collegio* immediately voted its approval, which was seconded by the Senate with a two-thirds majority.

Unfortunately, certain members of the *Maggior Consiglio* were nowhere near as enthusiastic about the whole idea. These included a number of the poorer nobles, for whom the corrupt practices in Dalmatia had been a veritable godsend, allowing them to fill

their own pockets with ill-gotten gains while serving in the local *Reggimenti*. As usual, there were also the hawks, who insisted that the only way to solve such problems in the region was by imposing a state of martial law. After the first round of votes had failed to come up with the necessary majority, Marco Foscarini delivered one of the most famous speeches in his entire career.

Foscarini began by reminding his colleagues that 130 years had passed since the *Sindici Inquisitori* were last in Dalmatia. Furthermore, the province was just coming out from under 44 years of skirmishes and open warfare, which had seriously compromised not

the hackles of the local aristocracy, who saw their prerogatives gradually being stripped away by the new regime. The feudal overlords were equally alarmed at the prospect of being governed by a powerful foreign ruler who had no intention of allowing them the kinds of liberties that they had traditionally enjoyed. With regard to their administrative structure, the Venetians would resort to the same system that they were already utilizing in their maritime colonies. As we have said time and again, this involved a centralized government in which all important economic and political decisions were made by the Senate and the *Maggior Consiglio*, whose membership was restricted to the patrician class. The *Reggimenti* themselves, including the *Rettori, Podestà, Capitani* and *Provveditori*, as well as the various *Camerlenghi* and *Castellani* who were assigned to the major cities and towns, were also the exclusive purview of the Venetian aristocracy.

On the arrival of the insurgent forces of the League of Cambrai, all the resentment that had been building up on the part of the local nobility and their counterparts in the surrounding countryside would literally explode in the Republic's face. In fact, Count Leonardo Trissino, the aristocrat from Vicenza who represented Maximilian of Austria's cause on the mainland, was greeted with wild enthusiasm wherever he went. On June 6, 1509, the "citizens" (i.e., nobles) of Padua actually raised the two-headed eagle of the Hapsburgs *"cum maximo gaudio"* ("with the greatest of joy"), according to one chronicler, who likened the liberation of its populace to that of the Jews *"de servitute Faraonis"* ("enslaved by the Pharaoh").

The fact that her citizens were extremely cautious in their dealings with outsiders was reflected in the general attitude of the local merchants, who thought long and hard before actually collaborating with their peers. As far as the local populace was concerned, they were totally dedicated to the well-being of a city that they themselves considered the center of the universe.

The common people themselves, however, were totally opposed to the League and everything that it stood for. Niccolò Macchivelli, who was camped out at the imperial headquarters in Verona, was amazed by this phenomenon. In his own words, "Not a day would go by when one of them did not have himself put to death rather than abandon the Venetian cause. . . . Just last night, someone appeared before the bishop and announced that he had lived as a *marchesano* (a supporter of the Republic of 'St. Mark'), and wanted to die as a *marchesano*, and so the bishop had him hanged. . . . There is no way that these kings can hold on to this territory as long as the local peasantry is alive."

In Treviso, a commoner by the name of Marco Pellizzaro would manage to raise such a storm of protest that the local aristocrats were forced to declare themselves *marcheschi*. During the violent clashes in the Friuli that occurred between the *"strumieri"* (who supported the patriarch and the emperor) and the *"zamberlani"* (whose support of the Venetian cause was spearheaded by the Savorgnan family), it was the peasants themselves who formed the shock troops against the forces of the feudal lords that had gone over to the enemy camp.

The common folk had come to realize that the presence of the Venetian *Rettori* assured them of far greater protection than they had ever enjoyed under the rule of the local nobility and landed gentry. In fact, by the time of the League of Cambrai, the former had been relegated to a minor role in government affairs, while the latter had seen their power gradually erode as the result of actions taken by the *Provveditori*

Right: The 17th-century Customs House, or "Dogana da Mar," is situated on the point of land that divides the Grand Canal and the Giudecca Canal, which was once the site of a crenellated tower. It was here as of the year 1414 that merchandise arriving by sea was unloaded, and customs duties were paid. The building itself, which contains enormous warehouses and repositories, is surmounted by a tower with two kneeling statues of Atlas, who are holding up a gilded sphere on top of which is the revolving figure of Fortune. The Republic derived her income not only from customs duties, but also the sale of grain and salt. When combined with the profits from her trade in exotic goods from the East, these sources of revenue soon made the city a great commercial success. Opposite page, above: The 16th-century salt warehouses, near Customs House Point, from Jacopo de' Barbari's perspective map. Below: The public granaries, which were once located across from Customs House Point, as depicted in an engraving by Domenico Lovisa. Out of a total annual revenue of 1,150,000 ducats recorded during the 16th century, the salt market alone yielded a profit of 100,000 ducats. Under the terms of this state-owned monopoly, the salt manufacturers were obliged by law to sell their entire production to the Camera del sal (Salt Commission), whose officials were responsible for granting export licenses, and deciding to whom, and at what price, this precious commodity could be sold. The salt-pans themselves were centered around Chioggia.

sopra Feudi, whom the Republic had appointed with the specific intent of curbing their excesses. Despite its many defects, the system of justice that had been put in place by the Venetian authorities had proven to be more beneficial to their interests than that of the Carraresi, the Scaligeri, the Visconti, and the Sforza, not to mention the European heads of state or the Spaniards.

The loyalty and dedication of the Republic's less privileged subjects would survive until the very end of her empire, despite the obvious signs of decay and neglect that characterized her final years. These individuals had not forgotten what it was like to live under a regime that had found the means to avoid the ravages of famine and plague, and to guarantee better living conditions all around. Such circumstances more than compensated for their having been excluded from the decision-making process itself, which they and their counterparts throughout Europe had never been part of in the first place.

Although the Venetians had undoubtedly been mistaken in not having taken full advantage of their popular support in order to drive out the powerful ruling families of the Veneto and Lombardy, they had no way of knowing what the future might bring. In any case, when we contemplate the abysmal conditions of the working classes in 19th-century France and England, there is no denying that the Republic was at least three centuries ahead of her time in establishing child labor laws, and protecting the rights and privileges of the powerless and disenfranchised.

As far as we ourselves are concerned, there is no reason to engage in a lengthy defense of these policies, which were so harshly criticized some 200 years ago by the petty tyrants and imperialist powers of the time. The fact of the matter is that the level of civility exhibited by the Republic in her dealings with her subjects on the mainland, and her basic concern for human rights, are more than able to speak for themselves. Suffice it to say that in these respects, she literally towered above those of her European counterparts who had established dominions on the Italian peninsula.

Another major political mistake that has been attributed to the Republic was her failure to court the favor of the all-powerful members of the mainland aristocracy, who had long since allied themselves with the wealthy landowners in an attempt to suppress the rest of the population. Rather than involving them directly in the affairs of state, and making them feel that they were an integral part of the *"patria veneziana,"* she had chosen instead to alienate them completely, and even humiliate them in many instances, which led to their abandoning her cause once again in 1797, when their total lack of support would play a major role in her final defeat at the hands of Bonaparte and the *Armée d'Italie.*

When Venice made the decision to expand her territories to include those of the mainland, she was fully equipped to deal with the major political issues and administrative challenges that lay ahead. Despite these grand designs, she was also obliged to take into account the concerns of her own mercantile class, which was no longer in the exclusive hands of the aristocracy. The fact that her citizens were extremely cautious in their dealings with outsiders was reflected in the general attitude of the local merchants, who thought long and hard before actually collaborating with their peers. As far as the general populace was concerned, they were totally dedicated to the well-being of a city that they themselves considered the center of the universe. Like their counterparts in Great Britain, they were very much an "insular" race.

never intended that they be allowed to serve in any official capacity within the government itself, particularly the sanctum sanctorum of the Senate. There is no reason whatsoever why these outsiders, who were not born in the city of Venice, should be privy to the secrets of the Venetian state. . . ."

They were "outsiders" because they had not been "born in the city of Venice," and therefore were not to be trusted. The inevitable result of such a mentality was the tendency to exclude anyone who was considered even slightly "different" from the inner circles of power, both at the highest levels of government and in the colonial administration itself. (In the case of Savorgnan, the Senate eventually resolved the problem by making him *Collaterale*

Large quantities of salt were imported from Cyprus and the Balearic Islands as well. Venice was also the most important grain market in the northeast of Italy. Unlike salt, grain was not a state monopoly, and its price was therefore fixed according to the laws of supply and demand. Although most of the grain was produced locally, it could be bought in almost every port in the Mediterranean when necessary.

Besides being arrogant and overbearing, the mainland nobility were considered too "different" to be trusted. In this regard, Girolamo Priuli has left an interesting description of what happened when the Friulan aristicrat Girolamo di Savorgnan attempted to participate in the workings of the Venetian parliament in the year 1509. In recognition of his distinguished service to the Republic (he had courageously defended his homeland against the imperialist forces), Savorgnan had been admitted to the ranks of the Venetian patriciate, which theoretically entitled him to do so. However, when his grateful colleagues elected him to the Senate itself, and he began attending plenary sessions, Priuli was extremely concerned about setting such a precedent: "These individuals were made members of the Venetian nobility not only to reward them and to enhance their reputation in their own cities, but also to keep them well-disposed toward the Republic, and to ensure that they conduct themselves in a manner that befits their station. It was

Generale, or army chief of staff. This was not only a great honor, but it also kept him out in the field and far away from the capital.)

We have already seen how the Senate membership promptly rejected the proposal that Antonio Contarini put forth in 1411, which would have allowed the nobility of Zara to participate in the affairs of their own government In the year 1736, when Marchese Scipione Maffei suggested that they consider the advantages of electing 20 aristocrats from the mainland as delegates to the *Maggior Consiglio,* his proposal, which was not even taken into consideration, was never officially published until after the fall of the Republic.

However, if we examine certain public documents from the 18th century, we can see that many of the nobles from the mainland who had been admitted to the patriciate when the Golden Book was reopened to help finance the war against the Turks were actively involved in the affairs of state as members of both the

Right: The old walls of Cattaro, which wind their way up into the hills. Opposite page: Detail of the congregation, from Bartolomeo Vivarini's Our Lady of Mercy *(Church of Santa Maria Formosa, Venice). At one point in the 16th century, the gross revenue derived from the Republic's overseas colonies amounted to 200,000 ducats. In the same year, a new system of direct taxation yielded another 60,000 in profits. Below: Two plaques in memory of Venetian governors, which can still be seen on the walls of Capodistria.*

Maggior Consiglio and the Senate. Among those holding high office in the year 1797, there was the Paduan Giulio Antonio Mussati, a personal advisor to the doge whose family had just been approved by the *Avvogadori di Comun*. A member of the Benzon family from Crema, which had been admitted to the patriciate at a much earlier date, was part of the Council of Ten. Girolamo Silvio Martinengo of Brescia was a *Savio alla Mercanzia*, and Pattaro Buzzacarini of Padua was a *Scansador alle Spese Superflue*. Even Doge Lodovico Manin himself came from a mainland family that had been enrolled in the patriciate "for money!" (In fact,

when Manin was first elected, N.H. Pietro Gradenigo, the heir to one of the oldest patrician families, was heard to exclaim: "A Friulan has been made doge! The Republic is dead!")

How can such apparent contradictions be explained? Besides the fact that 200 years had passed since the Savorgnan affair, any number of mainland families who had been admitted to the ranks of the patriciate, whether for reasons of money or personal merit, had long since established permanent residency in Venice, where they had become completely assimilated.

However, in the provinces themselves, where the members of the *Maggior Consiglio* continued to reign supreme, the privileged classes had become so resentful of being excluded from the inner precincts of power that they were ready and willing to join forces with Napoleon in 1797. When they raised their "liberty banners" along with the French and proclaimed the principles of the Revolution, what they were really celebrating was the opportunity to regain the power that they had previously lost to the Venetians.

Once again, as at the time of the League of Cambrai, it was the common people who actually rose up and cried "Long live St. Mark!" Was this out of ignorance, superstition and backwardness, as has so often been suggested? In our own opinion, absolutely not. What happened in Verona, for example (where at least two local aristocrats, Augusto Verità and Francesco Emilei, also paid with their lives for their loyalty to the Republic), was undoubtedly in direct response to harassment and cruelty on the part of the French troops. More importantly, the commoners knew only too well that they were about to lose the rights and privileges that they had enjoyed as Venetian subjects in favor of the old regime.

St. Mark on the Mainland

Long before the Republic herself adopted a policy of expansionism on the mainland, her citizens had begun acquiring vast amounts of territory on terra firma in the capacity of private property owners. In fact, as times changed, and the risks involved in overseas trade and maritime investments increased, the Venetian patriciate would look more and more to the real estate market as an alternative source of income. Among the first to take advantage of such an opportunity were the enormously wealthy Contarini from San Trovaso and the Pisani from Santo Stefano, who would inspire their compatriots to join them in building the magnificent villas that still grace the Veneto

The Capitano Generale da Mar, *who was the supreme commander of the Venetian fleet, was elected by the Maggior Consiglio. The moment in which he was given the baton of office was the occasion of an elaborate ceremony attended by both the doge and the members of the Signoria. The illustration by Giacomo Franco depicts a part of these proceedings.*

tory as the author of a treatise on the merits of a lifestyle of moderation). According to Cornaro, the only way to avoid the chronic shortages of grain, which had forced the government time and again to pay inflated prices abroad, was to adopt a comprehensive program of agricultural reform. (To her lasting credit, Venice had always made sure that her citizens would never go hungry. In fact, when it was no longer possible to purchase grain from Candia, Negropont and the Peloponnese, she would actually turn to the Turks to meet her needs.)

Thanks to the initiatives that were taken by this same government, the agricultural industry would eventually be able to meet the needs of the population as a whole. Although the basic living conditions of the peasants in the Veneto were hardly ideal, with the exception of the terrible famine of the early 1500s, they were at least assured of the where-

countryside. Of all the important architects who participated in this extraordinary venture, the Paduan Andrea Palladio, who would eventually make his home in Vicenza, was by far the most celebrated.

At the same time that her private citizens were investing large amounts of capital in the mainland, the Republic herself began to take a more active interest in the benefits to be derived from a policy of land reclamation that would ultimately apply to the entire Veneto region. During the 16th century, one of the major proponents of this idea was Alvise Cornaro, the great friend of Palladio and patron of the famous satirist Angelo Beolco (who would also go down in his-

withal to survive. This was a far cry from the plight of their miserable counterparts on the European continent, who were most often left to starve to death.

The Republic has also been accused time and again of levying excessive taxes that drained the economy of the local countryside, and fostering protectionist policies that favored her own industries as opposed to those of her territories. In reality, the Venetians were no more rapacious than their European neighbors. Their subjects on the mainland certainly never experienced anything like the brutal exactions that squeezed the French peasants dry under Richelieu and Colbert, which were often accompanied by acts of violence and intimidation. Furthermore, even the most critical historians have been forced to recognize that their system of taxation was both equitable and comprehensive.

The city of Venice derived the major portion of her income from indirect taxes such as import, transit and excise duties, monopolies on tobacco and salt, and levies on the slaughtering and sale of meat. Unfortunately, in the last century of her existence, she assigned the task of collecting the majority of these taxes to independent contractors, or *"Partitanti,"* as was the practice here in Italy until several decades ago. This arrangement may well have benefitted the state treasury, but it most certainly was not in the best interest of the taxpayers themselves. In fact, a document from the year 1773, which is quoted by Berengo in his study of Venetian society at the time of the Republic's decline, describes these contractors and their agents as "carnivores, thirsting after the blood of the workers, wringing them dry, oppressing them, and ruining them to the fourth generation." Of all the *"Partitanti,"* those connected with the tobacco monopoly were undoubtedly the worst, as witnessed by the frequent fights that broke out between their agents and the local peasantry.

In any day and age, it is always a good idea to maintain some degree of objectivity when dealing with the complaints of taxpayers in general. Be that as it may, the exemptions enjoyed by certain feudal jurisdictions, and the special rights of redemption accorded to others, were definitely unjust, although common to every country in Europe.

As far as direct taxes were concerned, the most remunerative was the so-called *"campatico,"* which affected all arable land. Then there was the *"decima,"* which pertained to buildings, ship charters and personal earnings, the *"tansa,"* which regarded overall income (and which was so modest that it was commonly known as the *"insensibile,"* or *"imperceptible"* tax), and the *"taglione,"* which applied to the arts and crafts guilds.

Unlike the majority of her European neighbors, the Republic firmly believed in the principle of equality with regard to sharing the burden of taxation. The fact that there were no exceptions to the rule, including the clergy, guaranteed that her own subjects on the mainland would be spared a plight similar to that of the rural populace in France, who were so terribly exploited during the years of the *Ancien Régime*. It should also be mentioned that in times of fiscal crisis, the Venetians looked first to the magistrates, merchants and homeowners, whom they often taxed to the hilt. In short, it was the patricians who passed the very laws that hit them the hardest. This was most definitely the case in 1379, when they courageously adopted a series of emergency measures to finance the war against Genoa that literally sent most of them into bankruptcy.(Among those who eventually called for a moratorium to save themselves and their families from ruin was Doge Andrea Contarini, whose request was not granted.) In the end, the Republic did not ask anything of her "subjects" that she had not demanded to a far greater degree from the members of her ruling class.

With regard to the accusation that Venice fostered protectionist policies that favored her own industries as opposed to those of her territories on the mainland, which seems to be a favorite argument of her detractors, there is no evidence whatsoever to support such a claim. On the contrary, the region of Brescia would continue to function as one of the most important weapons manufacturers in all of Europe after having been annexed by the Republic. The textile industry, which had already moved out of the city, would make great headway on the mainland, where the Schio woolen mills were established as a free enterprise in the last century of the Republic. Instead of blaming Venice for the industrial crisis that occurred in the Veneto and Venetian Lombardy toward the end of the century, critics would do well to consider the impact of competition from the Austrians, and the general decline of the Venetian economy, whose main victims were the citizens of the city herself.

Even at the lowest point in her history, Venice would provide public assistance for those workers who had been hit especially hard by the economic crisis. Given the number of charitable organizations, mutual aid societies and local pawnshops, this welfare system was extremely effective in both the capital and the principal towns and cities on the mainland. However, this was hardly the case in the countryside, which was overrun by thieves and bandits until the end of the Republic and beyond. All too often, these individuals were former peasants whose only real concern was that of feeding themselves and their families. This phenomenon had become so prevalent by the year 1849 that the Austrians (who are still thought of as models of good government and bureaucratic efficiency) would use the notorious Este Commission as a means to rid themselves forever of such a scourge, at which point hundreds of these poor souls were rounded up, brought to trial, and condemned to death by firing squad.

Apropos of good government and bureaucratic efficiency, we should mention that the *Sindici Inquisitori* were sent not only to the Levant, but also to the mainland territories. Although these visitations would become less and less frequent over the course of time, major abuses on the part of the local *Rettori* were still thoroughly investigated by the Council of Ten and the State Inquisitors.

In accordance with the legal procedures that had already been established in the overseas colonies, the *Inquisitori* responsible for the mainland were also required to encourage "all individuals, irregardless of their social status, whose lives or possessions or reputations had been threatened in any way . . . to avail themselves of a judicial system that would allow them to sue for damages at no personal cost. . . ." (So said a proclamation of the *Sindicato* for the Levant in 1635.) Among those whose conduct was subject to constant scrutiny were the *Rettori* themselves, as well as other influential members of the community such as chancellors, lawyers and tax collectors, all of whom were answerable to charges of "trafficking, extortion, fraud and exploitation."

In order to guard against the harassment or intimidation of plaintiffs and potential witnesses, *ser* Carlo Contarini *(Sindico* for the Levant in the year 1635) issued the following proclamation: "Let no one attempt, by using threats, pleas, arguments or any other means, to prevent or dissuade, with words, signs, facial expressions or any other device, to hinder those who

intend to appear before us for whatever reason . . . on pain of death . . . including lawyers, solicitors and legal representatives. . . ."As far as the *Rettori* were concerned, the Senate had thought of everything, as is obvious from their instructions to the *Sindici Inquisitori* on how to ensure that these individuals were not publicly discredited before being proven innocent or guilty: "You must not look askance at those *Rettori* who have behaved badly, or show any ill-will toward them." The *Sindici* were also cautioned to inform the accused that they were entitled to name their own defense lawyers. Only in those instances where the gravity of the crime was such that there was the risk of the *Rettori* not showing up at trial did the *Sindici* have the right to arrest them and send them directly to Venice. (In any case, those *Rettori* who had committed a serious offense such as embezzlement or abuse of power were required by law to defend themselves against these charges before the Venetian court as soon as their terms of office expired.)

In all probability, the last *Sindicato* on the mainland was the commission appointed in 1769 "to identify and adopt whatever means are necessary to prevent the abuses, frauds and irregularities that have been committed to the detriment of the people and the public economy with regard to duties, monies and taxes. . . ." So reads the Senate decree. Once again, we can see that the Republic was not in the habit of disposing discreetly of such matters. She was also well aware that it had become common practice for penniless aristocrats who had been sent to some outlying territory as *Podestà* to supplement their meager income by dipping into the public coffers, or by accepting bribes and gifts. These crimes were severely punished, even on the grounds of suspicion alone, as opposed to the rest of Europe, where such activities were taken for granted. What was considered a natural prerogative abroad was treated as a serious offence in Venice.

Before leaving the mainland entirely, we should

The Venetians were way ahead of their time in many respects, even if the lack of adequate means and the circumstances of the moment sometimes prevented them from achieving all of their objectives.

COMMERCE AND INDUSTRY

Opposite page: Detail of The Molo and the Doges' Palace, *by Luca Carlevarijs, a vivid depiction of the amount of commercial activity in the harbor itself, which symbolized the Republic's position as the crossroads between East and West. The local demographics were yet another indication of her enormous prosperity. In the 13th century, when a city of 20,000 inhabitants was considered a veritable metropolis, the residents of Venice already numbered some 80,000. One hundred years later, the total population stood at 120,000. (At this time, only Naples and Paris were as densely populated.) Despite the terrible plagues that had decimated the whole of Europe, by the end of the 16th century, the population of the city would reach an all-time high of 190,000.*

THE TRADE ROUTES, GOLD AND SPICES, PIRACY AND DECADENCE

829 A.D. One year after the body of St. Mark the Evangelist had been removed by Venetian merchants from its final resting place in Alexandria of Egypt and brought back in triumph to the city on the lagoon. Theophilus, the Emperor of Byzantium, was standing at a window in the Great Palace that overlooked the Sea of Marmara, watching a large merchant vessel slowly make its way toward the harbor.

Out of idle curiosity, the emperor asked someone in the room if he knew who was the owner of such a magnificent ship. When he found out that it was none other than his wife, the empress, Theophilus flew into an absolute rage: "God made me an emperor, and now you, woman, want to make me a sea-captain!" The order then went out from the Great Palace to burn the ship and all of the merchandise on board.

Theophilus' anger was provoked by the fact that his wife had gone against the ancient Roman law that prohibited nobles from engaging in any form of commercial activity, "so that the plebeians and merchants can go about their business more efficiently." (As far as his own commercial interests were concerned, he had limited himself to levying enormous taxes on those same individuals.) In noting this particular episode, the historian Robert Lopez tells us that for centuries to come, Byzantine historians would praise what was to

be known as Theophilus' "act of justice." The last of these enthusiasts was actually a secretary of Alexius Comnenus, the emperor who had been forced to mortgage the economic future of his kingdom to merchants and Venetian shipowners!

In the same year of our Lord 829, Doge Giustiniano Parteciaco would make provisions in his will for the disposal of an enormous personal estate that included not only lands, domestic animals, vineyards, orchards, houses and servants, but also the substantial sum of 200 silver pounds, "provided that the coins themselves arrive safely in port." What this meant, of course, was that a highly respectable gentleman who had risked part of his capital in maritime trade could not have cared less about the ancient Roman law!

In February of 853, Orso, the Bishop of Olivolo, and therefore of Venice (Olivolo was the island in Castello where the bishop's cathedral and palace stood, and where the Church of San Pietro, which was Venice's own cathedral until 1809, can still be seen), would also make out his will. Along with the many legacies to churches and monasteries, however, he left a sack of pepper and another of *"olivano,"* which must have been some type of spice or drug. In other words, not even the bishop himself considered it beneath his dignity to engage in commercial endeavors!

Alps by means of long caravans on foot or on horseback. From the Friuli passes, these led to Styria and Carinthia, and then to Vienna, Breslau and Cracow. From the Brenner and Septimer passes, they led instead to Augsburg, Nuremberg and Ulm, even though most of the trade with Germany took place in the Rialto business district itself, where the local expatriot community existed in large numbers.

Then there were the "sea-going caravans," which were commonly called *"mude."* Heavily armed and under military escort, these convoys would set out one to four times a year for the main market-places at home and abroad. The *"Muda di Romania,"* which was the most important caravan, went first to Constantinople, and then on to Azov, Trebizond, and other ports on the Black Sea. There were also convoys to Cyprus and Armenia, Syria, Alexandria in Egypt, and even the Barbary Coast. Others stopped at ports in Apulia, Sicily and Calabria, and Marseilles and Aigues-Mortes in Provence. Finally, as of the beginning of the 14th century, there were *mude* that sailed the Atlantic as far as Bruges, Antwerp and Southampton.

Doge Giovanni Dandolo, was introduced well after the coinage of Florence and Genoa. Incredibly, until the very end of the Republic, the ducat maintained its original weight and purity, which was 3.56 grams of 24-carat gold, with the exception of two minor alterations that were made between 1491 and 1550, which reduced it to 3.49 grams. In today's terms, this corresponded to a value of $47.00, or £29. Most certainly, the solidity and stability of the local currency played a major role in the extraordinary wealth of the city, despite a series of economic crises and financial reversals.

As maritime conditions improved, the old seafaring routes were gradually replaced by new ones. Such was the case in 1282, when all restrictions were lifted with regard to *mude* headed for Apulia, Calabria and Terra di Lavoro. Prior to this, the armed convoys going to the Apulian ports would only take on ships that carried large sums of money in order to purchase

The Trade Routes

While the inland itineraries followed the course of the rivers as far as possible, the overland routes crossed the

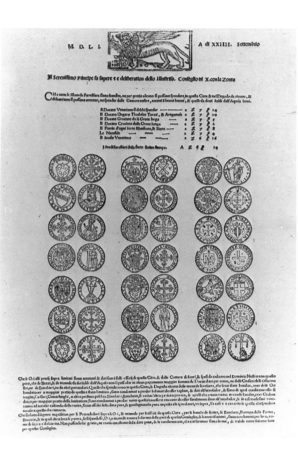

enormous quantities of grain. All other vessels would have to make their own way.

The *mude* were organized by the state, which auctioned off the contracts for the galleys themselves to both commercial shippers and private merchants. These rather small, narrow-beamed vessels, which were equipped with oars and sails, originally weighed no more than 90 tons. By the 15th century, however, especially after the establishment of the Atlantic route, they had reached a weight of about 300 tons.

Although the actual volume of merchandise carried by the convoys (which varied from 3,000 to 5,000 tons per year in the 13th century, 7,500 to 10,000 tons in the 14th century, and 10,000 to 12,000 tons in the 15th century) was not that extensive, the goods themselves were extremely valuable. According to the chronicler Morosini, between the end of the 14th century and the beginning of the 15th century, the overall value of the cargo carried by each convoy on both the outward and return voyage was somewhere around 250,000 gold ducats ($55,000, or £35,000). In certain cases, the cargo might even be worth double this figure. If we then consider that every *muda* made six to 10 round-trip journeys per year, we can easily calculate that the total value of the merchandise on board ranged from $330,000 (£80,000) to $550,000 (£350,000). While these figures are nothing compared with today's foreign markets, they are astronomical in terms of the medieval economy. We should also note that the average net profits from each convoy ran between 10 and 30 percent.

The bulk of the less valuable, but not necessarily less profitable cargo, such as salt, timber and any number of other raw materials, was transported instead by unarmed ships that did not have to follow a prescribed route. These particular vessels, which often sailed the seas for years at a time, were a good deal larger than the "merchant galleys." In fact, by the beginning of the 15th century, there were at least 300 of them that weighed over 120 tons. (Documents dating from the 13th century mention a sailing-ship named *La Roccaforte*, which actually weighed in at 500 tons. Com-

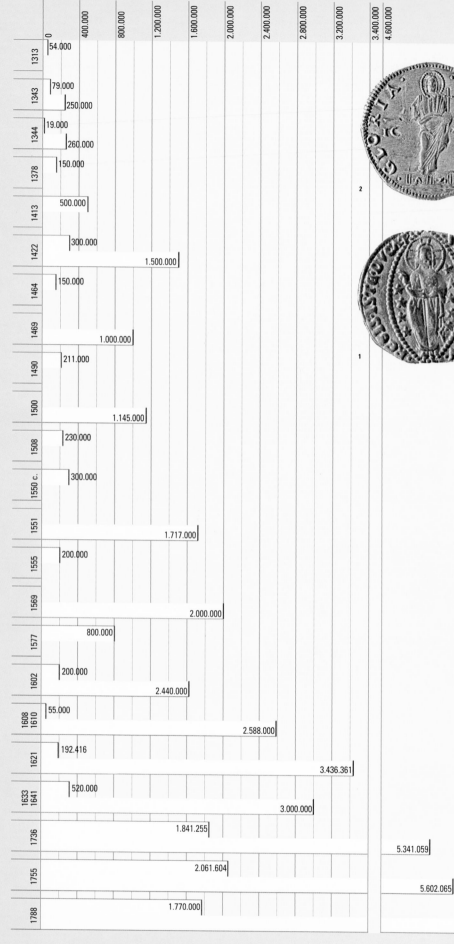

Chart axis labels (top): 0, 400.000, 800.000, 1.200.000, 1.600.000, 2.000.000, 2.400.000, 2.800.000, 3.200.000, 3.400.000, 4.600.000

Year	Value
1313	54.000
1343	79.000 / 250.000
1344	19.000 / 260.000
1378	150.000
1413	500.000
1422	300.000 / 1.500.000
1464	150.000
1469	1.000.000
1490	211.000
1500	1.145.000
1508	230.000
1550 c.	300.000
1551	1.717.000
1555	200.000
1569	2.000.000
1577	800.000
1602	200.000 / 2.440.000
1608 / 1610	55.000 / 2.588.000
1621	192.416 / 3.436.361
1633 / 1641	520.000 / 3.000.000
1736	1.841.255 / 5.341.059
1755	2.061.604 / 5.602.065
1788	1.770.000

Bottom axis: 6.000.000

COMPARISON OF STATE REVENUES AND LONG-TERM DEBT PAYMENTS

THE POWER
OF MONEY

When the gold ducat, or *zecchino*, was originally minted in 1284, it had the same weight and purity as the Florentine florin, which had already been in circulation for more than 30 years (1 and 2: gold ducats issued by Marco Barbarigo in the 15th century). In 1455, after its monetary value had been fixed at 24 small pieces of silver, it became known as the *zecchino* (from the word *"zecca,"* meaning "mint") in order to distinguish it from the new silver ducat.

Prior to the standardization of the ducat, silver coins were commonly referred to as *"le lire di grossi,"* or "large liras," which were used for major financial transactions, and *"le lire di piccoli,"* or "small liras," which were reserved for retail sales. At a later date, the lira itself would finally be minted (3 and 4: the half-lira, or *marcello,* which was issued by Andrea Vendramin during the 15th century; 5: the half-lira, or *mocenigo,* which was introduced by Pietro Mocenigo in the same century; 6: the *soldino,* which was minted by Francesco Dandolo in the 14th century).

Like most of her medieval counterparts on the European continent, Venice originally financed her military operations, which often represented an extraordinary economic burden on the state treasury, by borrowing on short loans that yielded between 12 and 20 percent interest. Unlike her contemporaries, however, she eventually decided to consolidate the public debt through a series of financial institutions known as the *"Monte Vecchio,"* which initially paid creditors an interest rate of five percent. As we can see from the graph to the right, which represents fluctuations in the amount of the public debt from the year 1262, when the "Monte Vecchio" was first established, until the beginning of the 15th century, the state treasury owed some half million ducats by the end of the second war with Genoa in 1299. This figure would double by the end of the war with Ferrara in 1313, and then decrease sharply in the following decades, only to skyrocket from two to five million ducats between the years 1379 and 1381, during the disastrous war with Chiog-

The bar graph to the left, which is based on Frederic C. Lane's exhaustive study of the history of the Venetian economy, compares state revenues to long-term debt payments for certain years between the beginning of the 14th century and the fall of the Republic.

It is interesting to note that even though the treasury office made widespread use of public borrowing, the balance between income and long-term debt payments remained relatively constant until the very end.

gia, which was subsidized by compulsory loans whose actual market value stood at a mere 18 percent. (In fact, the state was then in such dire financial straits that interest payments were suspended entirely in 1381. When they resumed in the following year, they would yield a paltry four percent.) By 1402, however, when the Venetians were expanding their territories on the mainland, the public debt had been reduced to 3.5 million ducats, while the market value of outstanding loans had risen to 66 percent.

The French Ambassador Philippe de Commynes was not alone when he declared at the end of the 15th century that Venice was the "wisest political head in Europe." One of the reasons for this accolade was the shrewd management of financial affairs on the part of the Republic's ruling class (7: A depiction of the *Camerlenghi di Comun,*" who were among the earliest financial officers of the city, from Livy's *First Decad,* which is now located in the Biblioteca Ambrosiana in Milan.)

The bar graph at the bottom of the page, which is also based on statistics compiled by Lane, compares state income and expenses in approximately the year 1500, when Venice was at the height of her power and influence as the most important maritime presence in the Mediterranean

and the largest republic in Italy. If we examine these figures carefully, we can see that while income and expenditures for the overseas colonies are virtually identical, the revenue derived from the mainland territories was considerably greater than expenses. As Lane himself has pointed out, "After the acquisition of the territories on the mainland, income derived from these sources offset the expenses of the overseas empire."

A system of direct taxation was introduced to sustain the costs of war at about the same time that these figures were recorded in order to replace long-term loans, which had involved serious difficulties. The huge sums available for special expenses helps to explain why neither the League of Cambrai nor the Turks themselves were able to defeat the forces of the Republic.

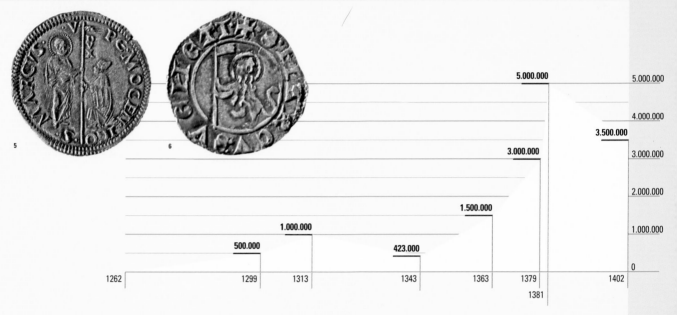

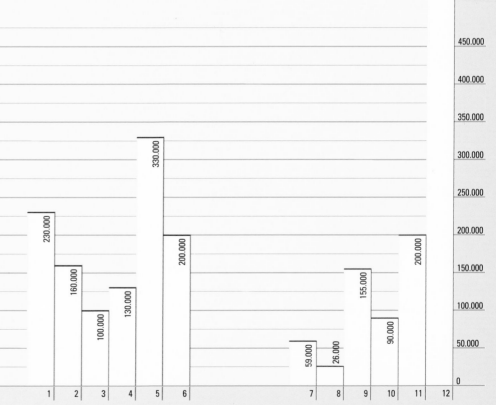

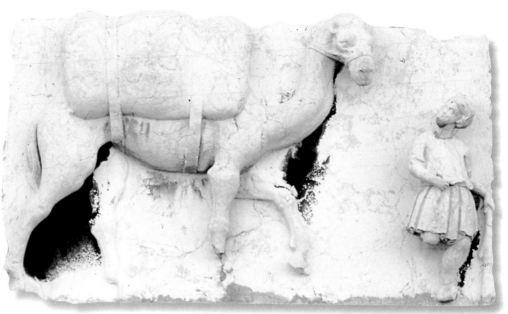

rewarded them with gifts that were worth at least twice the value. We also know the story of Simeone Avventurato and *ser* Lorenzo Viaro, who received nothing at all from the Khan of Persia in return for similar offerings. From other documents, we know that *ser* Francesco Loredan left for China in 1344 with some 300 *lire di grossi* in his pocket, and that two business partners named Andreolo Balanzano and *ser* Francesco Condulmer arrived on the Chinese mainland before 1350. Finally, we know that there were both patricians and commoners that went as far east as Japan, whose boundaries were considered the ends of the earth at that time.

Besides the usual commodities, merchants sometimes offered what would be referred to today as "specialty items."(Perhaps the most curious of these were the eunuchs that Venetian slave traders once supplied to the harems of Moslem potentates.) First and foremost were the precious objets d'art produced by local artists and skilled craftsmen, which fascinated the entire foreign market. Mehmed II, the barbaric sultan who had conquered Scutari, Negropont and Constantinople, was so intrigued by Venetian painting that he actually invited Gentile Bellini to be a guest at his court. However, when he presented poor Bellini with the severed head of a slave in order to show him exactly how he wanted him to portray the decapitation of John the Baptist, the terrified artist accepted his farewell gift of a magnificent gold chain, and promptly departed for Venice.

Among the Venetians' "exclusive clientele," there was Suleiman II, whose jewelry suppliers included none other than *ser* Francesco Zen, the *Bailo* of Constantinople. In fact, Zen was instrumental in persuading the sultan to buy a gold ring with a repeating watch, and a fabulous jewel-encrusted helmet, which the chronicler Sanudo described as "incredibly expensive." Then there was Ulugh Ali, the most daring of the Turkish admirals, who was patiently planning his revenge after having miraculously survived the Battle of Lepanto. Even he would eventually order a precious jewel case for his women from the goldsmith Battista Rizzoletti, whose shop was located on the Rialto under the sign of Jesus. However, by the time the casket actually arrived in Constantinople in 1598, the admiral had already died. According to the local diplomats, this inspired the *Bailo* to give it to the sultan himself, who was thrilled beyond belief.

Gold and Spices

We have already seen to what extent the Venetian diplomatic corps was actively involved in promoting foreign trade, especially with regard to opening up new markets abroad. The same was true of private individuals, whether they themselves were engaged in commercial activities, as was the case of Marco Polo, or whether they had a very different purpose in mind, such as the Blessed Odorico da Pordenone, whose missionary zeal led him to cross the entire continent of Asia between the years 1318 and 1330.

The list of these adventurous souls is endless. There was Marino Sanudo Torsello (1270-343), a wealthy patrician who made five separate journeys to China, and whose rather curious treatise on geography, nautical science, trade and economics, entitled *Liber secretorum fidelium Crucis*, proposed the annihilation of the Saracens, the annexing of Egypt, and a continental blockade against the Moslems (a project that would actually be carried out by Napoleon at the expense of the British Empire). Then there was Niccolò Zeno, who was shipwrecked on his way to Flanders in the late 13th century, and ended up in the Faroe Islands and Greenland, where he learned about the coast of North America from listening to the accounts of Scandinavian fishermen. There was Niccolò de'Conti, whose amazing experiences during his 25 years in Arabia, the Persian Gulf, the Malabar Coast and the Ganges were memorialized by the humanist Poggio Bracciolini. There was also *ser* Pietro Querini, who discovered the Lofoten Islands and crossed all of Scandinavia together with his friends Niccolò Michiel and Cristoforo Fioravanti after a terrifying journey over the turbulent waters of the Atlantic. Finally, there was Alvise da Mosto, who was the first European to explore the Cape Verde Islands in 1445 after having sailed down the west coast of Africa while in the service of the *Infante* of Portugal.

Above: State officials contracting out galleys to shippers in St. Marks's Square, as depicted by Gabriele Bella (Fondazione Querini Stampalia, Venice). Overseas trade involved both cargo ships leased by the state, which were guaranteed and protected, and vessels owned and operated by private individuals. Many of the merchants formed partnerships to share the enormous costs associated with purchasing goods, and equipping and manning the ships. The prices charged for the leasing of state-owned galleys varied according to the length of the voyage and market demand. Right: Two shipping contracts from 1488–89, the first of which refers to voyages to Aigues-Mortes, and the second to Beirut (Archivio di Stato, Venice).

One of the more interesting phenomena to emerge from all of this activity was the dispersion of the Venetian dialect throughout the Mediterranean Basin and beyond. It is up to the philologists themselves to decide how much of it survives to this day not only in the overseas colonies, but also on the mainland. What we do know for sure, however, is that a good half of the vocabulary used in spoken Greek is pure Venetian. Furthermore, almost the entire navigational terminology comes from the dialect as well *(orza, molla, drizza, finestrino, etc.)*. Even the word *"meltemi,"* which refers to the notorious mistral, the bane of all sailors during the summer months, derives from the Venetian for *"bel tempo,"* or *"good weather,"* since the wind itself disperses the clouds.

Besides the magistrates elected directly by the Senate, who handled major policy issues regarding commerce and trade, there were any number of minor officials who dealt with every possible contingency. As we have already seen, the state itself regulated duties and tariffs, acted as an intermediary in various financial negotiations, contracted out the merchant galleys, and assured them protection against the countless dangers lurking in the Mediterranean, whose waters were infested with adventurers, pirates, plunderers, rivals and enemy forces. In fact, the government knew only too well that the Republic's economic survival depended entirely on state control of the markets themselves, and the availability of vast sums of money to cover the staggering costs of maintaining her maritime supremacy.

What those who were violently opposed to Doge Francesco Foscari's expansionist ambitions feared most was the possibility that government resources would be diverted from the overseas colonies in favor of the mainland itself. In his last official speech, Foscari's predecessor, Tommaso Mocenigo, who led the opposition party, reminded his colleagues that it had always been the Republic's policy to "cultivate the sea and leave the land alone." Only by avoiding direct involvement in the chaotic events taking place throughout the Italian peninsula, driven by power-hungry potentates at constant war with one another for ultimate territorial control, would Venice actually be able to sustain her position as the "mistress of all the gold in Christendom."

In the end, the Venetians felt obliged to take over certain mainland territories, if for no other reason than to create a protective barrier between the fragile boundaries of the lagoon and the rest of the European continent in order to ensure that they would not become the victims of a universal conspiracy. This policy would eventually lead to a century or more of interminable wars that seriously depleted the gold reserves of both the *Serenissima* and her private citizens. Later on, when their worst nightmare had come true, and they were forced to defend themselves against the great continental powers, they had no choice but to hire the services of mercenaries in order to reinforce their own troops. At this point, they would find themselves teetering on the brink of bankruptcy, which proved to be disastrous for the financial community.

Despite these dire circumstances, the resources

of the Republic would not evaporate as rapidly as her enemies might have wished. In fact, in response to Pope Alexander Borgia VI's statement to the effect that Venice had finally lost her economic power, Cardinal Ascanio Sforza felt it necessary to reply: "Most blessed Father, the Venetians have more money than ever. . . . The collapse of the banking industry was due to bad management on the part of the bankers themselves rather than any deficiency of the central government. I guarantee that Your Holiness will hear an entirely different story from the Republic herself within the next several days."

Not even the violent attack unleashed by the Turks (which initially met with little resistance on the part of the Venetian fleet) would be enough to weaken the Republic's economy. Nor would Vasco da Gama's discovery of a trade route around the Cape of Good Hope in 1498, which gave Portuguese merchants direct access to the overseas spice markets, and allowed them to carry merchandise back to Lisbon without having to pay the heavy trans-shipment costs and customs duties imposed by intermediaries such as the Sultan of Egypt. Despite stiff competition from the Portuguese, which marked the end of her monopoly of the spice market, she would continue to trade actively with the

Egyptians. In fact, it was not until the 17th century, when the Dutch would form the powerful East India Companies, that she was actually excluded from trading in spices.

Between the time of Vasco da Gama's famous voyage and the arrival of the Dutch, there are those who

continue to insist that the Republic missed two extraordinary financial opportunities. In the first case, the circumstances speak for themselves. In 1499, when the Venetians learned that da Gama's ship had arrived in Lisbon laden with spices from the Orient, they immediately put diplomacy into action. However, when the King of Portugal cordially invited them to trade with him instead of the Egyptians, they refused his offer, not only because this would have meant losing the advantages of their monopoly in Alexandria, but also because trade with the East still represented the bulk of their commercial activities. What they agreed upon instead was to try and improve general conditions in Egypt, and set themselves up in direct competition with the Portuguese.

Once again, the wisdom and farsightedness of the Senate would play a critical role in deciding the fate of the Republic. At one point, there was even serious discussion about the possibility of digging a canal to take ships cross the Isthmus of Suez, which would have shortened the trade route considerably, and given the Venetian merchants a distinct advantage over their Portuguese rivals. Although this project was the subject of much debate on the part of the *Pregadi,* in the end, for reasons that were completely beyond the Republic's control, it would not be carried out. The second occasion presented itself in 1581, when Phillip II, the King Of Spain, offered the Venetians exclusive rights to the distribution of the enormous quantities of spices that had been traded by the Portuguese before their defeat at his hands. However, in this case as well, the Senate was less than enthusiastic about the offer: Not only did the state lack the proper fleet for such an endeavor; there was also the problem of too few shippers, and too little credit. Finally, there was the danger of being attacked by Phillip's enemies. In fact, they still refused when the offer was renewed, this time with guarantees that included military protection.

Was this really a golden opportunity to revive the Republic's sagging economy? First of all, it would have meant giving up trade in the Levant, which would have directly affected the lives of at least 4,000 Venetian expatriots. Furthermore, the volume of trade with the East was still enormous. In 1603, for example, some 105 years after the voyage of Vasco da Gama, the profits from trade with the city of Aleppo alone amounted to a million and a half gold ducats.

Be that as it may, the events that followed would prove that not only the Venetians had been right in rejecting Phillip's offer, but so had the Florentines, Genoese and Milanese. In fact, after the great German banking houses had accepted the offer instead, and had invested huge sums in the entire operation, they failed to reap the profits they had hoped for. As far as military protection was concerned, the resounding defeat of the *Invencible Armada* would show the world that the Atlantic was even more danger-

Left: Bill of lading for a galley trading with the Barbary Coast under the command of Giacomo Contarini (Archivio di Stato, Venice). State-controlled commerce employed armed galleys that traveled in convoys to Mediterranean and Atlantic ports at specific times of the year. During the 14th century, these so-called mude, which consisted of eight to 11 vessels, were generally used only for valuable cargo because of the greater security they offered.

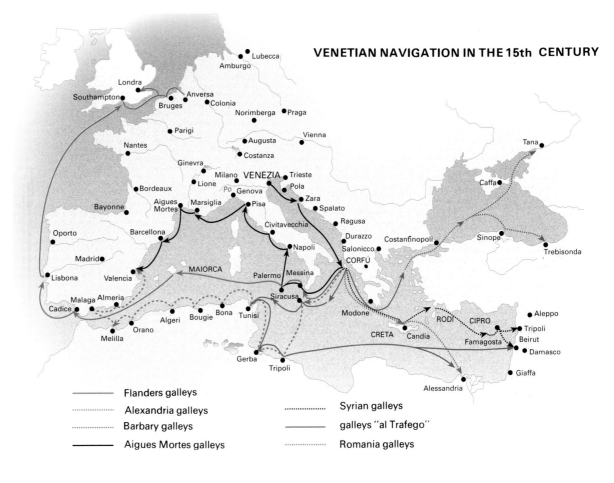

VENETIAN NAVIGATION IN THE 15th CENTURY

——— Flanders galleys
·········· Alexandria galleys
·········· Barbary galleys
——— Aigues Mortes galleys

·········· Syrian galleys
——— galleys "al Trafego"
·········· Romania galleys

ous than the Mediterranean for anyone carrying Spanish goods, whether directly or indirectly.

Piracy and Decadence

While Spain was enjoying her golden age in both literature and the arts, the Atlantic Ocean had become the setting for the adventures of such violent individuals as Drake, Raleigh and Morgan, all of whom were eager to grab as much as they could of the extraordinary riches arriving from the New World. In the Mediterranean, although pirates and plunderers had been problem for as long as anyone could remember, what had once been the province of daredevil ship-

owners and commanders of private vessels had now become a form of out-and-out warfare. In fact, privateering was being used by rulers and potentates not only as a means of acquiring ill-gotten gains, but also for ruining the fortunes of political rivals, and ridding the waters of dangerous competitors. For the Moslems and Saracens, who were merely following the commandments of the Prophet, as well as the Knights of Rhodes (and Malta), who were dedicated to waging a holy war against the infidels, it was even a way to get to heaven. The same principle inspired the Uzkok pirates, who justified the plundering of certain ships because they were carrying goods belonging to Moslems and Jews.

Among the most celebrated Genoese pirates of

medieval times, who were particularly colorful characters, we have already mentioned Enrico Pescatore, the Count of Malta, who attempted to hold out on the Island of Crete against the forces of the *Serenissima*.

We have also noted the grisly fate of Leone Vetrano, who ended up swinging from the mast of a galley in Ranieri Dandolo's fleet as punishment for having tried to keep Corfu for himself. Other names that have gone down in history are those of Guglielmo Guercio, Guglielmo Porco, Almanno da Costa and Raniero di Manente (who was actually from Pisa). Besides these legendary figures, there were the countless hordes of minor predators, some of whom were actually ships' captains themselves.

In later times, privateering became a powerful weapon in the arsenal of every monarch in Europe and beyond. Along with the King of Spain, the Archduke of Austria personally financed the excursions of the Uzkok pirates, whom he used repeatedly to undermine Venice's monopoly of the Adriatic. The Republic herself captured or sank more than one Barbary ship (the Berbers, who were Arabs from Maghreb, were incorrigible pirates), whereupon Constantinople never failed to take offense and threaten serious reprisals. The Spaniards themselves, for whom Venice's independence had always been a thorn in the flesh, armed their own pirates as well. However, the most enterprising of all the "powers that be" was the Grand Duke of Tuscany, who used the pretext of a "holy war" to assure Leghorn of an unending supply of galley slaves. In fact, he went so far as to found a religious order along the lines of the Knights of St. John of Jerusalem (better known as the Knights of Rhodes and Malta), which he called the Knights of St. Stephen. Under the banner of the cross, they captured countless slaves on the high seas, who were then put on the block in the Tuscan port.

As of the 16th century, the slave trade in the West no longer catered to the same market. Forever gone were the Tartar peasants who had tilled the Cretan soil, and the Circassian women who had warmed the beds of Venetian and Genoese merchants. In their place were galley slaves, who were used as the "motor power" of the time. (In the case of Venice, they were also employed to drive the great galleasses. These long, narrow vessels, armed to the teeth, would be the main protagonists in the victory of Lepanto in 1571, which finally put an end to Turkish dominion in the Mediterranean.)

In any case, once a pirate ship had appeared on the scene, the lives of those who were traveling by sea, whether they were merchants or pilots, captains or galley slaves, noble cross bowmen or pilgrims to the Holy Land, literally hung by a thread. Although some of these poor souls actually died by the sword, most of them ended up being sold as slaves in places like Tunis, Algiers, Jedda and Saana. This sorry state of affairs led to the founding of two religious orders, the *Mercedari* and "The Most Holy Trinity for the Redemption of Slaves," whose mission was that of procuring the release of such "prisoners." Their members, who wear a red and blue cross on their breasts to this day, have donated enormous sums of money in an effort to ransom thousands of hapless individuals, most of whom have been captured at sea.

Apart from the coastal pirates, there was also the imported variety, most of whom were English. At this point, the Mediterranean Sea, whose waters had always been dangerous, now became virtually impassable. In fact,

the scourge of piracy and privateering during the 17th century would mark the beginning of the end of the Venetian economy.

Although the name "Petrus Flabianus phiolarius" (phial-maker) is featured in a document dating from as far back as 1090, he was most certainly not the first glass-blower in Venice. In fact, excavations have shown that the glass-making industry had flourished from the earliest of times. We also know that the facilities were transferred to the Island of Murano in the year 1292 because of the serious risk of fire.

According to the notes accompanying the 18th-century drawings by Jan Grevembroch, which are displayed on these two pages, "Venice has become famous for her skilled craftsmen, who produce a quality of glass superior to that of any other nation.... The glass itself is blown over an open fire by a workforce of more than one thousand men, who move about half-naked and soaked in sweat ... and who toil night and day except for the months of August and September ... when they are free to amuse themselves with such activities as the running of the bulls and other rowdy sports ... and at certain times during Carnevale, when they participate in sumptuous banquets, which are accompanied by music and dancing...."

Every possible effort was made by the central government to ensure that the secrets of the trade were not revealed to their foreign competitors. In fact, those workers who chose to use their skills to the detriment of the state were ordered to return home immediately, after which their entire family was imprisoned, and they themselves were murdered by hired assassins. Other protective measures included a special government dispensation that allowed any male offspring of a marriage between a member of the nobility and a glass-blower's daughter to participate in the proceedings of the *Maggior Consiglio*.

As is still the case today, the craftsmen of Murano produced not only such exquisite items as plates, bowls, goblets, cups, glasses and jugs in both clear and colored glass, many of which were decorated with the likes of enamel, filigree and *millefiori*, but also a wide variety of mirrors and window panes. The basic tool of the trade was the kiln itself, as depicted in a 16th-century engraving from Georg Bauer's famous *De re metallica* (5), which was inspired by the facilities at Murano. Each opening in the oven contained a crucible from which the worker (1) would remove a certain amount of molten glass with his rod. The object in question was then shaped by blowing through the rod itself, with the help of a marver, or marble slab, on which the glass was rolled as it was crafted.

The other tools of the trade were relatively simple (4), beginning with the rod itself (a), which was

700 YEARS OF GLASS-MAKING ON MURANO

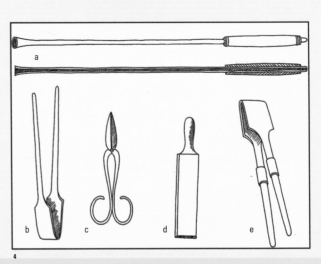

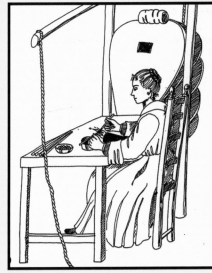

basically a metal tube with a funnel-shaped handle known as the *"morso."* Then there were the metal pliers (b), equipped with wooden handles (e), the *"ferrabate"* (d), which were utilized to shape the glass itself, and finally the shears (c), whose purpose was to cut an object down to the required size (3). This last procedure often involved the assistance of an apprentice, whose services were also used to "pull out" the tubes of glass in order to obtain the desired length and thickness (9).

One of the main sources of income for the industry as a whole was the production of window panes, as was noted in the 12th century by the monk Theophilus in a work entitled *Diversarum artium schedula*. The manufacturing process itself involved shearing a glass cylinder at both ends, and then slitting it down the side with a red-hot iron (2), whereupon it was placed in front of a flattening kiln (6) with the slit facing up, and gradually pushed inside. As the heat softened the glass, the cylinder opened up, after which it was flattened out with a pole.

The glass bead industry, which has also survived to this day, employed the skills of craftsmen known as *margariteri* (7), who produced small beads for embroidery and beadwork, and *perleri* (8), who manufactured beads for jewelry and trimmings. Once again, the notes accompanying Grevembroch's drawings tell us that the "diligent work" of the *margariteri* consisted in "carefully heating, cutting and shaping the (glass) tubes made in Murano . . . thereby producing beads that are . . . even admired on the continent of India." As for the *perleri*, "While the glass is melted over a low flame, the craftsmen turn out beads of incredible symmetry, in a thousand different styles."

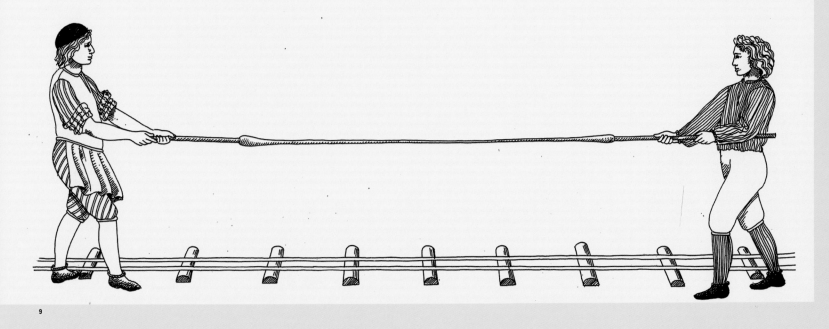

If we go back through the city's history, we can see that there were pirates at every turn, starting with the Slavs themselves, although there is still some doubt as to whether the legendary Gaiolo, who supposedly carried off the brides at Santa Maria Formosa, was actually Slavic or Triestino. Next came the Narentines, who would learn the hard way that Doge Pietro II Orseolo was out for blood. Then there were the Ragusans (who were actually merchants by trade, but who occasionally bent the rules), the Almissans and the Dulcignoti, all of whom were camped out on the opposite side of the Adriatic. There were also the Saracens and Normans, who would eventually be defeated by the Emperor of Byzantium. Finally, there were the hordes of Genoese and Pisan pirates, followed by the Greeks, who were sworn to avenge their captivity at the hands of the eastern Latin empire.

In the middle of the 14th century, the barbaric Catalan pirates would enter the picture as well when they attacked Attica and its surrounding territory, whereupon the Byzantine Emperor, John Cantacuzene, committed the colossal error of bringing the first contingent of Turks from Asia to Europe. In fact,

these marauders would soon establish a reign of terror in the entire Aegean, during which islanders, merchant seamen and feudal lords alike were captured and held for ransom. To make matters even worse, the Algerian pirate Khair-ad-din, known to the world as Barbarossa, would devastate over half of the Mediterranean Basin in the name of the sultan (though at his own risk), and even challenge the might of the Hapsburgs. While those who followed in his footsteps would pale by comparison, his own legacy would endure for many years to come. In fact, the last naval campaign against the Berbers was launched by the *Provveditore Straordinario* Angelo Emo in 1784.

Despite all of the above, it was not until the 17th century that acts of piracy would reach an all-time high. By that time, the Uzkoks, who sailed the turbulent waters of the Quarnaro in long, narrow boats that resembled the "drakkars" of the early Normans, had proven to be so troublesome that *Provveditori* and military commanders alike would pursue them mercilessly on land and at sea, often losing their own lives in the bargain.

The historian A. Tenenti, who has described privateering as the most flourishing industry in the

Portrait of Suleiman the Magnificent wearing the fabulous crown manufactured by Venetian goldsmiths in the year 1532 (from an anonymous woodcut). In his personal diaries, Marin Sanudo describes the object in question as follows: "This very morning, I, Marin Sanudo, saw the most remarkable item on the Rialto. It was a beautiful gold helmet that had been crafted by Caorlini, with precious jewels and four different tiers. The plume, which was absolutely exquisite, was adorned by four large rubies and diamonds. The diamonds themselves were worth 10,000 ducats, and the pearls were each 12 carats in size. There was also a very fine emerald, and a large turquoise stone, both of which were extremely valuable. The plume was made from the delicate, colorful feathers of a bird that is native to India, which are also very costly. Rumor has it that this helmet will be sold to the Turkish lord for more than 100,000 ducats. The object itself was crafted by several different individuals, including the sons of both Sier Piero Zen and the Turkish orator, Sier Jacomo Corner, as well as Sier Piero Morexini, and the above-mentioned Caorlini. It will be sent to Constantinople in the care of Sier Marco Antonio Sanudo, who will be paid a salary of 2,000 ducats over a period of eight months, as well as living expenses, and two percent of the profits from the sale. . . . He is scheduled to leave within the next two weeks, whereupon he will go by ship to Ragusa, and then proceed by land to Constantinople under a heavy military escort."

Mediterranean in the 1600s, has also painted a tragicomic picture of the comings and goings of the pirate ships, which were so numerous that the waters themselves must have looked like a crowded railroad station. Witness the case of the Venetian consul at Milos, in the Cyclades, who informed the Senate in July of 1607 that *bertoni* (rapid, easily maneuverable pirate ships) had been passing by right under his nose since the previous November. First there had been the *Golden Lion,* which had sailed by on November 12th, with a crew of 150 and 50 cannon, commanded by a certain Antonio Carara. On November 18th, Antonio Rucaforte's *bertone* had been sighted, armed with 30 cannon and 300 musketeers. On December 10th, two French *bertoni* had appeared on the scene, with 20 artillery and 180 soldiers each. On December 24th, a Dutch bark named *St. John* had passed by, fitted out in Sardinia and commanded by the French knight Monsieur de Roville, with 140 men and 40 cannon on board. On February 29th, the galleon *San Spirito,* commanded by Simon Galia, had shown up with 50 cannon, 400 soldiers, and an escort of three *bertoni* and a ship from Ragusa. On April 13th, the galleon *Il Sole,* commanded by a captain from Nice, had docked in Milos itself, followed by the ship *Zena.* The following day, Count Alfonso di Montecuccoli had arrived with 14 vessels belonging to the Grand Duke of Tuscany. Shortly thereafter, another 18 *bertoni* had been sighted offshore.

Given the current state of affairs, maritime trade literally declined overnight, due mainly to the fact that the merchants were no longer willing to run such enormous risks. As far as the sailors themselves were concerned, local recruitment had come to a dead halt, and the situation in Istria and Dalmatia was not much better. Furthermore, now that the patricians were safely ensconced in the green fields and gently rolling hills of the Veneto, Brescia and Bergamo, they saw no reason whatsoever why they should not abandon the traditions of their ancestors in favor of agriculture and real estate investments. After all, hailstorms were a lot less dangerous than the Uzkoks, and sudden frosts could not even begin to compete with the Algerians or the Knights of Malta and St. Stephen.

This was the prelude to the economic decline of the Republic herself, which would eventually lead to a major political crisis. In fact, as of the end of the 16th century, the members of the Venetian nobility, who had once been the mainstay of commerce and trade (as opposed to their "foolish" counterparts in the provinces, who would actually go to the extent of excluding anyone engaged in commercial activities from participating in parliamentary debates) would turn in on themselves, having chosen to rely instead on a regular income from farming and property ownership. Gone were the days of dealing with China, India, England and the Berbers. Times had changed, and the heirs of the great merchant families were more than content to retreat to the bucolic life of the mainland. What had once been the exclusive realm of the great doges, from Giuliano Parteciaco to Sebastiano and Pietro Ziani (whom the economist G. Luzzatto has compared to the Rockefellers and the Aga Khan in terms of their enormous wealth), and the pride and joy of the Cornaro and Mocenigo, was of little or no interest to their descendants, who were extremely critical of Doge Nicolò Sagredo's involvement in his family's lumber business at the end of the 17th century. Gone as well were the famous patrons of the arts.

Aside from the private practice of law, which involved only a small percentage of the aristocrats despite the profits to be gained, active participation in the affairs of state had also gone by the boards. By the

Below: The cesèndelo was a small lantern used to light one's way through the dark streets at night. Above: A plate with Apollo and the Muses. Both pieces are from the 16th century (Museo d'Arte vetraria di Murano (Venice).

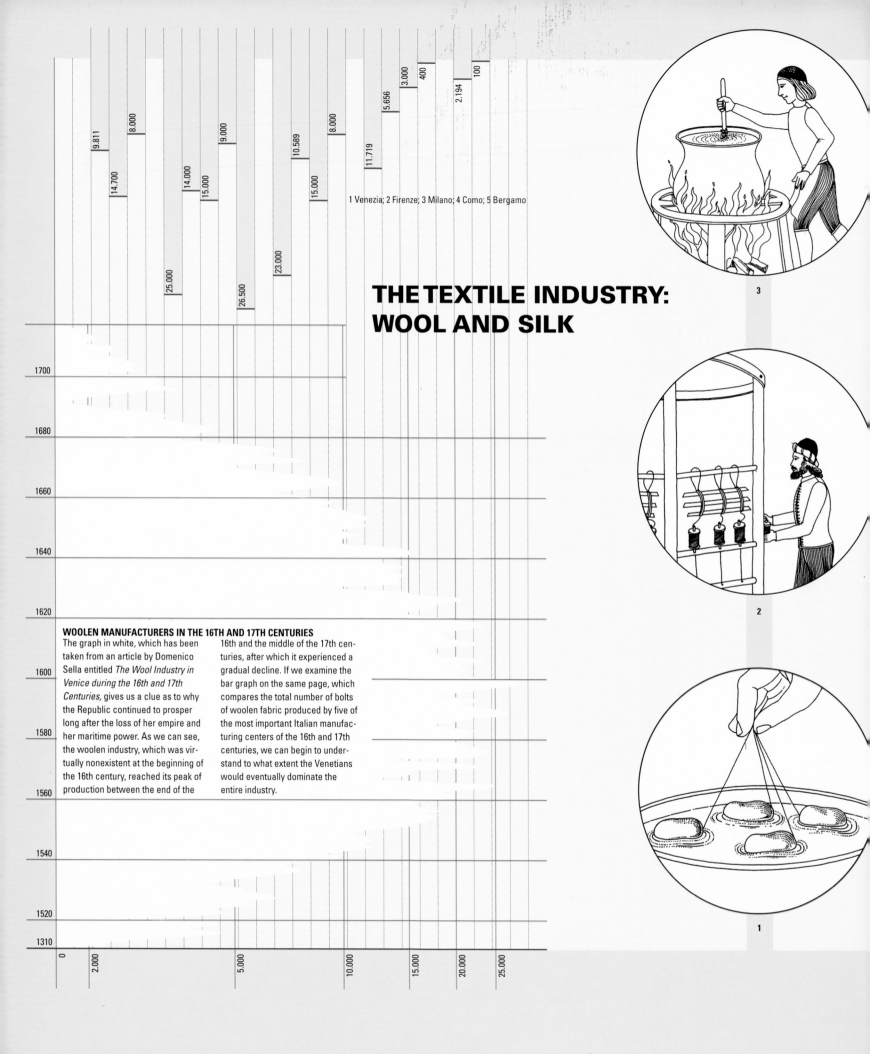

9.811

14.700

8.000

25.000

14.000

15.000

9.000

26.500

10.589

23.000

15.000

8.000

11.719

5.656

3.000

400

2.194

100

1 Venezia; 2 Firenze; 3 Milano; 4 Como; 5 Bergamo

THE TEXTILE INDUSTRY: WOOL AND SILK

3

2

WOOLEN MANUFACTURERS IN THE 16TH AND 17TH CENTURIES

The graph in white, which has been taken from an article by Domenico Sella entitled *The Wool Industry in Venice during the 16th and 17th Centuries,* gives us a clue as to why the Republic continued to prosper long after the loss of her empire and her maritime power. As we can see, the woolen industry, which was virtually nonexistent at the beginning of the 16th century, reached its peak of production between the end of the 16th and the middle of the 17th centuries, after which it experienced a gradual decline. If we examine the bar graph on the same page, which compares the total number of bolts of woolen fabric produced by five of the most important Italian manufacturing centers of the 16th and 17th centuries, we can begin to understand to what extent the Venetians would eventually dominate the entire industry.

1700

1680

1660

1640

1620

1600

1580

1560

1540

1520

1310

1

0

2.000

5.000

10.000

15.000

20.000

25.000

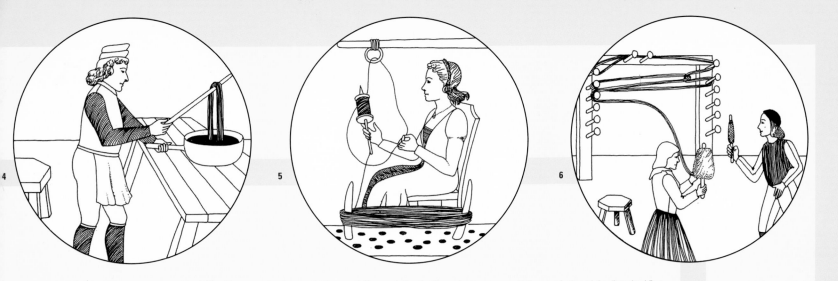

4   5   6

The textile workers were as important to the Venetian economy as the glass-blowers, shipbuilders, sugar and wax refiners, and numerous arts and crafts associations. While the woolen industry was not fully developed until the 16th century, which was considerably later than in other Italian cities, the silk manufacturers provided one of the main sources of income for the state from the 13th to the 15th centuries.

Wool and silk were actually "cottage industries," since the craftsmen involved in the various stages of the manufacturing process worked out of their own homes. The entire production schedule was in the hands of certain merchants, who were responsible for everything from providing the necessary capital to purchasing the raw materials to making sure that the work itself was delivered from one craftsman to the next. In fact, a document from the 16th century describes a particular piece of silk as having passed through "16 hands," meaning that 16 different workers had been involved in the production process.

1 The first step in the production of silk, which was called "reeling," involved unwinding the filaments from several cocoons at a time after they had been soaked in boiling water. The cocoons themselves were imported from Spain, Sicily and the Far East.
2 Two to three strands of silk were then twisted together by a master craftsman known as the "maestro da filatoi," who used his own twisting frame in the process.
3 After twisting, the silk was boiled in large vats to remove any sticky substances. The workmen who performed this particular task were called "cocitori."

4 The next step in the process was dyeing the skeins themselves.
5 The silk was then wound onto bobbins by female workers known as "incannaresse." This was one of the preparatory stages for weaving.
6 Before it was woven, the silk was divided into batches by means of a warping machine. Whereas today, one batch usually consists of 80 strands, in earlier times, there were at least 400 strands per batch for satin, and 300 for damask.
7 The weavers themselves (as depicted in a painted insignia from the Weavers' Guild) were divided into two groups: the "vellutai," who

produced velvet, and the "samitari," who worked with silk. When the fabrics contained designs, the heddles were prepared by female workers known as "imbarbaresse" and "levaresse."

Right: Detail from an illuminated "mariegola," or "rule book," of the Weavers' Guild, showing how raw wool was actually weighed.

7

the exception of those whose financial circumstances offered them no other alternatives. (As we have already mentioned several times, the most prestigious government posts were also the most expensive.) Rather than serving out their time in the likes of Padua, Verona, Brescia or Bergamo, the members of the aristocracy were only too happy to pay the prescribed fine, which was a pittance compared to what they would have spent to fulfill their civic responsibilities.

In the end, only the wealthiest of the patricians could actually afford to hold high office. (Not only the *dogado*, but also ambassadorships and important overseas posts had become so financially burdensome that the government itself would have little choice in the matter.) In fact, those of their colleagues who lacked the necessary funds to compete on an equal basis were obliged to serve as members of the *Quarantie*, perhaps, or as lower-level bureaucrats in the colonies. As far as the *Barnabotti* themselves were concerned, who represented the majority in the *Maggior Consiglio*, there was nothing left for them but the bottom of the barrel. This resulted in the establishment of an oligarchy within the ranks of the aristocracy itself, which would play a major role in the ultimate demise of the Republic.

beginning of the 18th century, public offices that were considered "hardship duty," such as the *Reggimenti* themselves, would attract fewer and fewer nobles, with

religious fervor, and even a few strokes of political genius. As for the permissive nature of their society, which has been so severely criticized by moralistic historians, they were certainly no more licentious than their European neighbors. If anything, they stood out among their 18th-century contemporaries for their love of music and the theater, their style of painting, which would influence artists throughout the continent, and their passion

Before the end actually came, however, the Venetians enjoyed a magnificent Indian summer marked by a flourishing of arts and letters, waves of for architecture (the so-called *"mal della pietra,"* or "stone fever"), which would leave the world a lasting legacy of palaces and churches.

Above: Eighteenth-century engraving by G. F. Costa, depicting Lizza di Fusina, which is situated at the mouth of the Brenta River. Here we can see a number of different types of boats, including gondolas, punts, scows, barges and lighters. Left: The so-called "Carro di Fusina," which was used to transport canal boats from one water level to another. Opposite page: Caccia in valle (Duck-hunting in the Marshes), by Vittore Carpaccio. Due to her unique location, Venice was one of the few cities that were not fortified by walls. The lagoon itself served not only as a line of defense, but also as a means of communication and an important source of food.

Above: Novices on Their Way to Visiting Convents *(Gabriele Bella). Opposite page: Interior of San Nicolò dei Mendicoli.* Although the Venetians had traditionally followed the teachings of the Catholic Church, they were equally dedicated to the well-being of the Republic. In fact, the laws of the land stipulated that whenever ecclesiastical issues came up for debate in the Maggior Consiglio or the Senate, the first order of business was to remove from chambers the so-called "papalisti" (those who had

Under the direction of such celebrated composers as Vivaldi, Porpora and Cimarosa, the local "conservatories," which were state-subsidized homes for orphaned girls, encouraged their wards to become virtuoso musicians. Giambattista Tiepolo traveled to Milan, Würzburg and Madrid, where he demonstrated the same imaginative skills that he had used to create the extraordinary frescoes for the Palazzo Labia and the Villa Pisani. Goldoni took his comedies to Paris, where they enjoyed an enormous success, along with the plays of Gozzi and Chiari. Thanks to the initiatives of Gasparo Gozzi, the art of modern journalism was born.

Then, of course, there was the Venetian *Carnevale,* the great *kermesse* that lasted almost the entire year.

Monarchs and adventurers poured into the city, protected by the anonymity of the carnival masks, which made everyone equal, whether male or female, rich or poor, honest or dishonest, native-born or foreign. There were also celebrations the likes of which the world had never seen before. When King Gustav III of Sweden made a state visit to Venice, the Pisani family put on such a feast in his honor at their villa in Stra that they ruined themselves financially, and their astonished guest openly confessed that he would never be able to repay such magnificent hospitality in his own kingdom. At a ball in honor of King Frederick IV of Denmark and Norway, the pearl necklace of his dancing partner broke, scattering the beads across the floor. When the king himself bent down to help

gather them up, the lady's husband, who was a Querini, nonchalantly trampled the precious jewels under his feet.

In the midst of all these excesses, however, there were also the worthy bourgeois of Goldoni's comedies, who were just as loyal and law-abiding as ever. Among the patricians themselves, there were still any number of simple souls, such as a certain Grimani, who was

observed (by none other than a spy in the service of the State Inquisitors) lunching on a slice of hot polenta after he had come out of an important political meeting. Then there were the members of the *Maggior Consiglio*, many of whom would traipse over to the famous *"malvasia"* at the Ponte del Rimedio for a glass of Cyprus wine and a piece of cake while still dressed in their wigs and robes.

relatives high up in the church, or who were in any way beneficiaries of the papacy).In such cases, the official minutes would always begin with the phrase, "Cazzadi (cacciati) i papalisti . . ." ("The followers of the pope having been removed . . .").

WARS, ARMIES, VICTORIES AND DEFEATS

VENICE AND THE TURKS, THE VENETIAN ARMADA, FORTRESSES AND GENERALS, NEUTRALITY AND THE END

Pirates and privateers in the Mediterranean were not the only enemies that Venice had to contend with. In fact, her entire history was an endless succession of armed conflicts that involved everything from establishing and protecting certain markets to conquering and defending an empire. Above all else, there was simply the need to survive.

We have already mentioned the Franks, hungry for new territory, who went down to defeat after having dared to attack the lagoon, and the Hungarians, greedy for spoils, who had eventually met the same fate. But the biggest battles of all were fought against the *comuni* and *signori* on the mainland, who would have been perfectly content to see the Venetians drown in their own salty waters.

Even before he attempted to piece together a continental state for himself, Mastino della Scala, the lord of Verona, would put his own merchants and customs officials right on the border of the lagoon. The Visconti of Milan, who were intent upon conquering the whole of northern Italy and Tuscany, would begin looking eastward after having taken possession of Genoa. The most pernicious of these enemies, however, were the Carraresi of Padua, who were also the most perfidious.

Although the Carreresi had originally appealed to the Venetians for help in ousting the Scaligeri family, who were then the rulers of this ancient city whose roots supposedly went back to Antenor, they would turn their backs on their former allies soon after they had

taken over the reins of power. In fact, Francesco il Vecchio, who was known as the "Carrarese fox," had imperialist designs of his own, starting with his efforts to destroy the Venetian economy by competing directly in the all-important salt market. (Thanks to the profits from agriculture and local industry, and a prosperous banking community, he had more than enough financial resources to do so.) Not only did he begin acquiring enormous quantities of salt from the Archbishop of Salzburg (whose mines would lend their name to his official seat), but he also decided to establish refineries at the edge of the lagoon itself. This was tantamount to beating the Venetians on their own turf.

Then there was the Patriarch of Aquileia, who planned on taking control of Istria, and the Archduke of Austria, who had his heart set on Feltre, Belluno and Treviso, which he considered part of his realm. And let us not forget the King of Hungary, who actually laid siege to Dalmatia, and somehow managed to hold on to it for a number of years.

As far as the mainland was concerned, Venice had no one to count on but herself. After the war against the League of Cambrai, when her citizens had invaded terra firma to defend Padua from the Emperor Maximilian (who would lose both the war and his own reputation), her only alternatives were allies who were less than reliable, and mercenaries who were less than loyal.

Despite these circumstances, however, she would have her moments of glory, as in 1438, when she trans-

Fragment of the tomb of Raimondo Lupi di Soragna (Oratorio di San Giorgio, Padua). Although she reigned supreme in the Mediterranean, Venice still had to defend herself tool and nail against the cities on the mainland, which lusted after her wealth and maritime power. Among the local signori who gave her the most trouble were Mastino della Scala, the lord of Verona, the Visconti of Milan, and the Carraresi of Padua, all of whom attempted at one time or another to attack her borders. The Republic was forced to entrust her security on terra firma to allies who were not always reliable, and mercenaries who were not always loyal. Along with the great military leaders in her pay, such as Bartolomeo Colleoni and Bartolomeo d'Alviano, there were also the likes of the Count of Carmagnola, who was condemned to death for treason.

ported an entire fleet over hill and dale to Lake Garda in order to do battle with the Visconti in the Bresciano. According to a nautical engineer by the name of Sorbolo, she succeeded in hauling two galleys (others would say six), several frigates, and a score of large boats over the terrain by means of teams of oxen. This entire operation, the likes of which had never been seen before, would end up costing the equivalent of £3,300,000,000. In the end, the members of the *Signoria* were obliged to admit that the money had been well spent.

The rest of the Republic's wars would be fought under the leadership of the great mercenaries of the day, from Bartolomeo Colleoni, who willed his huge estate to Venice, to Bartolomeo d'Alviano, Renzo da Ceri, Niccolò Orsini, and Francesco Bussone, the Count of Carmagnola, who was condemned to death

for treason after being tried before the Council of Ten (and whose sentence was more than justified, despite all the tears shed by Alessandro Manzoni). The Venetian high command was occasionally represented by "honorary" patricians, such as Girolamo di Savorgnan, who were given the rank of "*Collaterali Generali*," but more often than not, it was assigned to the so-called "*Provveditori in Campo.*" Although certain of these officers were totally inept, as was the case of Zaccaria Sagredo, who abandoned his troops entirely in Valeggio in the year 1630, most of them proved to be extremely efficient, despite their lack of experience in fighting on terra firma. Among these were Giovanni Dolfin, who was elected doge in 1356 while under siege by the Hungarians in Treviso, and who left the city with banners unfurled to return home and take over the reins of government, and Andrea Gitti, who dedicated his life to recouping the losses suffered during the war against the League of Cambrai.

During the 1400s, the Venetians would score one military after another, including a skirmish at Barberino di Mugello in Tuscany. (This was quite a distance from home for those whose "sea-legs," which were the butt of jokes by everyone from Boccaccio to Ariosto, supposedly made them incapable of riding horses or walking on dry land!) In the 1700s, when the Republic had already adopted a policy of neutrality, she entrusted her territorial defense to the "*Cernide,*" or "Home Guard," whom Ippolito Nievo so delighted in poking fun at in his *Confessions of an Italian*. With all due respect to that great writer and patriot, we also owe a little respect to the *Cernide* themselves. Admittedly, they were a scruffy bunch, and anything but efficient. However, these ordinary townspeople and peasants, who were responsible for protecting the homes and fields of country folk, were the forerunners of the "National Guard" that played such an important part in the democratic process during the years following the French Revolution.

The other 18th-century militias, such as *bombisti* and artillerymen, were obviously far more professional. As far as the regular army was concerned, most of its members came from the ranks of the mainland provinces, whose infantry regiments bore the names of their principal cities. There were also cavalrymen, dragoons, and cuirassiers, all of whom were stationed in strongholds and forts, including the great fortress at Verona, which was the site of the famous military college as well.

Despite all of the above, the survival of the Republic herself would always depend on battles fought on the high seas. In fact, among the most treacherous of her enemies, there were the Saracens and Normans, whom she eventually defeated in collaboration with the emperors of Byzantium. Then there were the deadly Narentine pirates, whom she was forced to war against in order to protect the navigation lanes and trade routes from their constant assaults. Her worst enemy, however, was the powerful city-state of Genoa, which she fought for over 200 years.

The mortal combat between these two relentless rivals began in the waters of Greece and Sardinia, and then shifted to Curzola in the Adriatic, where Lamba Doria defeated the Venetian fleet in 1298 during the most bloody battle in her history. In fact, so many galleys were eventually captured that it was impossible for Doria to tow them back to Genoa, Instead, he had them burned on the spot. In the end, the Venetian admiral, Andrea Dandolo, would crush his own skull against the side of the Genoese galley on which he was being held prisoner to atone for this terrible loss.

In 1379, when their ships invaded the lagoon as far as Poveglia and Malamocco, in sight of the bell-tower of St. Mark, the Genoesi actually showed up on the city's doorstep, whereupon they promptly took possession of Chioggia. At the same time, she was in danger of being attacked from the mainland by the combined forces of the Lord of Padua, the Patriarch of Aquileia and the King of Hungary. After mobilizing her military forces, and mustering all the courage that was needed to face such a dire situation, she would finally emerge victorious in 1381. As a result, Genoa disappeared forever from the international political scene, despite her enormous wealth and influence.

No sooner had the Genoesi been defeated, however, than the Venetians were confronted with serious problems in the East, including the terrible Catalan pirates, who had set about sacking the whole of Greece. Then there were the Ottoman Turks, whom the Republic would battle without interruption for the next 400 years both on land and at sea. After it was all over but the shouting, both sides were still in their own corners of the Mediterranean "boxing ring," worn out and thoroughly discouraged.

For any number of reasons, Venice's longstanding relationship with the Turks was neither simple nor straightforward. Aside from their powerful presence in the Mediterranean, where they would eventually take over the entire Arab world, including North Africa, after having driven the Mamelukes out of Egypt, they were a major force to be reckoned with in the Balkans. During the first stage of Ottoman expansionism, the Venetians would find themselves battling the Turks all the way from Smyrna, where the *Capitano Generale da Mar,* Pietro Zeno, was murdered at the foot of the altar while attending Mass, to Negropont, to Constantinople, which was conquered by Mehmed II in 1453, when

Fourteenth-century drawings by Giannino Cattaneo of cavalrymen engaged in combat, from Livy's First Decad.

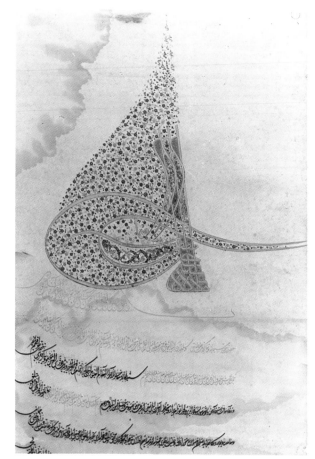

what reluctantly by the King of France could not even begin to hold a candle to the Venetian forces themselves. When we consider the actual size of the Ottoman Empire, and the infinite resources available to the wealthy, powerful European states, which provided only meager support in the defense of the island itself during the 25 long years that it was under siege, the military exploits of the Republic, who was basically left to her own devices, were unparalleled in the annals of modern history.

Throughout the course of some 400 years of open warfare, guerilla attacks, battles, skirmishes, and occasional forays, the dedication and depth of vision demonstrated by the Venetian commanders themselves is well worth mentioning. There were notable exceptions to the rule, of course, as was the case of the *Capitano Generale* da Canal (whom Sanudo referred to as the *"General Dottor"*), a highly educated gentleman who was condemned to a life in exile after his inexperience and ineptitude as a military commander had proven to be at least partially responsible for the loss of Negropont. (As Sanudo himself would point out, however, the poor man had been appointed for purely political reasons, and the ultimate blame lay with those who

had entrusted him with such a position.) Then there was the rather pathetic example of Antonio Grimani, "the ruination of the Christians," who lost to the Turks in the waters of Sapienza in 1499 after a half-hearted attempt at defending the interests of the Republic. (He himself had been elected to the supreme command because he was the only one available who was willing or able to pay the entire crew in cash.) Unfortunately, there were also a number of other admirals who were either too cowardly or too unprofessional to fulfill their required duties.

Then there were the men whose intelligence, organizational skills and extraordinary courage made them truly great military leaders. Such was the case of Lazzaro Mocenigo, a young, high-spirited patrician of the 17th century, who returned to Venice as soon as his term as admiral was over in order to re-join the fleet as a simple *Venturiere*, which was the title given to former commanders who were willing to serve their country without the benefit of a commission or rank. In 1657, however, he was re-elected *Capitano Generale da Mar* (commanders-in-chief were among the candidates who were actually elected by the ballot system rather than being nominated for office) as part of a plan to take

the war against the Turks to Constantinople, the capital of the Ottoman Empire, with its military bases and arsenals, by gaining access to the Sea of Marmara and the Bosphorus via the Strait of the Dardenelles. Tragically, at the very moment when it looked as if he would actually succeed in this daring attempt, Mocenigo's skull was crushed by the standard that had been hoisted onto the top of the mast, which had been shattered by cannon fire. The circumstances of his heroic death, which marked the end of the enterprise, were commemorated in an ode from the "Book of Merops," which is part of the work by Gabriele d'Annunzio entitled *In Praise of the Sky, the Sea, the Earth and Their Heroes*. Although the poet himself is out of fashion these days (not entirely without reason), in this author's opinion, these verses are a worthy tribute to Mocenigo's memory: ". . . on the same galley that was left/with only the horror of the blackened debris/on the same galley whose prow would turn/and plow to earth the cowardly Mehmed/the victorious Lazzaro Mocenigo/returned from the Dardenelles/while the shaft of the standard on the mast/ that cleft his poor skull in two/cried softly in the wind. . . ."

A similar campaign had been launched at a somewhat earlier date by Admiral Lorenzo Marcello, who also lost his life in the process. Although future attempts would fail as well, in the case of Cyprus, Crete and Corfu, and the waters of the Aegean, Ionian and Mediterranean, the commanders of the final naval battles would prove to be as brilliant as the legendary *condottieri* of the Republic's golden age, among whose ranks were the brave admirals that led the Venetian fleet to victory in the war against Genoa at Chioggia. There was Vetter Pisani, the "father of all seamen,"

whose humanity and generosity inspired his men to plead with the *Pregadi* for his reinstatement as supreme commander after his term of office had expired in 1380. There was also Carlo Zeno, who was as refined a man of letters as he was an adventurer on the high seas. Finally, there was Andrea Contarini, who took command of the navy while acting as head of state when he was already well into his eighties.

Besides the extraordinary series of paintings in the Doges' Palace, which serve to celebrate the daring feats of these great men, there are the commemorative statues on the tombs of the heroes themselves, many of which are located in the Churches of Santa Maria Gloriosa dei Frari and SS. Giovanni e Paolo. They are an impressive lot indeed, stretched out on their sarcophagi or standing atop their funerary monuments, dressed in breastplate and cuisses, with their fists clenched around the rod of command. In SS. Giovanni e Paolo, underneath the superb Renaissance statue of Pietro Mocenigo, who was elected doge after his military victory at Smyrna, we can read the inscription, *"ex hostium manubiis"* ("paid for with plunder from the enemy"). Another Mocenigo, Alvise Leonardo, who was carried out of the besieged town of Candia at the head of his troops after he had fallen seriously ill, now lies in state on a magnificent tomb in the Church of San Lazzaro dei Mendicanti. Francesco Morosini, who would go down in history as the conqueror of Attica and the Peloponnese, was the last of the doges to serve as supreme commander of the fleet. After his death in Nauplia (Napoli di Romania) in 1694, the Turks themselves ordered a cease-fire in honor of their great adversary, as they had already done once before during the funeral of Alvise Leonardo Mocenigo. His

the Turks were somewhat in awe of the Republic's western culture, which represented everything that their religion and moral code militated against, but which they had come to regard as far more civilized than their own

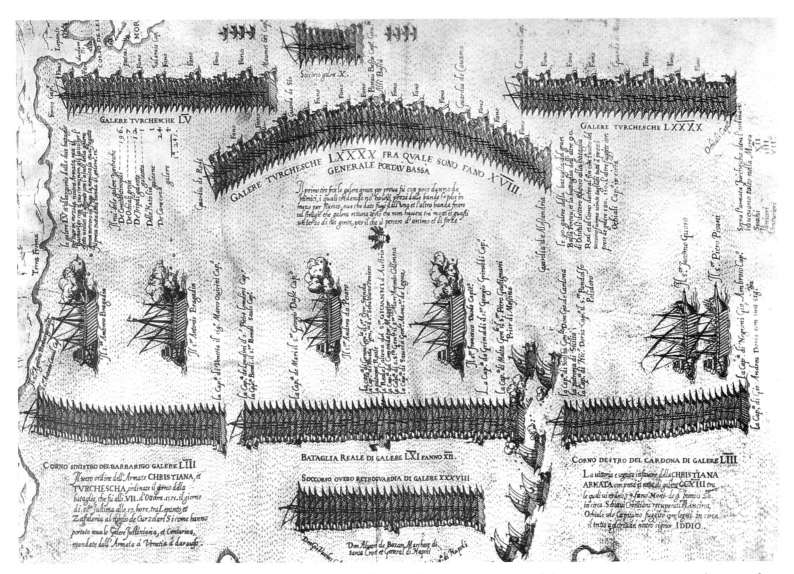

own funerary rites are commemorated in a rather curious series of paintings from his palace in Campo Santo Stefano, which are now on display in the Museo Correr.

The last of the great admirals of the *Serenissima* was Angelo Emo, who would launch a military excursion against the marauding Berbers of the Maghreb barely 10 years before the fall of the Republic. In fact, it was his own indomitable spirit that finally succeeded in rallying the troops of the "Venetian armada," who were anchored in the port of Corfu. Given the general laissez-faire atmosphere of the times, only a powerful personality such as himself could have managed to instill enough enthusiasm among the ranks to actually create a fighting force. After his death, however, life in general resumed its normal pace, in anticipation of the end, which many citizens of the Republic now felt was imminent (and others hoped would come sooner rather than later).

Emo's failure to receive governmental support for a massive land reclamation project in the *Valli Veronesi* during the time that he was serving as *Inquisitore alle Acque* is yet another indication of the sad state of affairs that existed in the final years of the Republic. In fact, he was denied these funds because the monies that had been set aside by the state for this specific purpose had already been spent to defray the costs of his own military campaign against the Barbary pirates.

The Venetian Armada

The actual structure of the Venetian armada would vary from one generation to the next in accordance with the changing of the times. In the early years, when the doge was the sovereign head of the state, he

FRAN. MOROS. CAP GNALE. CON POCHE GAL. E QVATRO NAVI DA LA FVGA A 17 NAVI TVRCHES
DA GVERRA, NE FA ROMPERE, E NAVFRAGARE DVE, E NE PRENDE VNA CARICA DI MILIZIE.
TERMINA COSI LA CARICA LI CAP GNALE LA PRIMA VOLTA, E SE NE RITORNA A VENEZIA DOPO ESSERVI
STATO LONTANO CON L'ARMA IN MANO LO SPAZIO DI 23 ANNI CONTINVI, SENZA MAI RIVE. LA
PATRIA NE PVR PER MOMENTI E SVBITO ANZI VIENE SPEDITO PROVER GNALE STRAORDIN IN FR PER VNA
TEMVTA IRRVCION DI TVRCHI IN QVELLA PROVINCIA MAGGIO 1661

Francesco Morosini's victories over the Turkish fleet in the Morea at the end of the 17th century, which were literally part of the Republic's "last stand," are commemorated by the artifacts contained on the current page. Above left: Canvas depicting a naval battle between the Venetians and the Turks. Above right: Three-branched lantern from Morosini's own galley. Below: Morosini's prayer book, complete with a loaded pistol.

not only devastated the Genoese colonies of Kaffa and Phocaea, but had also commanded the Venetian forces in the war against Ferrera. Other great *Capitani Generali da Mar* who would be elected to the dogeship were Lorenzo Celsi, Marco Corner, Giovanni Bemo, Francesco Molin and Alivse II Mocenigo.

Among the few exceptions to this rule, there was Doge Cristoforo Moro, who reluctantly agreed to take command of the naval fleet in 1463 at the behest of Pope Pius II, who was intent upon launching a new crusade to the Holy Land. When the pontiff's own death led his allies to abandon the mission, history tells us that Moro himself was more than relieved. As far as the ultimate fate of poor Doge Francesco Erizzo was concerned, he would eventually be exempted from having to serve once again in the capacity of *Capitano Generale da Mar* in 1645 due to advanced age and mental illness. In the case of Francesco Morosini, the so-called "Peloponnesian," who was twice elected *Capitano Generale da Mar,* and who actually died during his second term of office, the Venetian state would choose to set aside all the usual protocol involved in providing for the absence of the doge in view of the fact that his experience and charisma were deemed indispensable to the defense of the Republic.

During the last two or three centuries of the Repub-

was also the commander of the fleet. This was the era of the great warrior doges, from Pietro II Orseolo to Domenico Michiel to Enrico Dandolo, who was the driving force behind the Fourth Crusade, despite his blindness and advanced old age. (If the chronicles of Villehardouin and Clari are to be believed, when Dandolo embarked on this particular mission, he was still a model of physical and moral strength.) In those instances in which the doge himself could not take command, his own son, or perhaps his nephew, would be allowed to take his place.

In later years, when the doges were relegated to the position of mere servants of the Republic, the laws of the land would preclude the vast majority of them from serving as commanders of the fleet as well. The reverse situation was true of the admirals themselves, many of whom would eventually be elected as doge. Such was the case of Giovanni Soranzo, who had

The struggle between the Venetians and the Turks, which dragged on for centuries, finally came to an end in the 1720s because both sides had completely exhausted their resources. Throughout these many years of victories and defeats, more than one hero would give his life for the cause. As far as those who had failed in their duty, the punishments were harsh indeed. Above left: A stone marker in the portico of the Doges' Palace stands as a permanent reminder of the cowardice of Girolamo Loredan and Giovanni Contarini, both of whom descended from doges, whose surrender of the Fortresss of Tenedos to the Turks in 1657 "to the detriment of all Christendom" led to their being banished forever from Venice. As for those who had acquitted themselves well in battle, there were also great rewards. Above right: A drawing by Giambattista Tiepolo showing a Venetian admiral receiving the keys to an enemy city (Fondazione Horne, Florence). Opposite page: The former Palazzo Dandolo, which is now the Hôtel Royal Danieli.

lic's existence, the highest-ranking peacetime naval officer was the "Provveditore Generale da Mar" (there was also a commander permanently stationed in Candia until the actual loss of Crete), along with the "Provveditore Generale" of Dalmatia and Albania with headquarters in Zara, and the "Capitano in Golfo," who was responsible for the overall security of the Adriatic.

The armada itself was divided into two branches, the "armata grossa," or sailing fleet, which was composed of ships, and the "armata sottile," or rowing fleet, which used galleys instead. The "Provveditore d'Armata" was the second in command of the rowing fleet after the "Provveditore Generale," while the "Governator de' Condannati" was in charge of the galley crews themselves. Whereas each of the galleys was under the command of a "Sopracomito," whose second in command was the "Nobile di Galera," the galleasses were commanded by a "Governatore." The supreme commander of the sailing fleet was the "Provveditore Estraordinario," followed by the ships' commanders themselves, also known as "Governatori," who were aided by one or two "Nobili di Nave." All of the above were members of the patriciate who had been elected to office by the Maggior Consiglio.

Subaltern positions, which were not assigned to patricians, included the "Almiranti" (those who commanded the generals' ships), "Comiti" and "Piloti." Finally, there were the "Aguzzini" and "Aguzinotti," who were directly responsible for the galley crews. As we have already mentioned, from the second half of the 15th century onward, these poor souls were no longer volunteers, but rather Turkish and Barbary prisoners and condemned criminals, who were actually chained to their posts. The only exceptions to this rule were the few individuals chosen by lot from among the natives of Venice, Dalmatia and the Ionian Islands.

In times of war, the supreme commander of the fleet was the all-powerful "Capitano Generale da Mar," followed by the "Provveditore Generale," the "Provveditore d'Armata," and the "Capi da Mar," who together made up the "consulta," or advisory council. (Although the orders sent by the Senate would arrive on board at least 10 to 15 days after they had been issued, the commander-in-chief was still obliged to discuss them with his advisors, even if they no longer applied!) Apart from the Senate's directives, it was up to the persuasive powers of the commander himself to ensure that his own military strategy would be approved by the council. This is yet another example of the Republic's ultimate concern with a democratic system of government. In fact, there were situations in which the opinion of everyone on board was required, including the crewmen themselves.

Naval officers dressed in a breastplate and coat of mail, over which they wore a mantle called the "romana," whose luxuriousness varied according to their rank. This was fastened on the shoulder with large, oval buttons made of metal. On their heads they wore the characteristic "berretto a tozzo," or "a tagliere," and in their hands they carried the rod of command, which was occasionally made out of tortoiseshell and gold

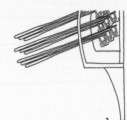

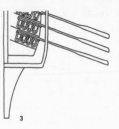

The main distinction between the longships and cogs, which were the two types of vessels that were used throughout the Republic's thousand years of history to sail the waters of the Mediterranean Sea, lay in their methods of propulsion. More specifically, while the cobs proceeded only under sail, the galleys used both sails and oars. These last were employed only while maneuvering in port, when the wind was slack, and during active combat.

Although the differing functions of the two vessels complemented each other for hundreds of years, in the long run, the technical improvements made to the cogs in order to permit them to sail the Atlantic Ocean would result in their replacing the galleys almost entirely. (While there were still a number of galleys

MASTERING THE SEA: THE LONGSHIPS

in the Arsenal at the time of the fall of the Republic, the French ship *Pyroscaphe* had already sailed up the Saône under steam in 1783.) These advantages included more cargo space and smaller crews.

The long, slender lines of the galleys were designed to accommodate as many oarsmen as possible in order to allow for maximum use of manpower. Until the mid-16th century, these crews were made up of volunteers, as opposed to the so-called *"galleotti,"* who were generally Turkish and Barbary prisoners and condemned criminals.

As we can see in Figure 1, the oarsmen were originally grouped in twos or threes on benches that were set at an angle (2). By the 16th century, however, there were three to four men to a bench (3). The oars themselves, which were longer and heavier, required much less skill and coordination on the part of the crew.

The galleys carried one (1), two (7) or three (4) masts, each of which was lateen rigged. By the 18th century, the galleass was no longer armed with a bow ram, which had become outmoded with the advent of the cannon, but rather with a bowsprit on which a jib could be hoisted in front of the foremast (7).

Galleys were also used for trading purposes, since they could be propelled by manpower when the wind dropped, and their large crews provided a strong defense in case of attack. Toward the end of the 14th century, the Venetians introduced a larger version of the same vessel, known as the galleass, which could hold up to 200 tons of cargo, and carried a crew of 200 men. (Figure 5: Engraving by Reuwich from Breydenbach's *Peregrinatio*, dated 1483-84, in which not all the details are perfectly clear. The enclosure on the starboard side near the stern itself was used to hold live animals, which served as a food supply.)

The six Venetian galleasses that were positioned in front of the 202 galleys during the famous Battle of Lepanto would play a critical role in the Holy League's conquest of the Turks. Although slower than the galleys themselves, these vessels were taller, heavier and larger than their counterparts, and armed with any number of cannon on the forecastle. Among the various diagrams of galleasses contained on these two pages, there is an 18th-century drawing by Coronelli (6), and another illustration from the same period (4), which depicts the ship under sail, with its oars raised (or *"acconigliati,"* as they were called in Venetian dialect). Figure 7: Cross-section of a two-masted galleass by Coronelli, showing its internal construction.

4

6

7

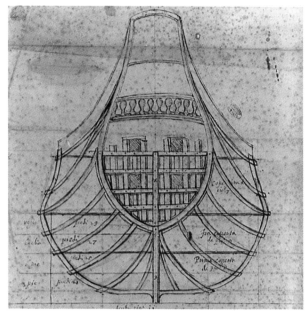

(like the one that belonged to Francesco Morosini), but which was more often crafted from ebony or ivory. (Interestingly enough, Sebastiano Venier, who was the ultimate victor at Lepanto, went into battle wearing some rather strange garb, including bedroom slippers, because he had a bad leg. He was also armed with a pike, which came in very handy during the assault on Ali Pasha's command ship.)

Under normal circumstances, the *Capitano Generale* himself was camped out on one of the so-called "*galere bastarde,*" which displayed not only an awning with red and white stripes, but also a beacon with three lights on the poop deck that indicated his rank. Among the most magnificent examples of these artifacts that have survived to this day, there is the exquisitely carved beacon used by the *Capitano Generale* Andrea Pisaro, who died in 1718 as a result of the explosion that destroyed the citadel at Corfu, which still graces the entranceway to his former palace, now

the site of the Venice Conservatory of Music. (Generally speaking, these precious mementos, some of which were actually wrought out of silver, were taken home by the "*Capi da Mar,*" along with their coats-of-arms and awnings, to decorate the atriums of their palaces.)

As far as the traditional warships themselves were concerned, the most agile and aggressive by far was the galley. Given its long, slender configuration, it sat extremely low in the water, which meant that the decks were often swept by waves, soaking the poor oarsmen themselves, who were confined to a few square inches of a wooden bench covered with cowhide on one of the most uncomfortable vessels that could possibly be imagined. Conditions were made even worse by the fact that the decks were also crowded with cross-bowmen and landing parties, all of whom ate, slept and defecated on board the small ship. Although a long voyage on a rough sea must have been an absolute

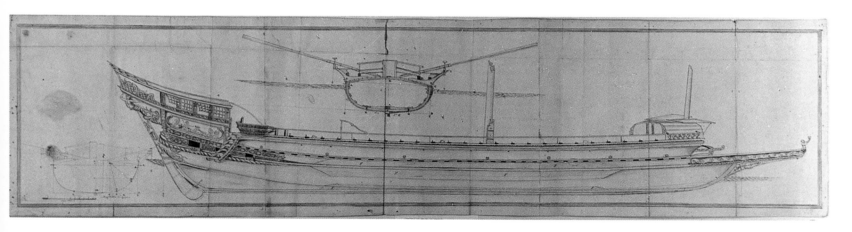

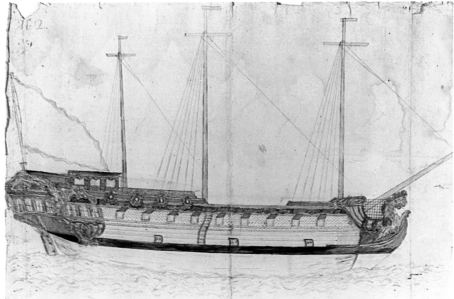

nightmare under the best of circumstances, there was always the call of the helmsman, and the rhythmic thud of the oars, which would have been somewhat reassuring.

There were also the galleasses, of course, which measured more than 100 meters in length. These powerful weapons of war, which were slightly broader than the galleys themselves, literally bristled with cannon.

The rations for the crewmen, sailors and slaves, as well as the crossbow-men, arquebusiers and gunners, consisted mainly of the biscuit prepared not only by the local bakeries that were situated close to the Arsenal, overlooking the Riva degli Schiavoni, but also by similar facilities scattered throughout the Venetian empire. The constant accusations of fraudulent practices involving the supply and distribution of this essential foodstuff, which was softened in olive oil and served in a broth that occasionally was mixed with sea water, were often the subject of heated debates in both the Senate and the *Maggior Consiglio*, as were

the illicit profits being made by certain of the ships' commanders. Even the heroic Leonardo Foscolo, who was proclaimed doge by the members of his own crew after having failed to be elected by the *Quarantuno*, was suspected of making a little something extra on the side.

In all probability, this last accusation was totally false, given the Republic's longstanding tradition of warring political factions, who delighted in arousing suspicions of ineptitude, insubordination, abuse of power, recklessness, and especially embezzlement on the part of the military commanders themselves. (As we have already noted more than once, this was one of the negative consequences of a parliamentary regime that was based on a system of checks and balances.) In fact, the highest-ranking naval officers had to be extremely careful about what they actually said or did. While some of them, such as the hapless *"General Dottor"* da Canal, whose fleet would never quite manage to arrive on time during the war in Negropont, were so intimidated by their lack of experience that they turned to their advisors for help in deciding the most trivial of matters, others were so terrified of making a fatal mistake that they never decided anything.

However, the paranoia that had literally paralyzed so many of these individuals would in no way prevent the great commanders such as Sebastiano Venier, Lazzaro Mocenigo and Lorenzo Marcello from making the most critical decisions of their entire careers. Perhaps the greatest example of this was Francesco Morosini, who chose to surrender Candia after a 25-year state of siege as a result of having been abandoned

Above left: Illustration of a trireme, from Cristoforo Canal's Milizia Marittima *(Biblioteca Marciana, Venice). Above right: Sketch of modifications to be made to a particular galley, which was part of an official dispatch from the* Provveditore Generale da Mar *in 1746 (Archivio di Stato, Venice). The Arsenal's extraordinary productivity was due not only to efficient management, but also to the skill of its specialized workforce. The technical and industrial sides of the operation were under the overall supervision of the "Magnifico Ammiraglio," who was in charge of the various department heads, or "Protomagistri." As a state-run enterprise, the Arsenal was administered by the "Eccellentissima Banca," which was comprised of three senators, the so-called "Provveditori dell'Arsenal," and three "Patroni," who were members of the Maggior Consiglio. Every two weeks, these last individuals took turns at sleeping in the Arsenal itself, where they were responsible for keeping the keys to the warehouses and workshops, and checking on the guard during the night.*

MASTERING THE SEA: THE BROAD SHIPS

"And the fleet they had fitted out was so fine and beautiful that no Christian had ever seen one finer or more beautiful." Such was Ville-hardouin's enthusiastic description of the Venetian squadron in the year 1202.

Aside from such personal accounts, documents regarding the Venetian shipping industry in the earliest centuries are both rare and difficult to interpret. However, there are several existing illustrations that serve to give us a general idea of what the Mediterranean cogs were actually like before the technical innovations that revolutionized the entire industry from the 14th century onward. From Figure 1, which is contained in a 14th-century manuscript, Figure 4, which is from a 13th-century Pisan relief, Figure 3, which represents a mosaic from St. Mark's, and Figure 2, which depicts a relief from the Arch of San Pietro Martire in Milan dated 1339, we can see that this vessel had a rounded hull, an upright stern and curved bows equipped with castles, a double rudder in the Roman style, from one to three lateen-rigged masts, and a crow's nest at the masthead. Figure 9, which is a reconstruction by Björn Landström based on the San Pietro Martire relief, gives us a more complete picture of the 14th-century cog itself.

From figures 5, 6, 7 and 8, which represent drawings from the late Middle Ages and the Renaissance, we can see the various changes that had occurred in shipbuilding techniques. Figure 5, which is taken from an early 15th-century painting, depicts a magnificent ship equipped with a mainmast and mizzenmast. Figure 6 is a reconstruction based on Jacopo de' Barbari's illustration of a large, four-masted ship, which is actually shown in Figure 8. Figure 7, which is taken from one of the panels in Carpaccio's *Legend of Saint Ursula* cycle, gives us a view of an elegant cog as seen from the stern. All of these vessels have two basic features in common, which derived from the ships that had been designed specifically for travel on the Atlantic. These were the central rudder, which was stronger and more easy to manage than the lee helms, and the square sail, which allowed not only for higher speed, but also for greater maneuverability. In Figure 8, we can see that the mizzenmast and foremast were still lateen rigged in order to be able to turn the bow into the wind when the ship was actually undergoing maneuvers. All four of these

2

3

drawings indicate the presence of a bowsprit as well. The cog in Figure 8 also carried a square spritsail that was unfurled beneath the bowsprit, as well as a topsail above the mainsail, as did the vessel depicted in Figure 7.

Although the cogs were used primarily for trade, and the galleys for the purposes of war, their traditional roles were often reversed. In fact, just as the galleys that traveled in convoys under military escort carried the most valuable cargo of all, the cogs themselves were powerful enough to be employed as warships when necessary.

5

8

9

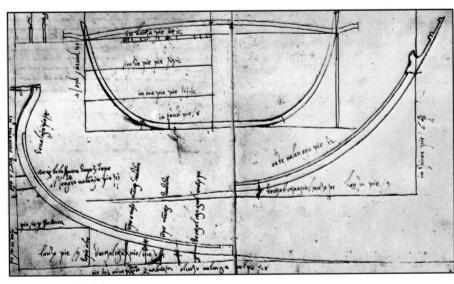

Fortresses and Generals

Among the various Venetian magistrates, there were also the *"Provveditori e Inquisitori alle Artiglierie e alle Fortezze,"* who were responsible for the construction of the magnificent fortresses that survive to this day on the islands of Crete and Cyprus, as well as in Greece and Dalmatia. Many of these fortifications were the work of experts who descended from mainland fami-lies that been admitted to the patriciate, such as the Martinengo, who had originally come from Brescia, and the Savorgnan, who were natives of the Friuli. However, there were also those civil engineers that descended from the great Venetian families themselves, such as Agostino Sagredo, who is credited with building the great Fortress of Palmede that overlooks the city of Nauplia (Nafplion), which the Venetians themselves referred to as "Napoli di Romania."

This kind of close cooperation between the Republic's nobility and the aristocrats of the mainland was particularly prevalent in times of war, when old animosities were forgotten in favor of a common cause. In fact, members of the Avogadro family from Brescia, as well as the Avogadro degli Azzoni from Treviso, were actually placed in command of certain Venetian warships. As for the infantry troops, who were sometimes called upon to reinforce the naval fleet, they themselves were under the command of the so-called *"condottieri,"* the last of the Renaissance military leaders, who would go down in history as the greatest mercenary soldiers of all time.

Among the more illustrious heirs to the powerful feudal families in the immediate area that produced these celebrated warriors (who were actually permitted to give their own name and coat-of-arms to their troops), there were the Counts of Porcia, and the Savorgnan, Colloredo and Strassoldo, all of whom came from the Friuli, as well as the Collato from Treviso, the da Porto from Vicenza, the Suardi from Bergamo, the Scotti and Martinengo from Brescia, and the Pompei from Verona. Then there were the members of noble families throughout the peninsula that had been in the employ of the Republic from time immemorial, such as the Orsini from Rome, one of whom was Paolo Giordano, the Duke of Bracciano, who commanded the infantry during the Battle of Lepanto. Finally, there were the foreign mercenaries, such as the Swedish Count of Koenigsmarck, who led the troops of Francesco Morosini when they disembarked in

Above: Painted panel from the Carpenters' Guild (Museo Correr, Venice). Below: Cross-sectional drawing used in the construction of galleys, from Pre' Todaro's Instructione sul modo di fabricare galere. *(Biblioteca Marciana, Venice).*

by the last of his French allies, and who would be made to pay in full for this heartbreaking decision despite the a priori approval of the Senate. In fact, he was brought up on charges of cowardice, desertion, and insubordination by the *Avogador* Correr, who also accused him of lying about the desperate state of affairs in Candia. Thanks to the superb defense of the politician Giovanni Sagredo, who was an avowed expert in eastern affairs, Morosini's actions would ultimately be vindicated by the vast majority of the *Maggior Consiglio* following a heated parliamentary debate. But the poor man's troubles were not yet over. Upon his election as a Procurator of St. Mark's, his swearing-in ceremony was boycotted by the populace at large, who bitterly resented his having conceded to the enemy whatever was left of the Cretan empire.

IDXVII·IN·TENPO·DE·MAISTRO·NICHOLO·DE·MARCHO·MARCHOVICHIO·DITO·DE·ANDRONICHO
GASTALDO·DE·LARTE·DE·REMERI·E·DISVO·9PAGNI

Left: Painted panel from the Oar-makers' Guild (Museo Correro, Venice). The fame of the skilled craftsmen employed by the Arsenal, who were known as the "arsenalotti," was so widespread that Czar Peter the Great himself attempted to hire their services in 1696. After having completed their apprenticeship on board one of the galleys of the Venetian fleet, the heirs to this cherished tradition, which was passed down from father to son, were taught the basics of reading, writing and arithmetic. In compensation for their rather modest wages, these workmen were accorded a number of privileges by the government, including state-subsidized housing, special allowances for wine, and permission to use leftover wood for their own purposes.

Greece, and ordered the famous cannonade that blew up the Parthenon, which the Turks were using as a powder store, and the Prussian General von der Schulenberg, who demonstrated extraordinary courage during the final siege of Corfu.

Neutrality and the End

In the last century of the Republic's existence, the government's policy of absolute neutrality with regard to the wars that were raging on the European continent would eventually lead to a series of circumstances that brought about her final demise, beginning with Napoleon's invasion of the Italian peninsula in the year 1796, which resulted in the immediate surrender of the all-powerful Piedmont region, an event that took everyone by surprise, and ending with his conquest of Austrian Lombardy, whose commander-in-chief, Marshal Beaulieu, would also cave in to Bonaparte's demands despite all expectations to the contrary. This state of affairs left Venice herself wide open to a sudden attack on the part of the armies of the French republic, whose leader had already demonstrated to the world at large that he had no respect whatsoever for the "rules of the game."

To make matters even worse, the same provincial *signori* that had totally abandoned the cause of the Republic during the war against the League of Cambrai would once again join forces with the enemy to throw off the so-called "yoke of Venetian domination." This time, however, their resentment at having been excluded from participating in the affairs of the

central government in Venice would result in such rebellious activities as echoing the slogans of the French Revolution, and raising the famous "liberty banners" in their own town squares. Naturally, the French aided and abetted them in every way possible, and actively encouraged them to stage further demonstrations whenever possible. The reaction of the rural peasants, who were the same *"marchesani,"* or "followers of St. Mark," that they had been in 1509, supplied Bonaparte with just the excuse he needed to accuse the Republic of having violated her own neutrality by inciting the people to rebel against his army.

The general himself demanded a great deal more of the Venetians than would normally be the case when dealing with a neutral power. In fact, whatever he wanted, he took, including provisions, arms, munitions, and even fortresses. On their part, the lack of military support, and the total inadequacy of the current governmental structure (both the Senate and the *Maggior Consiglio* had gradually been phased out, leaving the state in the hands of a series of *"consulte,"* or advisory councils"), forced the Republic's leaders to adopt a policy of appeasement toward the hot-headed Corsican, who always addressed them in threatening, imperious terms.

Although Venice's only hope of victory lay in the imperial forces, every general produced by the Austrians was outwitted by the military prowess of the young Bonaparte. Furthermore, the Republic's negotiators, who proved to be both inept and undiplomatic, were no match whatsoever for the wily general, which encouraged him to make even more outrageous demands. In the end, the popular insurrection known as the "Veronese Easter," during which a number of French-

1

2

FORTIFICATIONS
ON TERRA FIRMA

From the Adda to the Isonzo, the *Serenissima* would promote urban development and beautification projects in a continuing effort to improve the local environment of the towns and cities that lay within her domains. For those who are interested in discovering the "territories of St. Mark," we would like to suggest the following itineraries, the first of which involves the most impressive fortifications built by the Republic in defense of the major cities on the mainland, all of which are well worth visiting despite certain areas where the walls are either crumbling or completely destroyed. These include the magnificent city walls of Bergamo (A), which were constructed between 1559 and 1592, and which measure approximately three kilometers in length, the "new walls" of Padua (B), which were built under the direction of the famous *"condottiero"* Bartolomeo d'Alviano of Lugano, 5.418

Sammicheli (1).(Various of the underground fortifications that were built by the Republic would also serve as shelters for thousands of local residents during the terrible bombings that took place from 1944 to 1955.)

The second itinerary involves a tour of other significant examples of military architecture, including the great "Fortezza Stellare" of Palmanova, which is located in the Friuli (E). This masterpiece of military engi-

neering, which was approved by the Venetian Senate in 1593 as a means of defending the Republic's easternmost border against renewed attacks on the part of the Turks and the

Austrians during the second half of the 16th century, was designed by the renowned Friulano architect Giulio di Savorgnan (3).

kilometers of which are still intact, along with their splendid gates, the fortifications of Treviso (C), which were designed by the Veronese Fra' Giocondo, with the exception of the "Porta di San Tomaso," which is the work of Guglielmo Bergamasco, the "Porta dei Santi Quaranta" (4), which was built by Alessandro Leopardi, and the fortified walls of Verona (D), which were constructed by the great Veronese military architect Michele

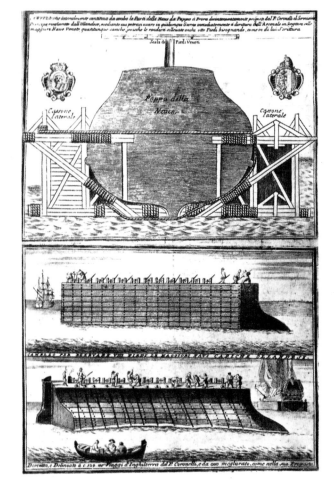

men were killed, and the incident provoked by the attempt on the part of a French ship to enter the port of Venice by force, which resulted in its being cannonaded and boarded by the soldiers guarding the harbor, were precisely the pretext that Bonaparte had been looking for in order to take decisive action against the Venetian nobility, whom he accused of the worse possible crimes.

In actuality, what the general was most concerned about was defending his rear guard during the eventual attack against Vienna, which meant assuring himself of the undivided support of the Republic herself in the person of men of his own choosing. His peremptory ultimatum to this effect, which led to an emergency session of the *Maggior Consiglio,* would force the membership to abdicate in favor of an elected popular assembly at the suggestion of Doge Lodovico Manin, who argued that this was the only possible means left to remedy the situation. While the gesture itself was a noble one, the circumstances that brought it about were anything but inspired. In fact, while still in session, the members of the *Consiglio* had mistaken the sound of gunfire on the part of Slavonian soldiers who

were being sent home for the beginning of a popular uprising, whereupon they hurriedly voted to end 500 years of aristocratic rule.

By May of 1797, when these events were taking place in Venice, Bonaparte himself had already come to an agreement with the emperor's representatives at Leoben with regarding to conceding the Venetian mainland to Austria. What actually persuaded the French general to finish off his handiwork several months later by conceding the city herself, as well as Dalmatia and Istria, is not our immediate concern. What does concern us, however, is the fact that even while he was supposedly upholding the ideals of democracy by forcing the Venetians to adopt a new constitution (although there was nothing at all democratic or representative about the so-called "Provisional Municipality," whose members had been chosen by Bonaparte himself upon the recommendation of the French diplomatic attaché in Venice), he was already intent upon wiping them off the map of Europe as a free and independent state. When the Treaty of Campoformido brought about the end of the Republic in October of 1797, those who were most horrified were precisely the individuals who had hailed the arrival of the French troops as the prelude to opening up a new democratic chapter in the history of Venice.

After Campoformido, Istria, Dalmatia and the mainland territories (with the exception of Bergamo, Brescia and Crema, which became part of the Casalpine Republic) were taken over by the Austrians, while the Ionian Islands went to the French. (These last would also fall to the English before being reclaimed by the Greeks.) So it was that the ancient Venetian order had come to an end.

The memory of the once-great Republic would be maligned from thereon in, first by the French general who had brought about her destruction, and then by the Austrians, who held Venice from 1799 to 1806, until Bonaparte reclaimed the city for his stepson, Eugène de Beauharnais, whom he appointed Viceroy and Governor General of the Kingdom of Italy. These years were perhaps the most desperate of all for the Venetian populace as a whole. Not only did the French soldiers set about systematically looting the city as they had done in 1797, but they also embarked on a campaign to destroy whatever happened to come across their path. The terrible state of poverty that affected every level of society would reach its nadir at the time of the continental blockade, which Napoleon used to isolate the English, and which had dramatic

repercussions on the economy of a city that depended for its very livelihood on its harbor facilities. In the year 1813, Venice was taken over yet again by the Austrians, who remained in control until 1866, apart from the brief interlude during which Daniele Manin would declare his "Revolutionary Republic." (Although this attempt was doomed to failure in the end, perhaps it served to tell the world that the strength and courage of the Venetian people themselves had finally vindicated the fatal resignation displayed by the nobility some 50 years earlier.)

The Republic would also be discredited by her new rulers in every way possible. While the French had engaged in spreading anti-Venetian propaganda on a rather minor scale (with the notable exception of Count Daru, a faithful follower of Napoleon, who took it upon himself to accuse the aristocratic government of the worst crimes imaginable in his monumental tome entitled *Histoire de la République de Venise*, in which he even went to the extent of falsifying documents in support of his opinions), the Austrians were bound and determined to destroy her reputation once and for all. As part of their plan, these same individuals who were so formal and correct in their dealings with one another began denigrating the local customs and traditions, which they felt were too deeply rooted in the hearts and minds of the Venetian populace.

Whereas Napoleon had ordered that all the statues and sculptural reliefs of the Lion of St. Mark be removed from the face of the mainland and the city herself, starting with those of the Doges' Palace, Austria made sure to wipe out everything that had once pertained to the privileges of the patrician class, including the title "N.H." ("*Nobil Uomo,*" or "Nobleman"), which was the only distinction that had ever been made among the members of the *Maggior Consiglio*. At a later date, the Austrians would give the patricians the option of adopting the same title that was used by the rest of the aristocracy under their rule, which meant eliminating the word *"uomo"* (giving rise to a certain amount of bitter humor), and simply calling themselves "nobles," or buying the title of "Count" or "Prince" of the Austrian Empire. (Given the sizeable sums of money involved, only the Erizzo and Giovanelli families would become princes.)

in the most ancient territories of the Empire, and especially on the Ionian Islands, the memory of the Republic is still etched in the minds of the local inhabitants, who recall with a touch of nostalgia what life was like under her regime . . . not only in terms of customs and traditions, but also the family names of the residents themselves, many of whom claim to be direct descendants of the Venetians

In the end, the various indignities suffered by the Venetian aristocrats would pale by comparison to what was actually done to the former Republic herself, starting with the Austrians' attempt to stir up the Slavs of Istria and Dalmatia against the Italians on the mainland, which ran counter to everything that the Venetians had worked so hard to achieve in their relations with these territories. Little did the imperialists know at the time, however, that their actions would eventually come back to haunt them. In fact, just as the Italians would be drawn to the political ideals of the Risorgimento (for which any number of Dalmatians and Istrians sacrificed their lives, beginning with Niccolò Tommaseo), the Slavs themselves would be caught up in the fervor of the pan-Slavic movement, which sought to reunite north and south under the banner of a Serbian nation, and which led to the disastrous circumstances that marked the beginning of the World War I.

Along with tragic consequences of the Second World War, these events would serve to erase the last traces of the Venetian presence on the Istrian and Dalmatian shores in terms of the local population. In fact, the descendants of those who had once called upon Doge Pietro II Orseolo for help in liberating them from oppression are currently in such desperate economic straits that they have been forced to emigrate en masse to the Italian mainland. Even if the architectural legacy left by the Republic is still more or less intact, the citizens themselves are no longer the heirs of the original inhabitants of the region.

Despite the *damnatio memoriae*, a number of Yugoslav scholars are now actively engaged in researching the history of the Republic's long-standing relationship with the Dalmatian Slavs. The same is happening in Greece, where historians are now referring to the years under Venetian rule as the "Venetocracy," and where the magnificent fortresses built by the Republic are in the process of being restored, thanks in part to funds made available by the *Serenissima* herself under the auspices of the *"Progetto Marco Polo."*

In the most ancient territories of the Empire, and especially on the Ionian Islands, the memory of the Republic is still etched in the minds of the local inhabitants, who recall with a touch of nostalgia what life

was like under her regime, not only in terms of customs and traditions, but also the family names of the residents themselves, many of whom claim to be direct descendants of the Venetians. Among the Greek intelligentsia, however, the Republic is primarily remembered for her valiant efforts to keep the Hellenic culture alive even in the worst of times. In fact, the Republic had created an official seat for the Metropolitan Archbishop of the Greek Orthodox Church, which was known as Philadelphia. In addition, she had encouraged the expatriots in her own community to establish the Scuola dei Greci as a place of worship, as well as the Collegio Flangini, whose purpose was to provide religious instruction for altar-boys and lay citizens alike. These institutions had also been responsible for publishing not only the standard Greek Orthodox texts, but also the great masterpieces of Greek literature.

ELEVEN CENTURIES OF INDEPENDENCE

Opposite page: Courtyard of the Palazzo Pisani in Campo Santo Stefano, renowned for its architectural features, which was begun in 1614, and completed in the mid-1700s. Although the moment in which it was built coincided with the decline of the Republic, the Pisani family would spend a veritable fortune to complete its construction. This was a classic example of the circumstances surrounding the city's imminent demise, when literature and the arts were flourishing once again.

Two hundred and two years have now passed since the fall of the Republic, and 1,302 years have gone by since the legendary Pauluccio Anafesto was elected as her first doge. What this tells us is that the Venetians enjoyed more than 11 centuries of absolute independence, during which time the 18th century alone represented a period of marked decline. These figures represent the "official endurance record" of the *Serenissima Repubblica di Venezia,*" which has yet to be challenged by any other country in the world.

The Republic's longevity, however, was only one of her great accomplishments. There was the incredible phenomenon of a society made up of fishermen, salt-workers and sailors, who would some day find themselves at the center of Mediterranean trade. Then, of course, there was the city herself, whose extraordinary beauty and enormous wealth was the direct result of the intelligence and ingenuity of her inhabitants, whose numbers never exceeded 180,000. Finally, there was an empire that extended from the Adda to the Isonzo, and the Alps to the Po, on the Italian peninsula itself, as well as Istria, Dalmatia, a portion of Albania, the Ionian Islands, part of the Epirus, the Pelopennese and Attica, the Aegean Islands, and Crete and Cyprus, not to mention the military strongholds and port cities both near and far, from Ferrara to Constantinople, and Trebizond to San Giovanni d'Acri.

Most importantly, perhaps, was the fact that the city on the lagoon was able to stand up to the most powerful monarchs on earth, whose territories were at least one hundred times more extensive and densely populated than her own. As for the papal authorities themselves, who were famous for exploiting the resources of their most formidable allies in an effort to establish political supremacy, the Venetians would hold out against them as well, despite their dedication to the Catholic faith.

How could all of this have possibly come about? Perhaps this is the right moment for us to consider some of the actual circumstances that contributed to such a magnificent legacy.

First and foremost, there was the basic need to survive. From the earliest times, the city's very existence would depend on her natural environment. The lagoon, which proved to be a valuable source of income from the salt-pans, and an endless supply of fresh fish, also provided a natural defense against foreign invaders. At the same time, however, it represented an ever-present danger. In the case of Malamocco, the former capital city, high tides and shifting currents eventually eroded its foundations to the point where we are not even sure where it was actually located. As for the rivers that flowed into the lagoon, they not only carried an enormous amount of silt, but they also affected the delicate ecological balance of the swamps, which poisoned the atmosphere for the local inhabitants. Then there

Detail of a painting by Gaspar van Wittel depicting maritime traffic on the Grand Canal (Galleria Doria Pamphili, Rome). While the discovery of new trade routes in the 15th and 16th centuries would initially threaten the stability of the Republic's economy, she would soon learn to adapt herself to the changing circumstances, and continue operating on a different scale.

the mainland, severing ties that had existed for centuries. In later years, as Venice grew in wealth and influence, the world outside would become even more hostile and aggressive. After the Longobards, the Franks and the German emperors, there would be the great feudal lords, followed by the signories, city-states and national monarchies, all of whom were dedicated to her destruction. Not only was she elusive and unconquerable; her very lifestyle, and the enormous amount of power that she had somehow managed to accumulate, were intangibles that deeply troubled her neighbors. The fact that she herself cultivated these "differences" made her even more subject to the hatred and hostility of others.

were the islands, whose foundations were rarely on firm ground, and which had to be shored up, reinforced and protected before any attempt could be made to build upon them. In fact, in the dark night of prehistory, among the most remote regions of the Veneto marshes, the territory was painstakingly conquered, often by the most rudimentary means, such as fencing and palisades constructed of rushes, and primitive land reclamation efforts.

This constant struggle for survival would also strengthen the character of the people themselves. Long before the days of the huge hydraulic projects for which the Venetians would become famous, the inhabitants of the lagoon set about building dams and diverting rivers and canals, bending the forces of nature to their own needs, and learning what it meant to turn even the most difficult situations to their own advantage.

What lay beyond the lagoon in those early years was an increasingly hostile and alien world. Although the actual circumstances of their exodus were undoubtedly less dramatic than legend would have us believe, the first refugees to reach the islands would choose to separate themselves from the social and political life of

The Republic's ultimate reliance on the sea was favored by many factors. First, there were the nearby forests, which provided the basic materials for the building of her ships. Then there were the beaches, whose natural harbors would become part of the great emporium between East and West. Finally, there were the vast stretches of water that protected her from the assaults of the Normans and Moslems. Even here, however, she would be obliged to defend her maritime "territory" against seemingly impossible odds.

And so it was until the very end of the Republic's existence. In later times, when the threat of Spanish aggression had finally faded, there would be the Hapsburg dynasty, which forced her to maintain a constant state of vigilance, and to compete fiercely on the commercial level with the Austrian ports of Trieste and Fiume. On the high seas themselves, there would be the need to defend herself against enemies from all four corners of the globe, including the ships from the western maritime powers, who had literally overwhelmed the waters of the Mediterranean. Even the Russians would eventually send a naval attachment to

The Greek Favorite in the Harem, *by Francesco Guardi, one of the many works of Venetian art that present a nostalgic view of the East (Von Tyssen Bornemisza Collection, Lugano). The taste for the exotic, which was widespread in 18th-century Europe, had its origins in the Venetians' longstanding relationship with the Levant.*

the Adriatic, at which point the Venetians contemplated strengthening diplomatic ties with this enormous empire in light of the imminent threat of an Austrian invasion. But by then it was too late to engage in such an ambitious undertaking. The war against the Turks, and the loss of most of the Levant, had severely weakened the former queen of the seas, and the might of the emerging European superpowers was so far superior to her own resources that she would be unable to compete on an equal basis with them in the end.

During their thousand years of history, however, the fact that the Venetians had been forced to maintain a constant state of emergency would contribute to their sense of total involvement in every aspect of their lives, from politics to diplomacy to waging war. This attitude was motivated by their awareness that there was no other way that they could possibly endure. They had also learned that part of their strategy for survival depended on taking the initiative when necessary, which meant assuming the role of the attacker rather than the attacked.

Another element that would prove essential to their independence was the government's policy of "public" over "private." With several notable exceptions, this phenomenon was in stark contrast to the prevailing mentality among the other states of Italy and Europe, where everything was oriented toward what the Florentine historians would call *"il particolare,"* or the interests of the individual himself.

Among the citizens of the Republic of Venice, from the doge himself to the most humble of men, no one was considered exempt from this obligation, which required a total willingness to sacrifice one's own personal concerns on behalf of the greater good. This tradition originated in the earliest of times, when the people came to realize that the prevalence of one political party over another, which had led to the establishment of dynastic rule, could be used to benefit the society as a whole. In fact, it may well be that the Parteciaco and Candiano families exchanged roles depending on whether the moment called for diplomatic skills or a strong military presence. At the time of the popular assemblies, the commoners would also learn to adapt themselves to the shifting political tides. Even the opposing factions would become accustomed

MAJOR EXHIBITIONS

L'Esposizione Biennale Internazionale d'Arte Contemporanea was established in 1895 at the initiative of the local government, which was headed by the poet Riccardo Selvatico, and organized by Antonio Fradeletto in his role as general secretary (6). Despite various political and organizational problems throughout the course of the century, the Biennale has continued to be the most important exhibition of contemporary art in

all of Italy and Europe. From its earliest years, when only paintings and sculptures were displayed, it has also been expanded to include architecture and the decorative arts. This has resulted in the need for additional exhibit space (some 30 pavilions are now part of the exhibit, most of which are provided by other countries), including portions of the Arsenal and the gardens of Castello.

La Mostra Internazione d'Arte

Cinematografica, which was inaugurated in the mid-1900s, is now considered one of the most significant film festivals in the entire world (4). Since that time, the city has also sponsored a theater festival, as well as a festival of contemporary music, whose main purpose has been to

expose the public to the works of modern composers who have remained in relative obscurity.

As of the 1930s, the government has also organized any number of exhibits dedicated to the works of the great Venetian artists, as well as various aspects of the local culture. Among the more important of these were the Titian, Tintoretto and Paolo Veronese exhibitions that took place before World War II, and the spectacular post-war exhibits entitled "Five Centuries of Venetian Painting," and "Masterpieces of the Museums in the Veneto." In later years,

there were exhibitions dedicated to Giovanni Bellini (1949), Lorenzo Lotti (1953), Giorgione (1955), as well as the landscape artists of the 18th century (1967). The most significant exhibits of the past decades include "From Titian to El Greco" (1981), the exhibitions dedicated to the work of Titian (1980) and Tiepolo (1997), and "The World of Giacomo Casanova," which was mounted in 1998.

The Giorgio Cini Foundation, which was established by Vittorio Cini on the Island of San Giorgio Maggiore in honor of his late son, has continued to sponsor exhibits in conjunction with its role as a research facility for students of Venetian history, including the show entitled "Venezia da State a mito" in commemoration of the 200th anniversary of the fall of the Republic. The Palazzo Grassi (3), which recently mounted an exhibition on the Mayan civilization, traditionally draws large numbers of visitors, thanks to its exceptionally talented curators. The Peggy Guggenheim Muse-

31

um (2), which is famous for its collection of modern art, has also been responsible for important exhibitions.

In addition to all of the above, there are the extraordinary municipal museums themselves, including the seemingly endless array of art and artifacts contained in the Doges' Palace, and the priceless treasures of the Accademia Gallery, which make it one of the most celebrated museums in the world (7). Among the other museum facilities, there are the Treasury of St. Mark's Basilica, the *Museo Marciano,* where the original bronze horses of Byzantium are currently on display, the Correr Museum, which houses not only a collection of important paintings, but also artifacts relating to the history of the Republic, and the Querini Stampalia Collection, whose treasures include a curious series of paintings by the 18th-century artist Gabriel Bella. There are also a number of specialized facilities, such as the Historic Naval Museum, the fascinating Glass Museum of Murano (5), the Diocesan Museum at Santa Apollonia, the Archeological Museum, and the National Library. Finally, among the museums that are currently closed for restoration, there is Ca' Rezzonico, which is the site of the magnificent Museum of the 18th Century, as well as Ca' Pesaro, and the Fondaco dei Turchi, which is now the Museum of Natural History.

Above: Gouache by Francesco Guardi showing the Grand Canal, the Church of the Scalzi, and the canal that was later filled in to create the Lista di Spagna (Ecole des Beaux Arts, Paris). Opposite page: La Scala dei Giganti. No other city on earth has ever been celebrated by its artists with more enthusiasm and affection than Venice herself. In their various depictions of daily life in the squares and on the canals, which date back at least to the 15th century, one can always sense a feeling of intimacy between the painter and his subjects.

to forgetting their differences when the well-being of the entire city was at stake.

As of the closing of the Great Council, the Republic would enjoy 500 years of aristocratic rule during which the parliamentarians never once lost sight of the ultimate goal of serving the state. (In reality, the nobility had been in power for at least and century and a half before this event took place, judging from the constant repetition of the same names in those documents dealing with major decision-making on the part of the government.) In fact, historians have yet to identify another aristocratic regime that concerned itself with curbing and controlling its own power on behalf of the common good.

When we consider the harshness of the taxes and surcharges that were imposed on the patricians in times of fiscal crisis and national emergency, from the wars with Genoa and the Carreresi until the campaign in Crete and Morosini's military expedition against the Turks, we realize that the ruling class carried a heavier burden of responsibility for the well-being of the state than those who were excluded from the inner circles of power. This is just one of the many examples

of those measures adopted by the government that affected the nobility far more severely than the lower classes.

Certain scholars have observed the fact that public documents from various stages in Venetian history always use the adjective "our" when referring to the state, implying that the aristocracy had a strong a sense of solidarity with the rest of the society. In other words, their role as political leaders was not a matter of class privilege, but rather of civic pride. The word "our" also occurs in a number of documents pertaining to the other social strata, including the affirmations, contestations, acclamations and protests that were so much a part of their daily lives. This feeling of participating in a common cause is undoubtedly one of the major reasons that the Republic eventually wielded such power and influence, and managed to survive for so long a period of time.

Another of the factors that contributed to Venice's ability to maintain her freedom and independence, as opposed to the fate of the rival city-states of Genoa and Florence, was the code of ethics adopted by the members of the patrician class with regard to their role as public servants. Both before and after the *serrata,* the aristocrats had always considered themselves the delegated representatives of the populace as a whole, as witnessed by the last decree issued by the members of the *Maggior Consiglio* at the time of the abdication in May of 1797, which formally "restored" the power that had been invested in them by the will of the people. This philosophy was also the driving force behind the severity of the rules and regulations concerning the personal conduct of the ruling class. Although certain punishments were undoubtedly excessive, as was the case of Senator Andrea Morosini's son, who was condemned to death after having been found guilty of kissing a girl from the lower class, and stealing a piece of her jewelry, such measures protected the rest of society from the oppression of the privileged few.

By the same token, the Inquisitors and the Council of Ten, who were ultimately responsible for enforcing these rules, never once hesitated to suppress the "public enemies" who had put their private interests ahead of those of the state. Among those individuals who were punished severely for such acts of oppression, there were a number of corrupt nobles who were obliged to pay with their lives for having perpetrated crimes against their fellow citizens. Although these sentences were carried out in the strictest of secrecy, they were always subject to the approval of both houses of parliament.

The government's concern with ensuring that equal justice was accorded to one and all is yet another reason for the Republic's longevity. Goethe himself, who was not particularly fond of the city of Venice, tells of having been present at a trial involving the morganatic wife of Doge Paolo Renier, who actually lost the case in question. He also notes that the Venetians themselves seemed quite proud of the fact that the consort of the head of state was seated on a bench in the *Quarantia* along with all the other litigants, as a member of society at large.

In comparison with the practices of the other city-states on the Italian peninsula, the Venetian judicial system was famous for the scrupulous manner in which trials were conducted. We have already mentioned the tragic fate of Doge Antonio Venier's son, who died in prison after having been found guilty of the crime of offending the honor of one of his peers. This was hardly the case in Paris, where a member of the de Rohan family would escape the charges of having Voltaire himself severely beaten.

The importance that was placed on the ultimate well-being of the state, as opposed to the interests of any particular individual, was also the basis for the lack of official recognition on the part of the central government with regard to specific instances of bravery, or years of dedication spent in the service of the Republic. The fact that there were only two monuments erected by the Venetians in honor of Sebastiano and Francesco Venier literally speaks for itself.

The above painting by Jacobello del Fiore, which dates from the beginning of the 14th century, portrays the figure of Venetian Justice, armed with her sword and scales, and flanked by the Lions of St. Mark (Gallerie dell'Accademia, Venice). Throughout the Republic's long history, her extraordinary system of justice would play an important role in assuring her survival as an independent state. Opposite page: Detail from Giovanni Battista Tiepolo's personification of the city herself in a painting entitled Neptune Offering Venice Gifts from the Sea (Doges' Palace, Venice).

(In those instances where the great statesmen and heroes of the day wished to leave a lasting memory of their accomplishments, they were expected to pay for it out of their own pockets.) However, when a member of the aristocracy actually chose to break the laws of the land, his name was published far and wide. To this very day, on the walls of the Doges' Palace, under the porticos which once served as an informal meeting-place for government officials when parliament was in session, there are still a number of plaques commemorating crimes such as the embezzlement of government funds, and abandoning military strongholds to the enemy.

Leaving aside for a moment our dedication to the principles of representative democracy, which were established as a result of the French Revolution (and which Winston Church once described as the worst possible form of government, despite the fact that a better system has yet to be found), there is no denying the reality that the much criticized *serrata* of the Maggior Consiglio in 1297 was the driving force behind the Republic's ability to survive as an independent state. While the rival city-state of Genoa would suffer at the hands of both domestic and foreign powers some 500 years before the fall of the Republic, the

Venetians themselves would go one to enjoy at least 400 years as a major European presence, and nearly 300 years as one of the great superpowers of the day.

Following the dramatic events of 1297, Venice would continue to reap the benefits of a strong, stable government, which eventually saved her from the likes of the chaotic demagogy that led to Genoa's demise at the hands of the Visconti, the French and the Spaniards. While we ourselves may be accused of certain prejudices in favor of the Republic, there are any number of foreign scholars, such as the renowned French historians Yves Renouard and Frédéric Chabod, who have reached the very same conclusions. (Perhaps we should also remember that the times were not ripe for a democratic regime. In fact, the popular assemblies themselves, which were exposed to the influence of one political leader after another, were certainly no foundation for the establishment of a true democracy.)

Another factor that contributed to the stability of the Republic was the government's concern for the welfare of the underprivileged, including the enactment of specific legislation to protect the interests of the working class and the poor, and the willingness to listen to the complaints of the local peasantry. Thanks to these enlightened policies, which were well ahead of their time in comparison with the other sovereign states of Europe, the ultimate collapse of the Republic would be a sad occasion indeed for the most humble of her subjects, as opposed to the sense of relief experienced by so many members of the nobility, who were only too eager to be free of the traditional constraints.

Such was the case throughout her former territories, where the resentments and frustrations that had existed for centuries among the privileged classes would finally rise to the surface. This was hardly the case among the lower classes, however, who were fully aware of the fact that they had been treated in a manner that was far more humane that anything they could ever have imagined. Despite all the rhetoric to the contrary, the farewell ceremony performed by the *Bocchesi* of Perasto, during which they buried the banner that bore the image of the winged lion beneath the mensa of the high altar of their church, was an extraordinary act of love and devotion. Even more poignant was the accompanying document: "For 377 years you have been our protector, St. Mark, for which we have willing given our lives in your service. We have always blessed the fact that you were with us, and that we were

PROTECTING THE NATURAL ENVIRONMENT

One of the most critical problems facing the Venetian government today is the decreasing population. In fact, during the last half of the 20th century, the city has actually gone from a total of 150,00 inhabitants to approximately 70,000. This phenomenon, which was due primarily to the closing on the part of the *Marina Militare* of the various workshops that formed part of the Arsenal, has forced thousands of workers to seek employment on the mainland. In addition, the dismal living conditions in the district of Castello, which once housed the majority of these workers, were such that they had no choice but to abandon their old neighborhoods in favor of a healthier and happier environment. As for those who have selected to remain in the city, there is the ever-present problem of a lack of adequate housing, as well as the exorbitant rents that are now being charged by absentee landlords to wealthy members of the expatriot community.

Any number of local manufacturers have moved to the mainland as well, leaving the city in the hands of the tourist industry, which is now her basic means of survival. This in turn has led to the abandonment of many longstanding customs and traditions in favor of the major "tourist attractions."

In an effort to combat this massive exodus, the local government has now embarked on a building campaign, particularly in those areas that once housed the manufacturing trades, with the ultimate objective of providing reasonably priced living quarters for the city's remaining res-

idents. At the same time, the University of Venice has established an international campus on the Island of San Servolo, which will eventually include a number of student dormitories.

Despite all of the above, the municipal authorities have still not come up with a comprehensive plan to combat the negative effects of international tourism, especially with regard to the hordes of "day tourists" who have literally invaded the city in the last several decades. (In 1990, for example, a rock concert that attracted thousands of young people from around the world resulted in serious physical damage to both the Piazza and Piazzetta.) There is also the overwhelming problem of tour groups themselves, which are often left free to wander the city without any form of guidance.

As of the early 1950s, the city's main tourist attraction has been the Venetian "Carnevale," which is celebrated in St. Mark's Square, where any number of longstanding traditions, such as the "flight of the dove," are re-enacted in honor of the occasion. For days on end, the Piazza is also filled with thousands of individuals in costume, who spend most of their time parading around in search of more fantastic get-ups than their own!

During the heyday of the Venetian "Carnevale," which occurred in the 18th century, theatrical performances

played an important part in the city's celebrations. As opposed to the nine theaters that were then available to the general public, there is only one that is still in existence today. However, while the painful process of restoring the Fenice to its former splendor will most probably go on for an extensive period of time, the newly renovated Teatro Malibran promises to delight audiences for years to come.

Right: Banquet in honor of Clement, Duke of Bavaria and Archbishop of Cologne, in the Casino Nani on the Giudecca (School of Longhi, Ca' Rezzonico, Venice). Opposite page, above: Banquet in celebration of the Polignac wedding in the Gradenigo villa at Carpenedo, as portrayed by Francesco Guardi (Museo Correr, Venice). Opposite page, below: Detail of portrait of a young woman with parrot, by Giambattista Tiepolo, who might well have been the model for the voluptuous feminine beauties described by Pietro Aretino as follows: "The Venetians want solid stuff, not the creatures of Petrarch's fantasies." During the 18th century, Venice attracted visitors from around the world for her famous joie de vivre, including Frederick IV of Denmark and Norway, who was the guest of the Foscarini, the King of Poland, who was received by the Pisani, Corner and Mocenigo families, the Duke of York, Emperor Leopold II, the Queen of Naples, Emperor Joseph II, Pope Pius VI, and any number of foreign aristocrats, all of whom were welcomed with open arms. Despite the fact that the city seemed to have turned her back on the glorious past in favor of endless entertainments, behind the facade itself, there was perhaps a bit of nostalgia for what once had been, and even a sense of what lay ahead.

with you. . . ." What other nation on earth could have received such a final tribute?

The Venetians' understanding of the basic mentality of their subjects was another factor that played an important role in their ability to survive. (In terms of today's sensibilities, the word "subjects" is far from "politically correct." Let us not forget, however, that many of the modern states in Europe and beyond came into being as a result of oppression.) Aside from the popular rebellions in Zara and on the Island of Crete, the vast majority of the uprisings on the part of the peasants were directed toward the local landlords and members of the nobility, rather than the Republic herself.

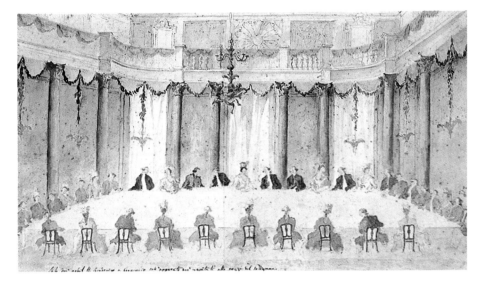

The final element that determined the fate of the Republic was her ability to use economic opportunities to her advantage. In fact, she would follow the example of her own merchants and seamen, whose boundaries were seemingly limitless, and who knew how to take advantage of the circumstances despite their religious ideals.

As we have seen, Venice was incomparable in so many ways, as was the Venetian state, in terms of her constitution, her laws, and her entire history. What if anything remains of that incomparable city?

It is extremely difficult to visualize the Venice of yesterday in the Venice of today. As a result of the incredible damage that she suffered during the years in which she was under foreign occupation, including the destruction of more than 70 churches and 100 palaces, and the loss of hundreds of thousands of precious works of art that are now scattered across the face of the earth, the city as we know her today is but a mere shadow of what she was before the events that took place in May of 1797. Nevertheless, her unique environment still survives to this day despite the constant assaults of both nature and mankind.

What is perhaps most upsetting of all is the fact that the ambience itself has changed so drastically. Among the various events that have contributed to this situation, there is the mass exodus of the local population, who seem to prefer the modern conveniences of the horrible suburb of Mestre to the discomforts of living in the historical center, which is the same phenomenon that occurred not only after the fall of the Republic, when the nobility abandoned the city herself in favor of the more tranquil provinces, but also during the Italian-Austrian War, whose last battles were fought but a short distance from St. Mark's Square, when the commoners themselves were forced to run for their lives.

In the 1880s, the city's main harbor facilities,

PRESERVING THE CITY AND THE LAGOON

As a result of the Republic's demise, her artistic treasures suffered great damage at the hands of the enemy, beginning in 1797, when the French themselves carried the spoils of war back to Paris, including the four bronze horses from the Basilica (which were eventually returned to Venice after Napoleon himself was defeated) (4). Between 1806 and 1814, when the city was part of the Kingdom of Italy, more than 70 churches in the historic center and on the outlying islands were desecrated, countless works of art were either stolen or destroyed, and magnificent palaces were razed to the ground. Although the Kingdom of Italy deserves a certain amount of credit for having established the gardens of Castello and the Cemetery of San Michele, it was directly responsible for the systematic destruction of many of the city's inner canals, even more of which were filled in by the Austrians, who also demolished two churches and any number of palaces in the process of constructing the Ferrovia Milano-Venezia (Santa Lucia) and the first railroad trestle (3) in 1847. (The causeway that links Venice to the mainland was actually built in 1930.)

After the city was annexed by the Italian republic, the local authorities demolished still other architectural masterpieces to make room for main thoroughfares such as Via XXII Marzo, Via Mazzini and Via Vittorio Emanuele (now known as "Strada Nova").

The Port of Marghera (1), which was established after World War I, has been the source of serious environmental problems for the city herself since its very inception. After becoming part of the petro-chemical industry, it has also been responsible for air pollution, which has affected not only the lives of those residing in the immediate vicinity, but the health and well-being of the urban infrastructure as well.

Among the many elements that have destroyed the delicate ecologi-

cal balance of the lagoon, there are the direct effects of industrial pollution, the excavation of too great a number of canals, including the Petroli Canal, which now cuts the lagoon itself in half, the landfills that have changed the course of the tides, and the shoring up of the "valli da pesca." These same factors have been largely responsible for the flooding that has devastated both Chioggia and the historic center of the city herself in recent years. In fact, the famous flood of 1966 (5) that would threaten the very survival of Venice was due primarily to exceptionally high tides and the strong winds of the scirocco, which eventually broke through the barriers of the Lido and Pellestrina.

In the wake of this catastrophe, some 27 private committees from 10 different nations, operating under the auspices of UNESCO, would assume the financial responsibility for restoring the countless paintings, sculptures and monuments that had been damaged by the flood waters. Many of these same organizations are still actively involved in the ongoing process of preserving the city's artistic heritage. In addition, the central government passed special legislation in 1973 and 1984 to provide substantial funding for the same purpose.

The serious problem of flooding, however, has yet to be resolved. Apart from the installation of the single mobile flood gate that is now commonly known as "Mose" (2), the city remains defenseless against the force of the high tides. Despite the endorsement of both the local authorities and experts from around the world, the Ministries for Environmental Protection and the Fine Arts in Rome have voted down the project in favor of other priorities, and have left the entire matter in the hands of an executive committee headed by the Prime Minister. Perhaps the constant pressure exerted by the international community will yield more positive results.

4

Detail of Canaletto's Campo di Rialto, *which depicts workers repairing a roof (Staatliche Museen zu Berlin, Stiftung Preussicher Kulterbesitz, Berlin). Some two centuries after the fall of the Republic, the city is fighting for her very survival. Thanks to the continuing efforts on the part of the international community at large, she may be able to conquer this latest challenge as well.*

which had also suffered enormous damage at the hands of the French and the Austrians, were diverted to the Port of Marghera, which remains a topic of heated debate between those who have chosen to dedicate themselves to the preservation of the city's artistic treasures, and those who understand the economic importance of the petro-chemical industry.

During the first half of the 20th century, the city would be the setting for the series of urban development projects initiated by Giuseppe Volpi, who was perhaps the very reincarnation of the Venetian merchants of ancient times in terms of the wide variety of his interests. Volpi's activities were also the focal point of other industrialists and financiers of the times, including Vittorio Cini, who established the important cultural institution that is known as the Giorgio Cini Foundation.

In place of those extraordinary individuals who determined the city's fate from the earliest moments

in her history, who unfortunately no longer exist in today's world, there is the international community at large, which has offered ideas, proposals, funds and expertise in a continuing effort to restore the city's paintings, sculptures and monuments, and to guarantee that they are properly preserved for the generations to come. Most of this responsibility lies in the hands of the 27 private restoration committees from 10 different nations, which were formed as a result of the devastating floods of 1966, and which now operate under the auspices of UNESCO.

This latest phenomenon tells us that the ideals of the Republic of Venice still live on in the hearts and minds of today's citizens from around the world, who have come to appreciate her incredible accomplishments, and who have joined together in order to ensure that the manifestations of her greatness will survive until the end of time.

CHRONOLOGY, DOGES, PATRICIAN FAMILIES, "REGIMENTS" AND PLACE NAMES

CHRONOLOGY

Venice's incomparable history as an autonomous state, which began some time during the early Middle Ages as a result of the collapse of the Western Roman Empire, went on for more than 1,100 years until the tragic events of the Napoleonic era. The city at first lay on the fringes of the Byzantine Empire, acting as a center for shipping and trade in the lagoons themselves, as well as the rivers of the Po Valley. After the year 1000, she also emerged as a great Mediterranean naval power, whereupon her role as the crossroads between East and West was further strengthened. With the conquest of Constantinople in 1204, she became the dominant force in the entire Levant. Her extraordinary system of local government also led to her supremacy on the Italian peninsula. In fact, as of the beginning of the 15th century, she pursued a policy of expansionism on the mainland itself. The rise of the great modern European monarchies, which would not only transform international politics but also bring an end to the medieval city-states, was only one of the challenges to the Republic's survival. In addition to Spain, and eventually Hapsburg Austria, she was constantly under pressure from the Ottoman Empire. However, thanks to her diplomatic skills, her ability to adapt her commercial policies to the conditions created by the new trade routes that had opened up on the Atlantic, and her flourishing manufacturing industries, she continued to enjoy great wealth and influence. Venice's history is far more Mediterranean than Italian, given her close ties to the Balkan peninsula, the Danube, the Levant, the Holy Roman Empire, the Roman Catholic Church, the maritime republics of the Tyrrhenian Sea, and the great powers of western Europe. The following is a summary of the most significant events that took place in her thousand years of existence.

ORIGINS
During the sixth century, the inhabitants of the lagoon were primarily boatmen, fishermen and salt-workers, as we can see from a letter written by Cassiodorus (537-538) in which he urged the local population to supply Ravenna with the precious commodity of salt. "They live just like the water fowl," he observed, "sometimes perched on land, and other times on the sea." He also mentioned that their main source of income was salt, given the fact that "the man has yet to be born who does not want salt. . . ." The Longobard invasion of Italy in 568, and their occupation of what was then the Byzantine province of Venetia, forced any number of inhabitants of the mainland to seek refuge among the islands in the

lagoon, which extended from Cavarzere to Grado. When the capital city of Oderzo fell to the invaders in 639, the Byzantine governor transferred his headquarters to Cittanova in the lagoon, which he renamed Herecliana, or Heraclea, in honor of the emperor Heraclius. In fact, an inscription on the foundation of the Church of Santa Maria on the Island of Torcello, which dates from these early years, cites not only the name of Heraclius, but also that of Isaac, the exarch of the Italian diocese, whose seat was located at Ravenna, and the local governor, Marurizio.

697 THE FIRST DOGE
According to local legend, Venice was able to establish her independence from Byzantium as of the very first days of her existence. Legend also has it that the first doge, Paoluccio Anagesto (more commonly known as Paulicius) was elected in the year 697. According to the historian Roberto Cessi, however, this particular individual was actually Paul, the exarch of Ravenna.

727–740 REBELLION AND RECONCILIATION
As a result of Pope Gregory II's outspoken protests against the edict issued by the iconoclast emperor Leo III in 727, which ordered the destruction of all holy images, the armies of Byzantine Italy decided that it was time to elect their own dukes. As far as Venice was concerned, this individual may have been Orso, who is third on the traditional list of the doges. This crisis was eventually overcome, however, and when the Lombard king Liutprand invaded Ravenna in 740, the exarch sought refuge in the lagoon, from where he was able to reconquer his capital with the help of the venetici themselves.

742 FROM CITTANOVA TO MALAMOCCO
From what little we actually know, we may assume that the doge's seat was transferred from Cittanova to Malamocco as a result of political crises within the Byzantine kingdom in Italy as well as crises at home. Despite this state of affairs, the merchants, landowners, seamen and farmers who comprised the population of Venetia went on with their daily lives undisturbed by the turbulent events of the time.

810 KING PIPPIN AND THE REALTINE ISLANDS
By the end of the eighth century, the Italian political situation had substantially changed in light of the Frankish conquest of the Lombard kingdom, and the coronation of the emperor Charlemagne, which took place in Rome in the year 800, whereupon his son Pippin, whom he had proclaimed the king of Italy, attacked both Dalmatia and the lagoon itself. Although he was soundly defeated by the venetici in 1810, many of the local inhabitants had already left their original settlements in the lagoon for the Realtine Islands, where they were afforded greater protection. At the election of Doge Agnello Parteciaco (or Partecipazio), the duchy itself was transferred to the same islands, which led to the founding of the city herself. As a result of the pax Nicephori, which was signed by the two emperors in the year 814, the integrity of the territories that stretched from Grado to Chioggia was ultimately guaranteed.

828 THE BODY OF ST. MARK THE EVANGELIST

After the Venetian merchants Rustico da Torcello and Buono Tribuno da Malamocco had purloined the body of St. Mark from Alexandria in Egypt and brought it back in triumph to the city in 828, the precious relic was placed in the private chapel of the doge's palatium until such time as it could be transferred to the Basilica of St. Mark's, which was built between the years 829 and 832 during the reign of Giovanni Parteciaco. This was also the moment in which the legend was born concerning St. Mark's final resting-place, which was supposedly told to him by an angel while he was dreaming("Pax tibi, Marce, evangelista meus"). At the synod of Mantua, which had taken place the previous year, Maxentius, the Patriarch of Aquileia, whose political affiliations lay with the Western Empire, had obtained permission to suppress the Patriarchate of Grado. At a later date, however, this decision was reversed. The fact that the city was now in possession of the body of one of the founding fathers of Christianity, who was neither Byzantine nor Roman, symbolized her independence from both the eastern and western empires.

840 PACTUM LOTARII

At the behest of Doge Pietro of Venice, the Frankish-Byzantine treaty that ensured respect of one another's territories (814) was renewed by a decree of the emperor Lothair. As a result, the Venetian fleet was entrusted with the defense of the Adriatic, since there was no imperial fleet in existence, and the Byzantine naval forces lay elsewhere.

866 THE SACK OF COMACCHIO

In her role as a Byzantine city situated on the edge of the Western Empire, Venice became the crossroads for trade with Constantinople. As her commercial interests expanded, she began to consider Comacchio, which had assumed the same role in the Po Valley after the fall of the Roman Adriatic ports of Aquileia and Ravenna, as a serious threat to her economic well-being. This situation led to her sacking the city not once but twice. At the time of the second assault in 932, which was carried out by Doge Pietro II Candiano, the city's inhabitants were deported as well.

946 OR 948 THE ABDUCTION OF THE BRIDES

The mainstay of Venice's trade with Constantinople consisted of precious goods from the East, which were destined for the inland market, and basic commodities such as salt, fish, timber and slaves. While her maritime activities were increasing in the Adriatic, however, she would find herself faced with the serious problem presented by the Narentine pirates, whose headquarters were located at the mouth of the Narenta (Neretva). As was typical of her dealings with the Byzantines and the Turks, she would continue to maintain both commercial ties (particularly in terms of the slave trade) and hostile relations with these individuals despite the face that Doge Pietro I Candiano himself had perished in an armed encounter with them in 887. Local legend also has it that the Narentines were responsible for kidnapping a number of Venetian brides on the occasion of a mass wedding that was held in the Church of Santa Maria Formosa in either 946 or 948.

976 FIRE AND REBELLION

As part of the violent rebellion staged by the local populace in 976, Doge Pietro IV Candiano was assassinated, and the palatium, the Basilica, the Church of San Teodoro, and over 300 private dwellings, most of which were made of wood, were totally destroyed by fire. The people themselves then elected Pietro I Orseolo as doge in the Church of San Pietro di Castello. This bloody episode may have been caused by the political ambitions of the Candiano dynasty, who employed foreign mercenaries during their assaults on the mainland. These tactics were viewed as not only oppressive, but also as a betrayal of Venice's dedication to overseas trade.

1000 DUX DALMATICORUM

According to a document from the end of the 10th century, the Venetians were seen as "people who do not plough, sow, or harvest grapes, but who are able to buy grain and wine in every port of the kingdom, and in the markets of Pavia." This comment, which reflects the fact that the city's prosperity was not founded on the land and the agricultural industry, is well illustrated by the reign of Doge Pietro II Orseolo. On the one hand, Venice maintained peaceful relations with the Ottonian Empire in order to ensure that the transport of goods along the Po, Adige, Piave and Livenza rivers was guaranteed, since these were the main routes by which salt was carried to the mainland. On the other hand, she attempted to control the Adriatic trade routes that communicated directly with the Levant. On Ascension Day of the year 1000, Orseolo set sail for the Dalmatian coast, whereupon he received a pledge of support from the local inhabitants of Ossero, Veglia, Arbe and Zara.

From his headquarters in Zara, he successfully fought the Croats, after which he stationed himself in Spalato (Split), where he forced the Narentines to concede the islands of Curzola and Lagosta. In so doing, he rid the high seas of the Slavic pirates, and placed the Dalmatian coast under his own protection, which led to his bearing the title dux Dalmaticorum.

1032 THE FIRST ADVISORS TO THE DOGE

At the time of the overthrow of the Orseolo dynasty, whereupon Domenico Flabianico was elected as doge, two individuals were elected to serve as his personal advisors, one from each side of the Grand Canal. This action was intended not only to deter the future leaders of the city from entertaining any thoughts of establishing an absolute monarchy, as had been the case of the Candiano and the Orseolo, but also as a basis for imposing further restrictions on the doge's powers.

1042 THE NEW BASILICA OF ST. MARK'S

Although the church that had originally been constructed by the Parteciaci, which had suffered serious damage during the revolt of 976, was rebuilt during the reign of Pietro I Orseolo, it is difficult to ascertain to what extent it was actually restored to its former state. The present church, which was designed along the same lines as the Church of the Apostles in Constantinople, was begun in 1042 by Doge Domenico Contarini, and was completed in the year 1071. According to a local chronicler, the church "resembles the marvelous construction of the church in honor of the twelve apostles that is situated in the city of Constantinople."

1081 ASSISTING THE CAUSE OF BYZANTIUM

After the Norman Robert Guiscard had taken over the Apulian ports of Bari, Brindisi and Otranto, he launched an attack on the Byzantine Empire itself from the eastern coast of the Adriatic, at which point the Venetians agreed to lend their military support to the emperor Alexius I Comnenus because of the threat to their interests in the Adriatic trade routes, and their strong commercial ties with Byzantium. Accordingly, in 1081, the Venetian fleet launched a counter attack off the coast of Durazzo, which was occupied by Guiscard, and succeeded in defeating the Normans, who were under the command of his son Bohemud. However, the Normans managed to hold on to Durazzo, and further Venetian military excursions in the waters of Corfu, which began in 1082, were unable to resolve the situation until Guiscard's death in 1085. In gratitude for the Venetians' assistance, Alexis I Comnenus issued a chrysobull in 1082 , which not only granted them greater exemptions from tariffs and customs duties and additional trading posts throughout the empire, but also officially recognized the Venetian expatriot colony in Constantinople.

1099–1100 THE RELICS OF ST. NICHOLAS

After setting out on its first crusade in 1099, the Venetian fleet wintered on the Island of Rhodes, where it was forced to do battle with the Pisan fleet, which had intended to do the same. Following the Pisans' defeat, during which time their men were only released as prisoners after swearing not to venture out again into the waters of Romania (the Byzantine Empire), the Venetians left Rhodes at the end of May, 1100. At Myra in Asia Minor, they purloined the relics of St. Nicholas, the patron saint of sailors, after which they signed an agreement with Godfrey of Bouillon in Jaffa stating that they would assist him in extending his control over the coast in exchange for the right to establish an expatriot community in each of the cities conquered. Only the city of Haifa was actually taken, however, and the fleet returned to Venice before the end of the year.

1104 THE ARSENAL

The Arsenal, which was founded in 1104 during the reign of Doge Ordelaf Falier, was once described by Dante as the place where "sticky pitch boils throughout the winter." Although it originally housed an arms magazine, naval equipment and provisions, as well as repair shops and a protected base, it occupied only a small portion of the space that it does today. The facilities were first enlarged in the early 1300s, when the fortified area was quadrupled in size. It was also at this time that the Arsenal became a construction site as well, although there were still dockyards scattered throughout the city and on the islands of the lagoon. Further renovations took place during the Renaissance.

1122–1124 DOGE DOMENICO MICHIEL'S EXPEDITION TO THE EAST

In late spring of 1123, the Venetian fleet set sail under the command of Doge Domenico Michiel, headed once again for the Levant. During the 20 years that had passed since the last expedition to the region, things had not been going well. Not only had the King of Hungary established his rule over certain cities in Dalmatia, but Doge Ordelaf Falier himself had been assassinated near Zara (Zadar). The Byzantine emperor John Comnenus had also refused to honor the privileges that had been granted the Venetians by his predecessors. Off the coast of Jaffa, the Venetians gave chase to the Egyptian fleet, which had just withdrawn from the city, and defeated it at Ascalon on May 30, 1123. After turning south, the Venetians then captured a number of merchant ships that were laden with spices and other precious cargo. Finally, they took part in the siege of Tyre, which fell to the crusaders on July 7, 1124, in return for which they were granted their usual privileges. During the voyage home, the Venetian fleet also sacked the Byzantine ports in the Aegean and the Adriatic, which led Comnenus to restored their rights once again.

1143 CONSILIUM SAPENTIUM

According to records that are still in existence, the year 1143 marked the institution of a new political entity known as the Consilium Sapentium, or Council of Wise Men, who were elected "for the honor and benefit and salvation of our country." This legislative body, which was presided over by the doge, was the nucleus of the Maggior Consiglio. As of the 13th century, it was composed of 35 members.

1145–1153 "TOTIUS ISTRIAE DOMINATOR"

Venice's relations with the Istrians, which were founded on her role as their defender, were strengthened during the reign of Pietro II Orseolo. In the year 932, Capodistria had surrendered to the Venetians after attempting to wage an economic war, whereupon the city became a protectorate of the Venetian state. Later on, however, a series of accords were signed, first with Pola and Capodistria in 1435, and then with Pola, Rovigno, Parenzo and Umago between 1148 and 1153, which recognized Venice's dominion over the mainland. At this time, the doge was also given the title of "Totius Istriae Dominator."

1171 THE CRISIS IN THE EASTERN EMPIRE

The Venetian merchants shared their privileges in Constantinople with the Genoesi and Pisans, who also equaled them in numbers. However, as diplomatic relations between the Italians and Byzantines fluctuated, the three city-states began to employ the tactics of sacking and plundering as a means of ensuring that their various privileges were renewed or extended. The Greeks' resentment of these practices turned into an open crisis in 1171, when Manuel Comnenus destroyed the Genoese quarter and dispersed the Venetian colony, during which time he also arrested the residents and confiscated their possessions.

1172 THE DEATH OF DOGE VITALE II MICHIEL AND THE ELECTION OF SEBASTIANO ZIANI

In retaliation for the actions of the Byzantine emperor, Doge Vitale II Michiel set sail for the Aegean in 1172. However, when he returned home after his crew had been decimated by the plague without having achieved his goal, there were immediately rumors of treacherous behavior on his part, whereupon a number of rebels broke up a session of the Council of Wise Men, and pursued the doge through the streets of the city, finally killing him near San Zaccaria. His successor was Sebastiano Ziani, who was then the wealthiest individual in Venice. At that time, the government would begin using an indirect method of election, which involved the participation of 11 electors, whose choice then had to be ratified by the Council. In later years, the election system would become far more complicated.

1177 THE POPE, THE EMPEROR AND THE DOGE: THE CONGRESS OF VENICE

"Safe on all sides, fertile, abounding in all things, pleasant, and with a quiet and peace-loving people." Such was Venice in the year 1177, when it hosted a meeting between Pope Alexander III and the emperor Frederick I Barbarossa, both of whom were received by Doge Sebastiano Ziani in St. Mark's. It was during this historic encounter that the war between the cities of northern Italy and the Church on the one hand, and the Hohenstaufen empire on the other, was finally brought to an end in anticipation of the Peace of Constance. Legend has it that it was on this occasion that Pope Alexander III presented the doge with the ring that was used during the ceremony known as the "marriage with the sea," which had already been long in existence.

1178 THE SIX ADVISORS TO THE DOGE

The voting system that had been instituted in 1172 was altered in the year 1178 at the time of Doge Orio Mastropiero's election in order to provide for 11 individuals who would then designate 40 electors. It was also at this time that the six advisors to the doge were first appointed from the six sestieri of the city.

1201–1204 A QUARTER AND A HALF OF THE EASTERN EMPIRE

The events of the Fourth Crusade would not only have surprising results, but would also prove to be extremely favorable to the Venetians. At the beginning of the expedition, the Count of Champagne, along with other great feudal lords of France, appealed directly to Venice for her assistance. After negotiations had taken place between the doge and their envoys, who were led by Geoffroy de Villehardouin, the final terms of an agreement that was drawn in April of 1201 stipulated that Venice would transport more than 33,000 to the Holy Land in exchange for the enormous sum of 44,000 pounds of silver. Although the ships themselves were ready by the spring of 1202, many of the crusaders had already chosen not to honor the Venetians' request, whereupon Doge

Enrico Dandolo decided that the balance of the debt should be paid out of future booty. He also asked the French to assist him in recapturing Zara from the Hungarians.

Thereafter, the same individuals made the decision to attack Constantinople in support of the pretender Alexius IV, the son of Isaac II, who had been overthrown by his brother, Alexius III. Consequently, in July of 1203, the Venetian fleet, fired by the 90-year-old Enrico Dandolo, who was also blind, sailed up the Golden Horn, where they succeeded in taking the walls of the city. In the end, Alexius V Ducas Mourtzuphlos was proclaimed emperor as opposed to Alexius IV, who had proven to be extremely weak and ineffectual as a leader. After Mourtzuphlos had sworn to liberate Constantinople from the crusaders, they staged a second assault in April of 1204, during which time the city was sacked and plundered for three entire days.

The Venetians and the crusader barons then established the Eastern Latin Empire, whose first emperor, Baldwin, the Count of Flanders, was given a quarter of the Byzantine kingdom, while the remaining three-quarters were divided up between Venice and the barons themselves. According to the specific terms of the contract, the Venetians received three-eights of the city of Constantinople, as well as Negropont in Euboea, Modon and Corone on the southern tip of the Peloponnese, and the Island of Crete, which was actually captured from the Genoese pirate Enrico il Pescatore, the Count of Malta, in the year 1212. Marco Sanudo, who was a nephew of Doge Enrico Dandolo, also set up the Ducy of Naxos in the Aegean Islands.

CA. 1220 THE QUARANTIA

During the first decades of the 13th century, a new council was formed under the general heading "pro proficuo et utilitatis Comunis Venecie." This 35-member body, which was known as the Quarantia, or Council of Forty, was elected in the same manner as the Council of Wise Men. At a later date, the Quarantia itself, as well as the heads of the individual magistracies and other important government officials, were made ex officio members of the Maggior Consiglio, and the Council of Wise Men was increased in size. The stage was now set for the so-called serrata (closing) of the Maggior Consiglio in 1297.

1240 CONTROL OF THE PO

After the lord of Ferrara had joined forces in the year 1240 with the Hohenstaufen emperor Frederick II, the pope requested the Venetians' assistance in laying siege to the city. Following the defeat of the Ferraresi, Venice signed an agreement with the new rulers, which not only gave them control over all trade between the city and the coast, but also stipulated that merchandise shipped from the Adriatic to Ferrara would first have to pass through the port of Venice.

1255 THE PREGADI

According to official documents, we know that as of 1255, the Consiglio dei Rogati, or dei Pregadi, was already in existence. This legislative body was more commonly known as the Senate, which served as the upper house of parliament. At a later date, when the Maggior Consiglio had increased in size, the Senate membership was elected by the Great Council itself.

1255 THE MARITIME CODE

In the year 1255, Doge Ranieri Zeno issued a new maritime code whose regulations included the responsibilities of shipowners, the rights of sailors, crewmen and merchant-seamen, and fixed the dates for contracts to be let out for the galleys that formed part of the convoys known as "mude," as well as their times of departure.

1257–1270 THE PILLARS OF ACRI AND THE FIRST WAR WITH GENOA

The Genoese community in Acri was as large as that of the Venetians, which led to a series of bloody incidents between the citizens of these two maritime republics. In 1257, Venice's Levantine fleet was joined by warships under the command of Lorenzo Tiepolo, the son of the doge, whereupon the Venetians broke the chain that barred the port of Acri, and fired on the Genoese ships. The following year, the great naval battle that took place between the warring rivals resulted in a heavy defeat for the Genoesi. Before returning home, the Venetians purloined the pillars that now adorn the southern side of St. Mark's. These events marked the beginning of constant wars between the two city-states, which would go on for another century. Several years after Acri, the Byzantine emperor Michael Paleologus, who had allied himself with the Genoesi at Nymphaion in 1261, succeeded in taking the city of Constantinople in the month of July, thereby putting an end to the Eastern Latin Empire, and conceding the suburb of Pera to the Genoesi. Nevertheless, the Venetians won the last two major naval battles against Genoa, first at Settepozzi in 1263, and then at Trapani in 1266. In 1268, Michael Paleolgus permitted the Venetians to return to Constantinople despite the fact that they were still at war with his Genoese allies.

1261–1295 MESSER MILION: THE POLO FAMILY AND THE FAR EAST

In 1261, the brothers Nicolò and Matteo Polo, who were Venetian merchants with commercial interests in the Crimea, set out to investigate the possibility of trading with the hinterland in the wake of the establishment of the Mongol regime. When they failed to reach Tabriz by way of Sarai and Bukhara, they crossed central Asia in order to pay a visit to the Great Khan of the Mongols, Kubilai, who sent them back to Venice with a message for the pope to the effect that he was interested in forming an alliance with the Christians against the Moslem empire. During their second journey in 1271, they were accompanied by Nicolò's sono Marco, who would later travel extensively in the easternmost parts of the Mongol empire, at times on diplomatic missions for the Khan.

The three Polos finally returned home in 1295, after 25 years spent abroad. When Marco himself was taken prisoner during a naval encounter with the Genoesi, he dictated the book entitled *Il Milione (The Travels of Marco Polo)* while sharing a jail cell with the Pisan man of letters Rustichello. Despite the controversy that still surrounds this fabulous tale of adventure, his accounts were essentially truthful. In fact, as he lay dying in 1324, he is alleged to have said, "Non scripsi medietatem de hiis que vidi" ("I did not write half of what I saw").

1268 IL QUARANTAUN

Election procedures, which were codified in 1268, stipulated a series of alternating votes and lotteries that finally led to the appointment of the "Quarantaun," who were the 41 individuals who actually elected the doge. This extremely complicated and complex system, which was used for the first time at the election of Lorenzo Tiepolo, would remain unchanged thereafter.

1284 THE VENETIAN GOLD DUCAT

Genoa and Florence, which were the first of the western cities to mint gold coins in 1252, bought the precious metal from the markets of North Africa. Venice's own silver and gold coins were minted in Byzantium until 1284, when she introduced the gold ducat (later known as the "zecchino"), which had the same weight and purity as the Florentine florin.

1294–1299 THE SECOND WAR WITH GENOA

The long-standing feud between the two great maritime powers of Venice and Genoa once again resulted in all-out war at the end of the13th century. The first Genoese victory was scored in 1294 off the coast of Laiazzo, which had become the most important Asian trading post after the fall of the Eastern Latin Empire. When the Venetians retaliated by attacking Pera, 80 Genoese ships under the command of Lamba Doria arrived in the Adriatic in 1298 with the intention of ravaging the Dalmatian coast. Although Doria won the great battle of Curzola, he had suffered such heavy losses that he was unable to pursue the retreating Venetians as far as the lagoon itself. In the end, a peace treat that was signed in 1299 gave Genoa the coast of Liguria, and Venice the Adriatic coast. However, as far as the East was concerned, their differences would remain unresolved.

1297 THE "CLOSING" OF THE MAGGIOR CONSIGLIO

The reforms enacted in 1297 during the reign of Pietro Gradenico originally restricted the composition of the Maggior Consiglio to those individuals who were currently members or had been members within the past four years, subject to the approval of the Senate by at least a 12-vote majority. As new members were admitted, however, the Council more than doubled in size to a total of over 1,000 participants. Consequently, the rules for admission were made even more restrictive. In the year 1323, Council membership became solely hereditary. In the words of one Bartolo di Sassoferrato, "Although they are few in number when compared with the rest of the population, they are many when compared with the rest of the world's rulers, and so the people themselves willingly accept this form of government."

1308–1313 THE WAR WITH FERRARA AND THE INTERDICT

In 1308, the Venetians decided to consolidate their control over the Po Valley by taking over the city of Ferrara, at which point the pope, who was their feudal overlord, issued an interdict against Venice from his headquarters in Avignon. After the Venetians had begun negotiations with the Veronesi in an effort to create a waterway that would link the Adige to the Po, thereby avoiding Ferrara entirely, the papal excommunication orders were lifted in the year 1313.

1310 THE TIEPOLO CONSPIRACY AND
THE COUNCIL OF TEN

Among the patricians who actively opposed Doge Pietro Gradenigo's expansionist policies with regard to the mainland were Marco Querini, Baiamonte Tiepolo and Badoero Badoer, who eventually engaged in a conspiracy to overthrow the government in favor of their own regime. When the doge himself was finally alerted as to what was afoot, he not only summoned those of the aristocrats whom he felt he could trust in the middle of the night, but also gave the alarm to the Arsenal, and ordered the podestà of Chioggia to stop Badoer in his tracks. After the rebels had been defeated, Querini was sentenced to death, Tiepolo and Badoer were exiled, and the Querini and Tiepolo palaces were razed to the ground. The Council of Ten, which was formed as a result of these tragic events, was considered provisional until the year 1335.

1329 GALLEYS UP FOR AUCTION

Between the end of the 13th and the beginning of the 14th centuries, important innovations would take place with regard to the shipping industry that allowed vessels to travel during the winter months. In the late 1300s, both a larger version of the original galley and a large, square-sailed vessel known as the "cog" were introduced. As of 1329, the state began sponsoring the voyages of the heavily armed galleys, which set out twice a year under military escort for the Eastern Empire (the Aegean, Constantinople and the Black Sea), Cyprus and Syria, and Alexandria in Egypt and Flanders. The galleys themselves were auctioned off to the highest bidder in St. Mark's Square. Such a system also ensured that the huge industrial complex that comprised the Arsenal would be provided with enough work. In addition to the galleys, there were countless numbers of private merchant vessels as well.

1339 THE ACQUISITION OF TREVISO

Treviso, which was the first city on the Veneto mainland to come under Venetian rule, was then in the hands of the Della Scala family from Verona, who had risen to such heights of power and influence that the Republic considered them a serious threat to her security.

1340 THE GREAT COUNCIL CHAMBER

As the membership of the *Maggior Consiglio* increased in numbers, the state realized that it was time provide the lower house of parliament with new facilities. This project, which took 10 years to complete, involved the total renovation of that part of the Doges' Palace that faced onto the Molo, after which its walls were adorned with frescoes by the Paduan artist Guariento depicting the *Coronation of the Virgin* between 1365 and 1367.

1347–1348 THE PLAGUE

The Bubonic Plague, which was raging among the ranks of the Tartar soldiers who were laying siege to Kaffa in the Crimea, was brought back to Italy in the autumn of 1347 by a Venetian vessel. Within the short space of 18 months, the city would lose three-fifths of her inhabitants.

1350–1355 THE THIRD WAR WITH GENOA

In the year 1530, the Venetian fleet, which was then under the command of Marco Ruzzini, attacked a number of Genoese galleys in the port of Castro near Negropont, several of which actually managed to escape the onslaught because the Venetian crewmen, who were by and large Greek and Dalmatian mercenaries, began to plunder too early in the day. After gaining reinforcements from the allied fleets of Catalonia and Byzantium, the Venetians set out once again for Pera. Although the two sides never actually made physical contact, there was a bitter and bloody encounter in the Bosphorus during the winter of 1352, after which the Venetian fleet was forced to retreat. In 1353, the combined forces of the Venetians and the Catalans won a great victory over the Genoesi off the coast of Alghero. Later on, however, the Venetian fleet suffered a surprise attack by Paganino Doria as it was wintering at Portolongo near Modon, during which Nicolò Pisani, who was the commanding officer, was captured by the enemy. In the end, however, Genoa would be taken over by Giovanni Visconti, the lord of Milan, in 1355.

1355 THE DOGE BEHEADED

Internal strife following the defeat at Alghero brought Genoa under Milanese subjection. The Venetian defeat at Portolongo led to an attempted dictatorship by the newly-elected doge, the septuagenarian Marino Falier. In Venice, however, the outcome was quite different. The Dogal Councillors were warned by denunciations, and summoned the Council of Ten. Among the conspirators who were at once arrested and condemned was Filippo Calendario, a building contractor, who has wrongly been credited with the construction of the Doge's Palace. When the doge's involvement was discovered, he was sentenced and beheaded on 17 April 1355. In the series of portraits of the doges in the Hall of *Maggior Consiglio*, there is a black curtain in Marino Falier's place.

1358 DALMATIA CREEDED

The cities, ports and islands of Dalmatia had been in Venice's possession since the profitable crusade of doge Pietro II Orseolo three and a half centuries before. However, the kings of Hungary had cast their eyes on these lands in the course of their expansion over the Slav hinterland towards the sea. The cities of Dalmatia were themselves turbulent and often rebelled against Venetian rule. At the end of 1355, after the peace with Genoa, Venice had to deal with the "whole of Slavonia in tumult." Arrayed against Venice in 1356 were the dukes of Austria, the partiarch of Aquileia, the Carrarese lord of Padua, and worst of all, the Hungarians, who were laying seige to Zara (Zadar). Zara fell, Traú (Trogir) and Spalato (Split) went over to the Hungarians, and in June 1358 Venice ceded her claim to the possessions in Dalmatia to the Hungarian crown.

1363–66 THE REVOLT OF CANDIA

A local revolt led by John Kalegris was joined by a group of noble Venetians who had settled on the island, including members of the Venier, Gradenigo, Sagredo and Molin families. The rebels were thrown back but not eliminated by a Venetian fleet with the land army of Luchino dl Verme and the governor Pietro Morosini. The rebels reorganized in the mountains and made renewed attempts, until their leaders were captured and beheaded in April 1366.

1378–81 THE WAR OF CHIOGGIA, AND THE FOURTH WAR WITH GENOA

The origins of the fourth war with Genoa lay in rivalry over the conquest of the island of Tenedos, which was a potential base commanding the straits coveted by both Venetians and Genoese. The Venetians occupied it in 1376; war was not far behind. Against Venice were Genoa, the Carraresi of Padua, and the king of Hungary, while Dalmatia, ceded in 1368, could not longer be counted upon; indeed the Dalmatian bases and strongholds were now the preserve of Venice's enemies. In 1378 the Venetian fleet under Vittor Pisani sailed on an offensive war to the West, achieved a brilliant victory, and returned to winter at Pola. Here they were attacked by the Genoese in the spring of 1379. Pisani was lured into a trap, and his victory was turned into defeat. Returning home, he was thrown into prison. The Genoese were reinforced, and attacked the coast of the lagoon with the help of the Paduans on 16 August 1379. Never had Venice stood in greater danger. all reserves were moblized. The populace and sailors forced the release of Vittor Pisani, "the chief and father of all the seamen of Veniexia." During the night of 22 December 1379, the aged doge Andrea Contarini and Vittor Pisani blockaded Chioggia, the cutting off the occupying forces from both the Paduans and the Genoese fleet. Meanwhile another Venetian squadron under Carlo Zeno which had left on a plundering expedition before the battle of Pola was inflicting heavy damage on Genoese trade in the Tyrrhenian and Aegean seas as far at Beirut and Rhodes. Zeno returned home on 1 January 1380, just in time to join the blockade of Chioggia. Failing in an attempt to subdue the mercenaries employed by the Venetians who were beseiging them, the Genoese in Chioggia surrendered six months later in June 1380, allowing the Venetians to sally forth and regain control of the Adriatic. On land they tried to win over Gian Galeazzo Vosconti as an ally. alarming the count of Savoy, who was in favor of a compromise. The peace of Turin of 1381 seemed to favor Genoa more than Venice, but Venice's greater political stability meant that she emerged victorious from the centuries of conflict. Thirty new families were ad-

mitted to the *Maggior Consiglio* after the peace, drawn from those who had most distinguished themselves in the war effort.

1386 THE OCCUPATION OF CORFU

The island of Corfu was occupied with the consent of its rulers in 1386; legal rights of possession were later obtained from Charles, pretender to the throne of Naples. Corfu was strongly fortified and became a very important base, commanding the lower Adriaic. It remained in Venice's possession until the end of the Republic.

1389–1420 EXPANSION OVER THE MAINLAND OF THE VENETO

Venice was a seafaring and mercantile power, whose main interests were trade and commerce. Just as in the Adriatic and in the Levant Venice's policy was to control ports, bases and trading-stations, so in the hinterland of the lagoon her policy was to keep the roads free so that her trade could flow unhindered. So long as there was only a sprinkling of communes to its rear, the Republic felt no great need to exert its rule over them, but with the flowering of the age of the great lords ruling over large stretches of land and ambitions of the different lords against each other was that Venice became involved herself in the struggle for the territory, eventually becoming one of the five great states of the 15th century. There were three main powers in Venice's game, the Scalligeri of Verona, the Carraresi of Padua, and the Visconti of Milan. Farther to the East were the lands of the patriarch of Aquileia, and here it was necessary to keep and eye on the ambitions of powers north of the Alps.

The first stage in Venice's expansion over the mainland was the recovery of Treviso, which had previously belonged to Venice but had been ceded to the dukes of Austria during the war of Chioggia, in order to keep the Carraresi at a distance. The alliance of Venice and the Visconti against the Carraresi in 1388 created the opportunity for the surrender of Treviso to Venice in 1389. On the other hand, although the Visconti were farther off than the CArraresi, they represented a far greater threat, especially when Gian Galeazzo ambitiously attempted to unite the whole of northern Italy under him. His death from the plague in 1402 left Venice facing Francesco Novello di Carrara. Vicenzia, Belluno, and Bassano submitted to Venice in 1404. In 1405 Padua and Verona were conquered. Francesco Novello and two other members of his family were thrown into prison and strangled by order of the Council of Ten.

Within the lands of the patriarchate, the house of Savorgnan at Udine held firm with the Venetian support, but here too the Carraresi had made attempts to expand, and Trieste had been given over to the dukes of Austria in 1382. When the emperor Sigismund of Hungary, with whom Venice was also fighting over Dalmatia, intervened, the military campaign of 1418–20 broke out. On 16 June 1420, Tristano di Savorgnan entered Udine bearing the banner of St. Mark. Venice now possessed almost the whole of the modern Veneto and Friuli.

1409–20 DALMATIA REGAINED

At the beginning of the 15th century there were two kings of Hungary, Sigismund of Luxemnorg, son of the emperor Charles IV and himself emperor from 1411 (who effectively held the state), and Ladislas of Anjou-Durazzo, king of Naples, who was in possession of Dalmatia which he had conquered in an expedition against Zara (Zadar) in 1403 as part of his strugle to acquire the throne of Hungary. In January 1409 Venice regained its rights over Dalmatia, ceded in 1358, from Ladislas who was in difficulties. Less than a third of the initial asking price of 300,000 ducats was paid. The little which Ladislas retained, principally Zara, was handed over to Venice, and the rest, Traú, Sebenico, Spalato, Cattaro, Curzola (Trogir, Sebenik, Split, Kotor, Korcula), and the other islands she won in the war with Sigismund in 1420.

1423 THE ELECTION OF FRANCESCO FOSCARI

The formula, "If he is pleasing to you," with which the doge was presented to the populace recalled the fact that the election of the doge had originally been subject to the approval of the popular asembly, although it had been a pure formality. In 1423 the formula was abolished; henceforth the Maggior Consiglio alone, and the patriciate which constituted it, was the sovereign master. In 1423 Francesco Foscari was elected doge to succeed Tommaso Mocenigo, who had in vain warned the Maggior Consiglio not to choose him: "the said Francesco Foscari spreads rumors and many other matters without any basis, and stoops and climbs more than a falcon." The Foscari led Venice into costly wars with Milan to which Mocenigo had been opposed; meanwhile Turkey was growing inot a great sea power. Thus while Mocenigo looked to the sea, Foscari looked to the mainland.

1424–30 THESSALONICA

The Turks had occupied nearly all of the Byzantine Empire with the exception of Constantinople. The city of Thessalonica entrusted its defense to Venetian sea power, and the Republic dispatched a fleet there under Pietro Loredan. It was he who in 1416 had destroyed a Turkish fleet at Gallipoli in the first naval battle between the Turks and the Venetians. Thessalonica was soon lost, however (in 1430), while Venice was caught up in the wars in Italy against Milan.

1425–54 THE WARS IN LOMBARDY

"I counsel you to pray to the almighty power of God who has inspired us to make peace, as we hae done, and to follow Him and render Him thanks. If you follow my advice, you will see that from now on we will be lords of all Christendom; the whole world will revere and fear you. Beware of the desire to take what belongs to others, and of making unjust war, for God will destroy you." These were the wrods of the aged doge Tommaso Mocenigo shortly before his death in 1423. Soon afterwards Venice was caught up in 30 ears of war, precisely to "take was belongs to others," *i.e.* Lombardy. This carried Venice's frontiers to Adda, convulsed the whole of Italy and ended in compromise with the Peace of Lodi in 1454 which brought 40 years of peace to Italy, but not to Venice. The

prelude to the war against the rule of the Visconti house in the person of duke Filippo Maria (wars therefore of supremacy, or from the other point of view, to protect the balance of power in Italy which was threatened by the expansion of the Visconti), was the League between Venice and Florence of 4 May 1425. There were four wars. In the first, (1425–26), Venice took Brescia with an army led by Carmagnola, and the fleet on the Po advanced as far as Padua. the second (1427–28) saw a Venetian victory at Maclodio on 4 October 1427, and ended with Venice being granted Bergamo as well as Brescia. In the third war of 1431–33, the Po fleet was defeated at Cremona but Venice won a naval victory over Genoa, which was at that time a dependency of the Visconti, at San Fruttuoso on 27 August 1431. Carmagnola failed to act, and was suspected of having come to terms with the enemy. He was recalled from the field by the Council of Ten for consultation, arrested in March 1432, and tried. A month later he was beheaded between the two columns of the Piazzetta.

The peace of Ferrara in 1433 left things as they stood. In the fourth war Venice's sea-captains were first Gattamelata, and later Francesco Sforza, while the Visconti side ws led by Niccolò Piccinino. Sforza and Piccinino were in fact fighting a personal war in which the interests of the opposing powers were secondary. Piccinino laid seige to Brescia in 1438 and penetrated the Veronese defenses. Venice's response to the crisis was the transportation of six galleys and other lesser craft by land from the Adige to Lake Garda, more than 2,000 oxen being used in the operation(1439). On the field of Cavriana, Sforza acted as mediator between the two sides accomplishing the act for which Carmagnola had lost his head. No territorial changes were made in the ensuing Peace of Cremona of 20 November 1441.

None of these treaties was more than a truce, and no general accord between the Italian states was reached, as Venice would have preferred. Instead, important political changes occurred. Francesco Sforza entered the service of Visconti and married his daughter, while Florence took a new turn under Cosimo de' Medici. Visconti died in 1447, and in May 1450 Francesco Sforza entered Milan in triumph, after the demise of the short-lived Ambrosian Republic (in 1449 Venice had acquired Crema). Two coalitions were now formed, Sforza Milan with Medici Florence on one hand, against Venice and Aragonese Naples on the other. The main theater of war was still Lombardy, where Venice clashed with Francesco Sforza. Worn out, both sides joined in the Peace of Lodi in May 1454, a peach which formed the basis for a general accord betwen the four contenders, Venice, Milan, Florence and Naples, under the leadership of the pope.

1463–79 THE TURKISH ADVANCE

On 3 April 1463, ten years after the capture of Constantinople, the Turks seized the Venetian fortress of Argos in a surprise attack. A long war ensued from which Venice emerged defeated. At first the Venetians launched a counterattack by sea and land with the help of their Hungarian allies, and gained some posistive results (1463–68). In spring

1470 the Turks attakced the base of Negropont in force with both land and sea troops. Poorly supported by the naval squadron commanded by the hesitant Nicolò Canal, the base fell, along with the whole of Euboea. During the course of fruitless negotiations, Turkish squadrons sailed into Friuli in 1471, repeating the attack in 1477 and 1478.

Venice had meanwhile succeeded in drawing the Shah of Persia into the war, and attacked the coast of Asia from the sea. However the Persians were put to rout (1472–74). The Turks began to press on the lower Adriatic, where the Venetians put up a tenacious resistance in Scutari. The peace of 24 January 1479 was humiliating: Venice lost Argos, Euboea and Scutari, and had to pay an annual tribute of 10,000 ducats. The Turks went on to attack peninsular Italy, landing at Otranto, but were unsuccessful in this attempt. The death of Mehmed II brought Turkey to a period of crisis, which allowed Venice to take and hold Zante in the Ionian islands, and to improve the terms of the treaty. The tribute was abolished, duty was lowered from five to four percent, and the privileges and immunities of the Venetian *bailo* in Constantinople were renewed.

1473 CYPRUS ACQUIRED
During the course of the disastrous war with the Turks, Venice managed to consolidate her hold on the island of Cyprus, where there were strong Venetian, and specifically Corner, interests. The king of Cyprus wa sGiacomo II Lusigano, who married Caterina Corner in 1472. A revolt against the queen broke out on the king's sudden death in 1473, with the aim of giving the throne to a natural son of Ferdinand of Naples. Venice reacted promptly and energetically, calling back Barbaro with his Venetian fleet from Asia to take charge of the island, and of the interests of Giacomo Lusignano's widow. The kingdom remained in the possession of Caterina Corner and of her baby son Giacomo III Lusignano, who died in 1474, under strict Venetian control until she was forced to abdicate on 24 February 1489. She ceded the island to the direct administration of Venice and was granted the signory of Asolo, where she continued to maintain a brilliant court.

1484 THE POLESINE
The pope had sought Venice's help against the king of Naples, leaving her a free hand against Ferrara (1482). He subsequently became alarmed by Venice's success, however, and while Florence and Milan intervened in Ferrara's favor, Sixtus IV had recourse to and interdict in order to stop Venice. At the peace of 1484 Venice was allowed to retain the Polesine, which she had conquered. A year later the French ambassador, Philippe de Commines, wrote of Venice, "It is the most splendid city I have ever seen, and the one which governs itself the most wisely."

1495–1503 BETWEEN LAND AND SEA
Charles VIII of France's descent into Italy in order to conquer the kingdom of Naples in 1494 is one of the turning points in Italian history. It marks the beginning of the crisis of Italian freedom. Venice was one of the architects of the anti-French league which, however, failed to destroy the French king's army at Fornovo in 1495 as it returned home. Nevertheless Venice occupied the Apulian prots, important strategic bases commanding the lower Adriatic and the Ionian islands. A few years later in 1499 Venice allied itself with Louis XII against Milan, and gained Cremona. In the same year the Ottoman sultan moved to attack Lepanto by land, and sent a large fleet to support his offensive by sea. Antonio Grimani, more a businessman and diplomat than a sailor, was defeated in the sea battle of Zonchio in 1499. The Turks once again sacked Friuli. Preferring peace to total war both against the Turks and by sea, Venice surrendered the bases of Lepanto, Modon, and Corone in 1499. Her supremacy in Italy seemed to be in peril, and her ambitions on the mailand won the day. Some believe that this decision, and this period were the critical point in Venice's fortunes.

1508–17 THE LEAGUE OF CAMBRAI
The area which had tempted Venice to divert her attention from her maritime position, with its promises of expansion, was the Romagna. This Venice hoped to remove from the control of the pope, now that Malatesta lords of Rimini were passing through a period of crisis, and the meteoric career of the duke of Valentinois, Cesare Borgia, son of pope Alexander VI was over. Venice's power was at its height, but this brought her enemies. Eager to take some of Venice's lands, these all joined in the League of Cambrai in 1508. The pope wanted Romagna, the emperor Friuli and the Veneto, Spain and the Apulian ports, the king of France Cremona, the king of Hungary Dalmatia, and each of the others some part. The offensive against the huge army enlisted by Venice was launched from France. On 14 May 1509 Venice was defeated at Agnadello in the Ghiara d'Adda; the city was in the gravest danger. French and imperial troops were occupying the Veneto, but Venice extricated herself by her efforts and her political skill. The Apulian ports were ceded in order to come to terms with Spain, and pope Julius II was placated when he perceived how much more dangerous Venice would be destroyed than powerful. The citizens of the mailand rose to the cry of "Marco, Marco." Andrea Gritti recaptured Padua in July 1509, and successfully defended it against the beseiging imperial troops. Spain and the pope broke off their alliance with France, and Venice regained Brescia and Verona from France also. After seven years of ruinous war, Venice regained her domains on the mainland up to the Adda, which she held until the end of the Republic.

1520–30 "THANKS TO THE VIRTUE AND WISDOM OF OUR ANCESTORS"
In 1544 Gasparo Contarini, politician and Venetian diplomat, and later a cardinal, wrote his *De Magistratibus et Republica Venetorum*. In this work, he expressed the approval and interest which surrounded Venice's constitutional arrangements, not only among the patricians of Venice but

throughout Italy and in foreign lands, where men were astonished at Venice's greatness, her long independence, her resistance to Italy's tragic loss of freedom, and, not least, her emerging unscathed from the war against the League of Cambrai. In this work Contarini suggested that the secret of Venice's greatness lay in the co-existence of Aristotle's three types of government, monarchy, oligarchy, and democracy. In his opinion, the *Maggior Consiglio* was the "democratic" part, the Senate and the Ten were the oligarchy, while the doge represented the monarchy. The combination of these three principles in the Venetian government came as close as was possible to perfection in the mechanism of government. At the same time the patrician Marino Sanudo, a politician who had a remarkable career, and a celebrated diarist, was bewailing the corruption which resulted from the great number of poor or impoverished patricians. "Votes are sold for money. . . . May God help this poor Republic. . . ."

1538 PREVEZA

When the struggle for supremacy in Italy between France and Spain was resolved in favor of Spain, ruled by the emperor Charles V Hapsburg, Venice found herself caught between the Turks and Spain (and later between Hapsburg Austria and the Turks). To this her only possible response was to put up a long, tough, and often skillful defense. the interests of Spain and Venice were united against the Turks, although only in part. Venice's maritime aid was potentially useful to Spain, but not to the point of allowing her to reinforce her position in the Levant, which would increase her strength in Italy as well, where she was practically the only Italian state not subject to Spain. In the Turkish war of 1537–40, Venice was allied to Charles V. Andrea Doria was the emperor's admiral and commander of the allied fleets. He was unable to fulfill his instructions successfully, and was defeated at Preveza in 1538. In 1540 Venice made peace, and the Turks took the Aegean duchy of Naxos from the Sanudo family. After Preveza the supremacy of the sea passed to Turkey.

1539 THE THREE INQUISITORS

The State Inquisitors, later known as the Supreme Tribunal, were instituted, and their duties laid down, in a law of 1539. There were three Inquisitors, one known popularly as *il rosso,* "the red one," who was chosen from the Dogal Councillors, who wore scarlet robes, and two from the Council of Ten, known as *i negri,* "the black ones." They began as a security body at the difficult time Venice felt herself encircled by the Hapsburgs, and gradually assumed some of the powers of the Council of Ten. By means of espionage, counter-espionage, and internal surveillance, they made use of a network of informers and "confidants."

1545 ENFORCED GALLEY SERVICES

Until 1545 the oarsmen in the galleys were free sailors enrolled on a wage. They were originally Venetians, but later Dalmatians, Cretans and Greeks joined in large numbers. Because of the difficulty in hiring sufficient crews, Venice had recourse to conscription, chaining the oarsmen to the benches as other navies had already done. Cristoforo da Canal was the first Venetian to command such a galley.

1556 THE *PROVVEDITORI AI BENI INCULTI*

This office was founded in 1556, and was established for the improvement of agriculture by increasing the acreage under cultivation and encouraging private investment in agricultural improvement. The consistent rise in the price of grain during the 16th century encouraged the transfer of capital from trade to the land.

1571 THE LOSS OF CYPRUS AND THE BATTLE OF LEPANTO

Venice's political situation now resembled that at the time of the battle of Preveza. Allied with Spain and the pope, she was able to assemble a grand fleet of 208 galleys, 110 of which were Venetian, equal in numbers to the Turkish fleet, under the command of John of Austria, half-brother of Philip II. The Venetians were commanded by Sebastiano Venier.

The Turkish fleet had sailed up the Adriatic as far as Lesina, and then returned to Lepanto in the Gulf of Patras for provisions. The Christian fleet had assembled at Messina and encountered the Turkish fleet off Lepanto on 7 October 1571. Lepanto was a great Venetian and Christian victory, and the victors divided up 117 galleys captured from the Turks. But the Venetians gained no strategic advantage. Philip II was concerned with the balance of power in the eastern Mediterranean and Africa, and was unwilling for the fleet to become involved in the Levant. Famagusta, the last stronghold on the island of Cyprus, had been attacked by the Turks in 1570 and had surrendered before Lepanto. The Turkish commander had had the Venetian *provveditore* Marcantonio Bragadin flayed alive. The loss of Cyprus was ratified in the peace of 1572.

1577 THE FIRE IN THE DOGE'S PALACE

On 20 December a fire broke out in the Doge's Palace and destroyed the Halls of the *Maggior Consiglio* and the *Scrutinio.* The *Signoria* summoned the 15 greatest architects of the time. Palladio's proposed new building in the classical style was rejected, and the contract given to Antonio Da Ponte, who completed the reconstruction in under a year. Guariento's great fresco of *The Coronation of the Virgin* was beyond repair, and Jacopo Tintoretto's huge canvas of *Paradise* was placed over it (1588–90).

1587 THE PUBLIC BANK

The first public bank was set up by the Venetian government in 1587 after the collapse of a private bank, amid public outcry. It was known as the Banco della Piazza. A second public bank, the Banco del Giro, was started in 1619, and in 1638 the Banco della Piazza was abolished. These banks played a very important role in financing the Republic's wars, by issuing representative money.

1593 THE STRONGHOLD OF PALMANOVA

After the war against the League of Cambrai, Venice had to cede Gradisca and retreat to the west of the Isonzo. Then came the Turkish incursions into Friuli. In order to reinforce the eastern border against the Turks and the Hapsburgs, Venie decided to build a fortress. In this way Palmanova was built to the design of Giulio Savorgnan, in a nine-pointed star. The first stone was ceremonially laid on 7 October 1593, on the twenty-second anniversary of the battle of Lepanto.

1605–7 PAOLO SARPI AND THE INTERDICT

The famous conflict between Venice and the Holy See began with the arrest of two members of the clergy who were guilty of petty crimes, and with a law restricting the Church's right to enjoy and acquire landed property. Paul V held that these provisions were contrary to canon law, and demanded that they should be repealed. When this was refused, he placed Venice under an interdict, which forbade priests from carrying out their religious duites and excommunicated the rulers.

The Republic paid no attention to the interdict or the act of excommunication, and ordered its priests to carry out their ministry. It was supported in its decisions by the Servite monk Paolo Sarpi, a sharp polemic writer who was nominated to be the Signoria's adviser on theology and canon law in 1606. The interdict was lifted after a year, when the French intervened and proposed a formula of compromise. Venice was satsfied with reaffirming the principle that no citizen was superior to the normal processes of the law. In 1607 Sarpi was wounded in an assault by three ruffians, and said that in the dagger which wounded him he recognized "lo stile(= the style, or the dagger) of the Roman curia." To him Venice also owed two essays on The Rule of the Adriatic in which he defended Venice's jurisdiction over this "enclosed and restricted sea, which has since time immemorial been owned and guarded at [great] expense and labor."

1613–17 THE PIRATES AND THE WAR OF GRADISCA

"The whole house of Austria is displeased and disgusted at the just rule of the Most Serene Republic over the Gulf, and it appears to [us] that they are disturbing Venice's peaceful jurisdiction and possession with the frequent raids of the Uzoks," so Venice wrote.

The Uzokzs were Christian refugees from Bosnia and Turkish Dalmatia who had been enlisted by the Hapsburgs to defend their borders after the peace between Venice and the Ottomans following the battle of Lepanto . They settled in Segna and lived as pirates in the Adriatic, causing Venice to worry that they would complicate relations with the Sublime Porte. When Venice acted against these *Uscocchi* in 1613, she found herself at odds on land with their protector, the archduke of Austria. An army was sent against Gradisca, which belonged to the archduke, and financial support was given to the duke of Savoy who was pinning down the Spanish army in Lombardy. The military operations on the eastern frontier were not decisive, but among the terms of the peace of 1617 the Hapsburgs undertook to solve the problem of the Uzoks, whom they moved inland.

1617–18 THE WAR OF OSSUNA AND THE MARQUIS OF BEDMAR'S CONSPIRACY

Whether on his own initiative, or supported by his king, the Spanish viceroy of Naples attempted to break Venetian dominance in the Gulf by sending a naval squadron to the Adriatic. His expedition met with mixed success in 1617, and he retired from the Adriatic. Rumors of sedition and conspiracy were meanwhile circulating in Venice, and there were disturbances between mercenaries of different nationalities enrolled for the war of Gradisca. The Spanish ambassador, the Marquis of Bedmar, was wise to the plot, if not the author of it. Informed of this by a Huguenot captain, the Ten acted promptly. Three "bravos" were hanged, and the Senate demanded the immediate recall of the Spanish ambassador.

1622 THE FOSCARINI AFFAIR

Antonio Foscarini, a senator and ambassador to England, was accused of acting for foreign powers during his time as ambassador and of spying for Spain after his return. He was tried, acquitted of the first charge, found guilty of the second and hanged from a gallows between the columns of the Piazzetta in 1622. A few months later the Ten discovered that he had been the innocent victim of a plot. He was rehabilitated, and the news circulated around all the chancelleries of Europe.

1628–30 THE MANTUAN SUCCESSION AND THE PLAGUE

On the death of Ferdinando Gonzaga, duke of Mantua and Monferrato, the succession developed upon a French prince, Charles of Gonzaga-Nevers. This changed the balance of power in northern Italy, which had until now been controlled by the Spanish through Milan. In the ensuing war, Venice was allied with France against the Hapsburgs and Savoy. The Venetian army was defeated in an attempt to come to the aid of Mantua which was under seige by German troops, and Mantua itself was savagely sacked. The peace which recognized Charles of Gonzaga-Nevers duke of Mantua and Monferrato was made practically without Venice's participation. War brought plague in 1630. In 16 months 50,000 people died in Venice, one third of the population. The first stone of the church of Santa Maria della Salute was laid as a thanksoffering for the end of the plague.

1638 VALONA BOMBARDED

While the Venetian fleet was cruising off Crete, a corsair fleet from Barbary consisting of 16 galleys from Algiers and Tunis entered the Adriatic. When the fleet returned, the corsairs reparied the Turkish stronghold of Valona. In spite of this Marino Cappello attacked the corsairs, bombarded the forts and captured their galleys, freeing 3,600 prisoners. The sultan reacted to the bombardment of his fortress by arresting the *bailo* Alvise Contarini. War was averted and the matter settled by diplomacy.

1644 THE SULTAN'S HAREM

The Knights of Malta raided a Turkish convoy route from Alexandria to Constantinople and captured part of the sultan's harem returning from Mecca. On their way home the Maltese landed on Crete. Christian pirates were no less active in the Mediterranean than Moslem ones, and Crete was an irritant to Turkish shipping. The sultan prepared a fleet to punish Malta, but it attacked Crete instead. So began the 25-year-long war of Candia.

1645–69 THE WAR OF CANDIA

In the middle of 1645 the Turks attacked the frontiers of Dalmatia and landed on Crete. On 22 August, Khania was forced to capitulate. Dalmatia too was heavily attacked but the Venetians were able to save their coastal positions because of their command of the sea. The greatest Turkish effort was directed against Sebenico (Sebenik), to which they laid seige in August–September 1647, but the seige failed, and in the succeeding year the Venetians recovered several fortresses inland, such as Clissa. In Crete, however, the situation was more serious. The Turks attacked the capital of Candia, which held out for 20 years. Throughout the long war the Venetian strategy was to blockade the Dardanelles in order to surprise the Turkish fleet on its way to supply troops on Crete. There were some signal successes, but they failed to alter the strategic situation. There were two victories in the Dardanelles, in 1655 and 1656. In the second of these battles on 26 August 1656, the Turks suffered their most crushing defeat since Lepanto, and the commander Lorenzo Marcello fell. The next year there was a three-day-long sea-battle (17–19 July 1657), in which the captain Lazzaro Mocenigo was killed by a falling mast. The battle was on the whole a defeat. With the end of the war between France and Spain in 1659, Venice received more aid from the Christian states that the small contingents which she had received in the first years. In 1666 and expedition to retake Khania failed, and in 1669 another attempt to lift the seige of Candia with joint action on land with the French contingent and by sea under Mocenigo, was also a failure. The French returned home, and only 3,600 fit men were left in the fortress of Candia. Francesco Morosini negotiated its surrender on 6 September 1669. The island of Crete was ceded, except for some small Venetian bases, while Venice retained the islands of Tinos and Cerigo, and its conquests in Dalmatia.

1667 THE LINE-OF-BATTLE SHIP

The backbone of the Venetian fleet had always been its galleys and galleasses. Naval battles were decided by boarding, as had been the case at Lepanto. But naval tactics had been revolutionized by the galleon, with rows of cannon on its sides, and by the line-of-battle ship, which derived from it. Venice chartered some Dutch and British ships, and adapted merchant ships to military purposes. After this the first line-of-battle ship was built in the Arsenal in 1667, to the design of a British battleship. In the next half-century 68 line-of-battle ships came from the Arsenal stocks.

1684–99 THE MOREA CONQUERED

In September 1683 John Sobieski routed the Turks beseiging Vienna. From this time the Ottoman power of expansion was broken, and the empire started the long course of its decline over the next few centuries. In 1684 Venice formed an alliance with Austria; Russia was later included in the league. Francesco Morosini occupied the island of Levkas and set out to recapture the Greek ports. Between June 1865 when he landed at Corone, and August when he occupied Patras, Lepanto and Corinth, he secured the Peleponnese for Venice. In September during the attack on Athens, a Venetian cannon blew up the Parthenon.

Venetian possessions were greatly increased in Dalmatia too, although the attempt to regain Negropont in 1688 was a failure. Morosini's successors failed to obtain lasting results in the next years, although large fleets were sent out, and in spite of some brilliant victories—at Mitylene in 1695, Andros in 1697 and the Dardanelles in 1698. The peace of Carlowitz in 1699 favored Austria and Russia more than Venice, which failed to regain its bases in the Mediterranean taken by the Turks in the last two centuries, in spite of its conquests.

1700 NEUTRALITY

New conflict was brewing over the question of the Spanish succession. Both France and the Hapsburg empire, the two European powers which had been fighting in Europe for 200 years, attempted to gain an active ally in Venice, despatching envoys with authority there in 1700. The Venetian government preferred to remain neutral rather than accept hypothetical advantages offered by interested parties. The Republic remained faithful to this policy of neutrality to the end, caught in unavoidable decline but living out its life in enviable luxury.

1714–18 THE MOREA LOST

In December 1714–18 the Turks declared war when the Peloponnese (the Morea) was "without any of those supplies which are so desirable even in countries where aid is near at hand which are not liable to attack from the sea." The Turks took the islands of Tinos and Aegina, crossed the isthmus and took Corinth. Daniele Dolfin, commander of the fleetm thought it better to save the fleet than to risk it for the Morea. When he eventually arrived on the scene, Nauplia, Modon, Corone and Malavsia had fallen. Levkas in the Ionian islands, and the bases of Spinalonga and Suda on Crete which still remained in Venetian hands, were abandoned. The Turks finally landed on Corfu, but its defenders managed to throw them back. In the meantime, the Turks had suffered a grave defeat by the Austrians at Petervaradino on 3 August 1716. Venetian naval efforts in the Aegean and the Dardanelles in 1717 and 1718 met with little success. With the peace of Passarowitz, of 21 July 1718, Austria, the conquering power, made large territorial gains, but Venice lost the Morea, for which her small gains in Albania and Dalmatia were little compensation. This was her last war with Turkey.

1733 LOSSES FROM RIVALS

In 1733 the five *savi alla mercanzia* wrote, "We have many ports in the Mediterranean which cause losses to our trade." Trade passed direct to Lombardy and Germany from Genoa, Venice's old rival, and Leghorn, created by the grand dukes of Tuscany and a staging-post for English trade in the Mediterranean. Still more injurious were the papal town of Ancona and Hapsburg Trieste, a free port since 1719, in the Adriatic, which no longer constituted a Venetian "Gulf." "Apart from the residue which is left to us, Ancona robs us of the trade from both the Levant and the West, from Albania and the other Turkish provinces. Trieste takes nearly all the rest of the trade which comes from Germany." Even the cities of the eastern mainland up to Verona got their supplies from Genoa and Leghorn."

1744–82 THE SEA WALLS

In 1744 the construction of sea walls was undertaken to protect the shore of the lagoon between Pellestrina and Chioggia to a plan drawn up by father Vincenzo Maria Coronelli, a cartographer to the Republic in 1716. The thick wall of Istria stone, 14 meters (46 feet) wide and four-and-a-half meters (15 feet) above mean tide level were in two parts. The sea walls of Pellestrina were four kilometers (two and a half miles) long, and were finished in 1751, while the walls of Sottomarina were 1200 meters (3/4 mile) long and were finished n 1782. They were "a work which recalls the greatness of the Romans, outdoing men, sea, and time" (1777). They were the last great public work of the Venetian state, which had always devoted its skill, its persistance, and its money to the defense of the lagoon.

1762 *TRIBUNALISTI* AND *QUERINISTI*

Angelo Maria Querini, *avogador del Comun*, had "intervened" in a sentence of the Supreme Tribunal (the three Inquisitors of State), and was arrested by order of the Inquisitors. In protest the *Maggior Consiglio* refused to vote in the elections for the Council of Ten, nominating four "correctors" to revise the laws. The head of the party of reformers, known as the *querinisti* was Paolo Renier, while the *tribunalisti*, those who upheld the power of the Supreme Tribunal, were led by Marco Foscarini. The parliamentary battle concluded with the vote of 16 March 1762, in the *Maggior Consiglio*, in which the "conservative" propsals of the correctors were accepted by a majority of only two votes. Marco Foscarini and Paolo Renier were both subsequently elected doge.

1766 THE BARBARY PIRATES: JACOPO NANI AT TRIPOLI

Venetian trade with the western Mediterranean was seriously affected by the wars of the Barbary pirates on the coast of the Maghreb, who were only nominally under the control of the Sublime Porte. In 1750 the *savi* lamented that "the pirates are multiplying their arms, losses are unceasing, and we are reduced to either remaining in port, or to sailing with excessive expenses in crew and safeguards, or else losing our ships and disgracing our nation." Diplomatic delegations between 1761 and 1765 to Algiers, Tunis, Tripoli and Morocco, led to agreements for which the Venetians had to pay large annual indemnities. The bey of Tripoli later caused further incidents, and Jacopo Nani's squadron was charged with undertaking military action. This turned out to be a simple demonstration of strength, since the bey hastily accepted the Venetian demands as soon as the fleet appeared. The goodwill purchases from the Barbary states bore fruit. From an original 40 Venetian vessels the number rose in 1774 to 303, and later to 405.

1779–80 ATTEMPTS AT REFORM

"All is in disorder, everything is out of control," exclaimed Carlo Contarini in the *Maggior Consiglio* on 5 December 1779. He was talking of a "commotion" in demand of a plan of reform also supported by Giorgio Pisani. The idea was to remove the monopoly of power enjoyed by the small number of rich patricians to the advantage of the very large number of poor ones. This gave rise to fears of "overturning the system" and the doge, Paolo Renier, opposed the plan. "Prudence" suggested that the agitations in favor of reform were a conspiracy. The Inquisitors took the arbitrary step of confining Pisani in the castle of San Felice in Verona, and Contarini in the fortress of Cattaro.

1784 THE LAMENT OF "EL PARON"

On 29 May 1784 Andrea Tron, known as *el paron* (the chief) because of his political influence, said that trade "is failing into final collapse. The ancient and long-held maxims and laws which created and could still create a state's greatness have been forgotten. [We are] supplanted by foreigners who penetrate right into the bowels of our city. We are despoiled of our substance, and not a shadow of our ancient merchants is to be found among our citizens or our subjects. Capital is lacking, not in the nation, but in commerce. It is used to support effeminacy, excessive extravagance, idle spectacles, pretentious amusements and vice, instead of supporting and increasing industry which is the mother of good morals, virtue, and of essential national trade."

1784–86 THE LAST NAVAL VENTURE

The bey of Tunis's Barbary pirates renewed their acts of piracy following claims of compensation for losses suffered by Tunisian subjects in Malta, due to no fault of the Venetians. When diplomatic efforts to reach an agreement failed, the government was forced to take military action. a fleet under Angelo Emo blockaded Tunis and bombarded Susa (November 1784 and May 1785), Sfax (August 1785) and La Coletta (September), and then Sfax and Susa again, and Biserta in 1786. These brilliant military successes brought no comparable political results in their train, and the Senate recalled Emo and his fleet to Corfu. After Emo's death on 1 March 1792, peace was made with Tunis by increasing the bey's dues.

1789 THE LAST DOGE

In January 1789 Lodovico Manin, from a recently ennobled mainland family, was elected doge. The expenses of the election had grown throughout the 18th century, and now reached their highest ever. The patrician Pietro Gradenigo remarked, "I have made a Friulian doge; the Republic is dead." In Valence Napoleon Bonaparte was serving the king of France as an artillery lieutenant.

1797 THE END

In spring 1796 Piedmont fell and the Austrians were beated from Montenotte to Lodi. The Italian army under Napoleon crossed the frontiers of neutral Venice in pursuit of the enemy.

By the end of the year the French troops were occupying the Venetian state up to the Adige. Vicenza, Cadore and Friuli were held by the Austrians. With the campaigns of the next year Napoleon aimed for Austrian possessions across the Alps. In the preliminaries to the peace of Leoben, the terms of which remained secret, the Austrians were to take the Venetian possessions as the price of peace (18 April 1797). Nevertheless the pease envisaged the continued survival of the Venetian state, although confined to the city and the lagoon, perhaps with the compensation at the expense of the papal states. In the meanwhile Brescia and Bergamo revolted to Venice, and anti-French movements were arising elsewhere. Napoleon threatened Venice with war on 9 April. On 25 April he announced to the Venetian delegates at Graz, "I want no more Inquisition, no more Senate; I shall be an Attila to the state of Venice." Domenico Pizzamano fired on a French ship trying to force an entry from the Lido forts. On 1 May, Napoleon declared war. The French were at the edge of the lagoon. Even the cities of the Veneto established provisional municipalities. On 12 May, the *Maggior Consiglio* approved a motion to hand over power "to the system of the proposed provisional representative government," although there was not a quorum of votes: 512 voted for, ten against, and five abstained. On 16 May the provisional municipal government met in the Hall of the *Maggior Consiglio*. The preliminaries of the peace of Leoben were made even harsher in the Franco-Austrian treaty of Campoformid, and Venice and all her possesssions became Austrian. The accord was signed at Passariano, in the last doge's villa, on 18 October 1797.

THE DOGES OF VENICE

The official list of doges includes 120 names, beginning with Paulicius, or Paoluccio Anafesto, who was supposedly elected in 697, and ending with Lodovico Manin, who witnessed the fall of the Republic in 1797. Included in their ranks are the *magistri militum,* who ruled the city from 737 to 742, the Tribune Caroso, the Patriarch Orso, who governed from 1031 to 1032, Domenico Orseolo, who was deposed after only one day, Orio Mastropiero, who refused his first election in 1172, Jacopo Tiepolo, who fled the city after being elected by popular acclaim in 1289, and Giovanni Sagredo, whose election in 1676 was declared null and void. The "traditional"names of certain individuals are given in parentheses.

697-717	PAULICIUS (PAOLUCCIO ANAFESTO)
717-726	MARCELLUS (MARCELLO TEGALIANO)
726-737	URSUS (ORSO IPATO)
737-742	MAGISTRI MILITUM: LEO, FELIX CORNICULA, DEUSDEDIT, JUBIANUS YPATUS and JOHANNES FABRIACUS
742-755	DEUSDEDIT YPATUS (DIODATO IPATO)
755-756	GALLA GAULO
756-764	DOMENICO MANEGARIO
764-787	MAURICIUS (MAURIZIO GALBAIO)
787-804	JOHANNES (GIOVANNI GALBAIO)
804-811	OBELERIO and BEATO
811-827	AGNELLUS PARTICIACUS (AGNELLO PARTECIPAZIO)
827-829	JUSTINIANUS PARTICIACUS (GIUSTINIANO PARTECIPAZIO)
829-836	JOHANNES PARTICIACUS (GIOVANNI I PARTECIPAZIO)
	REVOLT OF THE TRIBUNE CAROSO
836-864	PETRUS (PIETRO TRADONICO)
864-881	URSUS PARTICIACUS (ORSO I PARTECIPAZIO)
881-887	JOHANNES PARTICIACUS (GIOVANNI II PARTECIPAZIO)
887	PIETRO I CANDIANO
888-911	PETRUS TRIBUNUS (PIETRO TRIBUNO)
911-932	URSUS PARTICIACUS (ORSO II PARTECIPAZIO)
932-939	PIETRO II CANDIANO
939-942	PETRUS BADOVARIUS (PIETRO PARTECIPAZIO DETTO BADOER)
942-959	PIETRO III CANDIANO
959-976	PIETRO IV CANDIANO
976-978	PIETRO I ORSEOLO
978-979	VITALE CANDIANO
979-991	TRIBUNO MENIO (MEMMO)
991-1009	PIETRO II ORSEOLO
1009-1026	OTTONE ORSEOLO
1026-1031	PIETRO CENTRANICO
1031-1032	ORSO ORSEOLO, PATRIARCH OF GRADO
1032	DOMENICO ORSEOLO (doge for only one day)
1032-1042/43	DOMENICO FLABIANICO
1042/43-1071	DOMENICO CONTARINI
1071-1084	DOMENICO SILVIO (SELVO)
1084-1096	VITALE FALIER
1096-1102	VITALE I MICHIEL
1102-1118	ORDELAF FALIER
1118-1130	DOMENICO MICHIEL
1130-1148	PIETRO POLANI
1148-1156	DOMENICO MOROSINI
1156-1172	VITALE II MICHIEL
	ORSO MASTROPIERO (refused the office in 1172, only to accept it six years later)
1172-1178	SEBASTIANO ZIANI
1178-1192	ORSO MASTROPIERO
1192-1205	ENRICO DANDOLO
5 VIII 1205-3 VIII 1229	PIETRO ZIANI
6 III 1229-20 V 1249	JACOPO TIEPOLO
13 VI 1249-1 I 1253	MARINO MOROSINI
25 I 1253-7 VII 1268	RANIERI ZENO
23 VII 1268-15 VIII 1275	LORENZO TIEPOLO
6 VI 1275-6 III 1280	JACOPO CONTARINI
25 III 1280-2 XI 1289	GIOVANNI DANDOLO
	JACOPO TIEPOLO (fled after having been elected by popular acclaim in 1289)
25 XI 1289-13 VIII 1311	PIETRO GRADENIGO
23 VIII 1311-3 VII 1312	MARINO ZORZI
13 VII 1312-31 XII 1328	GIOVANNI SORANZO
4 I 1329-31 XI 1339	FRANCESCO DANDOLO
7 XII 1339-28 XII 1342	BARTOLOMEO GRADENIGO
4 I 1343-7 IX 1354	ANDREA DANDOLO
11 IX 1354-17 IV 1355	MARINO FALIER
21 IV 1355-8 VIII 1356	GIOVANNI GRADENIGO
13 VIII 1356-12 VII 1361	GIOVANNI DOLFIN
16 VII 1361-18 VII 1365	LORENZO CELSI
21 VII 1365-13 I 1368	MARCO CORNER
20 I 1368-5 VI 1382	ANDREA CONTARINI
10 VI 1382-15 X 1382	MICHELE MOROSINI
21 X 1382-23 XI 1400	ANTONIO VENIER
1 XII 1400-26 XII 1413	MICHELE STENO
7 I 1414-4 IV 1423	TOMMASO MOCENIGO
15 IV 1423-23 X 1457	FRANCESCO FOSCARI

30 X 1457-5 V 1462	PASQUALE MALIPIERO
12 V 1462-9 XI 1471	CRISTOFORO MORO
23 XI 1471-28 VII 1473	NICOLÒ TRON
13 VIII 1473-1 XII 1474	NICOLÒ MARCELLO
14 XII 1474-23 II 1476	PIETRO MOCENIGO
5 III 1476-6 V 1478	ANDREA VENDRAMIN
18 V 1478-4 XI 1485	GIOVANNI MOCENIGO
19 XI 1485-14 VIII 1486	MARCO BARBARIGO
30 VIII 1486-20 IX 1501	AGOSTINO BARBARIGO
2 X 1501-22 VI 1521	LEONARDO LOREDAN
6 VII 1521-7 V 1523	ANTONIO GRIMANI
20 V 1523-28 XII 1538	ANDREA GRITTI
19 I 1539-9 XI 1545	PIETRO LANDO
24 XI 1545-23 V 1553	FRANCESCO DONÀ
4 VI 1553-31 V 1554	MARCANTONIO TREVISAN
11 VI 1554-2 VI 1556	FRANCESCO VENIER
14 VI 1556-17 VIII 1559	LORENZO PRIULI
1 IX 1559-4 XI 1567	GIROLAMO PRIULI
26 XI 1567-3 V 1570	PIETRO LOREDAN
11 V 1570-4 VI 1577	ALVISE I MOCENIGO
11 VI 1577-3 III 1578	SEBASTIANO VENIER
11 III 1578-30 VII 1585	NICOLÒ DA PONTE
18 VIII 1585-2 IV 1595	PASQUALE CICOGNA
26 IV 1595-25 XII 1605	MARINO GRIMANI
10 I 1606-16 VII 1612	LEONARDO DONÀ DALLE ROSE
24 VII 1612-29 X 1615	MARCANTONIO MEMMO
2 XII 1615-16 III 1618	GIOVANNI BEMBO
5 IV 1618-9 V 1618	NICOLÒ DONÀ
17 V 1618-12 VIII 1623	ANTONIO PRIULI

8 IX 1623-6 XII 1624	FRANCESCO CONTARINI
4 I 1625-23 XII 1629	GIOVANNI I CORNER
18 I 1630-2 IV 1631	NICOLÒ CONTARINI
10 IV 1631-3 I 1646	FRANCESCO ERIZZO
20 I 1646-27 II 1655	FRANCESCO MOLIN
27 III 1655-30 IV 1656	CARLO CONTARINI
17 V 1656-5 VI 1656	FRANCESCO CORNER
15 VI 1656-29 III 1658	BERTUCCI (ALBERTO) VALIER
8 IV 1658-30 IX 1659	GIOVANNI PESARO
16 X 1659-26 I 1675	DOMENICO CONTARINI
6 II 1675-14 VIII 1676	NICOLÒ SAGREDO
	GIOVANNI SAGREDO (election was declared null and void)
26 VIII 1676-15 I 1684	ALVISE CONTARINI
26 I 1684-23 III 1688	MARCANTONIO GIUSTINIAN
3 IV 1688-6 I 1694	FRANCESCO MOROSINI
25 II 1694-5 VII 1700	SILVESTRO VALIER
16 VII 1700-6 V 1709	ALVISE II MOCENIGO
22 V 1709-12 VIII 1722	GIOVANNI II CORNER
24 VIII 1722-21 V 1732	ALVISE III MOCENIGO
2 VI 1732-5 I 1735	CARLO RUZZINI
17 I 1735-17 VI 1741	ALVISE PISANI
17 VI 1741-7 III 1752	PIETRO GRIMANI
18 III 1752-19 V 1762	FRANCESCO LOREDAN
31 V 1762-31 III 1763	MARCO FOSCARINI
19 IV 1763-31 XII 1778	ALVISE IV MOCENIGO
14 I 1779-13 II 1789	PAOLO RENIER
9 II 1789-12 V 1797	LODOVICO

THE VENETIAN PATRICIATE

EXISTING FAMILIES (as of 1999)

AVOGADRO A feudal house of Brescia admitted to the *Maggior Consiglio* in 1438 for distinguished service to the Republic.

BADOER Perhaps the oldest family in Venice, descended from the Parteciaci, or Partecipazi, who produced seven doges, including Agnello, elected in 811 after the Frankish invasion, and the transfer of the capital to the islands that comprise modern-day Venice.

BAGLIONI Prominent members of the printing industry who were admitted in 1716.

BALBI One of the families that remained in the *Maggior Consiglio* after the *serrata* of 1297.

BARBARO An illustrious family that produced, among others, the humanist and politician Marc'Antonio, and his brother Francesco, Patriach of Aquileia, both of whom were patrons of Palladio and Veronese.

BAROZZI One of the 12 "apostolic families," whose heirs included a patriarch of Grado, and who held the fiefdom of Santorini in the Cyclades.

BEMBO An "old" house descended from the tribunes, whose members included Doge Giovanni, elected in 1615, and Cardinal Pietro, the celebrated humanist and poet.

BON One of the families admitted to the patriciate before 1297, whose numbers included two procurators of St. Mark's and several distinguished diplomats.

BONLINI A family from Brescia, two branches of which were admitted in 1667 and 1685.

BRAGADIN One of the "old" families, perhaps descended from Doge Orso Ipato (d. 737), who produced eight procurators of St. Mark's, one cardinal, and a number of other illustrious heirs, including Marc'Antonio, who courageously defended Famagosta against the Turks in 1572.

BRANDOLINI A military family from Romagna that was admitted in 1686.

BUZZACCARINI A noble Paduan family that was admitted in 1782.

CAISELLI Aristocrats from Udine who were admitted in 1779.

CANAL or DA CANAL One of the "new" families, who produced two naval commanders, four procurators of St. Mark's, and the famous 13th-century chronicler Martino.

CAPPELLO A "new" house whose heirs included 10 procurators of St. Mark's, and any number of ambassadors and naval commanders. Bianca Cappello was Grand Duchess of Tuscany from 1578 to 1587.

CARMINATI A family from Bergamo that was admitted in 1687.

CICOGNA One of the "newest" houses, admitted in 1381 for distinguished service to the Republic during the war against Genoa, whose numbers included Doge Pasquale (d. 1595).

CIVRAN One of the "new" families that remained in the *Maggior Consiglio* after the *serrata* of 1297.

COLLALTO An illustrious feudal family from Treviso, admitted in 1306 for distinguished service to the Republic, who produced any number of military heroes.

CONDULMER Admitted to the patriciate in 1381, the family produced two cardinals, one of whom became Pope Eugenius IV in 1431.

CORNER One of the oldest houses in Venice, probably of Roman origin. Among its members were four doges, 22 procurators of St. Mark's, nine cardinals, and many distinguished ambassadors and generals. Caterina, the wife of King James II of Cyprus, ceded the island to Venice in 1489.

CORRER A "new" house that produced seven procurators of St. Mark's and two cardinals, one of whom became Pope Gregory XII in 1406. In the early part of the 19th century, Teodoro Correr founded the art museum that bears his name.

DOLFIN One of the most illustrious of the "old" families, whose heirs included one doge, 14 procurators of St. Mark's, six cardinals, and any number of distinguished citizens.

DONÀ A "new" house with two separate branches, one of which was called Dalle Rose after the flowers on its coat-of-arms. Among its members were three doges, including Leonardo, who was one of the most significant figures in Venetian history. The family also produced eight procurators of St. Mark's, one cardinal, and a number of distinguished men of letters.

DONDI DALL'OROLOGIO An old Paduan family admitted to the *Maggior Consiglio* in 1653.

EMO A "new" family that produced a number of important political figures, including Angelo, who won the last great naval victory in the history of the Republic (1784-1786).

FOSCARI The most famous member of this illustrious family was Doge Francesco, who was the driving force behind Venetian expan-

sionism on the mainland. After he abdicated in 1457, the tragic fate of his only son Jacopo, whose story was immortalized by Byron and Verdi, became the torment of his old age. Although the family was excluded from the ranks of the patriciate at the end of the 18th century as the result of a marriage that was not approved by the *avogadori di Comun,* they continued to use the title count, which the Republic had already conferred on them. They were also renowned for their magnificent Gothic palace on the Grand Canal, which now houses the University of Venice, and their Palladian villa in Malcontenta.

FOSCOLO — Among their many distinguished family members, the procurator Leonardo achieved lasting fame as a great naval commander. During the Middle Ages, the Foscolo were the feudal overlords of the Island of Amafi in the Cyclades.

GHERARDINI — A Veronese family of Florentine origin admitted in 1652.

GRADENIGO — One of the 12 "apostolic families," whose heirs included three doges (one of whom, Pietro, was responsible for the "closing" of the Great Council in 1272), 14 procurators, two cardinals, and any number of distinguished diplomats and soldiers.

GRIMANI — One of the most illustrious of the "new" families, who produced three doges, 21 procurators, three cardinals, and several distinguished diplomats and admirals. The extraordinary collection of archeological findings acquired by Cardinal Domenico, Patriarch of Aquileia, which he bequeathed to the Republic upon his death, formed the nucleus of the Museo Archeologico Marciano.

LOREDAN — Another of the great "new" families, whose members included three doges, 12 procurators of St. Mark's, and any number of naval commanders. Doge Leonardo, who was at the very center of the resistance movement against the League of Cambrai, also built the magnificent palace on the Grand Canal that now bears the name Vendramin Calergi.

MANIN — An influential family from the Friuli who had their roots in Florence. Among the heirs to the families admitted to the patriciate in the 17th century as a result of having donated 100,000 ducats to the war effort against the Turks, Lodovico Manin was the only one to be elected doge.

MARCELLO — A "new" house, probably of Roman origin, which produced one doge, six procurators, the celebrated 18th-century musician Benedetto, and a number of famous admirals, including Lorenzo, who lost his life during the naval attack on the Dardanelles in 1656.

MARIN — Among the illustrious members of this ancient family was Carlo Antonio, who achieved lasting fame for his treatises on the Venetian economy.

MEMMO — One of the 12 "apostolic families," whose heirs included Doge Marcantonio, elected in 1612, and probably Doge Tribuno Menio, who was deposed in 991, as well as five procurators of St. Mark's, one of whom was Andrea, a distinguished diplomat and personal friend of Giacomo Casanova.

MINIO — One of the families that remained in the *Maggior Consiglio* after the *serrata* of 1297, whose members included senators and ambassadors.

MINOTTO — An "old" family whose numbers included Giovanni, the *Bailo* of Constantinople, who perished while defending the city against the Turks in 1453.

MORO — A "new" house that produced one doge and six procurators of St. Mark's.

MOROSINI — One of the 12 "apostolic families," whose heirs included four doges, 27 procurators of St. Mark's, and two cardinals. During the 10th century, the two opposing political factions in the city were the Morosini, who were in favor of maintaining close ties with Byzantium, and the Coloprini, who supported a policy of rapprochement with the Holy Roman Empire.

MOSTA (DA) — A "new" family that counted among its more illustrious members the famous navigator Alvise da Ca' da Mosto, and the historian Andrea, a renowned paleographer and chronicler of the history of the doges.

NANI — One of the "newest" houses, admitted in 1381, whose numbers included six procurators of St. Mark's. Perhaps their most illustrious heir was Battista, who achieved lasting fame during the 17th century as a skilled diplomat and student of history.

ORIO — An "old" family who once owned part of the property on which the Rialto district was built in the 12th century.

PASQUALIGO — A family with two separate branches, one of which was admitted to the *Maggior Consiglio* in 1297, and the other in 1381. Among its more distinguished members were three procurators of St. Mark's, and several ambassadors and admirals.

PERSICO — A family from Bergamo that was admitted in 1685.

PIZZAMANO — A "new" house whose members included Domenico, who defended the port of Venice against the French in 1797.

PRIULI — One of the most illustrious of the "new" families, who produced three doges, 14 procurators of St. Mark's, and five cardinals.

QUERINI — An "old" house that claimed descent from Doges Maurizio and Giovanni Galbaio. Along with the Tiepolo and Badoer families, they were the organizers of a plot to overthrow the government in the year 1310. Among the most illustrious members of the family were 15 procurators of St. Mark's, and Cardinal Giovanni, who was the last feudal overlord of the Island of Stampalia in the Dodecanese.

REDETTI — A family from Rovigo that was admitted to the *Maggior Consiglio* in 1698.

RENIER — Admitted to the patriciate in 1381, the family produced Paolo (d.1789), who was the next to the last doge of Venice, and Giustina, the wife of Marcantonio Michiel, who achieved lasting fame as a learned writer and brilliant polemicist.

ROMIERI   One of the "newest" families, admitted in 1689.

SANDI   A family from Feltre, admitted in 1685, whose members included Vettor, a famous historian of the 18th century.

SORANZO   An "old" family whose heirs included one doge and 16 procurators of St. Mark's.

SPATAFORA or SPADAFORA   A feudal house of Sicily, admitted in 1409, whose members included several prominent politicians.

TIEPOLO   One of the most illustrious of the 12 "apostolic families," whose heirs included two doges and seven procurators of St. Mark's. The organizers of the infamous plot to overthrow the government in 1310 were led by Baiamonte, popularly known as the "grand gentleman."

TREVISAN   One branch of the family remained in the *Maggior Consiglio* after the *serrata* of 1297, another was admitted in 1381, and a third was inscribed in the "Golden Book" in 1689. Among its more distinguished members were one doge and 10 procurators of St. Mark's.

VALIER   One of the oldest houses in Venice, undoubtedly of Roman origin. Among its members were two doges and two cardinals.

VAN AXEL   A family of wealthy Flemish merchants, admitted in 1665.

VENIER   One of the most distinguished of the "new" families, who produced three doges, including Sebastiano, who defeated the Turks at the Battle of Lepanto, and 21 procurators of St. Mark's.

VERONESE   A noble family from Treviso, admitted in 1704, who produced one cardinal.

ZORZI   An "old" family whose heirs included one doge, one cardinal, 11 procurators of St. Mark's, and the feudal overlords of Curzola in Dalmatia, Lampsacus and Karistos in Greece, and Levkas in the Ionian Islands.

PRINCIPAL FAMILIES THAT ARE NOW EXTINCT

BARBARIGO   One of the most illustrious of the "new families," who produced two doges, 10 procurators of St. Mark's, and four cardinals, including Gregorio, Bishop of Padua, who was canonized by Pope John XXIII.

BARBO   An important family that produced four procurators of St. Mark's, and Cardinal Pietro Barbo, who became Pope Paul II.

BERNARDO   A distinguished "new" family whose heirs included four procurators of St. Mark's. They are also remembered for their two magnificent Gothic palaces, one of which is on the Grand Canal.

CAVALLI   One of the "newest" houses, whose members included Jacopo, Marino and Sigismondo, all of whom were distinguished ambassadors, and Jacopo, who was a famous general.

CELSI   An influential family that produced two procurators of St. Mark's, and Doge Lorenzo, who died in 1365.

CONTARINI   One of the most illustrious of the 12 "apostolic" families, who produced eight doges, 44 procurators of St. Mark's, and Cardinal Gasparo, the leader of a profound reform in the Catholic Church that was 400 years ahead of its time.

DANDOLO   One of the noblest houses of Europe, which produced four doges, including Enrico, who conquered Constantinople during the Fourth Crusade, and Andrea, a famous chronicler and man of letters who was a personal friend of Petrarch. Other distinguished family members included 12 procurators of St. Mark's and a patriarch of Grado.

DIEDO   A "new" house whose heirs included three procurators of St. Mark's and a number of other distinguished citizens.

DUODO   A "new" family that counted among its more illustrious members four procurators of St. Mark's.

ERIZZO   A "new" family whose heirs included one doge and four procurators of St. Mark's. Two of its most famous members were Paolo, who defended Negroponte against the Turks, and Niccolò Guido, who was one of the few capable and courageous politicians left in the last days of the Republic.

FALIER   One of the most ancient of the "apostolic families," probably of Roman origin. Among the three doges that it gave to the Republic, Marino has gone down in history for his aborted attempt to proclaim himself Prince of Venice in 1355, for which he paid with his head.

FOSCARINI   An "old" house that produced one doge (Marco, a famous man of letters, who died in 1763), 14 procurators, and any number of distinguished generals, diplomats and politicians.

GRITTI   A "new" house whose members included Doge Andrea, the general who won the final victory over the League of Cambrai, and whose features were immortalized by none other than Titian.

LABIA   A house admitted in 1646, renowned for their magnificent palace frescoed by Giambattista Tiepolo, and for the famous line, "L'abia o no l'abia, sarò sempre Labia" ("With or without the money, I'll always be a Labia"), which was supposedly delivered by a family member as he heaved a gold plate out of the window.

LANDO   A family that gave the Republic one doge, four procurators, and distinguished members of the clergy.

LEZZE (DA)   A family of diplomats and soldiers whose heirs included seven procurators of St. Mark's.

MALIPIERO   A "new" house whose members included one doge and three procurators of St. Mark's.

MICHIEL   Another of the old families that produced three doges, 12 procurators of St. Mark's, one cardinal, and any number of influential politicians and members of the military establishment, including Marcantonio, who is remembered for his extraordinary courage in the last days of the Republic.

MOCENIGO   One of the grandest of the "new" houses, whose numbers included seven doges, 25 procurators, and admirals Alvise Leonardo and Lazzaro, renowned for their victories over the Turks.

MOLIN (DA) A prominent family whose heirs included one doge, nine procurators of St. Mark's, and any number of politicians, generals, and influential members of the merchant class.

NAVAGERO Among their more illustrious heirs were Andrea, a noted diplomat and poet, and Cardinal Bernardo.

ORSEOLO A famous dynasty whose members included Doge Pietro I, who would later become a Camaldolese monk and a saint, Pietro II, the conqueror of Istria and Dalmatia, Ottone, and Orso, Patriarch of Grado and Regent of the Ducato. Connected by marriage with the Byzantine rulers and the family of St. Stephen, King of Hungary, it became extinct in the 14th century.

PARUTA One of the "newest" houses, whose members included Pietro, a famous historian and procurator of St. Mark's.

PESARO A distinguished family whose heirs included one doge and seven procurators, and whose magnificent palace on the Grand Canal was designed by Baldassare Longhena.

PISANI Wealthy merchants and bankers whose numbers included Vettor, Commander of the Fleet in the War of Chioggia against Genoa, 16 procurators of St. Mark's, and Doge Alvise, who built the grandiose 17th-century Villa Pisani.

POLANI One of the 12 "apostolic families," whose heirs included Doge Pietro (d. 1148).

POLO A famous family of adventurers and explorers whose members included Niccolò, Matteo and Marco, the celebrated author of "The Travels of Marco Polo."

PONTE (DA) An influential family that produced three procurators of St. Mark's, and the distinguished diplomat Doge Nicolò, who died in 1585.

REZZONICO A family from Como, admitted to the *Maggior Consiglio* in 1687, who produced two procurators of St. Marks, and two cardinals, one of whom became Pope Clement XIII.

RUZZINI One of the "old" families, who produced two procurators of St. Mark's, and Doge Carlo, who achieved lasting fame as an exceptionally shrewd diplomat.

SAGREDO St. Gerard of Csanad, bishop and martyr, was the first of the family's many illustrious heirs, whose ranks included one doge and seven procurators. Others who achieved lasting fame were Giovanni, a learned historian and man of letters, and Agostino, a 19th-century scholar.

SANUDO A very ancient family who claimed direct descent from the Candiani, and who produced five doges in the ninth and 10th centuries. Among its most distinguished heirs were Marco, a nephew of Doge Enrico Dandolo, who conquered the Duchy of Naxos in the Cyclades, and Marino the Elder, known as "Torcello," who was a famous merchant, writer and

geographer. Marino the Younger was the author of the monumental Renaissance chronicle entitled "The Diaries."

SAVORGNAN An illustrious Friulan house admitted in the 14th century whose heirs included Girolamo, remembered for his heroism in the war against the League of Cambrai.

STENO An influential family that produced three procurators of St. Mark's. Michele, who died in 1413, was the first doge to promote a policy of expansionism on the mainland.

TRON An illustrious house that produced one doge and seven procurators of St. Mark's, including Andrea, a *savio del Consiglio* who wielded enormous political power in the mid- 18th century.

VENDRAMIN One of the "newest" houses, renowned for its extreme wealth, whose members included Doge Andrea (d. 1478), three procurators of St. Mark's and one cardinal.

VITTURI A distinguished family who were feudal overlords in Dalmatia.

ZANE One of the wealthiest of the "old" houses whose heirs included five procurators of St. Mark's.

ZENO An "old" family whose male line only recently became extinct. Among its many illustrious members were one doge and 13 procurators of St. Mark's. Other distinguished heirs were Cardinal Giovanni Battista, whose magnificent tomb is in St. Mark's Basilica, the navigators Nicolò, Antonio and Catterino, and Carlo, who became a national hero in the Middle Ages during the wars against Genoa.

ZUSTINIAN or GIUSTINIAN One of the illustrious "old" families, only recently extinct, who produced one doge and 27 procurators of St. Mark's. Among its most celebrated heirs were San Lorenzo, a Patriarch of Venice, the Blessed Paolo, a leader of the reform movement in the Catholic Church, Angelo Lorenzo, *provveditore* in Trieste in 1797, who made a courageous stand against Napoleon, and Leonardo, the greatest of Venetian poets.

PRINCIPAL NON-VENETIAN FAMILIES ADMITTED TO THE PATRICIATE

At various times, certain of the noble houses of Europe were also inscribed in the "Golden Book," such as the Bourbons of France, the Bourbons of Parma, the Wittelsbachs of Bavaria and the Dukes of Brunswick. The same was true of the Italian nobility, including the House of Savoy, the Estensi, Dukes of Ferrara and later Modena, the Gonzaga, Marquises and later Dukes of Mantua, the Medici of Florence, later Grand Dukes of Tuscany, the Cybo Malaspina, Marquises of Massa, the Pico della Mirandola, the Pio da Carpi, the Sforza, Dukes of Milan, and the Pallavicino, Marquises of the so-called "Pallavicino State." Other families were admitted because they held fiefdoms in the Veneto, such as the Carraresi of Padua and the Scaligeri of Verona. Still others were admitted in recognition of distinguished military service. Finally, there were the papal families, such as the Albani, Aldobrandini, Altieri, Barberini, Boncompagni, Borghese, Chigi, Colonna, Conti, Corsini, Ludovisi, Odescalchi, Orsini, Pamphili, Pinatelli, Rospigliosi and Savelli.

None of the above played an active role in the *Maggior Consiglio* with the exception of the Bentivoglio d'Aragona, an extinct branch of the family that had held the fiefdom of Bologna, and the Pepoli, who were also natives of Bologna. The so-called "Reggimenti" were the government officials in charge of administering the affairs of maritime and mainland territories belonging to the Republic.

VENETIAN "REGIMENTS" AT THE FALL OF THE REPUBLIC (1797)

Listed below are the titles and terms of office for each of the principal administrators in a given regiment.

DOGADO

CAORLE	*Podestà* (16 months)
CAVARZERE	*Podestà* (16 months)
CHIOGGIA	*Podestà* (16 months); *Saliner* (16 months); *Castellano* (16 months)
GAMBARARE	*Provveditore* (24 months)
GRADO	*Conte* (16 months)
LIDO	*Castellano* (16 months)
LOREO	*Podestà* (16 months)
MALAMOCCO	*Podestà* (16 months)
MARANO	*Podestà* (16 months)
MURANO	*Podestà* (16 months)
TORCELLO	*Podestà* (16 months)

MARITIME REGIMENTS

ALBONA	*Podestà* (32 months)
ALMISSA	*Podestà* (24 months)
ARBE	*Conte* and *Capitano* (32 months)
ASSO	*Provveditore* (24 months)
BRAZZA	*Conte* (32 months)
BUDUA	*Podestà* (32 months)
BUIE D'ISTRIA	*Podestà* (32 months)
CAPODISTRIA	*Podestà* and *Capitano* (16 months); 2 *Consiglieri* (16 months)
CASTELNUOVO	*Provveditore* (24 months); *Castellano* (24 months)
CATTARO	*Rettore* and *Provveditore* (24 months); *Camerlengo* (32 months)
CEFALONIA	*Provveditore* (24 months); 2 *Consiglieri* (24 months)
CERIGO	*Provveditore* (24 months); *Castellano* (24 months)
CHERSO	*Conte* and *Capitano* (24 months)
CITTANOVA	*Podestà* (16 months)

CLISSA	*Provveditore* (24 months)
CORFÙ	*Bailo* (24 months); *Provveditore* and *Capitano* (24 months); 2 *Consiglieri* (24 months); *Capitano della Cittadella* (24 months); *Castellano della Cittadella* (24 months)
CURZOLA	*Conte* (32 months)
DIGNANO	*Podestà* (16 months)
ISOLA D'ISTRIA	*Podestà* (16 months)
KNIN	*Provveditore* (24 months); *Castellano* (24 months)
LESINA	*Conte* and *Provveditore* (24 months); *Camerlengo* and *Castellano* (24 months)
MACARSCA	*Provveditore* (24 months)
MONTONA	*Podestà* (32 months)
MUGGIA	*Podestà* (16 months); *Castellano* (16 months)
NONA	*Conte* (32 months)
NOVEGRADI	*Provveditore* (24 months)
PAGO	*Conte* (32 months); *Camerlengo* (32 months)
PARENZO	*Podestà* (16 months)
PIRANO	*Podestà* (16 months)
POLA	*Conte* and *Provveditore* (16 months); 2 *Consiglieri* (16 months); *Castellano di San Felice* (16 months); *Castellano di Castel Vecchio* (16 months)
PORTOLE	*Podestà* (32 months)
PREVESA	*Provveditore* (24 months)
RASPO	*Capitano* (32 months)
ROVIGNO	*Podestà* (16 months)
SANTA MAURA	*Provveditore* (24 months)
SCIM	*Provveditore* (24 months)
SEBENICO	*Conte* and *Capitano* (24 months); *Camerlengo* and *Castellano* (32 months); *Castellano di San Nicolò* (24 months)
SPALATO	*Conte* (32 months); *Camerlengo* and *Castellano* (32 months)
TRAÚ	*Conte* (32 months)
UMAGO	*Podestà* (16 months)
VALLE D'ISTRIA	*Podestà* (16 months)
VEGLIA	*Provveditore* (32 months); *Camerlengo* and *Castellano* (32 months)
VONIZZA	*Provveditore* (24 months)
ZANTE	*Provveditore* (24 months); 2 *Consiglieri* (24 months)
ZARA	*Conte* (24 months); *Capitano* (24 months); *Camerlengo* and *Castellano* (24 months)

MAINLAND REGIMENTS

ADRIA	*Podestà* (16 months)
ANFO	*Provveditore* (24 months)
ASOLA	*Provveditore* (16 months); *Castellano* (24 months)
ASOLO	*Podestà* (16 months)
ASSO	*Provveditore* (24 months)
BADIA POLESINE	*Podestà* (16 months)
BASSANO	*Podestà* and *Capitano* (16 months)
BELLUNO	*Podestà* and *Capitano* (16 months)
BERGAMO	*Podestà* (16 months); *Capitano* (16 months); 2 *Camerlenghi* (32 months); *Castellano della Cappella* (16 months)

BRESCIA	*Podestà* (16 months); *Capitano* (16 months); 2 *Camerlenghi* (16 months); *Castellano* (16 months)
CADORE	*Capitano* (32 months)
CAMPOSANPIERO	*Podestà* (16 months)
CANEVA DI SACILE	*Podestà* (16 months)
CASTELBALDO	*Podestà* (16 months)
CASTELFRANCO	*Podestà* (16 months)
CENEDA E TARSO	*Podestà* (16 months)
CHIUSA	*Castellano* (24 months)
CITTADELLA	*Podestà* (16 months)
CIVADALE DEL FRIULI	*Provveditore* (16 months)
COLOGNA VENETA	*Podestà* (16 months)
CONEGLIANO	*Podestà* and *Capitano* (16 months)
CREMA	*Podestà* and *Capitano* (16 months); 2 *Camerlenghi* (32 months); *Castellano* (24 months)
ESTE	*Podestà* and *Capitano* (16 months)
FELTRE	*Podestà* and *Capitano* (16 months)
GRISIGNANO	*Podestà* (16 months)
LEGNAGNO	*Provveditore* and *Capitano* (16 months)
LENDINARA	*Podestà* (16 months)
LONATO	*Provveditore* (16 months)
LONIGO	*Podestà* (16 months)
MAROSTICA	*Podestà* (16 months)
MARTINENGO	*Podestà* and *Provveditore* (32 months)
MESTRE	*Podestà* and *Capitano* (16 months)
MONFALCONE	*Podestà* (16 months); *Castellano* (32 months)
MONSELICE	*Podestà* (16 months)
MONTAGNANA	*Podestà* (16 months)
MOTTA DI LIVENZA	*Podestà* (16 months)
NOALE	*Podestà* (16 months)
ODERZO	*Podestà* (16 months)

ORZINUOVI	*Provveditore* (16 months)
PADOVA	*Podestà, Capitano,* 2 *Camerlenghi* and *Castellano della Saracinesca* (16 months); *Castellano del Castel Vecchio* (32 months)
PESCHIERA	*Provveditore* and *Castellano* (16 months)
PIOVE DI SACCO	*Podestà* (16 months)
PONTEVIGODARZERE	*Castellano* (32 months)
PORDENONE	*Podestà* and *Capitano* (16 months)
PORTOBUFFOLÈ	*Podestà* (16 months)
PORTOGRUARO	*Podestà* (16 months)
QUERO	*Castellano* (32 months)
ROMAN	*Podestà* and *Provveditore* (32 months)
ROVIGO	*Podestà, Capitano* and 2 *Camerlenghi* (16 months)
SACILE	*Podestà* and *Capitano* (16 months)
SALÒ	*Provveditore* and *Capitano* (16 months)
SERRAVALLE	*Podestà* (16 months)
SOAVE	*Capitano* (16 months)
TREVISO	*Podestà, Capitano* and 2 *Camerlenghi* (16 months)
UDINE	*Luogotenente* and 2 *Tesorieri* (16 months); *Maniscalco* (32 months)
VERONA	*Podestà, Capitano,* 2 *Camerlenghi, Castellano di San Felice* and *Castellano di Castel Vecchio* (16 months)
VICENZA	*Podestà, Capitano* and 2 *Camerlenghi* (16 months)

MILITARY REGIMENTS ELECTED BY THE SENATE

CATTARO	*Provveditore Straordinario*
IMOSCHI	*Provveditore*
PALMANOVA	*Provveditore Generale* and *Tesoriere*
SANTA MAURA	*Provveditore Straordinario*

A SHORT GLOSSARY OF PLACE NAMES

ABATE The "Corte (Courtyard) dell'Abate" took its name from several houses that belonged to the former Abbey of San Gregorio in Dorsoduro. The world "abate" also referred to the flag poles that once filled the city's squares.

ABAZIA The former "Abbey of Santa Maria della Misericordia" lent its name to a number of locations in the immediate neighborhood, including a fondamenta, sottoportico, campo and bridge.

ACCADEMIA The "Academy of Nobles," founded in 1619 to provide a proper education for young members of the patrician class, was situated on the Giudecca, where there is still a street that bears its name. The "Academy of Fine Arts" gave its name to the unsightly wooden bridge over the Grand Canal that was built some 60 years ago to replace an even more unsightly cast iron bridge constructed by the Austrians!

ACQUA DOLCE On their journey from the mainland, barges carrying "fresh water" for the city's wells often stopped over at a canal in the Santi Apostoli neighborhood, which still bears their name.

ACQUAVITA Among those who were allowed to sell "acquavitae" were the local café owners, one of whom lent his name to a neighborhood street and bridge.

ACQUE The city's first cafés, which were known as "spirit shops," are commemorated by a calle and sottoportico in the neighborhood of San Salvador.

ALTANA On fine summer evenings, family members would often gather on their rooftop terraces, which were enclosed by wooden fencing for purposes of privacy. These were also used as sun decks by Venetian women who bleached their hair, at which time they wore a crownless straw hat known as a "solana."

ANATOMIA The Anatomical Theater, which was established in 1761, gave its name to a courtyard and bridge near San Giacomo dell'Orio.

ARSENALE The word "Arsenale," which was used to define the complex of shipyards and boat basins that served the Venetian fleet, may have derived from the Arab word "darsina'a" (workshop), or perhaps from the Italian "darsena," (dock), or "arginato" (area protected by dikes).

ARZERE The local word for "argine," meaning dam or dike, eventually lent its name to a street and bridge.

ASEO A street and bridge in the neighborhood of San Marcuola were named after the "vinegar" factories of the 15th century.

ASSASSINI According to tradition, the rio and calle that bear this name were once the site of frequent murders, which prompted the government to ban the wearing of false beards (a favorite artifice of local criminals), and to order "cesendoli," or lanterns, to be hung by night in particularly dangerous areas of the city.

AVOGARIA A bridge, rio, ramo and calle in the San Barnaba neighborhood took their name from the Zamberti family, local residents who held offices in the "Avogaria di Comun," or Supreme Court of Appeals.

BACINO This word gave its name to St. Mark's Basin, where ships were moored, and the Orseolo Basin, on the other side of St. Mark's Square, which was created in the 19th century as a docking area for gondolas.

BALANZE A workshop in the San Luca area that once manufactured "balance," or weighing scales, lent its name to a local calle.

BANCO GIRO The first state bank in Europe, founded in Venice in the 17th century, gave its name to a sottoportico in the Rialto district.

BANDE In the neighborhood of Santa Maria Formosa, a local bridge still bears the name of the the "parapets" that were once used for protection.

BANDO The "pietra del bando" is the shaft of a column made of Syrian porphyry that is located in the south corner of St. Mark's Basilica. This is the site where all "bandi," or government decrees, were read posted.

BARBACANI These wooden corbels supported the upper floors of houses that projected out over the street. In the Calle della Madonna in San Polo, a stone corbel marked the maximum projection permitted by law.

BARBARIA DELLE TOLE Along the street that still bears this name, there were probably workshops where "tole" (wooden planks) were planed, or "shaved."

BARETERI In San Salvador, a bridge and rio commemorate the "beret," or "cap makers," who once had their workshops in the neighborhood.

BECCARIE These were the "butcher shops" of Venice. The public slaughterhouse, which was situated in dwellings owned by the rebellious Guerini family, gave its name to a calle, campo, bridge and rio in the Rialto district.

BERGAMA The inn known as "La Bergama," where residents of Bergamo often stayed when they were visiting Venice, gave its name to a nearby street and bridge in the neighborhood of San Simeone Grande.

BIASIO An embankment in the San Simeone Grande neighborhood commemorates the legend of "Biasio," a local grocer who supposedly ground up the bodies of young boys to make his own version of a pork sausage that is still considered a delicacy by local residents.

BISATI In the neighborhood of the Gesuati, there was once a vendor of "eels," who gave his name to a nearby sottoportico.

BISSA The "Calle della Bissa," which winds its way through the neighborhood of San Bartolomeo, may have taken its name from the word "biscia" (snake), or perhaps from the shops in the area that sold a particular type of silk known as "bisso."

BO The "Calle del Bo" (Ox) at the Rialto was once the site of an inn under the sign of a golden ox, which was later replace by an apothecary's shop.

BOCCA DI PIAZZA This is the main thoroughfare that leads into the east end of St. Mark's Square.

BOTERI These were the "bottai," or coopers, who gave their name to a street in the neighborhood of San Cassiano.

BOVOLO In the neighborhood of San Luca, "La Scala del Bovolo" was the name given to the magnificent "spiral staircase" in the courtyard of the Contarini Palace.

BRAGORA The Church of San Giovanni in Bragora may have taken its name from the Greek word "agorà" for marketplace, or from "bragolà," which has the same meaning in Venetian dialect, or even from bragolare, another local word that means "to go fishing."

BRESSANA This location in San Zanipolo was named after the official residence of the nuncio of Brescia. Bergamo, Chioggia, Lendinara, Vicenza, Badia Polesine and the Patria del Friuli e Feltre also had permanent representatives in Venice.

BURANELLI These were the inhabitants of Burano, who gave their name to a local street.

BURCHIELLE These small barges had a fondamenta and rio named after them in the Sant'Andrea district.

CA' The traditional abbreviation for "casa" signifies not only "house," but "family."

CA' DI DIO A riva, bridge and rio commemorate the hospice known as the "House of God," which was founded in the 13th century to accommodate pilgrims from the Holy Land, and whose premises are used today as a rest home.

CAFFETTIER The various streets that still bear this name recall the old "coffee shops" that once did business in the neighborhood.

CALCINA The warehouses of the "lime-sellers" were originally located on the Zattere, where a bridge and small square were named after them.

CALDERER These were the city's "coppersmiths," one of whom lent his name to a calle in San Marcilian.

CALEGHERI The "Shoemakers' Guild Hall," which was once located in San Tomà, gave its name to a nearby rio.

CALLE The Latin word "callis," meaning "street," gave its name to most of the main thoroughfares in Venice. Others took their names from the old Italian word "ruga," and its diminutive form "rughetta," while the streets that still bear the name "salizzada" were the first to be paved in "selce," or "salizo." Other thoroughfares, such as the "Lista di Spagna," were named for the white stones that marked the boundaries of diplomatic immunity in front of an ambassador's residence. Still others, such as the "Piscina San Samuele," were once the sites of bodies of water. Finally, there are a few modern boulevards that bear the name "via."

CALLE LARGA Wide street, or boulevard.

CALLESELLA A diminutive form of "calle," meaning "little street."

CALLETTA Another diminutive form of "calle."

CAMPAZZO A rather large square, such as the "Campazzo San Sebastiano" and the "Campazzo dei Tolentini."

CAMPIELLO A diminutive of "campo," meaning "little square."

CAMPO The classic Venetian terminology for "square." Only the "Piazza San Marco" uses the standard Italian word.

CANAL GRANDE The world famous "Grand Canal," which divides the Realtine Islands on which the city was built.

CANALAZZO The local term for the Grand Canal.

CANALI These are the 100 or so canals that separate the islands on which the city stands. In the lagoon itself, they are the channels that were excavated in the shallows, which are marked by wooden posts known as "bricole."

CANNAREGIO The name of this district derives from the Latin "canale-clum," meaning "wetlands."

CAPITELLO The word "capitello" refers to a small walled shrine in the "Merceria del Capitello," which leads from St. Mark's Square to the Rialto.

CARAMPANE This is the local dialect for "Ca' Rampani," which were several dwellings owned by the Rampani family in the neighborhood of San Cassiano that housed the city's prostitutes as of the beginning of the 15th century. A nearby calle and rio terrà still bear their name.

CARBON The "coal barges" that moored at San Luca on the Grand Canal, where they sold their goods wholesale, lent their name to a nearby riva, calle, ramo, sottoportico and traghetto.

CARIOLE A sottoportico and courtyard in San Zulian bear the name of a local carpenter who manufactured "wheelbarrows."

CARITÀ The Campo della Carità in Dorsoduro took its name from the nearby church and monastery, as well as the Scuola Grande di Santa Maria della Carità, which now houses the Accademia Gallery.

CARMINI The Church of Santa Maria del Carmelo in Campo dei Carmini is known locally as the "Carmini."

CARROZZE Strange as it may seem, carriages used on the mainland were manufactured in Venice until the end of the 17th century. A carriage-maker in the neighborhood of San Samuele gave his name to a local street.

CASARIA The local word for the Rialto "dairy market" took its name from the Venetian "casarol," which derives from the Latin "caseus," meaning "cheese."

CASIN DEI SPIRITI The "House of Spirits," which is located in the garden of the Contarini dal Zaffo Palace near the Sacca della Misericordia, may have been so named because it was the meeting place for humanists, philosophers and free thinkers at the beginning of the 15th century.

CASON The "Campiello della Cason" in Santa Apostoli commemorates the fact that each of the city's six districts once had its own "prison" for debtors and minor offenders.

CASSELLERIA A street in Santa Maria Formosa took its name from the shops that made "trunks" for transporting merchandise as well as "hope chests."

CASTELLO The name given to this district derived from the Roman fort, or "castle," that once stood on the Island of Olivolo. This was one of the earliest settlements in the lagoon, and the original site of the bishop's seat at San Pietro di Castello.

CAVALLO The workshop where the famous equestrian statue of Colleoni was cast in bronze gave its name to the "Corte del Cavallo" ("Courtyard of the Horse") in Madonna dell'Orto, as well as a street and bridge in San Zanipolo.

CELESTIA Near the site of the now demolished Church of Santa Maria della Celestia, a nearby campo and rio still bear its name.

CENERE The "ash deposits" from Istria and Slavonia, which were used to make soap and lye, gave their name to a local calle.

CERCHIERI In the neighborhood of San Barnaba, a ramo and calle are named for the "coopers" who once worked there.

CELERI A fondamenta in Santa Maria Maggiore commemorates the local candle-makers' shops.

CHIOVERE The Venetian "chiovere" originally referred to "fenced in pasturelands" (from the Latin "clauderiae"). Later on, it signified the patches of ground where dyed cloth was laid out to dry, which gave their name to the "Campiello delle Chiovere" in San Rocco.

COLONNE Two granite "columns" at the end of the Piazzetta facing the Molo, which were brought back to Venice from the East in the 12th century, serve as a magnificent gateway to the city. One is them is surmounted by the figure of St. Theodore, the first patron saint of Venice, and the other by the Lion of St. Mark. Executions also took place here at one time, which gave rise to the popular expression, "I'm between Mark and Theodore" to indicate that someone was in very serious trouble!

COLTRERA A courtyard in the Castello district may have been named for a local "blanket" manufacturer.

CORAZZERI In the area between Sant'Antonin and San Martino Castello, which was once the site of "armorers' shops," a calle, ramo and sottoportico still bear their name.

CORDARIA The "rope" manufacturers, whose shops were situated in the Rialto district, lent their name to a local street.

CORLI The familiar word for "wool-winders," which was also used to signify derelicts and vagrants, may have lent its name to a street in San Tomà because it was once the site of wool-workers' shops, or the precinct of local prostitutes.

CORTE The "courtyard" is a typical feature of many Venetian buildings.

CREA Streets in the neighborhoods of Spirito Santo and San Giobbe recall the fact that there were once "clay" deposits in these areas, which were used in making bricks.

CROSERA This is the local word for "crossroads."

CUORIDORO The craftsmen who manufactured "gilded leather" for binding books and covering walls and chairs gave their name to a courtyard and sottoportico in San Fantin.

DAI The Venetian word for "dice" can still be found on a bridge, sottoportico, rio and fondamenta in the San Marco district, where gambling houses were most prevalent. According to legend, they were so named because this was the war cry of the people who pursued a group of Baiamonte Tiepolo's co-conspirators across St. Mark's Square after their attempted coup d'etat on June 10, 1310.

DIAMANTER The "diamond-cutters," who were known as "diamanteri da duro," and those who cut other precious stones and gems, who were called "diamanteri da tenero," gave their name to a courtyard in Santa Fosca.

DIAVOLO According to Tassini, a courtyard and sottoportico in Santa Maria Mater Domini bear this name because of the almost "diabolical" darkness of the spot.

DOANETA The "Doaneta dell'Ogio," which was the "small customs house" where oil was stored and measured before being sold in the city, lent its name to a ramo in the neighborhood of the Frari.

DONNA ONESTA Legend has it that there were once two gentleman standing on a bridge in San Pantalon discussing the relative virtues of the female gender. Suddenly one of them pointed to the small head of a woman carved on the wall of a nearby house, and exclaimed that she was the only "honest woman" he had ever known! Other possible explanations for the local calle, bridge and fondamenta that bear this name may involve a married woman who killed herself after being raped, or even a neighborhood prostitute who plied her trade with a certain amount of discretion.

DORSODURO The name "Dorsoduro," meaning "hard back," may refer to the unusually hard subsoil of this particular district.

DOSE The house in Santa Marina where "Doge" Nicolò Marcello was born is commemorated by a nearby street, courtyard and fondamenta. This name is found elsewhere in the city, generally in reference to specific dwellings, or shops, that displayed the arms of the doge.

DUE APRILE The section of the Merceria in San Bartolomeo that bears this name recalls the events of April 2, 1849, when the Venetian parliament determined to resist the Austrians at all costs.

ERBERIA This is the wholesale fruit and vegetable market at the Rialto, which sells fresh produce from the neighboring islands and the mainland.

FABBRI The "Calle dei Fabbri" in San Moisè was named after the "Blacksmiths' Guild Hall."

FAVA Some residents believe that the "Calle della Fava" in San Lio took its name from a local miracle, while others insist that it refers to a former pastry shop that was famous for its "fave dolci," which were eaten on All Souls' Day. The Church of Santa Maria della Consolazione, which is situated in a nearby square, is also known as Santa Maria della Fava.

FELZI were the portable cabins that were used in gondolas during the winter to protect the more important passengers from the cold. The "Fondamenta dei Felzi, which is named after the cabin manufacturers, is located in the neighborhood of San Zanipolo.

FERALI In San Zulian, a bridge and rio are named after these "street lamps."

FIUBERA A calle and sottoportico in San Zulian took their name from the shops that sold "buckles."

FONDAMENTE These are the streets that run alongside the rii and canals, so called because they formed the "foundations" for adjacent buildings. Contrary to popular opinion, the correct spelling of the plural noun is "fondamente," and not "fondamenta."

FONTEGO This is the Venetian word for "fondaco," which referred both to local storage facilities, and the complex of warehouses, offices and living quarters of the more important foreign merchants, such as the "Fondaco dei Turchi," "Fondaco dei Tedeschi," and "Fondaco dei Persiani," which were situated in different areas of the city.

FORMAGIER A former "cheese shop" in San Canciano gave its name to a local street.

FORMOSA The Church of "Santa Maria Formosa" (from the Latin "formosa," meaning "beautiful") was supposedly founded in the seventh century by St. Magnus, Bishop of Oderzo, after the Virgin had appeared to him in the form of a "beautiful" young matron.

FORNER Any number of locations throughout the city bear this name in memory of the neighborhood "bakery shops."

FORNI The "Calle dei Forni" in San Giovanni in Bragora takes it name from the "military bakeries" that prepared the rations for the naval fleet during the 15th century.

FRARI The great Gothic church known as "Santa Maria Gloriosa dei Frari," or simply "I Frari," was built by the Franciscan "Friars."

FREZZERIA The calle where "arrows" were once manufactured is now a busy commercial street in San Marco.

FRUTAROL The several streets that bear the name "Calle del Frutarol," one of which is in San Fantin, were originally the site of "fresh fruit stands."

FURLANE In the district of Castello, the campo and calle "delle Furlane" may have taken their name from the local word for "Friulan women," or from the traditional dance known as the "furlana."

FUSERI The old neighborhood of the "spindle-makers" gave its name to a bridge, ramo, rio and calle in San Luca.

GATTE Before the construction of an official residence in San Francesco della Vigna, the papal "legates," or nuncios, who lived in the immediate area, gave their name to a salizzada, ramo and campo.

GESUATI This is the Church of Santa Maria del Rosario on the Zattere, which was built in the 18th century on the site of a monastery that had once belonged to the abolished "Order of Jesuats," whose adjacent church is still in existence.

GHETTO The Jewish "ghetto" was named after the "getto," or "foundry," that had originally occupied the same site. The German Jews, who were the first to settle in the neighborhood, hardened the sound of the "g" in "getto," which prompted the Venetians to change the spelling to "ghetto."

GIUDECCA This island, which faces the Zattere across the Giudecca Canal, is actually a series of eight small islands connected by bridges. The name "Giudecca" is thought to have derived either from the Jews ("Giudei") who once resided there, or from a "giudicato," or "judgment," in favor of former political exiles, who were allowed to occupy certain parts of the island during the Middle Ages.

GIUFFA This street in San Lorenzo may have been named after the Armenian city of "Julfa," whose merchants once resided in the neighborhood. It is more likely, however, that it took its name from "gajuffi," which was the local word for "gypsies."

GOBBO DI RIALTO The so-called "Hunchback of the Rialto" refers to the 16th-century statue of a supplicant who is crouched over the steps leading to a column in Campo di Rialto from which the "Comandador" proclaimed the laws of the land and made other public announcements.

GORNA The local word for "grondaia," which means "gutter," lent its name to the "Calle della Gorna" on the Fondamente Nuove, where there was a drain that channeled rainwater directly into the lagoon.

GUERRA The so-called "mock wars" between rival neighborhoods that took place on the city's bridges during public celebrations were fought with fisticuffs or sticks. Among the bridges that commemorate this tradition, there is the "Ponte dei Pugni" ("Bridge of Fists"), and the "Ponte della Guerra" ("Bridge of War") at San Zulian.

GUGLIE The "Ponte delle Guglie" on the Cannaregio Canal is named after the four small obelisks that adorn its parapets. Contrary to popular opinion, the "spires" on certain palaces were not meant to indicate the residences of naval commanders or admirals of the fleet.

INCURABILI The "Hospital for Incurable Diseases," located on the Zattere, was where both St. Ignatius of Loyola and St. Francis Xavier once worked. It also gave its name to a nearby bridge and square.

INDORADOR A sottoportico and courtyard in the neighborhood of Santa Marina took their name from a nearby "gilder's shop."

LAVADORI The "Calle dei Lavadori" at the Tolentini commemorates those whose task it was to "wash" the fleeces of sheep that had just been shorn.

LEONCINI These are the two "lions" carved out of red marble that gave their name to the section of St. Mark's Square that is now known as "Piazzetta Giovanni XXIII."

LIBRER The city's many "booksellers" are commemorated by the "Campiello del Librer" in San Polo.

LISTA This was the extent of "diplomatic immunity" permitted the foreign embassies in Venice, which was indicated by white stones that were placed in front of the ambassador's own residence. The famous "Lista di Spagna" recalls the original site of the embassy of the "Catholic King."

LISTON At the beginning of the 18th century, St. Mark's Square was repaved with "slabs" of trachyte from the Euganean Hills, and strips of white Istrian stone. The former may well have been the origin of the word "liston," which now refers to the "public promenade" in the square itself.

LOGGETTA This was the building designed by Sansovino at the foot of the "Campanile," which served in the 17th century as the headquarters of the Arsenal workers who were responsible for maintaining law and order during the sessions of the *Maggior Consiglio*.

LUGANEGHER The "pork butcher," who was once a familiar sight in Venice, is remembered by any number of place names in the city, including those in the Frezzeria and Sant'Aponal.

LUSTRAFERRI These were the workers whose job it was to polish the "ferri", which were the iron ornaments that decorated the prows of the city's gondolas. The "Bridge of the Lustraferri" is located on the Fondamenta degli Ornesini.

MADONETA The "Rio della Madoneta" is named after a bas-relief of the Madonna on the facade of one of the Donà family's palaces.

MALVASIA A number of streets still recall the town of Malvasia, which was the original source of a fine wine of the same name.

MANDOLER The "Calle del Mandoler" in San Tomà was once the site of a shop that sold "almonds."

MANGANER Those who washed fabrics made of silk and wool lent their name to the "Calle del Manganer" in Santi Apostoli. (Mamolo Manganer was the main character in a play by Carlo Goldoni entitled "One of the Last Nights of Carnival").

MARANGONA This was the name of one of the bells in St. Mark's Tower, which marked the beginning and end of the workday for the Arsenal's "marangoni."

MARANGONI These were the highly skilled "wood workers" employed by the Arsenale, whose name eventually became synonymous with carpenters in general. There are "Calli del Marangon" in every section of the city.

MARGARITERA The "Corte Margaritera" in San Martino di Castello took its name from the "margariteri," who manufactured the small beads of enameled glass that are still a part of the city's arts and crafts industry.

MARZER The city's many dry good stores lent their name to the "Calle del Marzer" in San Polo.

MEGIO In the neighborhood of San Giacomo dell'Orio, the warehouses where "millet" and wheat were stored for use in the case of a serious shortage gave their name to the fondamenta, bridge, sottoportico and street were they were originally located.

MENDICANTI   The Fondamenta and Rio dei Mendicanti were named after the Hospice and Church of San Lazzaro dei Mendicanti, which lent assistance to the city's "beggars."

MENDICOLI   This was another local word for "mendicanti," or "beggars," which gave its name to the old Church of San Nicolò dei Mendicoli.

MERCERIE   This is both a main shopping district of Venice, and a short cut from St. Mark's Square to the Rialto.

MILION   The word "milion" refers both to the courtyard in San Giovanni Crisostomo where the Polo family had their homes, and Marco Polo's world famous travelogue entitled "Il Milion," better known in English as the "Voyages of Marco Polo."

MIRACOLI   The Church of Santa Maria dei Miracoli, which was built in the Renaissance to house a "miraculous" image of the Madonna, lent its name to a number of places in the immediate vicinity.

MISERICORDIA   The various locations that bear this name refer to the Scuola Grande di Santa Maria di Valverde, or della Misericordia, which was one of the six most important guild halls in Venice.

MISTRA   The local word for "master craftsman" gave its name to the "Corte della Mistra" in San Barnaba.

MOLO   This is the famous wharf in front of the Piazzetta and the Doges' Palace.

MORI   The "Campo dei Mori" in Madonna dell'Orto was named after the sculptures of the three Mastelli brothers, traders from the "Morea" who dressed in Oriental style. The two bronze figures that strike the hours on top of the clock-tower in St. Mark's Square are also called "Mori," as are the four figures of the tetrarchs in red porphyry on the south side of St. Mark's Basilica.

MOSCHE   These were "beauty marks" made of black taffeta that Venetian women wore to bring out the whiteness of their skin. The campo, ramo and campiello "delle Mosche" in San Pantalon are named after the shop where these ornaments were made.

MUNEGHE   "Muneghe," nuns, and its diminutive form, "muneghette," gave their name to any number of locations that were once the site of nunneries, such as Sant' Alvise, Santa Marina and San Maurizio.

MURER   The "Calle del Murer" in the Incurabili took its name from the city's masons, whose guild hall was located in San Samuele.

NARANZERIA   This was the local name for the "orange market" and warehouse on the Rialto.

NOMBOLI   The "hindquarters" of beef and the small pieces of string that were used to make fuses. lent their name to a rio terrà and calle in San Tomà.

NONZOLO   In the neighborhood of Moisè, a sottoportico and courtyard were named after the church's "sacristans."

OLE   The "Street of Pots and Pans" is located in the district of Castello.

ORESI   The Venetian "goldsmiths" gave their name to a ruga and sottoportico in the Rialto.

ORIO   The Church of Santa Maria dell'Orio may have taken its name from a nearby "laurel tree."

ORMESINI   A fondamenta, calle and bridge in San Marcilian bear the name of the fabric that was originally imported from Ormuz, and then manufactured in both Florence and Venice.

OSTREGHE   The local word for "oysters" lent its name to a bridge, rio and fondamenta in Santa Maria Zobenigo.

PAGLIA   The "Ponte della Paglia" on the Riva degli Schiavoni is named after the docking area for the barges that carried straw to the city.

PALADA   The "piles" that once supported the "Fondamenta della Palada" on the Giudecca also gave their name to the adjacent bridge and rio.

PAPA   The "Corte del Papa" commemorates the birthplace of Pietro Barbo, who later became Pope Paul II.

PARADISO   According to Tassini, the Calle and Ponte "del Paradiso" in Santa Maria Formosa are so called because of their splendid illuminations on the occasion of Good Friday.

PARANGON   This place name is found in the Rialto district because it was here that silk cloth was manufactured according to such strict standards that it became the point of reference, or "paragon," for the entire industry.

PARROCCHIE   Although there are only some 30 parishes left of the 70 that once occupied the city, their original names (even in dialect, such as "San Trovaso" for "Santi Gervasio e Protasio") are still commonly used to indicate a specific street address. Since houses are numbered not by street but by sestiere (Santa Croce, which is the smallest district, has more than 2,000 dwellings, while Castello, the largest, has nearly 7,000), it is extremely helpful to know what neighborhood you are looking for!

PESCARIA   The "fish market" on the Rialto has lent its name to several places in the immediate area.

PESTRIN   A calle, rio and bridge in Santo Stefano took their name from local shops that sold milk, oil and cooking fat.

PIAZZA The word "piazza" refers solely to St. Mark's Square. All other city squares are called campi or campielli.

PIAZZETTA There are only two "piazzette" in Venice, one of which is the area that extends from the Libreria Sansovina to the Doges' Palace and St. Mark's Basin. The other, which is located on the north side of St. Mark's Basilica, was known as Piazzetta dei Leoncini before its name was changed to Piazzetta Giovanni XXIII.

PIETÀ The "Conservatorio della Pietà" on the Riva degli Schiavoni, whose musical director was none other than Antonio Vivaldi, was originally the site of an orphanage for abandoned and illegitimate children founded by Blessed Peter of Assisi.

PIGNATE The "Ponte delle Pignate," or "Bridge of Pots and Pans," is located in San Luca.

PINZOCHERE The "pious women" of Venice are commemorated by the "Corte delle Pinzochere all'Angelo Raffaele," which took its name from a tertiary order of Franciscan women, and a courtyard in Santo Stefano that was named after Augustinian tertiaries. Other locations that bear the same name were the site of hospices for elderly women with no family, which existed until some 40 years ago.

PIOVAN The "Fondmenta del Piovan" in the neighborhood of San Bartolomeo is one of the many locations named after the city's "parish priests."

PIRIETA A sottoportico and courtyard in San Bartolomeo took their name from the shops of local tinsmiths.

PISTOR A bridge and street in San Lio recall those whose task it was to prepare the dough for the bread-bakers themselves.

PONTI There are almost 400 "bridges" in the city of Venice, nearly an eighth of which are private property, and all of which have their own names. While some are still made of wood, and others that date from the 18th century are made of iron, the majority, which date from the end of the 15th century, are made of stone.

PROCURATIE Along the north side of the piazza is the colonnaded building known as the "Procuratie Vecchie," which was the official residence of the Procurators of St. Mark. At a later date, a new residence, known as the "Procuratie Nuove," was built on the south side of the square.

PROVERBI In the "Calle Larga dei Proverbi" in Santi Apostoli, the following "proverbs" can still be seen on the cornices of two balconies: *"Chi semina spine non vadi descalzo"* ("Those who scatter thorns should not go barefoot"), and *"Di de ti e poi di me dirai"* ("Speak for yourself before you speak for me.")

PUGNI The "Bridge of Fists" was the site of the so-called "mock wars" between the "Castellani," who were from Castello, and the "Nicolotti," who came from the parish of San Nicolò dei Mendicoli in Dorsoduro. These were finally prohibited in the 18th century in the interest of maintaining law and order.

QUARTAROLO The "Ponte del Quartarolo," which would later become the Rialto Bridge, took its name from the bridge toll, which was a "quarter" of a denaro.

RAMO This is the local word for a short calle that connects two other streets.

RASSE The "Calle delle Rasse" in San Provolo took its name from the black cloth that was used to cover the "felzi," or portable cabins, of gondolas. The word "rasse" is derived from "Rascia" (Serbia), where the fabric was originally manufactured.

REDENTORE The "Campo del Redentore" was named after the church that was erected in honor of the "Redeemer" in 1576 to commemorate the end of the plague.

REGINA The Palazzo Corner della Regina, which was once the home of Caterina Corner, the Queen of Cyprus, gave its name to a calle and ramo in San Cassiano.

REMER The workshops where "oars" were manufactured lent their name to a campiello and sottoportico in Sant'Agostino that was situated near the home of the famous rebel Baiamonte Tiepolo, as well as a courtyard in San Giovanni Crisostomo.

REMURCHIANTI The boatsmen who were responsible for towing other vessels gave their name to a campiello and calle in San Nicolò.

RENGHIERA This word refers to one of the bells of St. Mark's, which was used to convene the members of the "arengo," or popular assembly.

RIALTO The word "Rialto," which was derived from the Latin "rivoaltus," meaning deep channel, was the original name of the cluster of islands that we now call Venice. Today it refers to the Rialto district and its famous bridge.

RIDOTTO The Calle del Ridotto in San Moisè was named after the gambling house opened by Marco Dandolo in his own palace in 1638, which was closed down by the state in 1774.

RIELLO A diminutive form of "rio," meaning "small canal."

RIFORMATI The Franciscan friars who officiated in the Church of San Bonaventura lent their name to a nearby calle, rio and fondamenta.

RIO This is the common name for canals located within the city.

RIO MENUO Another diminutive of "rio," meaning "narrow canal."

RIO TERRÀ This are the canals that have been filled in to create new streets.

RIVA This word refers to both the banks of canals where goods are loaded and unloaded, such as Riva degli Schiavoni and Riva del Carbon, and the steps on a fondamenta or in front of a house where boat passengers embark and disembark.

RUGA There are still a number of thoroughfares in the city that are called "ruga," from the old Italian word for street, which is similar to the French "rue."

RUGHETTA A diminutive form of "ruga," meaning narrow street or alleyway.

SALUTE The "Campo della Salute" took its name from the Church of Santa Maria della Salute, which was erected in honor of the Virgin Mary for having delivered the population of Venice from the terrible plague of 1630.

SALIZZADA This local word, which derives from "salizo," meaning "paving," is still used to denote the earliest paved streets.

SAN BASEGIO Venetian dialect for San Basilio (St. Basil).

SAN BOLDO Venetian dialect for Sant'Ubaldo (St. Ubaldo).

SAN LIO Venetian dialect for San Leone (St. Leo).

SAN MARCILIAN Venetian dialect for San Marziale (St. Martial).

SAN MARCUOLA The local name for the Church of SS. Ermagora and Fortunato.

SAN PANTALON Venetian dialect for San Pantaleone (St. Pantaleone).

SAN POLO Venetian dialect for San Paolo (St. Paul). The Chiesa di San Polo gave its name to one of the city's sestieri.

SAN STAE Venetian dialect for Sant'Eustachio (St. Eustace).

SAN STIN Venetian dialect for Santo Stefanino. Although the Church of San Stin no longer exists, it gave its name to a nearby campo, rio and bridge.

SANTA CROCE The Church of Santa Croce, which was demolished together with its adjacent convent, lent its name to one of the city's sestieri.

SANT'APONAL Venetian dialect for Sant'Apollinare (St. Apollinaris).

SANTA TERNITA Venetian dialect for the Holy Trinity.

SAN TOMÀ Venetian dialect for San Tommaso (St. Thomas)

SAN TROVASO Venetian dialect for the Church of SS. Gervasio e Protasio and its various namesakes.

SAN ZAN DEGOLÀ Venetian dialect for San Giovanni Decollato.

SAN ZANIPOLO Venetian dialect for the Church of SS. Giovanni e Paolo and its associated place names.

SAN ZULIAN Venetian dialect for San Giuliano (St. Julian).

SAONERI The Calle dei Saoneri took its name from local soap-makers.

SARTORI Venetian tailors gave their name to a fondamenta, calle and ramo in the Gesuiti.

SCALETER The Calle and Corte del Scaleter were named after the city's "donut-makers," whose "scalete" bore a design that resembled a flight of stairs ("scala").

SCHIAVINE These large woolen blankets lent their name to the Calle delle Schiavine in San Luca.

SCHIAVONI The inhabitants of Dalmatia, formerly known as Slavonia, or "Schiavonia," moored their trading vessels along the "Riva degli Schiavoni."

SCOACAMINI The Calle and Rio dei Scoacamini took their name from the city's "chimney-sweeps."

SCOAZZERA The city's local "garbage dumps," which were walled in on three sides, gave their name to the Campiello della Scoazzera in Sant'Aponal.

SCUELLINI The manufacturers of soup-bowls gave their name to a campiello in the neighborhood of San Barnaba.

SCUOLA These were the Venetian "confraternities," some of which functioned as religious or charitable organizations, and others as trade associations and mutual aid societies. There are still any number of locations throughout the city that commemorate the six "Scuole Grandi," or Great Guilds, who took their names from their patron saints, such as the Scuola di San Rocco. The same is true for the crafts guilds, such as the Scuola dei Varotari (Tanners), and the fraternal organizations established by members of the expatriot community, such as the Scuola degli Albanesi. The city's synagogues, which were also called scuole, lent their name to the "Campo delle Scuole" in the Jewish ghetto.

SESTIERI Of the six "sestieri," or districts, that divide the city of Venice, San Marco, Castello and Cannaregio are located on one side of the Grand Canal, and Santa Croce, San Polo and Dorsoduro (which includes the Giudecca) are situated on the other.

SOCCORSO The fondamenta and bridge that bear this name commemorate a hospice for fallen women that was founded by the famous courtesan and poetess Veronica Franco in the neighborhood of Santa Maria del Carmine.

SOSPIRI The "Bridge of Sighs" connected the Doges' Palace with the "Piombi," or "lower prisons." Legend has it that the "sighs" were those of the condemned criminals, who were perhaps gazing on the city for the very last time.

SOTTOPORTEGHI The city's many "sottoporteghi," or "sottoportici," are narrow arcades built into the walls of private residences to accommodate pedestrian traffic.

SPEZIER The "Calle del Spezier" in the neighborhood of Santi Filippo e Giacomo took its name from a local apothecary's shop.

SQUARTAI According to local legend, the "Ponte dei Squartai" in the Tolentini was once used to display the bodies of criminals who had been "squartati," or "drawn and quartered," as an admonition to the general public.

SQUERO This local word, which means "construction site," lent its name to the "Calle del Squero" in San Moisè.

STAGNERI The "stagnai," or "tinsmiths," gave their name to a calle in the neighborhood of San Salvador.

STRAMAZZER The "Calle del Stramazzer" in San Giovanni Crisostomo took its name from a local mattress-maker.

STRAZZAROL This was the local word for "rag-man," or "used clothing dealer," which lent its name to the Calle del Strazzarol in San Zulian.

STRAZZE The Calle delle Strazze, or Calle dei Strazzeri, which is located in the San Marco district, was named after the "rag-pickers," or "second-hand clothing shops."

STRETTO Venetian dialect for a narrow passageway.

STUA The city's public bathhouses, which were generally considered dens of iniquity, lent their name to the "Sottoportico della Stua" in the neighborhood of San Giovanni Nuovo.

TAGLIAPIETRA Any number of locations throughout the city commemorate the Venetian "stonemasons."

TANA The "Rio della Tana," which passes through the Arsenale, is named after the "Casa della Tana," which was the workshop where ships' ropes were manufactured. The word "tana," meaning "hemp," came from the city of Tana (Azov), which exported the hemp to Venice.

TENTOR The Venetian dye works, which were an extremely important local industry, gave their name to any number of locations throughout the city.

TESTORI The "Calle dei Testori" in Sant'Andrea is named after the city's many "silk-weavers."

TETTE Legend has it that a bridge and fondamenta in San Cassiano were named after the "tits" of prostitutes, who bared their breasts in doorways and windows in order to attract new customers.

TOLETTA The word "toletta," which means "plank," refers to a gang-plank that once served as a bridge over a rio in the neighborhood of San Trovaso.

TROTTIERA This is the name of one of the bells of St. Mark's, which alerted the members of the nobility that they had better "put their horses to the trot" in order to arrive on time for a session of parliament.

TURCHETTE The Bridge, Calle and Fondamente "delle Turchette" recall the fate of young Turkish girls who were once kept prisoner in the area.

VAROTERI The Scuola dei Varoteri, which is located in the Campo Santa Margarita, was the guild hall of the city's "tanners."

VECCHI The "Corte dei Vecchi" in San Sebastiano is named after a hospice for "elderly men," who had to be "of good character, and without wife or sons, whether native born or foreign."

VENTIDUE MARZO The "Calle Larga Ventidue Marzo" in San Moisè commemorates the day on which the Austrians were driven from Venice, which was May 22, 1848.

VENTO Local residents say that the wind blows more strongly in the "Calle del Vento" in San Basegio than anywhere else in the city.

VERA DA POZZO Highly decorative "wellheads," which were once a common feature of Venetian architecture, are still found in courtyards, campi and campielli throughout the city.

VERGOLA This word, which refers to both snoods and fancy silk braids that were used to decorate articles of clothing, lent its name to a calle in the neighborhood of San Geremia.

VERIERA A sottoportico and courtyard in San Zanipolo were named after the local "glaziers' shops."

VOLTI The overpasses that connected certain city streets lent their name to the "Calle dei Volti" in the neighborhood of the Gesuiti.

VOLTO SANTO The "Corte del Volto Santo," situated in the old neighborhood of the silk-weavers from Lucca, took its name from an image of Christ's face, which came to symbolize the craft itself.

ZATTERE The fondamente on the Giudecca Canal are named after the "zattere," or "rafts," that were used to carry timber from the Piave River.

ZAVATER The neighborhood cobblers gave their name to the "Calle del Zavater," which is located in the area of San Marcuola.

ZIRADA The Ponte della Croce in the Tolentini was also known as the "Ponte della Zirada," or "turning point," as this was where the boats that were competing in the regatta started on the return lap.

ZITELLE The Fondamenta delle Zitelle on the Giudecca took its name from the Church of Santa Maria della Presentazione, which was known locally as the "Zitelle" in memory of the "conservatory for young girls" that was founded in the immediate vicinity in the year 1561.

ZOBENIGO The Church of Santa Maria del Giglio, which was founded by the Iubanico family, is also known as "Santa Maria Zobenigo."

ZUDIO The "Calle del Zudio" on the Fondamenta degli Ormesini took its name from an apothecary's shop that was under the sign of a Jew.

ZUECA This is the local word for the Giudecca, which is the southernmost island of Venice. AA. VV. *Venezia e le sue lagune.* 5 vols. Venice, 1847.

BIBLIOGRAPHY

ARGELATI, F. *Pratica del Foro veneto*. Venice, 1737.

ARMAO, E. *In giro per il Mar Egeo con Vincenzo Coronelli*. Florence, 1951.

BERENGO, M. *La società veneziana alla fine del Settecento*. Florence, 1976.

BRAUDEL, F. *La Méditerranée et le monde méditerranéen à l'époque de Philippe II*. Paris, 1966.

BRAUNSTEIN, P. and R. DELORT. *Venise: Portrait historique d'une cité*. Paris, 1971.

BRUNELLI, V. *Storia della città di Zara dal 1409 al 1797*. Venice, 1913.

CESSI, R. *Venezia ducale: Duca e popolo,* 2d ed. Venice, 1940.

—— . *Storia della Repubblica di Venezia*. Milano-Messina, 1940-44.

—— . *Le colonie medioevali italiane in Oriente*. Bologna, 1942.

—— . *La Repubblica di Venezia e il problema adriatico*. Naples, 1953.

DA MOSTO, A. *I Dogi di Venezia*. 2d ed. Milan, 1960.

DAMERINI, G. *Le isole Jonie nel sistema adriatico*. Milan, 1943.

DE BENVENUTI, A. *Storia di Zara dal 1409 al 1797*. Milan, 1944.

DORIGO, A. *Venezia: Origini*. Milan, 1983.

DUDAN, B. *Sindicato d'oltremare e di terraferma*. Rome, 1935.

—— . *Il dominio veneziano di Levante*. Bologna, 1938.

FOTHERINGHAM, J. *Marco Sanudo: The Conqueror of the Arcipelago*. Oxford, 1915.

GEROLA, G. *Monumenti veneti nell'isola di Creta*. 4 vols. Venice, 1905-32.

GUERDAN, R. *Vie, grandeur et misères de Venise*. Paris, 1959.

GUERRINI, E. *Venezia e la Palestina*. Venice, 1928.

KRETSCHMAYR, H. *Geschichte von Venedig*. 3 vols. Gotha-Stuttgart, 1905-34.

LANE, F. C. *Venice: A Maritime Republic*. New York, 1973.

"La Temi Veneta, Contenente Magistrati, Reggimenti e Altro per l'Anno 1797." Venice, 1796.

LEICHT, P. S. *Breve storia del Friuli*. Udine, 1930.

LOPEZ, R. S. *La révolution commerciale dans l'Europe médiévale*. Paris, 1974.

LUNZI, E. *Delle condizioni politiche delle isole Jonie sotto il dominio veneto*. Venice, 1859.

LUZZATTO, G. *Storia economica di Venezia*. Venice, 1961.

MARANINI, G. *La costituzione di Venezia*. 2 vols. Florence, 1927.

MOLMENTI, P. G. *Storia di Venezia nella vita privata*. 3 vols. Bergamo, 1929.

OSTOJA, A. "Gli istituti veneziani di diritto pubblico in Dalmazia." Doctoral dissertation, University of Bologna, 1930.

RENOUARD, Y. *Les villes d'Italie de la fin du Xe siècle au début du XIVe siècle*. Edited by P. Braunstein. Paris, 1969.

ROMANIN, S. *Storia documentata di Venezia*. 10 vols. Venice, 1853-60.

TENENTI, A. *Venezia e i corsari*. Bari, 1961.

THIRIET, F. *La Romanie vénitienne au Moyen Age*. Paris, 1959.

VENTURA, A. *Nobiltà e popolo nella società veneta del '400 e '500*. Bari, 1964.

ZORZI, A. *La Repubblica del Leone: Storia di Venezia*. Milan, 1979.

—— . *Vita di Marco Polo Veneziano*. Milan, 1979.

—— . *La vita quotidiana a Venezia nel secolo di Tiziano*. Milan, 1990.

INDEX

PICTURE CREDITS

THE AUTHOR AND PUBLISHER WISH TO EXPRESS THEIR GRATITUDE TO THE FOLLOWING PHOTO ARCHIVES FOR THEIR ASSISTANCE IN PROVIDING THE ILLUSTRATIONS CONTAINED IN THIS VOLUME:

ANDERS, BERLIN
ARCHIVIO ARNOLDO MONDADORI EDITORE, MILAN
ARCHIVIO ELECTA, MILAN
ARCHIVIO F.LLI FABRI, MILAN
ARCHIVIO SCALA, ANTELLA (FLORENCE)
OSVALDO BÖHM, VENICE
BULLOZ, PARIS
CAMERAPHOTO, VENICE
CAPRIOLI, VENICE
CARRIERI, MILAN
GIANCARLO COSTA, MILAN
DE BIASI, MILAN
EDITION ROBERT LAFFONT, PARIS
EMMER, VENICEEIKONOS, REGGIO EMILIA
FARABOLAFOTO, MILAN
FOTO CINE BRUNEL, LUGANO
FOTOFLASH, VENICE
FOTO LABOR COLOR, BERGAMO
FOTO LEANDRO, TREVISO

GIACOMELLI, VENICE
IMAGE BANK, MILAN
INTERPRESS PHOTO, VENICE
GIORGIO LOTTI, MILAN
LUCCHETTI, BERGAMO
LUFIN, ABANO TERME (PADUA)
MAGNANI E BARONI, MILAN
MAIRANI/GRAZIA NERI, MILAN
MARZARI/EMMER, VENICE
MORI, MILAN
NEW PHOTO CENTER, VENICE
NICOLINI, MILAN
PINEIDER, FLORENCE
REALY EASY STAR, TURIN
RENARD, VENICE
RICCIARINI, MILAN
STEFANO SACCOMANNI, VERONA
SAPORETTI, MILAN
FRANCA SPERANZA, MILAN
OSCAR SAVIO, ROME
TORTOLI, TAVARNUZZE
TOSO, VENICE
VISION, VENICE

OUR THANKS GO AS WELL TO THE VARIOUS MUSEUM ARCHIVES AND GOVERNMENT AGENCIES IN ITALY AND ABROAD.

FINALLY, OUR HEARTFELT THANKS TO THE VENETIAN STATE ARCHIVES FOR HAVING ALLOWED US UNLIMITED ACCESS TO THEIR SPECIAL COLLECTIONS.